Towards Smart World

Towards Smart World

Homes to Cities Using Internet of Things

Edited by

LAVANYA SHARMA

CRC Press

Taylor & Francis Group

Boca Raton London New York

CRC Press is an imprint of the
Taylor & Francis Group, an **informa** business

A CHAPMAN & HALL BOOK

Library of Congress Cataloging-in-Publication Data

Names: Sharma, Lavanya, editor.
Title: Towards smart world : homes to cities using Internet of Things / edited by Lavanya Sharma.
Description: First edition. | Boca Raton : C&H/CRC Press, 2021. | Includes bibliographical references and index.
Identifiers: LCCN 2020030249 (print) | LCCN 2020030250 (ebook) | ISBN 9780367521608 (hardback) | ISBN 9781003056751 (ebook)
Subjects: LCSH: Internet of things. | Smart cities.
Classification: LCC TK5105.8857 .T69 2021 (print) | LCC TK5105.8857 (ebook) | DDC 307.760285/4678–dc23
LC record available at https://lccn.loc.gov/2020030249
LC ebook record available at https://lccn.loc.gov/2020030250

ISBN: 9780367521608 (hbk)
ISBN: 9781003056751 (ebk)

Typeset in Palatino LT Std
by KnowledgeWorks Global Ltd.

Dedicated to My Dada Ji

(Late. Shri Ram Krishan Choudhary Ji)

Ek prerna mayeh Vyaktitavh…

Contents

Preface...ix

Acknowledgments xi

Editor Bio...xiii

Contributors..xv

Part 1

1. The Rise of Internet of Things and Smart Cities...3

   Lavanya Sharma

2. System Architecture of Internet of Things and Its Connectivity Challenges.........15

   Aakanksha Sharma, Venki Balasubramanian

Part 2

3. Design of Internet of Things-Based Accident Detection System...............................35

   Satyam Tayal, Harsh Pallav Govind Rao, Suryansh Bhardwaj, Samyak Jain

4. Smart Healthcare in Smart Cities...45

   Vukoman Jokanović

5. Portable Smart Home Device for Personalized Interior Display 73

   Aamna Shahab, Neetu Mittal

6. Importance of Augmented Reality and Virtual Reality in Our Daily Life..............83

   Vallidevi Krishnamurthy, D. Venkata Vara Prasad, Ganesh Kumar, B. Surendiran,
   Arjith Natarajan, Akshaya Natarajan, Dattuluri Rushitaa

Part 3

7. Internet of Things and Artificial Intelligence..99

   Shailja Gupta, Mayank Khattar

8. Convergence of Artificial Intelligence of Things: Concepts, Designing,
   and Applications..119

   Divya Upadhyay, Shanu Sharma

9. Internet of Things and Image Processing 143

   Xiao Yuan Yu, Wei Xie

10. Internet of Things Enabled by Artificial Intelligence 173
Rinku Sharma Dixit, Shailee Lohmor Choudhary

11. Cloud Computing and Internet of Things Towards Smart World for Real-Time
Applications 197
Sugandhi Midha

12. The Convergence of Internet of Things and Big Data 215
Shailee Lohmor Choudhary, Rinku Sharma Dixit

13. Moving from Cloud to Fog: An Internet of Things Perspective 235
Sudhriti Sengupta

Part 4

14. The Architecture of Internet of Things with Applications and Healthcare
Working Models 255
Dr. T. Venkat Narayana Rao, Vivek Kapa, Vinutha Kapa

15. Diagnostic of the Malarial Parasite in RBC Images for Automated Diseases
Prediction 269
Karanjot Singh, Sudhriti Sengupta

16. Design of a Multipurpose Android-Controlled Robotic Arm for a Smart City 279
Satyam Tayal, Harsh Pallav Govind Rao, Suryansh Bhardwaj, Shreyansh Soni

17. From Moving Objects Detection to Classification and Recognition:
A Review for Smart Environments 289
Sirine Ammar, Thierry Bouwmans, Nizar Zaghden, Mahmoud Neji

18. Human Detection and Tracking Using Background Subtraction in Visual
Surveillance 317
Lavanya Sharma

19. The Future of Smart Cities 329
Lavanya Sharma, Mukesh Carpenter

Index 341

Preface

This book will provide an overview of basic concepts from rising of machines and communication to Internet of Things (IoT) with artificial intelligence (AI), and critical applications domains, tools, technologies, and solutions to handle the relevant challenges. This book will also provide a detailed description to readers with practical ideas of using IoT with AI for smart cities to deal with human dynamics, the ecosystem, and challenges involved in surpassing diversified architecture, communications, integrity, and security aspects. IoT in combination with AI has proved to be most advantageous for companies to efficiently monitor and control their day-to-day processes, such as production, transportation, maintenance, implementation, and distribution of their products.

Overall, *Towards Smart World: Homes to Cities Using Internet of Things* helps readers to understand the value of IoT with AI to individuals as well as homes and organizations.

Acknowledgments

I am especially grateful to *my dada ji, my parents, my husband (Dr. Mukesh), Romeo Sharma, Vedant,* and *my beautiful family* for their continuous support and blessings. I owe my special thanks to *Samta Choudhary ji* and *Pradeep Choudhary ji* for their invaluable contributions, cooperation, and discussions.

I would like to thank to my husband *Dr. Mukesh Carpenter* (*General Surgeon*) for his continuous motivation and support throughout this project. Apart from his very busy schedule, he always motivated me and supported me.

Very special thanks to *Shri Parvesh Sahib Singh Verma Ji* (*Hon'ble Member of Parliament, India*) for their blessings and invaluable support. He simply gave only direction with hints and it inspired me to explore new ideas. Then, it comes to my Mama ji *Shri Surender Matiala Ji* for his valuable guidance and blessings.

I am very much obliged to *Prof. Pradeep K. Garg* for his motivation and support. This would not have been possible without blessings and valuable guidance from him.

Thank you to *Miss Aastha Sharma and Miss Shikha Garg*, CRC Press/ Taylor & Francis, for their cooperation and kind help during this project.

Above all, I express my heartiest thanks to *God* (The One to Whom We Owe Everything) *Sai Baba of Shirdi* for all blessings, guidance, and help by you and only you. I would like to thank *God* for believing in me and being my defender. Thank you, God Almighty.

Lavanya Sharma
September 29, 2020,
New Delhi, India

Editor Bio

 **Dr. Lavanya Sharma** is an Assistant Professor at Amity Institute of Information Technology at Amity University UP, Noida, India. She did her M.Tech (Computer Science & Engineering) in 2013 at Manav Rachna College of Engineering, affiliated to Maharshi Dayanand University, Haryana, India. She did her Ph.D at Uttarakhand Technical University, India, as a full-time Ph.D scholar in the field of Digital Image Processing and Computer Vision in April 2018, and also received the *TEQIP* scholarship for her Ph.D. Her research work is on Motion-Based Object Detection using a Background Subtraction Technique for Smart Video Surveillance. She has been a recipient of several prestigious awards during her academic career. She has more than 20 research papers to her credit including Elsevier (SCI Indexed), Inderscience, IGI Global, IEEE Explore, and many more. She authored book *Object Detection with Background Subtraction* (LAP Lambert Academic Publishing, 2018). She is also an editor of the book *From Visual Surveillance to Internet of Things* (CRC Press, 2019). She also contributed as an organizing committee member at Springer's ICACDS conferences 2016, Springer's ICACDS 2018, Springer's ICACDS 2019, and Springer's ICACDS 2020. She is an editorial member/reviewer of various journals of repute and also an active program committee member of various IEEE and Springer conferences. Her primary research interests are Digital Image Processing and Computer Vision, Artificial Intelligence, Mobile Ad Hoc Networks, and Internet of Things. Her vision is to promote teaching and research, providing a highly competitive and productive environment in academic and research areas with tremendous growing opportunities for the society and her country.

Contributors

Sirine Ammar
Lab. MIRACL, Univ. Sfax, Tunisia/Lab. MIA, Univ. La Rochelle, France

Dr. Venki Balasubramanian
School of Science, Engineering and Information Technology, Federation University Australia, Ballarat, Australia

Suryansh Bhardwaj
Thapar Institute of Engineering & Technology, Patiala, India

Prof. Thierry Bouwmans
Lab. MIA, Univ. La Rochelle, France

Mukesh Carpenter
Department of Surgery, Alshifa Hospital, Okhla, New Delhi, India

Shailee Lohmor Choudhary
Department of Business Analytics and Data Sciences, New Delhi Institute of Management, New Delhi, India

Dr. Rinku Sharma Dixit
Department of Business Analytics and Data Sciences, New Delhi Institute of Management, New Delhi, India

Ms. Shailja Gupta
Department of Computer Science Technology, Manav Rachna University, Faridabad, India

Samyak Jain
Thapar Institute of Engineering & Technology, Patiala, India

Vukoman Jokanović
ALBOS Ltd., Institute of Nuclear Sciences Vinca, Belgrade, Serbia

Vinutha Kapa
Department of Computer Science and Engineering, Sreenidhi Institute of Science and Technology, Hyderabad, India

Vivek Kapa
Department of Computer Science and Engineering, Sreenidhi Institute of Science and Technology, Hyderabad, India

Mayank Khattar
Department of Computer Science Technology, Manav Rachna University, India

Vallidevi Krishnamurthy
Department of Computer Science and Engineering, SSN College of Engineering, Anna University, Chennai, India

Ganesh Kumar
Department of Computer Science and Engineering, SRM University, Chennai, India

Ms. Sugandhi Midha
Department of Computer Science and Engineering, Chandigarh University, Gharuan, Mohali, India

Dr. Neetu Mittal
AIIT, Amity University, Uttar Pradesh, Noida, India

Akshaya Natarajan
Department of CSE, SSN College of Engineering, Anna University, Chennai, India

Arjith Natarajan
Department of CSE, SSN College of
  Engineering, Anna University, Chennai,
  India

Dr. Mahmoud Neji
Lab. MIRACL, Univ. Sfax, Tunisia

D. Venkata Vara Prasad
SSN College of Engineering, Anna
  University, Chennai, India

Harsh Pallav Govind Rao
Thapar Institute of Engineering &
  Technology, Patiala, India

T. Venkat Narayana Rao
Department of Computer Science and
  Engineering, Sreenidhi Institute of
  Science and Technology, Hyderabad,
  India

Dattuluri Rushitaa
Department of ECE, SSN College of
  Engineering, Anna University, Chennai,
  India

Sudhriti Sengupta
Amity Institute of Technology, Amity
  University, Uttar Pradesh, Noida, India

Aamna Shahab
AIIT, Amity University, Uttar Pradesh,
  Noida, India

Aakanksha Sharma
School of Science, Engineering and
  Information Technology, Federation
  University Australia, Ballarat, Australia

Dr. Lavanya Sharma
AIIT, Amity University, Uttar Pradesh,
  Noida, India

Shanu Sharma
Department of Computer Science &
  Engineering, Amity University
  Uttar Pradesh, India

Karanjot Singh
Amity Institute of Technology, Amity
  University, Uttar Pradesh, Noida,
  India

Shreyansh Soni
Thapar Institute of Engineering &
  Technology, Patiala, India

Dr. B Surendiran
Department of Computer science and
  Engineering, NIT Puducherry,
  India

Satyam Tayal
Thapar Institute of Engineering &
  Technology, Patiala, India

Divya Upadhyay
Department of Computer Science &
  Engineering, Delhi Technical Campus,
  Greater Noida, India

Wei Xie
College of Automation Science and
  Technology, South China University
  of Technology, Guangzhou 510641,
  China

XiaoYuan Yu
College of Automation Science and
  Technology, South China University
  of Technology, Guangzhou 510641,
  China

Nizar Zaghden
Tunisia, ESC, Univ. Sfax, Tunisia

Part 1

1

The Rise of Internet of Things and Smart Cities

Lavanya Sharma

Amity Institute of Information Technology, Amity University
Noida, India

CONTENTS

1.1 The Emergence of the Smart City from the Traditional City 3
1.2 Features of a Smart City and Its Components 4
    1.2.1 Smart Transportation 5
    1.2.2 Smart Energy Empowerment 6
    1.2.3 Smart Data 6
    1.2.4 Smart Networks and Connecting Devices 6
    1.2.5 Smart Quality of Life 7
1.3 Smart City Architecture 7
    1.3.1 Goals, People, and the Ecosystem 8
    1.3.2 Soft Infrastructure 8
    1.3.3 Hard Infrastructure 8
1.4 Smart City Tools and Technologies 8
    1.4.1 IoT and Big Data 8
    1.4.2 IOT and Computer Vision 9
    1.4.3 IoT and Remote Sensing 10
    1.4.4 IoT and Artificial Intelligence 10
    1.4.5 IoT and Machine Learning 10
    1.4.6 IoT and Fog Computing 10
1.5 Conclusion 11
References 12

1.1 The Emergence of the Smart City from the Traditional City

According to a 2014 United Nations (UN) report, more than 50% of the global population is urbanized [1-20]. In today's scenario, cities are home to more than 50% of the current world's population and are expected to add another 2.5 billion new inhabitants by 2050 [1, 2]. Every day, people are facing increased environmental burdens, infrastructure requirements, and increasing demands from populaces to provide a better quality of life, as shown in Figure 1.1 21–24. Smart tools and technologies can help cities meet these day-to-day issues or challenges, and they are already enabling the next wave of community investment; because cities, in all their complexity and scope, generate oceans of it [1–4]. Smart cities use information and communication technologies (ICT) to upgrade the quality of life of residents, the local economy, transportation, traffic management, the environment, and interaction

3

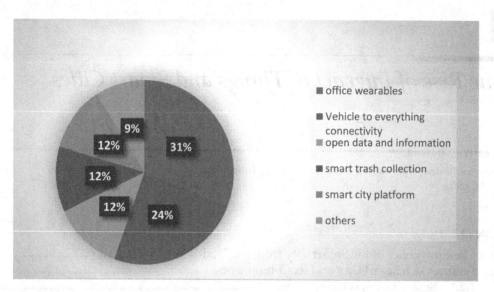

FIGURE 1.1
Global growth rate for smart cities (2017–2020) [5, 6].

with the government to plan for the future, as shown in Figure 1.2. Furthermore, by adding all the realistic data to the organization and community helps in empowering for better decision making and also plays an important role in improving the city's overall performance. When cities get smarter, they become more civilized and more responsive.

The idea of smart cities has attracted substantial consideration from researchers within multiple domains including information systems, smart homes, smart ecosystems, smart residents, smart governments, smart parking, and many more [5, 6]. Rapid growth of global urbanization has also put a lot of pressure on inhabitants' hubs, presenting a challenge for cities to deliver ecosystem sustainability, security, and safety of residents alongside a rise in crime and threats [7]. In order to avoid these upcoming challenging issues, cities seek a sustainable environment but also resist growth in terms of current development, as shown in Figure 1.1.

1.2 Features of a Smart City and Its Components

Generally, a city with a base of information and computer technology can be termed as a "smart city." ICT is the base of the entire city: its medium of communication, its property, and other services. The concept of "smart cities" comes from two campaigns in 2008 and 2009, namely the Smarter Planet initiative launched by IBM. Presently, various countries including India are taking effective control measures in order to develop smart cities. One of the best examples of a smart city is "Curitiba," a capital of Paraná in Brazil, where waste management was a big issue that led to the release of waste masses in the streets [8–10]. In this city, approximately 70% of the population actively participates in recycling of waste from streets and, as a result, the city has become much cleaner and was also rewarded by the government of Brazil. Some other companies also

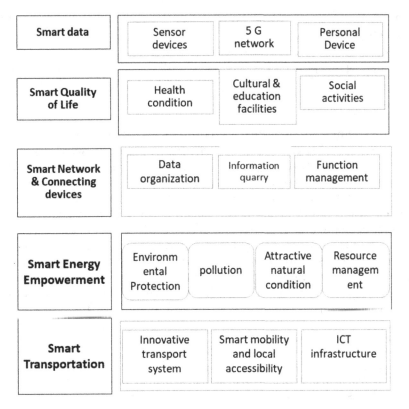

FIGURE 1.2
Features of a smart city and its components.

launched campaigns to develop cities like Singapore, Dubai, Amsterdam, Barcelona, and New York. All the listed cities are applying novel solutions to infrastructure in order to improve it [10–16].

There are various components present in literature that makes a city smarter. In general, this includes smart transportation, smart energy empowerment, smart data, smart networks, and smart quality of life, as shown in Figure 1.2.

1.2.1 Smart Transportation

This type of city has less traffic flow that results in ease of transportation of goods and individuals through numerous sources. Reducing the number of traffic results in less road accidents, less traffic congestion, a decrease in the level of air pollution, and also helps in promoting a better lifestyle [2, 10, 17]. There are various challenging issues in terms of smart transport development because various developing cities around the world are not able to make a balance between the supply of goods and demand of the urban transport system, as shown in Figure 1.2 and later in Figure 1.5. Some of the core challenging issues are listed here:

- Developing cities lag behind due to inadequate capacity to mobilize the large amount of funds that will be required to initiate the transport development projects.

- The rapid increase in population is one of the biggest challenging issues that has to be taken on a priority basis.
- Unlawful occupancy of automobiles on footpaths and bicycle traffic lanes is another important challenging issue.

1.2.2 Smart Energy Empowerment

Residential and commercial buildings are both efficient at using less energy. The saved energy is analyzed to collect relevant information. Intelligent networks are the entry point of a smart city and improve failure detection, collect relevant data and information, and carry out disaster management, field operations, and various techniques to upgrade the network. In this, the Internet of Things (IoT) plays an important role that results in smart home electric meters that allow the consumer to flexibly adjust power consumption, provide better network management, and provide a better distribution of energy. In smart cities, homes and energy suppliers can exchange data in a transparent manner to the consumer [2, 18, 19]. The energy empowered will be very challenging by the end of 2025 due to around 4.6 billion people living in metropolitan regions. These cities will consume approximately 65% of existing primary energy and count for around 70% of greenhouse gas emissions to supply energy for illumination, heating, cooling, and transportation [16, 20].

1.2.3 Smart Data

A smart city collects huge volumes of raw data to be promptly analyzed to provide valuable information to its people. Residents can install an open-data portal and publish online data based on cities. These data can be easily accessed and also used by data scientists for predictive analysis to identify forthcoming prototypes. The source of realistic data is increasing day by day with deployment of sensors and IoT devices to "sense" the city. In India, the "Smart Cities Mission-Ministry of Housing and Urban Affairs" intends to launch the "DataSmart Cities" strategy to leverage the potential of data to address multiple challenging issues in smart cities. This strategy will encourage cities to set up building blocks of data such as setting up the City Data Strategy, Smart City Data Alliance, and Smart Cities Data Network. It also aims to provide peer-to-peer (P2P) learning across various cities over the data-driven governance. The major smart city data challenge is the ability of gathering, managing, and manipulating data safely and effectively to produce fruitful outcomes [12, 13, 25, 26]. But in practice, it is a very challenging task if various councils have multiple sets of legacy IT systems and gaps in technical skills and data science need to be filled to unlock the importance from this exclusive asset.

1.2.4 Smart Networks and Connecting Devices

The analyzed data enables proactive maintenance and future-based enhanced planning. An intelligent infrastructure is required to handle this huge amount of data that involves the combination of various tools and technologies such as cloud computing, fog computing, IoT, big data, and many more. The data collected using these technologies will result in upcoming administrative changes. The IoT devices or sensor-based devices are a basic component of a smart city. The integrated sensors (ISs) in these devices collect valuable data or information that can be used to get valuable information [11–16]. This exchange of data between composite city systems will be managed and integration of this data analysis will also result in a reduction in the number of accidents and accidental consequences.

1.2.5 Smart Quality of Life

A smart quality of life or living standard is characterized by different cultural facilities available to both the largest and smallest communities. Advanced learning can be provided by smart schools, colleges, and universities, smart tourism, and smart healthcare with all the modern technology-enabled devices and equipment that provide a healthy lifestyle for all residents. Smart homes as well as social cohesion can be provided to every resident of the city. The graduate enrolment ratio (GER), Human Development Index (HDI), and level of qualifications are considered as one of the most important aspects of life [7, 27]. Smart people have a lifelong enthusiasm to learn things, to be social and traditional plurality. Nondiscrimination is another important aspect of smart residents, as it has the flexibility to change them according to ecosystem variations and also possess a democratic nature.

1.3 Smart City Architecture

Smart city architecture is a method of defining the context of infrastructure and the smart city system. It mainly comprises of five layers: Goals, People, Ecosystem, Soft Infrastructure, and Hard Infrastructure, as shown in Figure 1.3.

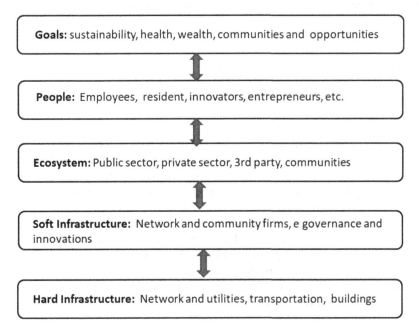

FIGURE 1.3
Smart city architecture.

1.3.1 Goals, People, and the Ecosystem

The smart city has a set of specific goals and is mainly focused on sustainability, residents or the community, and social and economic growth. Communities are an important element of an ecosystem and are living bodies of metropolitan life. The main challenge faced by architects in designing the smart city is to create infrastructure and facilities that can become part of the ecosystem of communities and residents, as shown in Figure 1.3. In order to solve this issue, interaction of cocreative dialogue should happen [7, 27, 28].

1.3.2 Soft Infrastructure

Soft infrastructure is created to understand the interactions of communities and people. If the process of conversations is broad, then that process and communities of the city can become part of soft infrastructure. Basically, soft infrastructure refers to all the organizations that are necessary to maintain the financial, health, cultural, and social standards of a nation, such as the healthcare system, education system, government policies, and the financial system, as shown in Figure 1.3.

1.3.3 Hard Infrastructure

Hard infrastructure refers to the large physical networks such as 4G or 5G networks that are required for functioning of a modern industrial country. The newly developed technology offers city systems transformation. These platforms comprise of wired or wireless networks and communication tools such as social media, telephony, and video conferencing, as shown in Figure 1.3. Other computational resources are also required such as cloud computing or big data and modeling tools that provide a detailed view into the performance of smart systems.

1.4 Smart City Tools and Technologies

1.4.1 IoT and Big Data

IoT is one of the most emerging technologies that any smart city project cannot exist without. In IoT, "things" refers to sensor-based devices that can collect the data for effective technological solutions for real-time scenarios such as water management, city lightening, smart traffic management, 5G connectivity, and many more, as shown in Figure 1.4. For example, a smart water meter measures the water usage, its quality, and also sends an alert to the water companies regarding leakage or contamination of the water. Smart city initiatives require big data analytics to make them functional. IoT will generate a large amount of data that can be analyzed and processed to implement services in smart cities. Big data is a major part of ICT infrastructure, because it is required to sort, examine, and process the data collected from IoT devices. City governance integrates ICT solutions to interconnect public services and, at the same time, engages people in local governance to promote cooperation, as shown in Figure 1.5. For example, the Greater London Authority initiative where City Hall is using an open common platform to share data with local residents or communities [27–31].

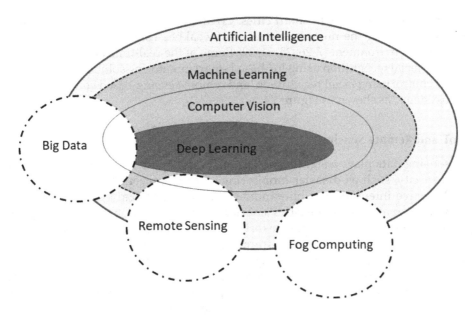

FIGURE 1.4
Different technologies for smart cities.

1.4.2 IOT and Computer Vision

Computer vision can be used to determine traffic congestion problems, hygiene issues, parking of automobiles, overcrowding, environmental variations, controlled access, theft identification and reduction, disease detection, forensic investigations, secure transactions, and many more. The computer vision process sets a new standard in the domain of

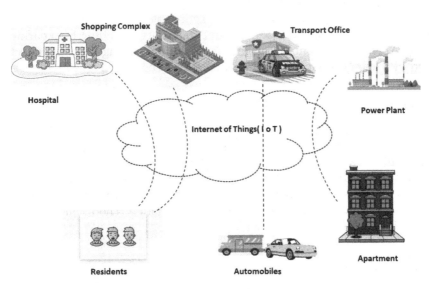

FIGURE 1.5
Role of IoT in smart cities.

security and safety measures in smart cities. Computer vision in the smart city can also be used in identifying the numerous strengths, weaknesses, opportunities, and threats deployed in the environment [7, 26–28, 31, 32]. Some of the real-time applications of smart cities include facial recognition using IoT-based smart monitoring solutions, IoT-based real-time traffic control using facial recognition, and remote-sensing-based computer vision for smart ecosystems, as shown in Figure 1.4.

1.4.3 IoT and Remote Sensing

Remote sensing data plays a significant role in several application domains, especially in the smart city, such as disaster monitoring, remote surveillance, and climate prediction. Effective integration of humanoid digital and physical systems can improve quality of life and also make the cities smarter and sustainable, as shown in Figure 1.4. For example, an Open Geospatial Consortium (OGC) white paper provides the foundations for a spatial information (SI) framework that integrates geographic information system (GIS) features, sensor-based observations, imagery, and social media. This remotely sensed information can be combined with location-specific data that can be collected locally or by using IoT devices and presents incredible future openings for smart city applications. High-resolution remote sensing data can be used by insurance firms and financial firms to track consumer expenditure and assist with consumer claims [17, 20, 28].

1.4.4 IoT and Artificial Intelligence

Artificial intelligence (AI) significantly supports the sustainable development of smart cities. The various growing domains of AI have contributed in transforming traditional cities into well-equipped smart cities [17, 20, 25]. The concept of providing better means of livings by incorporating technology into the daily life activities of citizens is the only purpose of the emergence of smart cities. In cities, data are collected using sensor-based devices for environment sensing, traffic sensing, smart meters, and automobiles, as shown in Figure 1.4. These data can be used to extract actionable insights where AI can shine [2]. For example, a driver may spend too much time in the city searching for a parking space, but by using AI techniques, smart parking can be built up using the data collected from various sensor devices, making a city more smarter, as shown in Figure 1.5.

1.4.5 IoT and Machine Learning

A smart city has several uses for machine learning (ML)-driven and IoT-enabled technology, from maintaining a better environment to advanced transportation and safety. By leveraging these two technologies integrated with IoT, enhanced and improved smart traffic solutions can be designed so that residents can move from one place to another in a safe and efficient manner [29, 31, 33]. ML can collect data from different points and transfer it to a central server for further analysis and implementation. Then, collected data can be utilized to make a city smarter, as shown in Figure 1.4.

1.4.6 IoT and Fog Computing

One of biggest challenges of a large amount of data generated, captured, and analyzed on a daily basis is that it has become difficult to manage this data, store it, and keep track of

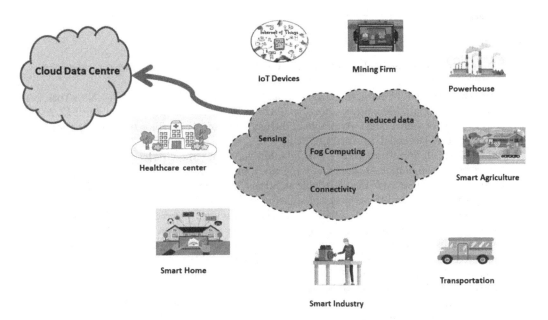

FIGURE 1.6
Fog computing for smart cities.

it. Transferring this large amount of data between the cloud and data sources is also very time-consuming and expensive. Therefore, the concept of fog computing arises that makes it possible to reduce the amount of data that needs to be sent to the cloud for processing, thereby improving efficiency. Smart cities can benefit by sending a minimal amount of data to the cloud. The main motive of this technology is to make big data smaller and more manageable. According to the International Data Corporation's 2019 forecast, it has been observed that data collected using connected devices will exceed 79 zettabytes (ZB) by the end of 2025 [26, 28, 32, 34, 36]. Fog computing is capable of reducing this large amount of data with the help of intelligent sensing and filtering applications, which allow the transmission of only useful data or information based on the knowledge available at nearby local fog devices, as shown in Figure 1.6.

1.5 Conclusion

The urban population is increasing day by day and it is adversely affecting both the quality and quantity of basic essential services provided to city residents. The emergence of smart cities provides effective solutions to existing problems. Several smart city projects by both public and private sector firms resulted in deployment of ICT to find sustainable solutions to the real-time challenges faced by cities in terms of education, health, unemployment, and crime, among others. This chapter highlights the emergence of the smart city from the traditional city. Architecture and its major characteristics are also discussed along with important technologies that play a vital role in making a smart city.

References

1. IoT for smart cities. Available at: https://www.visualcapitalist.com/iot-building-smarter-cities/ [accessed on April 12, 2020].
2. Lavanya. Sharma, P. K. Garg, (Eds.). *From Visual Surveillance to Internet of Things*. New York, NY: Chapman and Hall/CRC, https://doi.org/10.1201/9780429297922 [accessed on April 12, 2020].
3. Applications of smart cities. Available at: https://www.digi.com/blog/post/iot-applications-in-smart-cities [accessed on April 12, 2020].
4. Zaib Ullah et al., "Applications of Artificial Intelligence and Machine learning in Smart Cities," *Computer Communications*, Elsevier, vol. 154, no. 1, pp. 313–323, March 5, 2020.
5. Characteristics of Smart Cities. Available at: https://ecmapping.com/2017/03/31/top-6-characteristics-to-understand-the-concept-of-smart-city/ [accessed on April 15, 2020].
6. Challenges of Smart Cities. Available at: https://www.ifpenergiesnouvelles.com/article/smart-city-energy-challenges-facing-sustainable-cities [accessed on April 15, 2020].
7. Lavanya Sharma, P. K. Garg "Smart E-healthcare with Internet of Things: Current Trends Challenges, Solutions and Technologies," *From Visual Surveillance to Internet of Things*, Chapman and Hall/CRC, Vol. 1, p. 215, 2019.
8. Smart City Architecture. Available at: https://www.smartcitiesdive.com/ex/sustainablecities-collective/new-architecture-smart-cities/68921/ [accessed on April 15, 2020].
9. Yongmin Zhang, "Interpretation of Smart Planet and Smart City [J]," *China Information Times*, vol. 2010, no. 10, pp. 38–41, 2010.
10. Lavanya Sharma, Nirvikar Lohan, "Performance Analysis of Moving Object Detection using BGS Techniques in Visual Surveillance," *International Journal of Spatiotemporal Data Science*, Inderscience, vol. 1, pp. 22–53, January 2019.
11. Anubhav Kumar, Gaurav Jha, Lavanya Sharma, "Challenges, Potential and Future of Internet of Things Integrated with Block Chain," *International Journal of Recent Technology and Engineering*, vol. 8, no. 2S7, pp. 530–536, July 2019.
12. Yong Liu, Rongxu Hou, "About the Sensing Layer in Internet of Things [J]," *Computer Study*, vol. 2010, no. 5, p. 55, 2010.
13. Akshit Anand, Vikrant Jha, Lavanya Sharma, "An Improved Local Binary Patterns Histograms Techniques for Face Recognition for Real Time Application," *International Journal of Recent Technology and Engineering*, vol. 8, no. 2S7, pp. 524–529, July 2019.
14. Krassimira Antonova Paskaleva, "Enabling the Smart City: The Progress of City E-governance in Europe [A]," *International Journal of Innovation and Regional Development [C]*, vol. 2, pp. 405–422, 2009.
15. Gauri Jha, Pawan Singh, Lavanya Sharma, "Recent Advancements of Augmented Reality in Real Time Applications," *International Journal of Recent Technology and Engineering*, vol. 8, no. 2S7, pp. 538–542, July 2019.
16. Lavanya Sharma, Annapurna Singh, Dileep Kumar Yadav, "Fisher's Linear Discriminant Ratio Based Threshold for Moving Human Detection in Thermal Video," *Infrared Physics and Technology*, vol. 78, pp. 118–112, Elsevier, March, 2016.
17. Lavanya Sharma, Dileep Kumar Yadav, "Histogram based Adaptive Learning Rate for Background Modelling and Moving Object Detection in Video Surveillance," *International Journal of Telemedicine and Clinical Practices*, vol. 2, No. 1, pp. 74–92, Inderscience, June 2016 (ISSN: 2052-8442, DOI: 10.1504/IJTMCP.2017.082107).
18. Smart City Challenges: What Stands in the Way of Smart Cities?. Available at: https://mobility.here.com/learn/smart-city-initiatives/smart-city-challenges-what-stands-way-smart-cities [accessed on October 16, 2020].

19. Bhagya Nathali Silva et al., "Towards Sustainable Smart Cities: A Review of Trends, Architectures, Components, and Open Challenges in Smart Cities," *Sustainable Cities and Society*, Elsevier, vol. 38, pp. 697–713, April 2018.
20. Lavanya Sharma, Nirvikar Lohan, "Performance Analysis of Moving Object Detection using BGS Techniques," *International Journal of Spatio-Temporal Data Science*, vol. 1, No. 1, pp. 22–53, Inderscience, February 2019.
21. Andrea Caragliu, Chiara Del Bo, Peter Nijkamp, "Smart Cities in Europe," *Journal of Urban Technology*, vol. 18, no. 2, pp. 65–82, April 2011.
22. Vito Albino, Umberto Berardi, Rosa Maria Dangelico, "Smart Cities: Definitions Dimensions Performance and Initiatives," *Journal of Urban Technology*, vol. 22, no. 1, pp. 3–21, Feb 2015.
23. C. Harrison, B. Eckman, R. Hamilton, P. Hartswick, J. Kalagnanam, J. Paraszczak, et al., "Foundations for Smarter Cities," *IBM Journal of Research and Development*, vol. 54, no. 4, 2010.
24. Shubham Sharma, Shubhankar Verma, Mohit Kumar, Lavanya Sharma, "Use of Motion Capture in 3D Animation: Motion Capture Systems, Challenges, and Recent Trends," in 1st IEEE International Conference on Machine Learning, Big Data, Cloud and Parallel Computing (Com-IT-Con), India, pp. 309–313, 14–16 Feb 2019.
25. H. Schaffers, N. Komninos, M. Pallot, B. Trousse, M. Nilsson, A. Oliveira, et al., "Smart Cities and the Future Internet: Towards Cooperation Frameworks for Open Innovation," in *The Future Internet. FIA 2011. Lecture Notes in Computer Science*, Berlin, Heidelberg: Springer, vol. 6656, 2011.
26. J. Jin et al., "An Information Framework for Creating a Smart City Through Internet of Things," *Journal of IEEE Internet of Things*, vol. 1, no. 2, pp. 112–121, 2014.
27. Lavanya Sharma, P. K. Garg, Naman Agarwal, "A Foresight on e-Healthcare Trailblazers," *From Visual Surveillance to Internet of Things*, Chapman and Hall/CRC, Vol. 1, p. 235, 2019.
28. Lavanya Sharma, P. K. Garg, "IoT and its Applications," *From Visual Surveillance to Internet of Things*, Chapman and Hall/CRC, Vol. 1, p. 29, 2019.
29. Lavanya Sharma, Nirvikar Lohan, "Internet of Things with Object Detection," *Handbook of Research on Big Data and the IoT*, IGI Global, pp. 89–100, March 2019. (ISBN: 9781522574323, DOI: 10.4018/978-1-5225-7432-3.ch006).
30. Lavanya Sharma, "Introduction," *From Visual Surveillance to Internet of Things*, Chapman and Hall/CRC, Vol. 1, p. 14, 2019.
31. Lavanya Sharma, P. K. Garg, "Block Based Adaptive Learning Rate for Moving Person Detection in Video Surveillance," *From Visual Surveillance to Internet of Things*, Chapman and Hall/CRC, Vol. 1, p. 201, 2019.
32. Lavanya Sharma, P. K. Garg, "Future of Internet of Things," *From Visual Surveillance to Internet of Things*, Chapman and Hall/CRC, Vol. 1, p. 245, 2019.
33. A. Zanella and L. Vangelista, "Internet of Things for Smart Cities," *IEEE Internet of Things Journal*, vol. 1, no. 1, pp. 29–36, 2014.
34. A. Botta et al., "Integration of Cloud Computing and Internet of Things: A Survey," *Future Generation Computer Systems*, vol. 56, pp. 684–700, 2016.
35. S. Sicaria et al., "Security Privacy and Trust in Internet of Things: The Road Ahead," *Computer Networks*, vol. 76, pp. 146–164, 2015.
36. Industrial Internet of Things: Unleashing the Potential of Connected Products and Services, Jan. 2015. http://www3.weforum.org/docs/WEFUSA_IndustrialInternet_Report2015.pdf

2

System Architecture of Internet of Things and Its Connectivity Challenges

Aakanksha Sharma

School of Science, Engineering and Information Technology, Federation University Australia Ballarat, Australia

Venki Balasubramanian

School of Science, Engineering and Information Technology, Federation University Australia Ballarat, Australia

CONTENTS

2.1   Introduction 15
2.2   Background 16
2.3   IoT Applications 18
    2.3.1   5G Benefits 21
    2.3.2   Significant Benefits of Integrating SDN in IoT 21
2.4   A Proposed Framework for the IoT System 23
    2.4.1   IoT System Architecture 23
    2.4.2   Major Challenges in IoT System Architecture 24
    2.4.3   Connectivity Challenges 26
    2.4.4   Case Study: Results Analysis Using NetSim for University Environments 28
    2.4.5   Significance and Contribution 29
2.5   Conclusion 30
References 30

KEYWORDS: *internet of things, healthcare, quality of service, bandwidth allocation and computation offloading, software defined networks*

2.1 Introduction

The Internet of Things (IoT) is a network of smart devices with low capabilities that are able to collect, preprocess, and disseminate useful data to make a smart and efficient decision. The devices are embedded with electronics, software, sensors, actuators, and network connectivity. Today, there is a tremendous increase in smart devices that connect to the internet; it is usual for a person to have more than one smart electronic device featuring sensors, data loggers, and the Global Positioning System (GPS). Existing smart devices have software that enables them to provide specialized services for which they are designed; these devices can communicate among each other and also transfer data to the internet. The network of such devices is known as IoT and is used in many contemporary applications such as robotics, healthcare, mining, and transportation [1, 2]. IoT devices are highly heterogeneous in nature because the networks of smart devices are of different capabilities and are manufactured by different vendors. Therefore, the deployed devices gather data from the environment for the data compilation in various formats that need a common platform to compile that data. Due to the heterogeneous nature of devices, the bandwidth usage also varies invariably; when many devices are connected, it is a great challenge to provide bandwidth to all the connected devices.

2.2 Background

Over the last decade, IoT has been rapidly increasing, and this is expected to continue to grow exponentially in the coming years. As shown in Figure 2.1, the existence of smart devices was almost negligible in 2003, but within less than a decade, by 2010, the use of IoT was nearly double the world population. Likewise, by 2015, connected devices had increased to the stage where the world population was three times less than the connected devices. In the future, by the end of 2020, it is predicted that 50 billion devices will be connected to the internet and each person will have more than six devices connected that transfer or exchange data through the internet. Current network architecture cannot accommodate the increase in the number of smart devices expected in the future. Therefore, we need a scalable and trusted platform [2, 3–5].

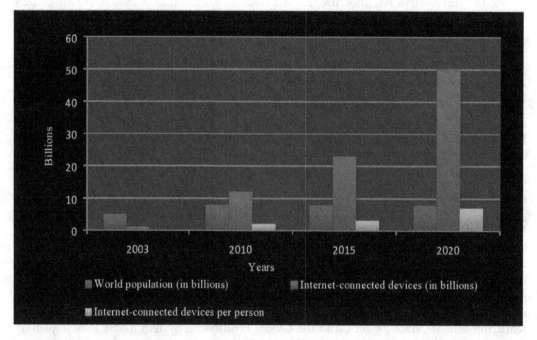

FIGURE 2.1
IoT growth. Global growth of world population, IoT devices [2, 3].

Connecting numerous IoT devices is the biggest challenge. A centralized server/client paradigm could serve tens or thousands of devices, but when the network grows to billions or trillions of devices, the centralized system will be unable to provide services to all of the devices [6]. To avoid a single point of failure, centralized systems need to migrate to cloud servers that can handle a huge information exchange to prevent any system breakdown.

- Traditional network technology is not capable of handling billions or trillions of connected devices. Thus, software defined networks (SDN), in which control and data planes are decoupled using forwarding devices, can fulfil the requirements of IoT effectively in terms of different network aspects with edge, access, core, and data center computing. A generic SDN has three layers: infrastructure, control, and application; with the SDN in place, the adequate control logic can be implemented on the physical devices, depending on application-specific requirements in real time [2, 7].

- Wi-Fi needs to be fast and reliable due to fast-growing mobility. An SDN was used to achieve highly scalable mobility in the Wi-Fi network by identifying two main issues: most vendors use proprietary protocols for communication between the controller and the access points that lack interoperability between products from different vendors. It can raise issues of the wireless local area network (WLAN) standard—Control and Provisioning of Wireless Access Points (CAPWAP), which allows protocols to manage access points modified by vendor extensions or not implemented in an interoperable way [8].

- The wireless body area network (WBAN) aggregates the data generated from the body sensors deployed on the human body or inside it. This aggregated data generates enormous traffic and hence increases the complexity to handle heavy traffic using traditional network architecture [9].

- The bandwidth allocation to all the energy harvesting devices is a challenge. The objective of providing QoS and bandwidth allocation is by proposing the Bandwidth Allocation and Computation Offloading (BACOFF) method. The results showed less memory limitations, data loss, and time sensitivity. In the same paper, the results of the BACOFF approach was compared with cross-layer control of data flows (CORAL), and it provided slightly better performance [2].

- The CORAL-SDN technology; it is an SDN solution for wireless sensor networks. It makes use of centralized control mechanisms, supports elasticity, maintains a scalable architecture, and it exhibits improved network management. But they do not consider mobility and radio signals [1].

- The paper concluded as this lack of information results in a large number of mobility issues. Many strategies have been proposed to connect the devices, but they are unable to provide effective results. Traditional network technology is not capable of handling the increase in IoT connectivity. SDN is used to fulfil the requirements of IoT in terms of edge, access, core, and data center [7].

- Interoperability, scalability, heterogeneity, and security need to be considered in future IoT connectivity [10]. IoT devices gather a massive amount of data; therefore, this needs to be appropriately managed and heterogeneous sensing and actuating technologies need to be supported. The future connectivity issues due to the increase in IoT devices, low power, long-range, and a large amount of data transmission is required [11]. The authors illustrated the use of Long Range (LoRa); it is used for low power consumption, long-range communication technology. Still, it cannot transfer a large amount of data.

- All connected heterogeneous devices generate a large amount of data. Allocating bandwidth to each sensor device is a challenging issue. Existing bandwidth allocation mechanism does not consider device constraints, gateways, and applications. IoT gateways have limited bandwidth, so allocation of bandwidth to connected devices while maximizing the throughput is also a challenging problem. The authors proposed the BACOFF method; it considers service-related properties of both IoT devices and the gateway with which they are connected [2].

- Mobility is considered as a significant issue in low-power wide-area networks LPWANs. Mobility is dependent on distance to gateway and vehicle speed. LPWANs get affected even by minor human movement. It is concluded that the mobility-aware protocol needs to be developed to address mobility issues [12].

- The personal digital assistant (PDA) is used as an SDN switch to review the heterogeneity for healthcare and concluded that heterogeneity demands standard communication technology and protocol with the capability to operate in a noisy environment [9].

- In [13], the authors raised the issues of QoS and proposed the backtracking algorithm. However, it is still not as successful because the number of steps in the backtracking algorithm for calculation of QoS is too much. Therefore, QoS needs to be considered in future.

IoT is expanded in almost all the areas. It provides enormous advantages in different fields such as smart shopping centers, smart transportation, and smart healthcare, such as remote patient monitoring. In spite of several benefits, it also suffers from growth obstacles.

Based on the background, a summary of connectivity issues (heterogeneity, mobility, bandwidth allocation, and QoS) for IoT is shown in Table 2.1.

2.3 IoT Applications

The leading IoT applications are shown in Figure 2.2. The uses of IoT are expanded in almost all areas, and a few are listed here:

1. **Healthcare:** The use of IoT in healthcare provides various benefits. Healthcare applications range from remote monitoring to surgical robots. It has benefited in terms of patients' safety. Now, physicians can deliver care to keep patients healthy. New tools advent with the usage of advanced technology such as fitness sensors [3–5, 14–19].

2. **Security:** This includes authentication and confidentiality of data. It provides data and device security. IoT devices work remotely without human interference, but this can lead to the chance of dangerous physical attacks. Few sensors have essential data delivered securely. In healthcare sensors, if this kind of data is hacked or corrupted, then patient health can suffer. Therefore, security is considered as a high priority, and it is crucial for future IoT [3–5, 13, 15].

TABLE 2.1

IoT Connectivity Challenges

Challenges in IoT Connectivity			
Heterogeneity	Mobility	Bandwidth Allocation	Quality of Service
Heterogeneous IoT refers to the platform that allows communication with a wide variety of devices using multiple protocols (MQTT, CoAP, Modbus, etc.)	Mobility in IoT can be defined as the allocation of information whenever the user demands and even during the user's movement	Allocating bandwidth to multiple connected devices is a challenge because of limited resources	QoS needs to be ensured by prioritizing the services. Real-time applications should be given high priority for the improvement in performance
Existing Issues			
Heterogeneity, mobility, QoS, security, scalability, data sharing, and requirement of low-power wide-area communication technology	Need to achieve heterogeneity, mobility, QoS, security and scalability	Connectivity problem, bandwidth allocation, to achieve QoS, memory constraint devices, CPU capability, and power supply	Delivering QoS, bandwidth allocation, heterogeneity, security, mobility, big data
Technology Used			
Software-defined wireless sensor networks, virtual Wi-Fi AP OpenFlow	Software-defined wireless sensor networks, virtual Wi-Fi AP OpenFlow	Wi-Fi, Zigbee, Z-Wave, 6LoWPAN, WLAN, Cellular, Bluetooth low energy (BLE), Thread, BACOFF method, long hop algorithm	Software-defined wireless sensor networks, software-defined IoT, BACOFF method
Main Contribution			
Provides elasticity and scalable architecture, Performance and resource utilization is improved.	Existing SDN-based approach is discussed to address different challenges of wireless sensor network, and performance and resource utilization is improved	Avoids memory limitations, data loss, and time sensitivity. Results of BACOFF provides better performance than the CORAL method. Long hop algorithm is used to prioritize the packets, and power connectivity is minimized by using low energy networks	It uses centralized control mechanism to support protocol functionalities. Provides elasticity and scalable architecture. Illustrates data loss and time sensitivity

3. **Smart Home:** The smart home is designed to provide convenience and security—a dream home for everyone. IoT currently offers various benefits such as it is used to control the lights of the house even if you are not physically present in the home; switching lights on/off helps from a security point of view. IoT also helps when a person comes back from a long working day and are not in a condition to stand and cook—with their smartphone, they can switch on the toaster and air conditioner [14, 16, 19].

4. **Transportation:** Transportation is improved with the use of IoT. There are mainly four significant applications in transportation: automobile, road, rail, and mass

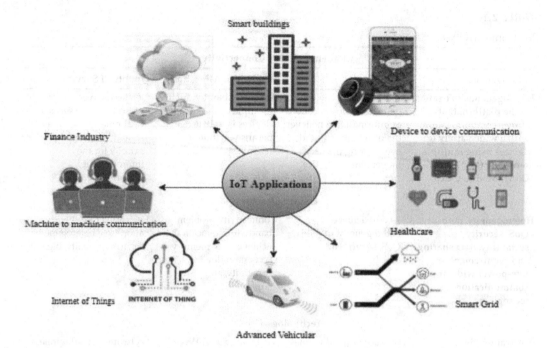

FIGURE 2.2
Applications of IoT.

transit/industrial transportation. IoT has improved private cars and makes them smart. The main concern is to control traffic by handling congestion, accidents, and parking. It helps to expand the commercial enterprise by optimizing transport [2, 4, 5, 14].

5. **Agriculture:** IoT is used in agriculture mainly for various purposes such as monitoring, irrigation, and automation. Sensors are used for smart irrigation to check forecasts or plant-care information, and so on. Intelligent cameras are used to monitor fields. Emerging GPS-based sensors are used for tracking the movement of cattle. The main motive of IoT in agriculture is to perform the required operations remotely. IoT provides relief to farmers because they can predict the weather, they can learn ways to grow new crops, and so on. IoT has helped in making smart agriculture and fruitful crops [2, 13, 19].

6. **Industry:** The industrial IoT is defined as a collection of various hardware objects communicating together through IoT to help improve industrial processes. The use of IoT in industry can be found by considering connected machines and devices in industries such as oil, gas, healthcare, and so on. An IoT system includes various devices—such as fitness bands to monitor the heart rate and smart home appliances—and these devices provide comfort for the user with an easy-to-use approach, but the limitation is that they are not totally reliable because they cannot handle an emergency if the system fails [4, 5, 13].

2.3.1 5G Benefits

The advent and deployment of the 5G network brings a large number of innovative network services and exceptional user experience by providing superior data rates. Altogether, 5G is a novel technology that differs from its predecessors and can naturally accommodate the growing number of users. 5G is a progressive version of cellular networks designed to cope with new situations [3–5, 15–20]. Usually, 5G is an intelligent network capable of managing the enormous amount of data from the trillions of heterogeneous devices. 5G technology provides a much fuller frequency band compared to previous technologies and a broader spectral bandwidth per frequency channel. Previous generation technologies (0G–4G) differ in terms of a substantial increase in peak bitrate, as shown in Table 2.2.

5G also reflects a rise in bitrate, making it different from 4G. But this is not the only reason why 5G is better than 4G; it also depends on various factors mentioned here [20]:

- Increase in peak bit rate
- System spectral efficiency is high
- More capable of coping with heterogeneous devices concurrently
- Battery consumption is low
- Can connect multiple devices at a time
- Developing infrastructure is cheap
- Reliable communications

2.3.2 Significant Benefits of Integrating SDN in IoT

An SDN is an emerging computer networking paradigm. SDN architecture can accommodate mobility and scalable for a more significant number of IoT devices by allocating dynamic bandwidth without modifying the underlying technology. The idea of SDN is to separate the data plane from the control plane to simplify network management, as opposed to a traditional architecture where the control plane and the data plane reside in the same device. The SDN control plane is centralized while the data plane is distributed.

TABLE 2.2

The Evolution of 5G Network Technology

1G	2G	3G	4G	5G
Started: In 1982 Technology: Analog Bandwidth: 2 Kbps Throughput: 14.4 Kbps Core Network: PSTN Switching: Circuit Service Primarily: Analog phone calls Web standards: -	Started: In 1991 Technology: Digital Bandwidth: 14.4 - 64 Kbps Throughput: 20 Kbps Core Network: PSTN Switching: Circuit, Packet Service Primarily: Digital phone calls and messaging Web standards: www	Started: In 2000 Technology: CDMA 2000, UMTS Bandwidth: 2 Mbps Throughput: 200 Kbps – 3 Mbps Core Network: Packet network Switching: Packet Service Primarily: Phone calls and messaging data Web standards: www(IPv4)	Started: In 2003 Technology: Wi-max, LTE, LTE advanced Bandwidth: 1 Gbps Throughput: 100 – 300 Mbps Core Network: Internet Switching: All packet Service Primarily: All IP based network services Web standards: www(IPv4)	Started: By 2019-20 Technology: WWWW Bandwidth: Higher than 1 Gbps Throughput: 1 -10 Gbps or higher Core Network: Internet Switching: All packet Service Primarily: High speed, high capacity and provide large broadcasting of data in Gbps Web standards: www(IPv6)

Traditional Network   **Software Defined Network**

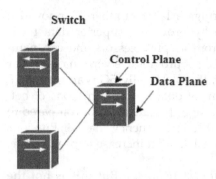
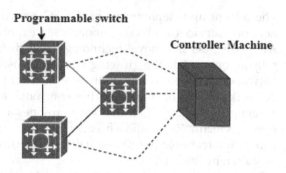

FIGURE 2.3
Traditional network versus an SDN.

The centralized nature of the control plane makes the network flexible and enhances flow forward decision making [7].

SDN, unlike the traditional method, brings many benefits:

- According to Figure 2.3, it is much easier to adapt to new network policies by using software because it is easier to add or modify network-level rules based on the controller using a program than to manually use a limited set of orders on this equipment.
- Moreover, managing the distribution of network equipment is no longer an obstacle with the introduction of an SDN, which relies on the benefits of centralized management and configuration of the network.

Figure 2.4 shows separated SDN data and control planes. Each data plane entity has its corresponding controller/s in the control plane. Similarly, the application and the management functions are also separated from the two bottom planes [21].

- SDN has the potential to route traffic and intelligently uses underutilized network resources. This will significantly enhance the network's ability, and therefore it will be much easier for systems to prepare for the data onslaught of IoT devices. This will eliminate bottlenecks to efficiently process the data generated by IoT devices without placing an enormous strain on the network, especially on the Wi-Fi network.
- The deployment of SDN in IoT will provide visibility of the network resources and management of access based on user, group, device, and application.
- SDN provides better results than the traditional network because it offers both a centralized approach and a distributed approach. But in traditional systems, different switches or routers are used to transfer data; they have the routing information installed in the physical device itself. If any device has to send the data, then it will be sent to all devices.
- If the centralized server is down, then the whole system will collapse. Also, if there is any update in the routing information of traditional networks, then it needs to manually update the information in all the physical devices [21].

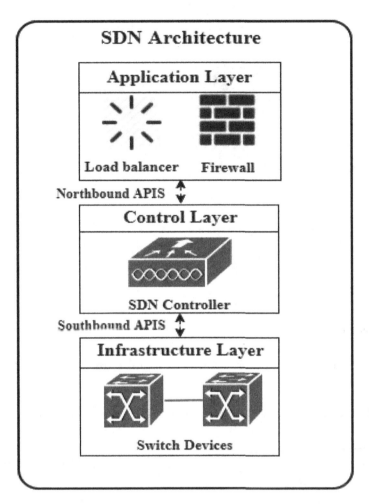

FIGURE 2.4
SDN architecture.

2.4 A Proposed Framework for the IoT System

2.4.1 IoT System Architecture

The ratio of wirelessly connected devices is increasing, leading to significant connectivity challenges and making the system error-prone. In future, massive connectivity of devices will bring lots of connectivity challenges like heterogeneity, mobility, security, bandwidth allocation, and QoS. Current network architecture cannot accommodate the increase in the number of smart devices expected in the future. With the growth in connected devices, there is a need for emerging technology and service applications. These are the first hop challenges because it is hard to change the existing infrastructure [2].

The sensors in IoT are used in smart homes, smart cities, buildings, and shopping centers. The data is collected by the sensors. The collected data is transmitted to the storage servers via the network components. The information is then processed and delivered as

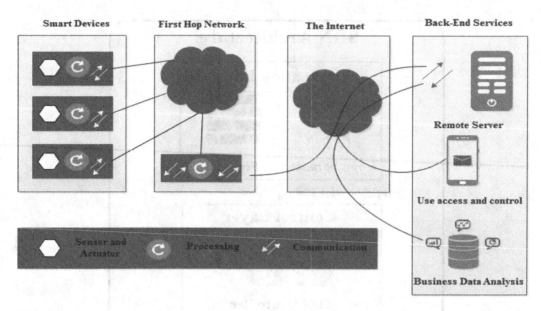

FIGURE 2.5
The system architecture of IoT.

a service to be used by the application. A generic architecture of IoT consists of four main parts, as shown in Figure 2.5.

- **Smart Devices:** A smart device is an electronic gadget that can connect, share, and interact with its user and other smart devices. Although usually small in size, smart devices typically have the computing power of a few gigabytes.
- **First Hop Network:** The local network that translates the device communication protocols to internet protocols.
- **The Internet:** The internet connects smart devices with backend servers.
- **Back End Server:** These are mostly data centers or client applications.

2.4.2 Major Challenges in IoT System Architecture

In the future, massive connectivity of devices will bring numerous connectivity challenges such as heterogeneity, mobility, security, bandwidth allocation, and QoS. The connectivity of internet-connected devices is the means of data sharing. Many methods have been used to consider connectivity by ensuring QoS, mobility, bandwidth allocation, and heterogeneity. During this process, few challenges were raised as mentioned here:

1. **Sensors:** In IoT, internet access and physical devices such as a sensor or actuator are the main components. Sensors are deployed to identify the objects and to collect the required information from the environment. These act as the front end and they are connected directly or indirectly with the IoT network. All sensors are not the same; different applications require different sensors, such as temperature sensors are needed to gather temperature information, humidity sensors are used

to check the quantity of water vapor in the air, and so on. With the growth of IoT, there is a need to deploy enormous sensors to monitor the area. Therefore, the next concern is the complexity raised by lots of sensors. A sensor's battery needs to be replaced with time. Therefore, another matter is the cost required to replace the battery of the sensor [14]. In the future, sensors could create lots of connectivity issues, and this scenario needs an answer. As deployment increases, more complexities will happen.

2. **Network Connection:** Sensors are connected through technologies such as 3G/4G, Bluetooth, and Wi-Fi; the collected information is transferred to the desired location through the internet. In [14], the authors addressed the need of LPWANs, as a first hop network, due to the limitations of existing technologies in terms of data rate and coverage.

3. **Web Storage and Data Retrieval:** Web storage and data retrieval is an issue raised due to the increase in the use of sensors. Various sensors have been deployed to gather the information from the environment; collected data is then transferred to the server using the communication network, as this way, a tremendous amount of information is gathered. According to [14], lots of data collected by sensors led to the issue of big data, which needs to be intelligently processed. It is a challenge to deliver the required data at the time necessary.

4. **Human Dependence:** Human independence is taking necessary action at any point of time without human involvement. The machines need humans to operate them; sometimes they can take action by themselves (e.g., robotics may be trained using machine learning to take some steps) but most of the time, they fail to take action by themselves. It is a challenge to model the SDN to tackle connectivity issues without any human involvement [14].

5. **Scalability and Object Identity:** IoT is increasing and requires object identity. The IPv4 standard is exhaustive and not sufficient to provide address space to the growing rate of IoT devices. IPv6 will provide enough address space globally, but the growth of IoT using IPv4 is a challenge [14].

6. **Heterogeneity:** Heterogeneity is considered as a significant challenge in IoT systems. This is mainly due to the different components present in the system, because they can generate different data. For example, various sensors present in healthcare can generate different data in different formats. The communication among sensors may be held using different protocols. It is difficult to uniformly process the data at a common platform because of issues like diverse components, varied data formats, and different protocols [22].

7. **Mobility:** Mobility in IoT can be defined as the allocation of information whenever a user demands it during the user's movement. Mobility as a big challenge in the growth of IoT [22].

8. **Security:** IoT devices provide a platform to share information, data, and device control processes that can be hacked by unauthorized people during data communication. The internet offers security mechanisms to protect data. Still, those mechanisms are not compatible with providing security for all devices due to the heterogeneous nature of IoT devices [2, 14].

9. **Bandwidth Allocation:** IoT connectivity faces significant challenges in terms of bandwidth allocation. Allocating bandwidth to many connected devices is a

challenge due to limited resources. The authors [6] ascertain that, until now, bandwidth has been expensive on the smartphone network when billions of devices connected by sending requests to a server. It leads to server clogging for handling extensive data.

10. **Quality of Service:** QoS is achieved by considering the time taken to deliver the messages between the sender and the receiver. In [23], the authors mentioned that in many applications, gathering data needs to be delivered within a specific time to the intended destination else the data will be of less value. The QoS requirements are met with differentiated services and delay management, packet loss, and bandwidth parameters on a network. Therefore, QoS needs research and stabilization for implementation, optimization, and control.

2.4.3 Connectivity Challenges

In this section, we discuss the main connectivity challenges in IoT environments, as shown in Figure 2.6.

1. **Heterogeneity:** Heterogeneous devices make the management and programmability of devices complicated. IoT best represents heterogeneity because it deals with the different devices and performs their functionalities. According to [24], it is a challenge to find an effective method to manage these devices without considering their nature. Heterogeneity of devices can be defined in various ways by using different technologies, sensing techniques, software, and processing methods. Heterogeneity can be determined according to different perspectives, such as:

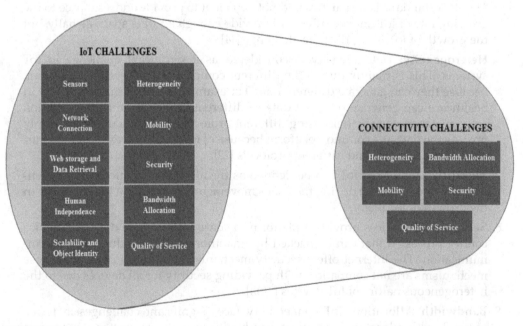

FIGURE 2.6
Connectivity challenges of IoT.

- **Operating Conditions:** The operating conditions of all sensor devices are not the same. They all work on various conditions like pressure, temperature, and voltage.
- **Functionality:** IoT devices can deliver data periodically and also as per demand.
- **Resolutions:** IoT devices may have the objective of tracking, monitoring, sensing, and actuating.
- **Hardware Platform:** Hardware used can vary according to the requirement of the device. It is based on architecture and design.
- **Services:** IoT services also differ in some scenarios, such as to calculate the packet size.
- **Implementations:** Various programming languages are used to design IoT applications. Different operating systems, like Android and iOS, are used to develop IoT applications [22].

2. **Mobility:** Mobility is the biggest challenge in the IoT network. Many IoT applications need IoT devices to be mobile such as vehicle tracking and patient tracking. The Wi-Fi faces client mobility with the movement of clients. Access points provide access to the client network when the client goes out of coverage from the system. An access point detects client signal strength is weak, and it needs to provide a new access point with the right coverage area. Sometimes, if the client gets connected to the new access point, then the Wi-Fi network takes time to get activated because the switches still use old routing rules and reconfiguration takes some time, leading to delay. Mobility also helps enterprises by allowing users to do their jobs from anywhere using a variety of devices and applications. It refers to the use of mobile devices like smartphones and laptops from anywhere to perform the required job. It provides flexibility and choice, which helps to increase productivity [8].

3. **Bandwidth Allocation:** Due to the increase in processing capabilities of IoT devices, edge networking is moving to IoT gateways and smart devices. It is not possible to fully process the data on-board due to the limited energy resources and processing capabilities. It needs to offload a few parts of the computation to the gateway and servers [25].

4. **Quality of Service:** QoS is one of the main requirements of IoT architecture to ensure quality service to users by prioritizing services. The real-time applications should be given high priority for the improvement in performance. It is measured using primary factors such as bandwidth and throughput. It needs to consider service models to check the degree of QoS for every internet service. Internet service models help in classifying internet services: first, is the ability to organize internet applications by assigning them priority and second, is to define the QoS service demands that are required to achieve user satisfaction. It is used in various areas such as smart healthcare, and to monitor traffic and human movement. In this case, reliable data delivery is essential without any delay [13].

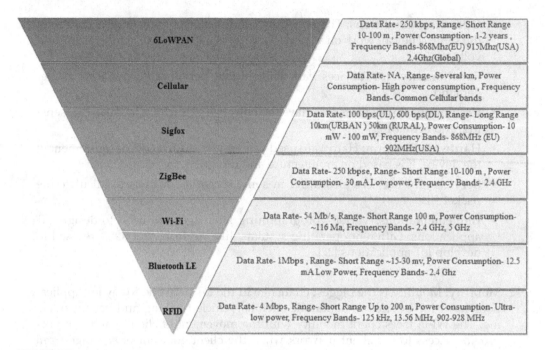

FIGURE 2.7
Technologies used in IoT.

2.4.3.1 Connectivity issues using various technologies

Various technologies are used to connect IoT devices. Primary techniques used in the past and present are Wi-Fi [26, 27], 6LoWPAN [26, 28], Zigbee [24, 28, 29], Bluetooth LE [28, 30], Sigfox [28, 31], cellular [26] and RFID [27, 28]. The features of all these technologies and the proposed technique to support connectivity challenges are mentioned in Figure 2.7.

2.4.4 Case Study: Results Analysis Using NetSim for University Environments

The aim is to accommodate the existing infrastructure, with minimal changes, for the growing number of connected IoT devices. IoT is expanding in almost all areas. It provides enormous advantages in different fields. In spite of several benefits, it also suffers from growth obstacles, as we have mentioned in this chapter.

To analyze device connectivity issues in terms of packet loss, throughput, delay, and jitter, we have used the systematic approach of simulation [32]. The simulation follows the eight-step methodology to identify deficiencies in the existing infrastructure. Literature ascertained that traditional Wi-Fi architecture is not flexible, and traditional WLAN architecture-based controllers are usually closed and not programmable.

For this, we set up a simulation network for a university in NetSim by connecting various IoT devices. During the transmission of data, we will identify the issues in terms of packet loss, delay, jitter, and throughput. The simulation will emulate a planned gathering of a large number of people for a conference or social event in a university or a confined place. The simulation will show how the existing infrastructure can withstand the normal

Results of University 1 and University 2					
University 1 Results	**Throughput (Mbps)**	**Delay(microsec)**	**Jitter(microsec)**	**Packet generated**	**Packet received**
Average	0.092142	60523.03025	3271.751611	7358	7356
Packet Loss	2				
University 2 Results	**Throughput (Mbps)**	**Delay(microsec)**	**Jitter(microsec)**	**Packet generated**	**Packet received**
Average	0.0453078	886367.3074	32025.46789	12899	2580
Packet Loss	10319				
Results comparison of University 1 and University 2					
	University 1	**University 2**	**Value difference**		
Throughput (Mbps)	More	Less	University 1 throughput is more than University 2 by value 0.0468342		
Delay(microsec)	Less	More	University 2 Delay is more than University 1 by value 825844.27716035		
Jitter(microsec)	Less	More	University 2 Jitter is more than University 1 by value 28753.7162765833		
Packet Loss	Less	More	University 2 Packet loss is more than University 1 by value 10317		

FIGURE 2.8
Comparison of results in NetSim.

population in the confined area and the large group of people in the same area. The reason for using simulation is due to the diversity of IoT devices (or heterogeneous nature); it is not feasible to develop a prototype with many IoT devices.

We set up a simulation environment for various heterogeneous smart devices such as a microwave, fridge, television, smartphone, laptop, and so on. During the simulation, these devices will start communicating; the issues will be identified in terms of packet loss, delay, coverage, and throughput. We have categorized the university in two scenarios as University 1 and University 2. In University 1, we have connected a few devices, approx. 10–15, and 3 applications are configured such as 1 FTP, 1 voice, and 1 video. After simulating, we calculated the throughput, jitter, delay, and packet loss, as shown in Figure 2.8. The results show that if a few devices are connected then there are fewer chances of packet loss. As per our findings, only two packets are lost. In this case, throughput is more but jitter, delay, and packet loss is less. In University 2, we connected more devices, approx. 200. In this, 20 applications are configured such as 6 FTP, 8 voice, and 6 video. After simulating, we calculated the throughput, delay, jitter, and packet loss. The results show that if more devices are connected, then there are more chances of packet loss. As per the results, 10,319 packets are lost. In this case, throughput is less but jitter, delay, and packet loss is more. Therefore, with the increase in device, packet loss increases and throughput decreases.

2.4.5 Significance and Contribution

The idea of IoT has enticed significant research attention, since the large connectivity of devices brings a variety of challenges and obstacles including heterogeneity, bandwidth allocation, QoS, and mobility. IoT creates billions of devices and networks with an extensive range connected to the internet. In many applications, gathered data need to be delivered within a specific time to the intended destination, else the data will lose its importance. Therefore, QoS needs in-depth research and stabilization for implementation, optimization, and control.

2.5 Conclusion

In this chapter, the various IoT challenges and connectivity challenges are discussed. We have mainly focused on connectivity challenges such as heterogeneity, mobility, bandwidth allocation, and QoS to the technology used. To conclude, as with the increase in the number of devices, there is a need for new technology to support the connectivity among devices. The main motive of this chapter is to provide an idea about the connectivity challenges and different approaches used so far to overcome them. This chapter introduces an overview of the IoT systems, discussing various applications and benefits of integrating SDN in IoT. This chapter also discusses generic IoT system architectures and different connectivity challenges in IoT. These challenges are defined concerning the technology used. This chapter also includes the complete introduction of IoT systems and the challenges they face.

References

1. Theodorou, T. & Mamatas, L. (2017). CORAL-SDN: A software-defined networking solution for the Internet of Things. IEEE Conference on Network Function Virtualization and Software Defined Networks (NFV-SDN), Berlin, Germany, November 6–8.
2. Sharma, Lavanya & Garg, P.K. (Eds.). (2019). *From Visual Surveillance to Internet of Things*, New York: Chapman and Hall/CRC.
3. Kumar, Anubhav, Jha, Gaurav & Sharma, Lavanya. (July 2019). Challenges, potential & future of IOT integrated with block chain. *International Journal of Recent Technology and Engineering*, 8(2S7): 530–536.
4. Sharma, Lavanya & Lohan, Nirvikar. (2019). Internet of things with object detection, In *Handbook of Research on Big Data and the IoT*, IGI Global, pp. 89–100. DOI:10.4018/978-1-5225-7432-3.ch006
5. Sharma, Lavanya. (2019). Introduction: from visual surveillance to Internet of Things, In *From Visual Surveillance to Internet of Things*, Chapman Hall/CRC, Vol.1, p. 14.
6. Sharma, Lavanya, Singh, Annapurna, & Kumar Yadav, Dileep. (2016). Fisher's linear discriminant ratio based threshold for moving human detection in thermal video. *Infrared Physics and Technology*, 78: 118–128.
7. Bera, S., et al. (2017). Software-defined networking for Internet of Things: A survey. *IEEE Internet of Things Journal*, 4(6): 1994–2008.
8. Stiti, O., et al. (2015). Virtual OpenFlow-based SDN Wi-Fi access point. Global Information Infrastructure and Networking Symposium (GIIS), Guadalajara, Mexico, October 28.
9. Sallabi, F., Naeem, F., Awad, M. & Shuaib, K. (2018). Managing IoT-based smart healthcare systems traffic with software defined networks. International Symposium on Networks, Computers and Communications (ISNCC), Rome, Italy, June 19–21.
10. Harit, A., et al. (2017). Internet of Things security: challenges and perspectives. Proceedings of the Second International Conference on Internet of things, Data and Cloud Computing, Cambridge, UK, ACM: 1–8.
11. Kim, D. H., et al. (2016). Low-power, long-range, high-data transmission using Wi-Fi and LoRa. 6th International Conference on IT Convergence and Security (ICITCS), Prague, Czech Republic, September 26.
12. Patel, D. & Won, M. (2017). Experimental study on Low Power Wide Area Networks (LPWAN) for mobile Internet of Things. IEEE 85th Vehicular Technology Conference (VTC Spring), Sydney, Australia, June 4–7.

13. Hassan, Z., Ali, H. & Badawy, M. (2015). Internet of Things (IoT): Definitions, Challenges, and Recent Research Directions. *International Journal of Computer Applications*, 128(1): 140–156.
14. Gupta, R. & Gupta, R. (2016). ABC of Internet of Things: Advancements, benefits, challenges, enablers and facilities of IoT. Symposium on Colossal Data Analysis and Networking (CDAN), Indore, India, March 18–19.
15. Sharma, Lavanya & Garg, P. K. (2019). Smart E-healthcare with Internet of Things: Current trends challenges, solutions and technologies, In *From Visual Surveillance to Internet of Things*, Chapman Hall/CRC, Vol. 1, p. 215.
16. Sharma, Lavanya, Garg, P. K. & Agarwal, Naman. (2019). A foresight on e-healthcare Trailblazers, In *From Visual Surveillance to Internet of Things*, Chapman Hall/CRC, Vol. 1, p. 235.
17. Makkar, Suraj & Sharma, Lavanya. (2019). A face detection using support vector machine: Challenging issues, recent trend, solutions and proposed framework. Third International Conference on Advances in Computing and Data Sciences (ICACDS 2019, Springer), Inderprastha Engineering College, Ghaziabad, India, April 12–13.
18. Sharma, Lavanya & Garg P. K. (2019). Future of Internet of Things, In *From Visual Surveillance to Internet of Things*, Chapman Hall/CRC, Vol.1, p. 245.
19. Sharma, Lavanya & Garg, P. K. (2019). IoT and its applications, In *From Visual Surveillance to Internet of Things*, Chapman Hall/CRC, Vol.1, p. 29.
20. Kabalci, Y. (2019). 5G mobile communication systems: Fundamentals, challenges, and key technologies. In E. Kabalci & Y. Kabalci (Eds.), *Smart Grids and Their Communication Systems* (pp. 329–359). Singapore: Springer
21. Bedhief, I., et al. (2016). SDN-based architecture challenging the IoT heterogeneity. 3rd Smart Cloud Networks & Systems (SCNS), Dubai, UAE, December 19–21.
22. Hussain, M. I. (2017). Internet of Things: Challenges and research opportunities. *CSI Transactions on ICT*, 5(1), 87–95. Doi: 10.1007/s40012-016-0136-6
23. Farhan, L., et al. (2018). A concise review on Internet of Things (IoT)—Problems, challenges and opportunities. 11th International Symposium on Communication Systems, Networks & Digital Signal Processing (CSNDSP), Budapest, Hungary, July 18–20.
24. Gazis, V., Goertz, M., Huber, M., Leonardi, A., Mathioudakis, K., Wiesmaier, A. & Zeiger, F. (2015). Short Paper: IoT: Challenges, projects, architectures. Paper presented at the 18th International Conference on Intelligence in Next Generation Networks, Paris, France, February 17–19.
25. Samie, F., Tsoutsouras, V., Bauer, L., Xydis, S., Soudris, D. & Henkel, J. (2016). Computation offloading and resource allocation for low-power IoT edge devices. Paper presented at the IEEE 3rd World Forum on Internet of Things (WF-IoT), Reston, Virginia, USA, December 12–14.
26. Frenzel, L. (2012). The fundamentals of short-range wireless technology. *Electronic Design*, October 11.
27. Kuzlu, M., Pipattanasomporn, M. & Rahman, S. (2015). Review of communication technologies for smart homes/building applications. Paper presented at the 2015 IEEE Innovative Smart Grid Technologies—Asia (ISGT ASIA), November 3–6.
28. Azamuddin Bin Ab, Rahman (2015). Comparison of Internet of Things (IoT) data link protocols (paper, Washington University, St. Louis, USA).
29. Samuel, S. S. I. (2016). A review of connectivity challenges in IoT-smart home. 3rd MEC International Conference on Big Data and Smart City (ICBDSC), Muscat, Oman, March 15–16: 1–4.
30. Hughes, J., Yan, J. & Soga, K. (2015). Development of wireless sensor network using Bluetooth low energy (BLE) for construction noise monitoring. *International Journal on Smart Sensing and Intelligent Systems*, 8(2): 1379–1405.
31. Raza, U., Kulkarni, P. & Sooriyabandara, M. (2017). Low power wide area networks: An overview. *IEEE Communications Surveys & Tutorials*, 19(2), 855–873. doi:10.1109/COMST.2017.2652320.
32. Ülgen, O., Black, J. J., Johnsonbaugh, B. & Klunge, R. 2006. *Simulation Methodology: A Practitioner's Perspective*, Dearborn, MI: University of Michigan.

Part 2

3

Design of Internet of Things-Based Accident Detection System

Satyam Tayal

Thapar Institute of Engineering & Technology
Patiala, India

Harsh Pallav Govind Rao

Thapar Institute of Engineering & Technology
Patiala, India

Suryansh Bhardwaj

Thapar Institute of Engineering & Technology
Patiala, India

Samyak Jain

Thapar Institute of Engineering & Technology
Patiala, India

CONTENTS

3.1 Introduction 35
3.2 Methodology of the Accident Alert System 37
3.3 Design of the Proposed System 37
    3.3.1 Detection of the Accident 38
3.4 Workings of the Software 39
3.5 Results and Discussion 41
3.6 Conclusion 41
Acknowledgment 43
References 43

KEYWORDS: *sensors, traffic accidents, Global Positioning System (GPS), Central Processing Unit (CPU), Internet of Things (IoT), Application Programming Interface (API), Radio-Frequency Identification (RFID), Global System for Mobile Communications (GSM)*

3.1 Introduction

Road accidents are continuously on the rise due to a large number of vehicles on the road. In India, due to rapid urbanization and fast road network expansion followed by high growth of vehicles, road safety is a serious matter of concern. This large increase in road traffic causes more accidents. In the majority of cases, the nearby hospital, police station, or family members are not timely informed. This delay of medical and other help may cause

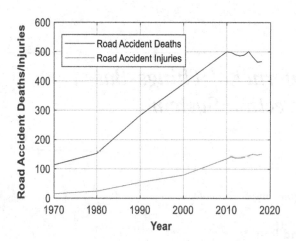

FIGURE 3.1
Road accident deaths/injuries in India [1].

a delay in the treatment of the suffering person and even the loss of life in severe cases. The number of road accidents in India from 1970 to 2018 are depicted in Figure 3.1.

In a large number of cases, the major cause of death is the delay in the intimation of the road accident to a nearby hospital [1]. Thus, the required medical help does not reach the accident site in time. In earlier techniques, accident information could be transferred without knowledge of the accident site. For successful treatment of an injured person, the accident location is required. Thereafter, a message to the nearby hospital and next of kin is sent [2–3]. There is a need for an automatic system to detect the accident location and quickly inform the nearby hospital and other concerned authorities [4–8]. This intimation time may be substantially reduced by application of modern Internet of Things (IoT) technology. This technology is changing at a rapid rate in the modern world. IoT technology uses a Radio-Frequency Identification (RFID) system, Wi-Fi, Global System for Mobile Communications (GSM), Global Positioning System (GPS), and cellular 4G, among others. [9–10]. IoT can be utilized to generate an automatic alert message sent to nearby concerned places or persons. IoT can be used in various industrial and domestic applications, including smart cities.

Smart cities are being planned to deliver cost-effective, quicker, and better amenities to the masses. A smart city integrates information and communication technology (ICT) with modern infrastructure [11–12]. The smart city offers increased quality of life through ICT, application of various sensors, higher energy efficiency, and availability of the latest technology.

To track a vehicle and generate an alert message using advanced IoT technologies, a system has been proposed in this chapter. The accident detection and alert system has been designed using various sensors, a microcontroller, a GSM modem, and a GPS receiver in a smart city environment. In the event of an accident, the emergency message is processed and directed to the closest hospital through designed IoT architecture. The GPS module [13] is used to determine the accident site coordinates. Based on these coordinates, the nearby hospital and the police station locations are determined by a server using an Arduino UNO microcontroller [14–16]. A short message service (SMS) alert and email messages are forwarded to the nearby hospital, police station, and a registered contact number by the GSM module [17]. This chapter is organized as follows: Section 3.2 discusses the methodology of the accident alert system. The accident has been detected using GPS and the GSM modules, and the complete design of the system has been included in Section 3.3. Section 3.4 consists of the working of the software, which is followed by the results and discussions. The last section is the conclusion.

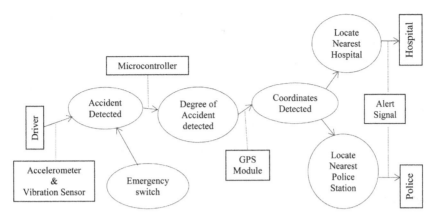

FIGURE 3.2
Flowchart of the working accident alert system.

3.2 Methodology of the Accident Alert System

The flowchart of the proposed accident alert system is shown in Figure 3.2. As soon as an accident occurs, the accident alert system identifies the coordinates of the accident location. Further, the system senses the severity of damage and vehicle passenger condition based on its algorithm. Thereafter, the system sends an alert message to the emergency services such as the nearest police station, hospital, and an emergency contact registered by the passenger.

The system is a small unit and can be embedded in a safe place inside a vehicle. It should be placed in a position with the least chance of damage. The system utilizes the Arduino UNO microcontroller as the Central Processing Unit (CPU). An accelerometer and vibrational sensors are used to predict the amount of damage to the vehicle and the condition of the passenger in the vehicle. A GPS module is used to determine the accident site coordinates. These details are sent to a server.

In order to determine the nearest hospital and the police station, the Haversine formula [18] is used by the server. Further, an SMS alert is sent to the nearest hospital/police station and a registered contact number by the GSM module. An email message is also sent to the emergency authorities for a quick response. If the accident is nominal and there is no need for emergency services, an additional emergency switch is provided for the passenger to terminate the detected accident alert [19–23]. The passengers have sufficient time to determine whether or not to call off the detected accident alert. Thus, this system provides an aid to the emergency facilities for road accidents in a feasible way.

3.3 Design of the Proposed System

The block diagram and components required for the design of the accident alert system are shown in Figure 3.3. The major blocks used in this work are: (1) microcontroller, (2) GPS module, (3) GSM module, (4) accelerometer, (5) vibrational sensor.

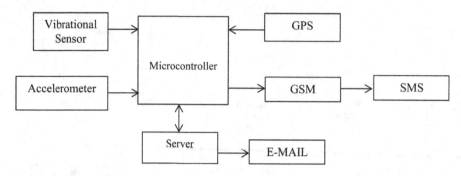

FIGURE 3.3
Block diagram of proposed system.

This circuit is designed using a microcontroller board used for embedded application. The interfacing components used are GSM and GPS modules, an accelerometer, and vibrational sensors. On occurrence of an accident, based on the stored information in the database, the accident intimation is sent to the next of kin of the passenger [24–26]. The nearby hospital and police station are also instantly informed about the exact location of the accident. The family member and hospital are informed using GPS and GSM modules.

3.3.1 Detection of the Accident

The road accident is detected using the accelerometer and the vibrational sensor. A triple-axis accelerometer ADXL335 (Figure 3.4) is used in the system. This sensor is a low-power device and can determine the static acceleration in three directions: X, Y, and Z. In occurrence of an accident, the angle of tilt of the vehicle with the horizontal can be determined with the help of the triple-axis accelerometer.

The vibrational sensor is also used to measure the impact of accident. This sensor is used to detect abnormal vibrations in the system. A vibrational sensor works on the piezoelectric effect. This measures the changes in force, temperature, pressure, and acceleration by changing to an electrical charge. This sensor sensitivity lies in a range of 10–100 mV/g. The vibrational and accelerometer sensors are used to determine the degree of the accident based on predefined threshold values. The threshold value depends on the type of vehicle used.

To compute the time and position, an SIM28 GPS module with GPS antenna uses a group of ground stations and satellites with an error up to 10–20 meters everywhere on Earth. This module has a six-channel GPS search engine and is highly power efficient. The SIM28 GPS module is a standalone L1-frequency module, operating at 1575.42 MHz. In

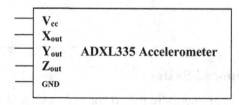

FIGURE 3.4
Triple-axis accelerometer (ADXL335).

FIGURE 3.5
Hardware implementation of accident alert system.

order to send the accident location coordinates to the emergency authorities, the SIM900A GSM module is also employed. It is one of the most commonly used GSM/GPRS modules. This module supports two frequency bands (900/1800 MHz) for SMS, voice, fax, and data. Its simple functionality makes it easier to integrate with a microcontroller. This module is utilized to direct an SMS to the emergency authorities.

For controlling the functionalities of all components, the Arduino UNO is utilized. The Arduino UNO board is constructed by using an ATmega328P microcontroller. The ATmega328P is an 8-bit microcontroller with 32 KB of in-system programmable flash memory. The Arduino UNO has 2 K bytes of SRAM and 32 K bytes of flash memory. It is highly versatile and one of the cheapest microcontroller-based boards. It can be easily programmed and a good choice to control the entire system. The hardware implementation of the proposed system is shown in Figure 3.5.

3.4 Workings of the Software

The software solution is implemented in different stages. First, detection of accident and detecting the degree of the accident. For implementing this, an algorithm is created taking into account the threshold values of the accelerometer and vibrational sensors. These values depend upon the type of vehicle used. The accelerometer and vibration sensors send data into the microcontroller, which, based on data received, predicts the amount of damage occurred to the person and, based on its damage level, it decides whether to send the accident alert or not. The accelerometer and vibrational sensors outputs are continuously checked and compared to the threshold values. If these values are beyond the threshold values, then an alert signal is generated. If the passenger finds the accident to be nominal and not an emergency, they are given sufficient time delay to press the "Ignore the Alert" button so that the fake alert is not sent to the emergency authorities. If the passenger doesn't hit the emergency switch within the allotted time, then the accident message along with the coordinates of the location are sent to the nearest hospital. Thus, medical help can be brought to the location as soon as possible and the lives of such people can be saved. Further, the police station and an emergency contact are also notified about the accident and its location.

TABLE 3.1

List of Registered Hospitals (Near Accident Location) and Their Coordinates

S.N.	Name of Hospital	Email	Latitude	Longitude
1	Max Super Specialty Hospital, Dehradun	xyz@gmail.com	30.37583	78.073598
2	Fortis Escorts Hospital, Dehradun	abcd@gmail.com	30.322459	78.05546
3	Kanishk Surgical & Super Specialty Hospital, Dehradun	uvw@gmail.com	30.292783	78.051644
4	Kailash Hospital, Dehradun	mlq@gmail.com	30.28907	78.064093
5	Shri Mahant Indiresh Hospital, Dehradun	pqr@gmail.com	30.306008	78.019757
6	Military Hospital, Dehradun	xyz@gmail.com	30.359546	78.035874
7	Jagdamba Hospital, Dehradun	abcd@gmail.com	30.298096	78.055979
8	Prem Sukh Hospital, Dehradun	uvw@gmail.com	30.320199	78.023959
9	MH, Dehradun	mlq@gmail.com	30.362433	78.038796
10	Synergy Hospital, Dehradun	pqr@gmail.com	30.340074	78.014922

The second function of the software is to locate the hospital nearest to the accident location using the Haversine formula. This is done by continuously communicating with a server storing all locations of hospitals registered with the proposed system. The server sends an email to the emergency authorities, providing another mode of communicating the alert and the location of the accident so that help can be provided by any mode at the earliest possible time.

Table 3.1 shows the list of all hospitals in close proximity of the considered accident location. The email is sent to the nearest hospital by using the Haversine formula. The mathematical expression for the Haversine formula is given by Equation (3.1):

$$d = 2r\sin^{-1}\left(\sqrt{\left(\cos(\phi_1) \times \cos(\phi_2) \times \sin^2\left(\frac{\lambda_2 - \lambda_1}{2}\right)\right) + \sin^2\left(\frac{\phi_2 - \phi_1}{2}\right)}\right) \qquad (3.1)$$

Equation (3.1) is valid for the Earth assumed as a spherical body. Here, d, r indicates the distance between two points on Earth and radius of Earth, respectively. The λ_1, ϕ_1, and λ_2, ϕ_2 indicates the longitudes and latitudes (in radians) of points 1 and 2, respectively.

In order to save the person, GPS is utilized to determine the accident location and a message is sent through GSM to the nearby hospital. The communication using the GSM module is initiated through AT commands. The location coordinates, a Google Maps link with the emergency message, are sent by the GSM module (Figure 3.6). The GSM module

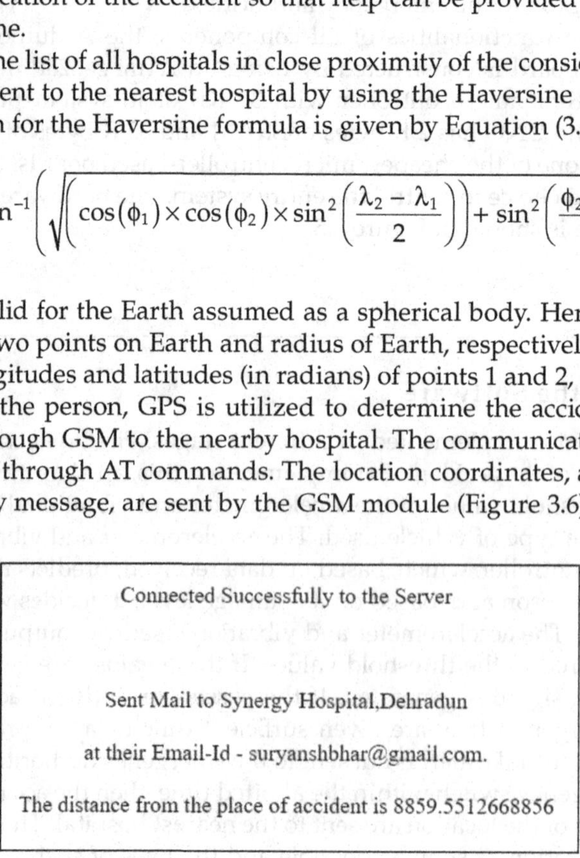

Connected Successfully to the Server

Sent Mail to Synergy Hospital,Dehradun

at their Email-Id - suryanshbhar@gmail.com.

The distance from the place of accident is 8859.5512668856

FIGURE 3.6
Email sent by server to hospital.

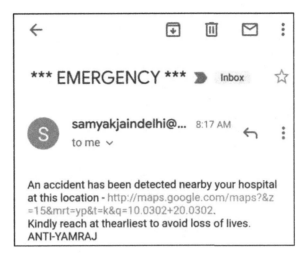

FIGURE 3.7
Email received by hospital.

is directed by AT commands. The Google Maps link is generated by using Google Maps Application Programming Interface (API). The email received by the nearest hospital is shown in Figure 3.7.

3.5 Results and Discussion

The proposed system can be placed inside a small box similar to a black box present in an aircraft. This accident alert system is implemented on a local host server. This can be implemented on the internet by purchasing a domain name for the server, hence, the server can be accessed from anywhere on the internet. The alert message is generated only when the accident is above the threshold limit. The threshold value depends on the type of vehicle used. The vibrational and accelerometer sensors are used to determine the severity of accident. The accelerometer sensor measures the angle of tilt of the vehicle with the horizontal on occurrence of the accident. The vibrational sensor detects abnormal vibrations in the vehicle. The SMS received by the nearest hospital is shown in Figure 3.8.

The longitude and latitude points captured by the GPS are also sent through email. Google Maps is also used to pinpoint and trace the exact location of the accident. The GPS location traced on Google Maps is shown in Figure 3.9. The location obtained may vary in a range of about 10–20 meters.

3.6 Conclusion

The death rate due to road accidents is continuously on rise. In the majority of cases, people die in road accidents due to the unavailability of instant intimation for medical help to the nearest hospital. The effective accident alert message can be generated and communicated

Latitude:30.42 longitude:77.97
Speed:0.0Knots http://maps
.google.com/maps?&z=15&
mrt=yp&t=k&q=30.416772+77
.966842

ICICI Bank ATM

30°25'00.4"N 77°58'00.6"E

FIGURE 3.8
SMS received by hospital.

in smart cities due to the availability of smart communication media. In this chapter, an accident alert system is designed to provide the real-time GPS coordinates of the vehicle to the nearby hospital, police station, and one emergency contact person in the event of an accident. The accelerometer and vibration sensors are used to judge the degree of damage to the vehicle and extent of injury to the passenger in the vehicle. The proposed system requires very small space and can easily be fitted by vehicle manufacturing companies inside any vehicle.

FIGURE 3.9
GPS location traced on Google Maps.

Acknowledgment

This research work is supported by the Thapar Institute of Engineering and Technology, Patiala, India. The authors are highly thankful to the Department of Electronics and Communication Engineering for providing laboratory facilities.

References

1. Ministry of Road Transport and Highways, Govt. of India. Road Accidents in India. 7–8. 2018. https://morth.nic.in/sites/default/files/Road_Accidednt.pdf
2. H. Singh, J.S. Bhatia, J. Kaur. Eve tracking based driver fatigue monitoring and warning system. India International Conference on Power Electronics (IICPE2010), Delhi, India, December 20–23, 2010, 1–6.
3. O. Rizwan, H. Rizwan, M. Ejaz. Development of an efficient system for vehicle accident warning. IEEE 9th International Conference on Emerging Technologies (ICET), Islamabad, Pakistan, December 9–10, 2013, 1–6.
4. S. Reeja, V.S. Jayaraj. An embedded based approaches for accident analysis using event data recorder. IEEE Conference on Electrical Instrumentation and Communication Engineering, Karur, India, April 27–28, 2017, 1–5.
5. C.V. Thota, L.K. Galla, R. Narisetty, U. Mande. Automated vigilant transportation system for minimizing the road accidents. Electronics Communication and Computational Engineering (ICECCE), Hosur, India, November 17–18, 2014, 179–183.
6. S.A. Shabbeer, M. Meleet. Smart helmet for accident detection and notification. 2nd International Conference on Computational Systems and Information Technology for Sustainable Solution (CSITSS), Bangalore, India, December 21–23, 2017, 1–5.
7. B.S. Anil, K.A. Vilas, S.R. Jagtap. Intelligent system for vehicular accident detection and notification. Communications and Signal Processing (ICCSP). 2014. 1238–1240.
8. D. Acharya, V. Kumar, N. Garvin, A. Greca, G.M. Gaddis. A sun SPOT based automatic vehicular accident notification system. Information Technology and Applications in Biomedicine (ITAB), 2008, 296–299.
9. Elprocus. RF module – Transmitter & receiver. 2019. https://www.elprocus.com/rf-module-transmitter-receiver/
10. Postscapes. IoT Technology Guidebook. 2019. https://www.postscapes.com/internet-of-things-technologies/
11. Z. Iqbal, M.I. Khan. Automatic incident detection in smart city using multiple traffic flow parameters via V2X communication. *International Journal of Distributed Sensor Networks*. 14. 11. 1–23. 2018.
12. F. Bhatti, M.A. Shah, C. Maple, S.U. Islam. A novel Internet of Things-enabled accident detection and reporting system for smart city environments. *Sensors*. 19. 9. 1–29. 2019.
13. Elliott D. Kaplan (Ed.). *Understanding GPS: Principles and Applications*. Artech House Telecommunications Library, London, 1996.
14. Krishna Kant. *Microprocessor and Microcontrollers*. Eastern Company Edition, New Delhi, India, 2007.
15. R.S. Gaonkar. *Microprocessor Architecture Programming and Application*. 5th Edition. Wiley Eastern Ltd, New Delhi, India, 2002.
16. [online] Available: https://store.arduino.cc/usa/arduino-uno-rev3 (Accessed on May 17, 2020).
17. G. Heine. *GSM Networks: Protocols, Terminology and Implementation*, Artech House Publishers, London, 1998.

18. [online] Available: https://en.wikipedia.org/wiki/Haversine_formula (Accessed on May 17, 2020).
19. R. Dias, V. Ghike, J. Johnraj, N. Fernandes, A. Jadhav. Vehicle tracking and accident notification system. 3rd International Conference for Convergence in Technology (I2CT), Pune, India, April 6–8, 2018, 1–4.
20. N. Kattukkaran, A. George, T.M. Haridas. Intelligent accident detection and alert system for emergency medical assistance, International Conference on Computer Communication and Informatics (ICCCI), Udupi, India, September 13–16, 2017, 1–6.
21. Michael Rosen, Method and system for automated detection of mobile telephone usage by drivers. *Electronics for You Magazine*. Akron, OH, 135, 2008.
22. R. Sujitha, A. Devipriya. Automatic identification of accidents and to improve notification using emerging technologies. International Conference on Soft-Computing and Networks Security (ICSNS), Coimbatore, India, February 25–27, 2015, 1–4.
23. S.J. Banarase, V.N. Jadhav, S.M. Sutar. Review on: Real time lane departure awareness system & maintenance in reducing road accidents. International Conference on Information Communication Engineering and Technology (ICICET), Pune, India, August 29–31, 2018, 1–3.
24. T. Kalyani, S. Monika, B. Naresh, Mahendra Vucha. Accident detection and alert system. *International Journal of Innovative Technology and Exploring Engineering (IJITEE)*. 8. 4S2. 227–229. 2019.
25. A. Kumar, V. Jaganivasan, T. Sathish, S. Mohanram. Accident detection and alerting system using GPS & GSM. *International Journal of Pure and Applied Mathematics*. 119. 15. 885–891. 2018.
26. K.L.S. Soujanya, Sri Sai Rajasekhar Gutta. Accident alert system with IOT and mobile application. *International Journal of Recent Technology and Engineering (IJRTE)*. 7. 5S2. 337–340. 2019.

4

Smart Healthcare in Smart Cities

Vukoman Jokanović

ALBOS Ltd, Institute of Nuclear Sciences "Vinca"
Belgrade, Serbia

CONTENTS

4.1 Introduction...45
4.2 Smart Healthcare 46
    4.2.1 Basic Information...46
    4.2.2 The Main Challenges 47
    4.2.3 Smart Healthcare Technologies 48
    4.2.4 Smart Homes 50
    4.2.5 Internet of Things 50
    4.2.6 S-Health and M-Health...53
    4.2.7 Electronic Health Record and Personalized Medicine................55
    4.2.8 Networked Healthcare System for Smart Cities...........................55
    4.2.9 Deep Learning and Smart Health Care...58
    4.2.10 Telecare Medical Information Systems...60
    4.2.11 Surgery in Space and Telesurgery..60
    4.2.12 Robotic Telesurgery 61
    4.2.13 Brain–Computer Interfaces 61
    4.2.14 Complex Nanoscale Geometry in Biology 63
    4.2.15 Relationship Between Physical Fields in Which Human Cells Emerge
           and Cell Geometry 65
4.3 Conclusion 67
References...67

4.1 Introduction

The up-growth of smart cities is mainly based on innovations in the data sciences with the aim of achievement of bettering people's life and viability in our highly citified population. Therefore, it is necessary to understand that we need new approaches and smart initiatives so we can connect all our databases to reach higher-ordered cities as unlimited, multisectorial, civil–environmental–infrastructural systems with numerous participants, preferences, and answers.

Taking in mind that by 2050, the number of people living in cities will probably increase to about 2.5 billion, while over 60% of urban areas will be built in Asia and Africa, it is clear that this must be followed by new infrastructure requirements. Besides, in existing cities worldwide, infrastructure essential for economic development, which assumes basic systems for supplying water, energy, and food, as well as healthcare, transport and information systems, waste disposal, and public sectors, is out of date, and it needs to be renovated and modernized [1, 2].

Infrastructure is very important for linking different aspects of human activity and everyday means of communication, which can be described from various aspects that include architecture, energy supply, transport, and management of the level of smart cities. A smart home, which is a home that combines diverse innovations for better solutions of everyday use, uses home sensors and actuators to enable full automation of numerous everyday functions, such as helping elderly and disabled people who often need help in their medicine intake management [3, 4].

As it is well known, medical data grows fast because the quantity of this information duplicates every two years. Furthermore, the quality of medical management systems enables significant contribution and accessibility of extensive medical databases, which allows quick collecting and filtering of the many results of their enquiries in order to detect and analyze the selected search information. Therefore, the main goal of healthcare is to maintain the degree of collective health and assure the needs for professional medical treatment [3, 4].

In this discourse, the main problems are influenced by the shortcomings of the concept of personal healthcare, which assumes the observation of each patient separately, because these results are dependent on specific characteristics, current state, and anamnesis. The next challenge is joined with the condition of the organisms that rapidly change over time, while each event should be considered as the consequence of other events. In order to use such technologies, raw medical data might be processed by deep learning models, using programs for the previous separation of vital data from the starting information to constitute them in ordinary formats. Therefore, a very efficient system is able to respond to the inquiry of administrative workers, fast and precise [4, 5].

Additionally, the various prescriptions with complicated medical names and several concomitant medications with similar drug delivery instructions and with various expiration dates and adverse effects are some of the specific issues addressed in smart healthcare services, in a so-called smart home, in which the central place belongs to the Magic Medicine Cabinet (MMC), which contains an automatic face recognition program, radio-frequency identification (RFID) smart tags (which enable the remote nodes of devices with which the readers and writers communicate), a healthy signs detector, and speech synthesis. Besides, the MMC contains the home personalized reminder that detects when a patient takes the wrong drugs and checks their vital functions. The specific database can be dedicated as an energetic approach and data in the relationship with the cell's geometry and its structure and substructure, which is suitable for deep learning methods as the base of the enhancement of medical healthcare. It increases opportunities for successful medical service on the significantly higher degree, through a close relationship of traditional medicine and exact medicine founded on the physical models briefly discussed in this chapter [4–6].

4.2 Smart Healthcare

4.2.1 Basic Information

Smart healthcare is a new communication technology based on the combination of smart mobile end electronic devices with everyday healthcare. Its crucial goal is the improvement of the medical treatment of the patient and completes their health, enabling enhancement of the quality of their life and good communication between patients and medical workers, over corresponding mobile and electronic providers. In this internet era, new medical knowledge, theory, and practical experiences are multiplied so quickly that the connection between healthcare and modern internet technologies becomes necessary. These technologies change everything because they are centered on the patient, joining medical staff and their information with the patients, regardless of where they are located [7–10].

Smart healthcare is the crucial phase in the idea of a smart city and planet from the standpoint of health, using technologies like Internet of Things (IoT) and supercomputers, with dynamic access to health information and treatments, with strong information networks, to ensure the best healthcare and decision making and rational use of health resources. It includes networking between patient disease and its prevention, diagnosis, medical treatment, and all other services inside of hospital and clinical centers, with diverse internet technologies, like IoT, cloudlet and cloud computing, big data, 4G and 5G networks, machine learning, and so on. All these technologies enable a very close relationship between patients and doctors, resulting in the best decisions from the aspect of patient treatment. At the same time, such approaches reduce the cost and medical risk, increasing the efficiency of medical support. Healthcare in practice is shared between clinical or scientific institutions, regional decision-making institutions, and patients [7–10].

4.2.2 The Main Challenges

The most important technologies for the development of smart healthcare are IoT-enabling transitions of all crucial data and decisions for patients regardless of the patient and provider locations and machine learning, which enhances their quality of care. These smart technologies are the core of smart healthcare, pushing their service to the edge, which is not limited by the physical location of any subject of this technology. The expanded databases give more useful and specific information about patients, enhancing their outcome and health efficiency, but the essential dilemma for healthcare institutions has balanced these outcomes with operative institutions' efficiency. These two responsibilities can sometimes be in opposition to each other. One has a direct impact on the patient community, while the other is more oriented to the medical organization's efficiency. The challenge is to balance both outcomes and integrate them over new communication technologies in a unified whole [7–10].

The digital front office primarily dedicated to the patient community enables healthcare providers' insight in the habits and necessary service of patients, where the experience of the patient is essential for an organization to learn from the patient's experience. The waiting time for the service ordered on the frequency of patient flow, and corresponding predictions, can be the most effective method for medical serving patients. Then, by using the small devices, the patients moving inside of the medical institution can be tracked, giving them adequate suggestions about the available requested staff at the hospital. To provide all these opportunities in the back office by internet technology behind of the main scene transforms patient experience into income for a healthcare institution, balancing between enhancement of the patient's outcome and efficiency of healthcare systems, enabling the most acceptable price for their healthcare service [7–10].

Enterprise resource planning (ERP) by appropriate software allows electronic asset tracking, which is labeled, by RFID. This enables optimization of resources, making rules that are flexible and ensuring efficient billing. Smart healthcare is oriented on care outside the hospital or clinic, extending the continuum of care, like telemedicine and all issues related to it, moving the boundary of healthcare using digital technologies and internet desktop infrastructure. It allows the collection of patient data from medical monitor systems. The same devices can give insight on where a patient is walking, or in bed, monitoring their activity level. On the base of specific data, they can evaluate the patient's health state from afar. These devices can measure blood pressure, temperature, or something else, enabling better diagnostics in real time and taking the necessary preventive measures if they are needed [7–10].

The back office is based on artificial intelligence and robotics, to improve the capabilities of the medical laboratories and pharmacy. Introduction of robotic devices make the analysis faster and more accurate and circulation of the data between a patient and medical institutions is more successful, with better outcomes for the patient and a diminished risk of possible error. Predictive capabilities are better, leading to better instrument calibration, and optimization of the needed drugs in the healing process. Diagnosing at a distance becomes much better. Social media also plays an important role, which can be used for spreading smart healthcare across a large geography, joining the healthcare system in various countries in one unique global system, and using all available capacities everywhere for the global enchantment of healthcare [7–10].

A crucial goal in this strategy is the collection of health data and the formation of suitable queries with all necessary questions. It particularly respects the nature of the queries, and data set questions, which are necessary for the patient's right answers. All obtained information is integrated with data from various devices, including patient monitoring, and other sources of knowledge. These data are important for fast exchange of information and data between various subjects in healthcare systems. Besides, the other managing components of these systems are their patient access, outcomes, and cost, and all of these must be satisfied for efficient functioning [7–10].

Machine learning systems and other artificial intelligence systems are often more precious than doctors and specialists for some areas of medicine, particularly in pathology and imaging, because they give a very reliable connection between clinical data and new scientific knowledge. Particularly, they are successful in the case of cancer and diabetes because algorithm-based devices improve diagnosis and support timely adequate medical treatment, which can be fully personalized [7–10].

Therefore, recent smart healthcare concepts should be enriched by macro guidance and program strategy to improve the benefit of the used resources. There are no uniform medical standards for medical institutions in various areas and their institutions, which makes communication between them very difficult. Besides, there are no compatibilities between various platforms and devices, because data sharing is very complicated. The legal norms from the aspect of risk are also missing because some healthcare technologies are in the experimental phase and request more knowledge and experience to be upgraded and maintained. Unified technical standards and a much higher degree of compatibility are necessary to achieve efficient exchanges of medical information, their data security, and transmission stability, through appropriate legislation rules and ethical standards [7–10].

4.2.3 Smart Healthcare Technologies

Wireless technologies, like Wi-Fi, Bluetooth, RFID, wireless sensor networks (WSNs), wearable medical devices, and smart mobile technologies are the main base of smart healthcare systems. They play an essential role in traffic information among different physical elements [11]. The RFID implant permits user recognition, motion detection, and automation, enabling an intelligent reaction in user identification, while the wearable sensor nodes are responsible for measurements of vital signs, like pulse, respiratory rate, and body temperature, which are crucial for the assessment of the health status. The smartphone and smartwatch will probably include reliable health technology sensors and abilities in future, which will enable distant monitoring of patients' health, including corresponding data collection, drug dosage, medication compliance, and access to medical documentation.

Beside typical smart functions in smart cities, such as government, education, transport, energy, control, environment, community, communication, payment, and commerce, smart healthcare is also one of the crucial priorities in the development of the smart city [12]. Smart healthcare (mobile and electronic) assumes sensing, networking, computing, RFID, WSNs, and artificial intelligence, including sensors, medicine dispensation, smart pills, smart surgeries, wearables, and new registration devices [13]. It combines smart technologies within the home, hospital, patient, and information exchange. Top healthcare technologies such as IoT, cloud computing, big data, deep learning, and advanced analytics transform traditional healthcare into smart healthcare.

IoT enables the extension of the utilities of the internet such as distant access, exchange data, and networking of various other application areas like healthcare, transport, parking, agriculture, and surveillance. IoT in healthcare technologies is also popularly known as the Internet of Medical Things (IoMT). It allows mutual connections of all entities through wired or wireless communication. Its primary goal is to connect doctors with patients through a smart device. This technology will revolutionize the gathering of healthcare data and care delivery [14]. This communication can be short-range communications and long-range communications. For example, electrocardiogram (ECG) data can be collected by a suitable registering node and transferred straight to the IoT cloud using Wi-Fi. IoT devices can also help the elderly to keep a close track of their medications and vitals like heart rate, glucose levels, and sleep patterns.

The healthcare industry is responsible for generating a considerable amount of so-called big data. This includes demographic data, historical data, illness-related information, test results, imaging data, costs, discharge summaries, pharmacies, insurance companies, medical imaging, genomics, social media, smartphones, wearables, sensors, and other IoT devices. These data are characterized by volume, velocity, variety, veracity, and value.

Cloud computing is a recent computing resource and ministration. It offers not only the colossal capacity of computing and storage, but also data sharing, and unlimited access to resources. Application areas of this technology include urgent medical healthcare, auxiliary healthcare, and telemedicine, incorporating storage, dividing, and progress of widespread medical resources. Cloud computing provides the following primary services: Software as a Service (SaaS), Platform as a Service (PaaS), and Infrastructure as a Service (IaaS). It can reinforce healthcare communities through the distribution of information such as electronic health records (EHR), suggestions, insurance data, and trial results. It enables easy archiving and uses patient records and medical images and collaboration into medical teams. It is expected that cloud computing healthcare will exponentially grow [15–17].

The other significant component of smart healthcare is machine learning (ML), which enables a computer's ability to learn without being explicitly programmed. This learning augments patient care and saves money because ML performs diagnostics or precious healthcare treatment plans. The application of ML opened up a new area in smart healthcare, where personalized care is the primary goal of smart healthcare solutions, which can be easily applied through machine learning [17, 18].

Smart home healthcare provides care in the home for outpatients, particularly for older people and people with disabilities. It allows communication between patients and doctors about their current health status. It enables the management of chronic illnesses of the elderly population. This technology is designed to assist the homes' residents in the realization of their daily living activities. It is cost-effective and allows elderly people considerable freedom and living standards, decreasing their potential social isolation. A robot at home mainly takes care of patients at home. Smart healthcare recording is needed to enable enhanced and total care to patients. Wireless body area networks (WBANs) are the crucial constituent of social healthcare recording, which is assisted by miniature sensors located on the patient's body to record different vital signs such as blood pressure, heartbeat, temperature, and prolonged electrocardiogram [19].

Online virtual clinics provide all-day access for patients over a smart mobile device called "Virtual Clinic" that allows doctors to answer the patient's questions very quickly. With internet-enabled smart devices, smart healthcare has become a reality in which patients can receive medical treatment from anywhere across the world, enhancing the standards of patient care and reducing healthcare cost; however, sharing patients' sensitive information over the internet leads to severe security and privacy concerns. Because confidentiality is an urgent security requirement in smart healthcare, due to sophistical cyberattacks, this is a significant challenge in the application of this technology in medical practice [17–20].

4.2.4 Smart Homes

Although the MMC is a very promising product, it is not optimally adapted for the requirements of elderly people. One of the problems is its interaction with the patient's medication, physicians, and healthcare providers. The smooth interaction of a smart home with the patient's physicians, pharmacists, and healthcare providers is desirable, enabling useful checking of adverse effects during drug distribution.

The Smart Medicine Cabinet (SMC) [21] and the Smart Box [22, 23] can widen the MMC by RFID and Bluetooth, to coordinate the requirements of the MMC by a wireless smartphone, enabling automatic updating of the SMC content, by RFID. In this way, the smartphone as a part of the SMC content helps to synchronize user information, reducing their intervention to a minimum.

Therefore, the Medicine Information Support System (MISS) and its subsystems, with all its interactions, have to be adapted for successfully managing the medical services and detection of possible conflicts, including a patient visit to the doctor and getting their prescription, when details are entered into medical documentation. Additionally, this system should have a possibility to check the conflict between various prescribed drugs and health conditions based on the patient's observations. After this consideration, the patient will be informed which prescription of drugs will be picked up. Based on this, the pharmacy will prepare drugs following the physician's instructions, double-checking the adverse drug effects and health status founded on the patient's report of the pharmacy. Finally, the patient consumes the drugs at the smart home, following the RFID-instructions, and uses the RFID-reader to check the appearance of the recent drugs into the smart home system. The smart home will then update its database and produce an ending verification of adverse effects contained in the drugs, including health status and eating habits. Therefore, an organized MISS coordinates the doctor, the pharmacy, the patient, and smart home [21–23].

4.2.5 Internet of Things

IoT enables a connection of various smart devices, such as smartphones, notebooks, sensors, and many other similar devices to send and receive information [24]. These objects can be used for diverse aims. A smartphone can be applied for the collection of data from sensors, monitoring environmental or patient body temperatures, transforming them in audio or video signals, and retrieving and storing these data in assistance of a cloud depository, while the application of these smart devices is unlimited. The application of IoT technology assumes the close connection between the patient and the smart home, smart city, and smart environment, which includes very fast monitoring of all data related to the health status of the patient (e.g., the temperature, activity, and position of the baby in the womb of the mother in her smartphone). Smart medicine assumes home safety attendance remotely or in the neighborhood on smartphones and sensor networks to record the weather, or anticipates some danger in time (earthquake, tsunami). Such smartphones include various sensors and devices (accelerometer, gyro, video, GPS, and RFID) for the identification of the resources in the healthcare system. This system can be particularly useful in undeveloped states where basic health services are not enough good, especially in rural areas; although everywhere in the world, mobile operators with wired or wireless infrastructure exist, including pastoral regions [25, 26].

Patients in smart health divisions can be medicated from a distance if the doctor or specialists are not available, because doctors online can make suggestions and recommendations to the patient in this unit via the internet using corresponding applications, enabling collection of patient data in real time by sensors, suggesting at the same time a mode of treatment and some further investigations. Therefore, patients do not need to visit clinics for regular or ordinary checkups. The patient will travel only when it is necessary. Besides the primary health facility, this smart health unit (SHU) will ensure the right decisions of the physician regarding travel. Artificial intelligence techniques will be applied for automatic decisions by using cloud services, which will make the distance depository possible and artificial intelligence learning will be used to improve the patient's database and enhance automatic actions. An SHU has a particular importance. This technique is feasible if sensors of an SHU are available to the tehsil headquarter hospital (HQH) and the HQH to the district headquarter (DHQ) as managing centers of regions by the internet that is afforded over the public switched telephone network (PSTN) or mobile operators with an IoT provider, which supports all services in the smart city [26–27].

IoT service providers should be joined with data collections of every medical institution in the city. These data collections contain data about available medical staff, physicians, pharmacists, specialists, beds, and rooms for the patient and the facility's total capacity for various types of patients. From the aspect of efficiency, during processing, the appliance must be adapted to support diverse file transfer protocols between various institutions. Besides, in the sensor sheet, the underlying interface sheet contact with a patient in an SHU and upper sheets. It collects health data about heartbeats, pulse rates, blood glucose degrees, and arterial and systolic pressure, and so on. Sensors are applied to transfer these data from the patient and their vicinity in an SHU through various protocols depending upon the inquiry [28].

Usual file transfer protocols at this sheet are Zigbee and Bluetooth. In an SHU, the information gathered from the patient's body is transferred to the cloud depository, by similar cloud services on the internet. The cloud depository data will be retrieved by remote from HQH, DHQ, or anywhere in the world, even if there are no physicians or medical workers in the HQH and DHQ. Communications with medical staff in such cases will be provided by smartphones or by a virtual private network (VPN), which can join the DHQ, HQH, and SHU. In cloud storage, the patient's health data can be retrieved by smart units in the HQH/DHQ by using specific inquiry applications.

IoT shall be capable of including plenty of diverse and miscellaneous networks, ensuring open access to essential subgroups of information for the growth of an abundance of electronic services. Constructing a basic infrastructure for IoT is a very complicated job, primarily due to the great diversity of devices, link layer technologies, and services entangled in such infrastructure. The urban IoT systems can be described over their particular application. They are designed to keep up the smart city vision, using the most enhanced information technologies to reinforce diverse services of the city and ordinary people [25–26].

IoT is a current communication model, in which the things of ordinary life will be connected with microcomputers, control centers for digital communication, and will be able to contact not only mutually but also with users, becoming a constitutive fragment of the internet [29]. IoT postulation enhances the strength of the internet, making it more fascinating and wide-spreading. Besides, IoT easy access and interlink with many diverse devices (household apparatus, supervision cameras, sensors, actuators, displays, vehicles) accelerates the expansion of many uses, potentially generating extensive quantity and diversity of information, enabling new services to ordinary people, firms, and administrations. This service becomes necessary in many different spheres, in all fields of people living in smart cities [30].

This difficulty can influence the expansion of various and, occasionally, conflicted programs for the applied recognition of IoT systems. Therefore, the establishment of an IoT network, together with the needed backup services and tools, is still absent due to its newness and complicity. Besides, the promotion of the IoT network is also obstructed by the absence of a clear and widely eligible business model for investments to encourage the disposition of these technologies [29–30]. IoT in an urban context is exceptionally important because it strongly forces governments to adjust their information and communication technology (ICT) results in management related to the sociopolitical area, to the smart city concept [25–29]. This concept includes better use of common resources, enhancing the quality of citizen services, and decreasing the serviceable costs of the government administrations. This goal can be accompanied by the disposition of an urban IoT, such as an information infrastructure to enable cooperative, easy, and functional access to an abundance of administrative services, thus releasing its full capacity and transparency to the citizens.

It is well-known that an urban IoT may induce many benefits in the management and optimization of traditional public services. Besides, the accessibility of various types of information, gathered by a ubiquitous urban IoT, may also induce the increase of the transparency and encourage the efforts of the local authorities to the citizens, improving the knowledge of the citizen about the real problems of their city, stimulating their active involvement in the management of public authorities, and inspiring them in the modeling of new services by IoT. Therefore, the application of the IoT model to the smart city is especially interesting to local and regional authorities, who should be the first to embrace such technologies, catalyzing its applications on a broader extent [25–29].

ICT has enormous significance in fundamental transformations of healthcare. Electronic devices play a crucial role because they allow medical treatments and monitoring of patients, known as mobile health (m-health). Due to the extraordinary development of IoT and similar technologies, the center of attention is shifted from mobile technologies to smart technologies, which can search, recognize, accept, and apply the context of patients as the foundation of smart health (s-health), built on the context of aware network and sensing infrastructures. All these changes enable better quality, lower prices, and expanded opportunities for medical research. Software for smart healthcare improves and simplifies citizen's potential to interact with increasingly complex and heterogeneous environments, analyzing people systems, and designing software to enable and improve their operations in such variable environments [29–30].

Software is normally oriented on machinery, while this software is created to be better adjusted to the machine. In the case of healthcare, this is a complex goal, contained from diverse context-sensitive inconsistencies and operations. This enables a software system to work as a central unit with central controls making healthcare systems more successful in the communication between medical professionals and patients [29, 30].

These systems support connections with diverse data origin and citizens into the hospital, frequently combining minimally invasive techniques, accelerating corresponding medical treatments because patients would be discharged earlier from the hospital, and greatly decreasing the cost of their treatment, advancing the accessibility of the user interfaces. This software should provide knowledge instead of data, overcoming drawbacks of the enormous amount of data, which blur the right information, filtering all received information taking into account the user's background knowledge. Innovations, which include anatomical models, improve analysis of patient diverse data, searching the most relevant elements for medical diagnosis or healing, while artificial intelligence learning, data collection, and processing change given data into useful information [31].

Nevertheless, correspondence questions are constantly present, causing usability challenges induced by the extra work if reentering data or by its manual transferring, because crucial data may be misplaced or corrupted in transcription, or lost interoperability between medical devices. In the case of contextual data, the integration problem can be very pronounced, causing additional problems from the aspect of the data characteristics (like velocity, variety, and volume). During a patient's life, they need more or less care, depending on their lifestyle. Usually, if they live healthier, they look for slight assistance to stay healthy, enabling the healthcare professionals to cooperate with them in safeguard programs, particularly adjusted to those people with a severe health risk. Symptoms of the severe disorder request intensive reactions between patients and medicals, particularly in the case of chronic diseases, which assumes aftercare and home care. In all phases, healthcare customers have to be more or less connected to healthcare professionals, and take complete responsibility for their health [31–32].

In emergency and monitoring cases during diagnosis and treatment, a real-time reaction is most important to decrease patient pain. Therefore, support in decisions includes sophisticated robots because the decision should be based on a great amount of data related to recent citizen health and their healthcare history. All this information is desirable to provide proper medical treatment, in which patients are at the center of the treatment process, mainly focused on prevention [33].

4.2.6 S-Health and M-Health

The conception of s-health is based on numerous health-supported data by mobile devices (m-health), which include the sensing capabilities of smart cities. While the user data in m-health arrives from the patients, in s-health, the information also includes complete smart city infrastructure as a new source of data. M-health is individualized, that is, useroriented (information is directed to the patient), while s-health is city-centric because of the information gathered by the patient's influence on the city behavior, including the safe arrival of an ambulance. S-health is focused on society, because all people during their lifetime will probably become a patient, participating in healthcare costs. S-health brings benefit to society by significant improvement of healthcare services, oriented to the establishment of a healthier community and a physical and nutritional routine inside of the feasible and green smart city. Citizens' benefits are better living conditions and independence, more productive and cheaper treatments, and decreasing deadlines and mortality rates. Due to a very efficient preventive, a patient will require fewer treatments; while the infrastructures of s-health based on big data and cloud computing will enable the collecting of unthinkable big quantities of data, which are very valuable for the professional community, increasing knowledge in diverse basic fields of human activity, healthcare, and engineering [34].

It assumes a change of behavior of many professionals who have work habits in the corresponding institution because they are not accustomed to sharing their knowledge to find multidisciplinary responses based on the concept of s-health. Therefore, the approach of s-health requests interaction and collaboration among governments, investigators, doctors, and specialists, to determine a common concept maximally adapted to the citizen in smart cities. Protection of confidentiality and protection of infrastructure is the essential problem of s-health for the research community, because from the gathered data in a smart city, it is possible to introduce citizens' customs, social position, and religion, including patient health information [35].

Taking in mind that big data can be principally explained by diversity, velocity, and volume in a smart city, data collected from the sensors, like temperature, pollution, and allergens, must be analyzed almost in real time to provide adequate service to citizens/patients (rate of information and the final decision about the best way to overcome given health problems). Since the amount of collected data is huge due to measurements every few seconds of thousands of sensors (volume), their collecting and processing in real time is an enormous problem in both bandwidth and storage, because it is necessary to use the cloud paradigm when inducing numerous implications related to privacy, security, and access control. Therefore, patient interaction with the city administration is attended with diverse problems, like designing better sensors, improving their compactness, weight, and autonomy. By simplifying interaction among them, their reliability will be improved. Besides, there are some other problems related to financial constraints, lack of the proper estimations of the technological difficulties, organizational problems, and weak interaction among various contributors (i.e., patients, physicians, analysts, sociologists, engineers, computer professionals). It assumes the use of infrastructure of smart cities, giving diverse possibilities for the development of new sanitary services [36].

Real-time collected data from patients about patient vital signals, habits, and health status, should be combined with city information obtained from sensors, cameras, and weather forecasts, and integrated for efficient use in s-health uses. S-health enables efficient precaution and healing of chronic and acute illnesses and injuries, identifying situations carefully when intervention is necessary, as in the case of cardiovascular severe events and accidents, providing an automatic and optimal solution for them, and directing patients in some cases to the nearby pharmacy or healthcare contributor when their life is in a dangerous situation. Besides, real-time analyses of gathered data provide not only efficient disease prevention and earlier detection of chronic illnesses, but also the identification of new health threats and risk factors [37].

Chronic patient's data, like their vital signs. abnormal heart rate, blood pressure, and blood glucose, can be combined with a patient's health state, living place, and recent animations to decrease potential health complications. S-health systems should connect long-term follow-up of the patient, medical documentation, and efficiency of the used methodologies with city sensors' information, as a key factor of the requested personalized therapy. Besides, environmental measured parameters such as temperature, contamination, moisture, and patients' daily routines should be applied for the final adjustment of required drug doses. The ability of the system for routine assessment to the patient increases the effectiveness of each intervention [37, 38].

For efficiency of s-health systems, public health management plays an essential role, which can "personalize" their policies and decisions to each town and region, taking into account information obtained from residents, and specifically, health risks such as climate and accessible infrastructure. S-health information and procedures can also improve the ability of detection and control infections or a pandemic, because patients' vital signals can be applied to predict new cases of epidemics by clear detection of regions of growing risk, and better managing not only the epidemic but also various other health risks (contamination or radiation) [39].

4.2.7 Electronic Health Record and Personalized Medicine

EHRs as a part of Healthcare IT (HIT), includes genetics/genomics in the clinical reports to enhance patient protection and outcomes, simultaneously diminishing medical treatment and healthcare prices. EHRs, due to enhanced performances, will enable better clinical decisions, quality assurance, and communication inside the healthcare network, and finally, fewer healthcare costs and improved patient outcomes. These data are crucial for clinical conclusions related to disease risk estimation and diagnosis, medical treatment, and risk assessment for an adverse drug reaction [40].

Also, EHRs allow fast and persistent learning from unified clinical genomic information for suitable and efficient replies on personalized medicine requests. Genomics permit EHRs to integrate genotype and phenotypic information, inserting them into the clinical work stream, and enabling further application of the information for outcome examination. National EHR authorities of health information in corresponding uniform forms then are transmitted to healthcare providers focused on systematic patient care [41].

Genetic/genomic implications include checks of efficiency for genomic-based drugs, their dose harmonized with differences in native drug metabolism of various clients, risk of side effects, health maintenance and risk evaluation, diagnostic programs, medication, medical prediction, and transmission of care. For some illnesses, EHR assumes patient genomic profiles, among other clinical data, organized in the form of a warehouse model designed to support the effective selection of patients with specific characteristics, supporting specific outcomes analysis, and clinical management [42].

4.2.8 Networked Healthcare System for Smart Cities

Smart city enhancements become the largest global challenge. Growing requests for pervasive and personalized healthcare with diminished risks and price require mobile cloud computing to fulfill the healthcare requests by providing fast analyses of patients' data. Ubiquitous healthcare firm, Ube Health, has the most advanced approach to s-healthcare, including advanced data processing, machine learning, big data, high-performance computing (HPC), and IoT. They serve to optimize network circulation, which consecutively over cloudlet and net sheets adjusts data speeds and storing, and daily outcomes. Advancements in s-healthcare ICT—cloud computing, IoT, broadcasting communications, WSN, WBAN, big data, robotics, artificial intelligence, and 4G/5G networks—has a significant impact in the advancement of healthcare because these techniques can provide anywhere, anytime connectivity, initiating the new generation of healthcare paradigms and services [43–48].

Bearing in mind that smart cities are a significant transforming driver of healthcare and many other industries because they involve the incorporation of various city systems like transport, healthcare, and research, their development is significant for distribution of as best as possible healthcare to the patients, regardless of where they live in the world. Ube Health assumes excellent service for patients at any time anywhere regardless of their location and without any problems related to the patients' mobility. It enables distant care for patients with any kind of disease, particularly for illnesses like diabetes, heart disease, arthritis, and lupus. IoT healthcare systems include improvement in all internet technologies—2G, 3G, WLAN, 4G, and recent 5G networks. Besides these technologies, cloud computing is of particular importance, which assures continual access anywhere to the data saved in a cloud, which significantly reduces the price of constructing a healthcare system, efficiently using the facility inside of the cloud. This technology can easily integrate IoTs with Mobile Cloud Computing (MCC). Also, MCC healthcare applications enable fast monitoring of the essential signs of patient healthcare vitals, and consequences of the other patient's activities, analyzing corresponding information obtained by the various detection devices and IoT tools at the principal cloud. MCC has many advantages because it allows limitless use of resources by electronic devices without any difficulties [43–48].

In recent times, cloudlets developed elsewhere as data centers enhanced the latency and bandwidth of the network. They enhance the quality of service (QoS) of an interconnected healthcare network through a decrease of the latency and enhancement of the network capacity, connectivity, and fault tolerance. Traffic classification helps in the identification of the diverse procedures and applying it inside the network, enhancing safety by identification and neutralizing malicious packages. Cloudlets, as a specific part of the central cloud, are mobile edge-based self-managing technology, which collect and integrate data of Wi-Fi or mobile base stations. It consists of the assembly of devices, cloudlets, and clouds. Networking of 5G network stations with cloudlets will decrease the latency to value < 1 ms, because they can mutually communicate during recovering possible faults and respond to the various user demands. In processing data, the particular position has deep neural networks (DNN) based on deep learning (DL) supported by the help of a specific softer, which consists of multiple processing sheets that enable learning and recognition of various specific cases by using a back-propagation algorithm for indication of how changes of computer internal parameters can improve information in the specification sheet from the data of the previous sheet, discovering all complex connections in and between the layers [49, 50].

This specific type of DNN that consists of neurons joined to arrange an acyclic graph is called multi-sheet/multi-layer perceptions (MLPs), with full connections between them when the outcome of a neuron in one sheet is entry to the neurons in the subsequent sheet. MLPs consist of a minimum of three invisible sheets, which form a profound neural network. Accordingly, MLPs consist of an incoming and outgoing sheet and multiple hidden sheets. The larger numbers of the hidden sheets make a more profound network [51].

Recurrent neural networks (RNNs) are a specific type of deep learning network that shows dynamic temporal behavior by using their internal memory. In RNNs, the invisible sheets of one neural network are joined to the invisible sheets of the subsequent neural network, linking in this way the current state with the previous state of layers. Long short-term memory (LSTM), consisted of input, output, and recurrent invisible layers, which consist of memory block instead of neurons, was upgraded to RNNs to solve some more complex gradient problems. Each package contains one or more storage cells and three exits—input, output, and forgets exit—because it can stock and retain the data for more extensive time to solve the disappearing gradient problem [52].

The adaptive flow of data is the main characteristic of the specific content-centric networks (CNNs), which enable significant improvement in the lifetime and efficiency of the mobile cloud networks known as Mobile Clouds for Assistive Healthcare (MoCAsH), consisting of mobile sensing, context-sensitive middleware, and procedure collaboration for resource utilization and distribution. Preventive smartphone healthcare needs an improved data speed and very low latencies, which are essential for its high interactivity and bandwidth of technology, which assumes prevision of the cyberspace, multimedia applications, and IoT. The difficulties in unloading considerable volume data, high latency, the necessity of data transference and service accessibility, fast processing, and sharing of healthcare information requests reliable smartphone communication networks. It assumes potential migration of the resources to various cloudlets when the user changes locations, which can be supported by a model virtual machine (VM) transfer, based on ant colony technologies for smartphone cloud computing. The proposed model is founded not only on the user mobility but also on the resource utilization of the cloudlets, with a central role of the master cloudlet that connects all other cloudlets. Besides, a master cloudlet is directly connected with a principal cloud, and with other cloudlets through it [53].

The latency as one of the main requirements of CCNs changes with a variety of use and the aspect of the user. Multimedia applies for distant diagnosis and surgery needs reciprocal audio and video transference, with latency less than 300 ms, while live distant surgery needs < 1 ms [53, 54].

Smartphone cloud health service assumes immense transportation bandwidth, capable of transporting top-quality medical images (MRI, CT-Scan), videotape, and sound for distant Voice over Internet Protocol (VoIP) connections. This technique enables speech communications via a high-speed internet instead of an ordinary (or analog) telephone connection, and other biomedical signs that are obtained from the patients. A satisfied VoIP connection demands a minimum of 80 Kbps, while high-resolution videos need bit speeds between 5 and 12 Mbps [55].

The rate of energy consumption of smartphones is a big problem because battery consumption can interrupt displaying data, which is a critical factor from the aspect of safety during surgery or other similar processes. Therefore, the network requests to be optimized with smartphones with minimal power consumption. The reliability of the network is also essential because the lacking range from a small disorder to a great life-threatening disturbance can be incorporated into the network because fault-tolerant techniques are requested to rapidly recover it from any mistakes [56].

Bearing in mind that the network consists of numerous equipment, software, and healthcare implementations, each working on diverse platforms with various equipment drivers, it can induce numerous security shortcomings that have not yet been detected. The program and controllers that control the security of the smartphone healthcare network mainly contains three main components located among four sheets: deep learning network, traffic analysis and prediction (DLNTAP) component; deep learning network traffic classification (DLNTC) component; and flow clustering and analysis (FCA) component. The first sheet includes all smartphone users (doctors and other medical staff) and devices at diverse residencies ensuring advanced broadcast healthcare services (health and illness recording, and distant control of surgery). The second cloudlet sheet contains the DLNTC component. Its construction enables connection of all smartphones and users with local cloudlets in the vicinity to the access points or smartphone networks to analyze, for example, the current two-way transportation. On the base of similar data, enhanced opportunities for prediction of traffic of the local area network results in greater QoS, controlling the information transmission rate between the cloudlet sheet and the cloud sheet [57].

The DLNTC component in this sheet at the internet service provider (ISP) is responsible for the distribution of the application procedures of the transit flows. Besides, it enables the detection of unacceptable traffic and illogical data and maintenance of the network, while FCA clusters register diverse contact signals, information, undesired, and unknown data packets. Cloud computing is provided by supercomputers, large-scale accelerators like GPUs and MICS, and servers for the accumulation of huge amounts of information; while for broadcast media, broadcast media servers and internet sites in web servers are used [58].

The adaptive content delivery (ACD) segment predicts the traffic, while the content delivery server (CDN) is responsible for distributing a low data stream or high data stream of broadcast media content [53, 54].

DLNTC is essential for any internet cloud networks for records of illogicality, and to provide QoS. Its application protocol assumes the application of various packets, over YouTube, Facebook, and Skype. All projected results then pass through FCA to take diverse steps enhancing the QoS of the network [57, 58].

4.2.9 Deep Learning and Smart Health Care

Smart cities assume powerful setups based on computers and computer-mediated technologies with the desire to connect cities' habitats and technology. This is important for the enhancement of the condition of patient existence, through their easier movability and access to better healthcare, proper administration, and feasibility of resources. This also supports the growth of the economy and the extension capacity of basic city needs. Therefore, the information is collected and refined continuously to produce other information necessary for a citizen's better life in smart cities. In this era of IoT, the interaction among internet networks, wireless transmissions, and expert systems enormously transforms humans, through diverse types of technological advancements, particularly in the processing capacity, speed of computer processing, and storage capacities [59].

With the discovery of virtual-physical systems, which includes the incorporation of physical assets with communication capabilities, a model of ordinary city conception is overcome in favor of a smart city, which is capable to offer various new services, like smart driving, homes, lifestyle, administration, and health. In the platform of the smart city, one of the most important issues is the change of health services by doctors and IoT supported by medical appliances and delivery to provide accessibility, omnipresence, and individual adjustment of services, and comfortable access to them [60].

The smartness of a smart city should be investigated from the technology aspect (i.e., digital, virtual, and pervasive and cyber city), the citizen aspect (creative, humane, learning, and comprehension), and the community aspect (smart community). The smart city assumes smart infrastructures, where devices use sensors and microprocessors; smart transport with excellent traffic networks and communication frameworks enabling efficient regulation and control; smart environments where ICT provides its monitoring; smart services to assure citizen health, tourism, education, and safety; smart administration, for proper distribution of management services; smart people who apply ICTs to increase their creativity; smart living where technology enables better quality of living; and smart economy, to provide an increase in business and growth of the economy [61].

A smart health system is one of the leading goals that ensures the well-being of the community. Unsatisfied health services lead to the spreading of diseases and infections, sometimes to an epidemic level. Smart health is the consequence of excellent health services, which use all advantages of the smart city. This is essential for the success of the smart city ecological community. Smart health assumes the application of sensors in smart devices and specially designed customizable sensors, like bio-patches for controlling the medical state of city life and the air quality monitoring inside of a smart city. As a basic part of the smart city, smart health systems use equipment with sensors for ecological and surrounding data gathering. All obtained data from sensors are transferred to the information centers as the intake during data and decision-making processing. Smart cities should provide rapid growth of the required framework for smart health, improving the quality of significant data acquisition and leverage them, upgrading a sustainable smart city structure, like a system for following patients with some specific complication issues. Besides, for ensuring air quality in a smart city, a cloud-based monitoring system is provided. The human body network can be used for ECG monitoring for warning patients of potential heart-related problems, like a cardiac arrest, and determination of various human actions, which can improve the quality of healthcare [62].

Data processing of citizens is also one of the applications of smart health in smart cities. Besides, the scope of smart health in smart cities is not only related to the physiological aspects of living bodies; it also includes the ambiance and constitutive elements of smart infrastructure. Structural health problems in smart cities should be addressed by using WSNs. Therefore, the application of the machine deep learning techniques and its combination with sensor and actuator networks is necessary for the processing of very challenging multimedia data. Deep learning upgrades ordinary artificial neural networks (ANNs) with many invisible neuromorphic sheets, which enable identifying hidden instructions. Through the enhanced computing capacity of information technologies and the improvement of cloud distributing models, machine learning actively enhances its analysis of numerous sensory data (multimedia data) improving our long-lasting choices. The essential aim of machine learning is mimicking the human brain. The sensors and actuators in the machine learning network receive corresponding entry and repeatedly transfer it through the following sheets until a suitable exit complies. Due to the iterative approach, the strength of connections of the network links is adjusted to correspond to the entry of the desired output in the period of the learning procedure, in which varying sensors of medical screening, invasive, or inserted sensors in smart equipment collect medical information. Therefore, deep learning becomes more present in smart healthcare, from diagnosis to the prediction of health state and health treatment [63, 64]. Deep learning assumes a group of computational operations that imitate the brain. Therefore, it includes learning over algorithmic steps, establishing hierarchical structures among more straightforward knowledge, and designing computers that can think. This learning is based on experience, applying a bottom-up procedure. Designed information forms the experience, which is then applied as an acquired entry inside the system where the learning process follows the previous experiences, through spam filtering [63–65].

By this technique, obtained data from sensors are fine-adjusted before applying any analytics method. This enables the formulation of the correct and satisfactory processing of information from the sensor and actuator networks. The outcome of machine learning can be used for decision making, treatment of sensory information by their classification, detection of errors, and prediction via learning and improving its quality with time. The challenges of deep learning techniques in smart health are the efficient collection of data, its quality, and capacity.

This generally results in excessive capacity data, which induces many difficulties through the process of the exercise data, leading to a longer timeframe for result derivation. Thus, it is very important to understand how much data is optimal for processing. Therefore, the existence of sensor and actuator networks and exact and adequate processing is crucial for obtaining the right decisions, prognosis, and advice for citizens in smart cities [65].

4.2.10 Telecare Medical Information Systems

A smart infrastructure system will be able to examine the habits of ordinary citizens and advise the relevance of this approach in exact medicine programs. Smart cities simplify the integration of transmission networks, which is one of the main parts of smart infrastructures. Like biological systems, they are flexible, predictive, accommodative, adjustable, and optimized, because they can register, gather, estimate, examine, and disseminate experience using data collected from separate sensors, taking action without human arbitration. Their infrastructure is characterized by complicity, coordination, hierarchy, independency, instant action, fast decision making, abundance, durability, and flexibility, having the same properties as ecological, taxonomic, genetics, physical, and development of self-organized and dynamic biological systems [66].

They are organized like biological systems that are constituted from molecules, organelles, cells, tissues, organs, individuals, families, populations, and meta-populations and which include various phases of life (from the embryo, over birth and reproduction, to death). These structures can make decisions, by dynamic changes without human intervention, induced by independent interactions of the component of these structures, following a process like Darwinian. Numerous resemblances between the biological organization and smart substructures enable capabilities of prediction, prevention, and management of various dangerous diseases like sickle cell anemia or cystic fibrosis, or systematic and sophisticated disorders like hypertension, type-2 diabetes, and asthma [66].

Variations among specific entities (factors) in simple subordinated systems can be examined using agent-based modeling (ABM), which includes both self-determining and interchanging objects in a surrounding, psychological issues, and adaptation and response to new environments based on their previous experience. Smart infrastructures are slightly different from ABMs, typically working on an extensive level like a society or ecosystems offering a more realistic figure of human disorders [55, 66].

Smart infrastructure, together with smart cloud computing shows limitless dimensions for the data store, and incorporation of a fast enough bio-sensor is a powerful tool for organization, analysis, and application results relating to human health. Its models are necessary for supervising and regulating large multisheet sophisticated systems, consisted of many interactive constituents, often joining the metropolis and local countryside. Self-learning computers could self-assemble diverse origins of data (without our arbitration), imitating the evolutionary process. Adaptation of these models to human health enables isolation, observation, and monitoring of people and specific ingredients (factors) of health or disease in the subordinated level inside of human populations, and their adaptation to the behavior of other people has specific importance [66, 67].

4.2.11 Surgery in Space and Telesurgery

Possible human migration to any closed place in the cosmos requests reasonable opportunities for life-sustainment and healthcare. Remote-controlled surgical robots could be adapted to the harsh environments both in space and on Earth. For such kind of requirements, a three-layered architecture can be applied for ensuring the maximal performances of telepresence for potential investigation missions. The three-layered concept gives efficient support for long-distance telesurgery. Telemedicine can be online or offline, vulnerable to the technological property of the internet network [68].

There are three main categories of telemedicine: (1) storage-and-delivery telemedicine that assumes only one-directional communication over time, and the distant evaluation of the therapeutic data offline and returning it to the requested site later; (2) gathering of patient remote information with sensors' various configuration; and (3) so-called interactive telemonitoring that enables enough fast communication between two places, which can be transformed in various models of communications, enabling physicians to invasively treat patients using robots and other teleoperated devices, although they are geographically separated from themselves. When the connection is predictable, and all technical tools are reliable, then the distant surgeon can still actively support the operation in another place, on nearly instant-time using video and voice in the operational location at another place. This technique is called telementoring. It includes classical mentoring and professional guiding [68, 69]. Currently, it is a dominant visual form of telemedicine because it ensures the maximal concentration of data [70].

4.2.12 Robotic Telesurgery

Small-sized, in-body robots provide significant improvement for a distance control of operations. Typically, the several millimeters-sized robots are equipped with a camera, which can quickly access the peritoneal cavity over a minor incision moving around the place of teleoperation without tissue damages. Some of them are self-organizing robots moved by exterior magnets. The average latency in their applications in very far distances is less than 400 ms. The primary problem with remote teleoperation is unsatisfied internet infrastructure because of precise and harmonized sensory feedback, which is crucial for efficient telesurgical treatment. The continual progress of internet broadcasting is crucial in a substantial decrease of normal latencies because it tends to be in the reduction of latency of 20 s, and less with an extreme value of about 2 s [71].

In the range of planetary distance, corresponding telesurgery techniques can be applied in the case of urgency, when useful algorithms can be used to grow the feasibility and capabilities of the human surgeon by robot-assisted surgery with maximal 2 s delay. Telementoring requires the trafficking of images, video movement, videoconferencing, internet conversation, and data file exchange, as a successful alternative to conventional teleoperation, allowing distant personnel to do jobs founded on the instructions obtained from the distant center.

Telementoring enables telepresence, with a 50–70 s waiting, inside of the distance order of 10 million km. The self-controlling surgical robot will have an essential influence in improving all quality of surgery: motion adjusting, flexible vibration filtering, electronic monitoring of organ functions, or automated suturing, reducing the risk of accidents [71, 72].

4.2.13 Brain–Computer Interfaces

A brain-computer interface (BCI) is a computer communications form that enables interaction between people and their surroundings, without peripheral nerves and muscle inclusion, by using a detector of signals induced by electroencephalographic (ECF) activity. Such an interface is very useful for people with serious physical and motoric disabilities because it can enhance their living conditions, decreasing the refunds of intensive care. As an artificial intelligence system, (AFS), it can identify patterns in brain signals through signal acquisition and reinforcement, extraction specific elements, their organization, and interface management. In the process of signal collection, AFS catches brain signals, while during a stage of their enhancement, it prepares the signal for additional processing. During the extraction specific elements, AFS recognizes specific messages in brain signals, recording them and mapping in specific forms from the other signals. The extraction process is very complex because these brain signals are disturbed with signals of other brain activities, frequently overlapping them in both time and space. In the classification stage, they are classified, selecting them from signals with the best discriminative features, which are essential for efficient pattern recognition. Finally, during the control interface phase, they are translated into desirable instructions for any integrated device, like a computer. Through the growth of very cheap computers that allow very complex online examinations during the last two decades, BCI researches have become very popular [73, 74].

BCIs use brain signals to collect information, measuring electrophysiological and hemodynamic brain activities, translating so obtained information into compliant electrical signals. Electrophysiological activity is induced by electrochemical transmitters that transfer instructions among the neurons, generating ionic currents that pass within and through neuronal assemblies. The broad diversity of current pathways can be presented by a one-way directing current between the source and sink across the dendritic trunk. These intracellular currents are recognized as primary, while extracellular current flows, generated as a consequence of conservation of electric charges, is known as secondary currents. The hemodynamically replay is a process where the blood releases glucose to active neurons more rapidly than in the location of inert neurons. These differences should be identified by neuroimaging techniques, like functional magnetic resonance and near-infrared spectroscopy [74, 75].

Most recent BCIs' relevant information is obtained from brain activity by ECF, by the most frequently used neuroimaging method, because it possesses high temporal resolution, is relatively cheap, easy portability, and low risk for the users. BCIs founded on ECF acquire ECF signals by corresponding sensors from different brain areas. Invasive monitoring techniques such as electrocorticography or intracortical neuron monitoring is used to enhance the properties of brain signals recorded by BCIs. It enables the movement by using prostheses with manifold grades of freedom, which will be enhanced soon. It is expected that further improvements in monitoring and evaluation technologies will raise the characteristics of these invasive or noninvasive devices [76].

In BCI electrocorticography, the electrodes are located outside of the cortex or dura mater (epidural electrocorticography) or under the dura mater (subdural electrocorticography), and intracortical neuron. Perhaps, in the future of nanotechnologies, nanodetectors will be embedded into the brain, providing correct everlasting invasive applications. Besides, an internet link between the microelectrode and the exterior computer is necessary to diminish health hazards [77].

BCIs enable their applicants to interact over exterior devices by brain signals over peripheral nerves and muscles. BCI investigations and development are the intention to ensure safe systems for seriously disabled people in everyday practice [77, 78].

Therefore, direct communication between the human brain and computers or robots is a subject of various academic speculation for many years. In the case of BCI, communication and control instructions are transmitted instead of the muscular contractions over brain signals. This technology is directed to the people suffering from diverse motoric disabilities, like amyotrophic lateral sclerosis (ALS), spinal cord injury, stroke, and other neuromuscular severe disorders or traumas. In these cases, the regeneration of necessary communication capabilities can considerably enhance the living conditions of these people, increasing their independence and reducing social isolation, and finally potentially reducing the cost of healthcare [78].

By replacement of the conventional neuromuscular output channels, BCI should ensure enough fast response to the recipient, optimizing the desired brain output. A diversity of neurophysiologic signals that reflect brain activities can be applied to initiate a BCI. These signals, depending on the signal source, are divided into electrophysiological, magnetic, and metabolic signals. Electrophysiological signals can be classified in agreement with the extent of invasiveness of the monitoring equipment into signs evaluated by noninvasive (EEG), cortical surface (ECoG), and intracortical monitoring equipment [79, 80].

Electrocorticographic (ECoG) signals are generated by surgically located electrodes outside of the cortex. Although these electrodes estimate the same signs as in EEG, due to their smaller distance from the brain they show higher amplitudes, more extensive sensitive frequency range, and better resolution [79, 80].

And finally, the intracortical method (ICM) is used for quantification of localized area potentials (LFPs) and neuronal action potentials (pikes). They perform the most invasive BCI methods, showing the brain's electrical activity by electrodes embedded in the brain. For both ECoG and ICM monitoring, the broad frequency interval, high topographic resolution, and excellent signal property are typical. Besides the obvious advantages of the ICM method, the surgery carries a risk of tissue injury and infection [81].

Magnetic and metabolic signals obtained by magneto-encephalography (MEG) are a new origin of the brain-acquired signals in BCI. MEG belongs to noninvasive methods. It can register frequency above those in EEG monitoring. It also shows a slightly better spatial resolution than EEG. MEG is based on measurements of tiny magnetic fields generated by the brain electrical activity [81, 82].

In current times, increasing interest is shown to BCIs based on metabolite signs generated in the brain by measurement of blood oxygen extent-dependent response, through functional magnetic resonance imaging (fMRI) or near-infrared spectroscopy. It was shown that during mental activation, the oxyhemoglobin increases, while deoxyhemoglobin decreases. Due to fMRI's high spatial resolution and improvement of the simultaneously gathering data and examinations, through visualization of complete-brain areas, it becomes possible to successfully train patients to achieve self-control of localized brain areas using a response from a real-time fMRI BCI [81–83].

4.2.14 Complex Nanoscale Geometry in Biology

As a potential base of new knowledge of smart medicine from the standpoint of clinical application nanomaterials, particular care can be dedicated to nanoscale geometry in biology and their mathematical modeling as a useful tool for anticipating and explaining nanoscale performances of live systems. The structural and electronic characteristics of various nanoparticles can be predicted with satisfying precision using quantum mechanical models based on density functional theory (DFT). This method improves the opportunity for optimal design nanoscale facilities for specific applications in the field of nanomedicine. Theoretically, nanoobjects can be designed to enable a unique combination of hardness, electrophilicity, and conductivity through the optimization of their physical and biological properties, such as bonding strength and the rate of release of drugs or the establishment of selective ion channels through the membrane of diseased cells. However, such a model is difficult to implement properly [84–87].

Simpler models have frequently been applied in researching the relationship among various nanoobjects and their medical characteristics. These models are based on the parameterization, instead of on the principles of quantum calculation, enabling successful treatment of more significant systems with greater efficiency. Mathematical models are highly applicable from the standpoint of context drug-nanoparticle interactions. Also, besides this being the most important aspect related to the nanoparticle drug delivery system, the application of the model to the treatment of a disease in biological organisms is welcomed.

For modeling of the efficiency of these systems, standard chemical techniques of modeling can be used because they are quantum chemical calculations and calculations of surface energy. The behavior of nanostructures inside biological systems is a very demanding subject because the biological systems are incredibly complex. These techniques show strong nonlinear physiological feedback induced by inherent noise. This is induced by the inhomogeneous multiscale space–time interaction and ultimately many components, even with a minimal description of the required variables, act discouraging because it wastes a huge amount of time for their solution [88, 89].

Therefore, mathematical models and particularly artificial intelligence end deep learning using the MoCAsH network can have an enormous significance for the development of the nano-bio system, which is mainly related to the spreading of IoT and cloudlets and sophisticated cloud networks for such type of systems. The complexity of the issues during modeling nano-bio systems and theoretical approaches used in the modeling framework belongs to the most challenging topics in the field of nanodesign of these systems for medical applications. The main factors, particularly essential and selective for the existences of a high degree of nonlinearity of their properties, are still the subject of much debate and different approaches inside different contexts of recurrent RNNs of these systems [84–88].

Numerous biological processes are naturally nonlinear due to the mutual interaction of various biological ingredients. This reaction includes numerous positive and negative feedback loops. Among them are intercellular signaling pathways, intercellular calcium oscillations, and genetic regulatory systems, because typical biological processes can be characterized by high nonlinear dynamics. Nonlinearity increases with repression and with negative feedback, generating resistance to noise and inducing particular advantages for biological organisms. Alan Turing and his associates showed that specific topology of the system induces the nonlinearity in the given reaction-diffusion systems, which can be widely applied. Irrespective of the evolutionary pressure that rises to the high level of nonlinearity in biological systems, the experimental results frequently show that such systems can only be interpreted by nonlinear dynamics [84–88].

This causes various problems in modeling due to two specific reasons. Primary, nonlinear systems are almost impossible to describe on the base of the experiment, while nonlinear systems show typical dynamic performance because they are particularly unsuitable for understanding and predicting on the intuitive level. Nonlinearity is not specific for biological systems. Mainly, many physical and chemical systems are also nonlinear. Besides, the nonlinearity is especially present in a biologic context, since the necessary mechanical interpretation of many management processes is little or completely unknown. Despite these drawbacks, a nonlinear description of biological systems is indeed an impressive tool, and in the case of its careful design, it can rationalize nanoscale performance of numerous biological systems. Therefore, it is ideal for the modeling and control of biological systems due to its correct estimation of the model structure and specific property for corresponding biological systems founded on sets derived from experiments data [84–88].

The calculations for linear systems are relatively simple, while for nonlinear systems they are more complex. Therefore, they request the addition of the a priori assumptions for the set of nonlinear functions, which enable a correct description of the dynamics of biological systems. Practically, good selections of sets of these functions depend on the system and the requested accuracy of the calculations. Therefore, certain functional forms can be considered as useful in terms of modeling and evaluation of the complex biological system. Models take mass activity (GMA) as the most intuitive value, based on the

N simple differential equations of rate. The equations define the dynamics of N diverse chemical constituents, which participate in M various chemical reactions [89, 90].

Alternative access to the GMA is the application of Hill's functions to express the reaction rates for a diverse biologically active species contained in a given biological system. Hill's functions have their solutions in the fundamentals of enzyme kinetics (kinetics which obey enzyme-catalyzed reactions), which was first explained by Michaelis and Menton in 1913. This approach has limitations. However, at the same time, it is a powerful tool that aims to predict the quality and handling, despite shortcomings in understanding of basic physical, chemical, and biological processes that primarily govern the nonlinear dynamic behavior. Another problem is related to the high nonlinearity of the most biological systems and their wealth of dynamic behavior. Nonlinear systems, even at equilibrium, show that they cannot generate linear systems. Multistability is frequently one of the main indications of some nonlinear systems. Additionally, the topic of many profound discussions is the multistability of these systems, which probably has a critical role in some genes and cell communications including the well-known lac operon [88–90].

An operon is a unit of genomic material containing the gene cluster under the command of an alone promoter or regulatory signals, wherein the genes are transcribed together into mRNA and translated in the regions along with the coil, passing through the cytoplasm or particularly processing RNA in eukaryotes in which the exons of two different primary transcripts connect with their ends one to another, forming a new chemical bond through the so-called "trans-splicing" [88–90].

Lac operon is the operon responsible for transport mechanisms in various types of lactose-digested bacteria, such as *Escherichia coli*. The general opinion is that the multistability in regulatory networks is extensively influenced by the decrease of noise caused by the perturbation. Particularly, at the level, its geometry, great variations in the repressor, and activator protein are probably present with their typical small number of copies in the cell. Although the multistability gene regulatory circuits are not inherent, these fluctuations can induce fast communication ("chat") between the involved "on" state and excluded "off" condition for the transcription of the genes, inducing less efficiency of the cells and leading to selective deficiencies. Multistability, together with the corresponding hysteresis, allows cells to take part in threshold chemical concentrations (limits) and turn them off at low enough concentrations. This enables the efficiency of penetrating power on/off the decision for gene transcription by the fluctuation of the concentration value of the repressor and activator [88–90].

Besides, nonlinear systems show numerous other conditions nontypical for a linear restriction process, like collective excitation and coherent oscillations. The addition of nonlinearity to the complexity of biological systems from the aspect of modeling indicates that biological systems possess great stability to noise and sensibility to particular coherent stimuli, which can be crucial for biological systems. Besides, the significance of nonlinear dynamics and dynamic phenomena is essential for the study of biological functions by the use of biological models on all scales. At the nanoscale, nonlinearity is particularly essential, because the noise is an essential subject of biological systems on a nanoscale, becoming a major driving power of selection in nonlinear biological systems [90].

4.2.15 Relationship Between Physical Fields in Which Human Cells Emerge and Cell Geometry

According to our theoretical models of ultrasonic and electromagnetic waves that describe the relationship between them and developed material structure under their influence on the micro and nano levels, our research published elsewhere shows that the approach in material design gives results with exceptionally high matching between theoretical expectations and experimental results. These models clearly show that it is possible (in any inorganic structure generating in such fields) to create entirely predictable structures on various levels of hierarchy (beginning from the particle as an entity and finally taking in account their subelements or subparticles), thus enabling full control of its development through all stages of the system generation [91–97].

Such investigations may be from essential importance not only for the new strategy of the investigations in material sciences but also in medicine, because these physical fields may induce positive influences to the closest surroundings, through distribution of precisely controlled data generated not only in a given material but also in the cell structures following the same principles of harmonization between related physical fields and their structures obtained during their generation inside these fields. It follows that these structures produced in periodical physical fields are some fingerprints of these fields in which they are created. From these facts, it can be assumed that a similar kind of relationship is not exclusive only for inorganic systems and that this approach is probably acceptable for any system, nevertheless of its origin, including living systems and human cells [97].

As the base for experimental testing of the model applicability on the cell geometry and "energy fingerprint" by which this geometry is established, numerous data found in the literature were used. These data relating to the various cell sizes enable the investigation of the potential applicability of this hybrid model to the cells, based on the relationship between cell geometry and physical fields of the environment in the cell vicinity, responsible for particular cell geometry, similarly found for inorganic systems [97].

In other words, cell geometry must contain diverse information in the discrete form about physical fields that induce the generation of such geometry. By using these models, the values of the frequencies corresponding to given cell geometry consequently follow their healthy behavior. Following the same logic, it seems that shifted values of the cell geometry (in comparison with the geometry of normal cells) indicate possible energy deviation from the normal state, and the cell disease, clearly showing that cell geometry and energy are very strongly interconnected. Also, it might significantly enhance the conventional way of cell observation, in agreement with this approach, in which the energy in the surrounding of the cells is the most important factor in the regulation of their behavior [97].

This approach is very close to the observed way of the living organism in traditional medicine because it is also based on energy as a leading factor in the treatment of cells. However, its enhanced opportunities are based on the exact calculation of the requested energy for optimal cell functions, from the other side, making it unique from the aspect of future perspective in the treatment of various diseases, bridging the gap between traditional medicine and other fields of modern medicine, such as molecular biology and genetics and particularly future perspectives of smart medicine healthcare in smart cities. Following such interpretation, it is possible to define suitable physical fields in cell vicinity for normal cell behavior and explain why the corresponding deviation of the energy field leads to cell disease, through the forced change of cell geometry, induced by the energy that is outside the limits for normal cell functioning [97].

This approach is analyzed in detail in the book *Bridge Between Nanophysics and Alternative Medicine* [97] in which is given a theoretically whole new approach that can be applied in energy treatment cells. This book join the fundamental aspects of cell physics and biology, in an interdisciplinary manner, showing a completely new concept to the energy treatment of different types of cells necessary for their healing, giving a very efficient tool for smart healthcare modeling on the base of physical and biological fundamentals by using adequate models drawn from that insight, advanced by using the MoCAsH network and recruiting deep learning for further enhancement of this auspicious approach. This approach can also be a great challenge for alternative medicine specialists for explanations of why the disease occurs and how it can be most effectively treated [97, 98].

4.3 Conclusion

The spread of ICT to the cities requests the appearance of various services of smart cities, such as smart healthcare. The smart cities and m-health concepts recently assumed a union of smart cities with electronic and smartphone health services. This chapter gives a critical review of this and s-health through the discussion of the main challenges for its implementation and development in the future. These technologies will probably dramatically improve the quality of medical services and treatments as a result of very efficient control and preventive measures after the early identification of disease. Application of IoT techniques in healthcare influences beneficial impacts to physicians and administrators to accessing broad orders of data sources due to their accessing various structures of IoT data in real time. Progress in ICT techniques such as 4G/5G communications, big data, IoT, HPC, robotics, and cloud computing influences a huge transformation of healthcare in smart cities. Besides, countries worldwide are trying to provide excellent healthcare convenient to their patients in the range of reduced budgets.

Networked healthcare enables the delivering of always and everywhere healthcare services at a distance, irrespective of the location of the patient and their mobility. Mobile cloud computing by its network latency, bandwidth, and reliability is the main recent challenge, which assumes a universal healthcare frame that includes deep learning, big data, HPC, and IoT. The DLNTAP component uses deep learning, big data, and HPC technologies for prediction of the network transport to adjust data speeds and its storing and consequent adequate decisions.

Particular care is dedicated to the new energetic approach in the healing of the deceased cell and tissues by using well-described physical periodical fields in the book *Bridge Between Nanophysics and Alternative Medicine* [97].

References

1. Ramaswami A, Russell AG, Culligan PJ, et al (2016) Meta-principles for developing smart, sustainable, and healthy cities. *Science* 352(6288):940–943.
2. Bibri SE (2019) On the sustainability of smart and smarter cities in the era of big data: An interdisciplinary and transdisciplinary literature review. *Journal of Big Data* 6:1–64.
3. Al Nuaimi E, Al Neyadi H, Mohamed N, Al-Jaroodi J (2015) Applications of big data to smart cities. *Journal of Internet Services and Applications* 6:1–15. https://doi.org/10.1186/s13174-015-0041-5
4. Sharma Lavanya, Garg P K, Agarwal Naman (2019) A foresight on e-healthcare Trailblazers, In: *From Visual Surveillance to Internet of Things*, Chapman Hall/CRC, Vol.1, p. 235.
5. Wing JM (2008) Computational thinking and thinking about computing. *Philosophical Transactions of the Royal Society A: Mathematical, Physical, and Engineering Sciences* 366:3717–3725. https://doi.org/10.1098/rsta.2008.0118

6. Mehmood R, Graham G (2015) Big Data Logistics: A health-care transport capacity sharing model. In: *Procedia Computer Science*. Paris, France, Elsevier B.V., August 29–31, 2017, pp. 1107–1114.

7. Wang F, Liu J (2011) Networked wireless sensor data collection: Issues, challenges, and approaches. *IEEE Communications Surveys and Tutorials* 13:673–687.

8. Giroux S, Pigot H (2005) From Smart Homes to Smart Care: ICOST 2005. In: 3rd International Conference on Smart Homes and Health Telematics. June 2005, IOS Press, Netherlands.

9. Lavanna G. (2013) The role of information and communication technology in planning the digital hospital. *World Hospitals and Health Services* 49(3): 4–6.

10. Sharma Lavanya (2019) Introduction: From Visual Surveillance to Internet of Things. In: *From Visual Surveillance to Internet of Things*, Chapman Hall/CRC, Vol. 1, p. 14.

11. Santos MY, Pendão C, Ferreira B, Gonçalves L, Moreira G, Moreira A, Carvalho JA (2015) MyHealth: a cross-domain platform for healthcare. In: SAC 15: Proceedings of 30th Annual ACM Symposium on Applied Computing, Salamanca, Spain, New York, NY, Association for Computing Machinery, 40–46.

12. Tian S, Yang W, Michael Le Grange J, Wang P, Huang W, Ye Z (2019) Smart healthcare: Making medical care more intelligent. *Global Health Journal* 3(3): 63–65.

13. Mshali H, Lemlouma T, Moloney M, Magoni D (2018) A survey on health monitoring systems for health smart homes. *International Journal of Industrial Ergonomics* 66:26–56.

14. Sharma, Lavanya, Garg, PK (Eds.) (2019) *From Visual Surveillance to Internet of Things*. Chapman and Hall/CRC, New York, NY. https://doi.org/10.1201/9780429297922

15. Paul A, Pinjari H, Hong W-H, et al (2018) Fog Computing-Based IoT for Health Monitoring System. *Journal of Sensors* 2018:7. https://doi.org/10.1155/2018/1386470

16. Qureshi F, Krishnan S (2018) Wearable Hardware Design for the Internet of Medical Things (IoMT). *Sensors* 18:3812. https://doi.org/10.3390/s18113812

17. Raghupathi W, Raghupathi V (2014) Big data analytics in healthcare: Promise and potential. *Health Information Science Systems* 2:3. https://doi.org/10.1186/2047-2501-2-3

18. Kuo AMH (2011) Opportunities and challenges of cloud computing to improve health care services. *Journal of Medical Internet Research* 13:e67.

19. Lee SI, Celik S, Logsdon BA, et al (2018) A machine learning approach to integrate big data for precision medicine in acute myeloid leukemia. *Nature Communications* 9:42. https://doi.org/10.1038/s41467-017-02465-5

20. Majumder S, Aghayi E, Noferesti M, et al (2017) Smart homes for elderly healthcare-recent advances and research challenges. *Sensors (Basel)* 17:2496. https://doi.org/10.3390/s17112496

21. Wan D (1999) Magic medicine cabinet: A situated portal for consumer healthcare. In: *Lecture Notes in Computer Science (including subseries Lecture Notes in Artificial Intelligence and Lecture Notes in Bioinformatics)*. Springer Verlag, Germany, pp. 352–355.

22. Floerkemeier C, Floerkemeier C, Lampe M, Schoch T (2003) The Smart Box Concept for Ubiquitous Computing Environments. In: Procedure of Smart Objects Conference, Grenoble, 118–121.

23. Siegemund F, Flörkemeier C (2003) Interaction in pervasive computing settings using Bluetooth-enabled active tags and passive RFID technology together with mobile phones. In: Proceedings of the 1st IEEE International Conference on Pervasive Computing and Communications, PerCom 2003. pp. 378–387.

24. Sharma Lavanya Sharma, Garg P K. (2019) Block based adaptive learning rate for moving person detection in video surveillance. In: *From Visual Surveillance to Internet of Things*, Chapman Hall/CRC, Vol.1, p. 201.

25. Kortuem G, Kawsar F, Sundramoorthy V, Fitton D (2010) Smart objects as building blocks for the Internet of Things. *IEEE Internet Computing* 14:44–51. https://doi.org/10.1109/MIC.2009.143

26. Mok E, Retscher G, Wen C (2012) Initial test on the use of GPS and sensor data of modern smartphones for vehicle tracking in dense high rise environments. In: *2012 Ubiquitous Positioning, Indoor Navigation, and Location Based Service*, Finland.

27. Fan YJ, Yin YH, Xu L Da, et al (2014) IoT-based smart rehabilitation system. *IEEE Transactions on Industrial Informatics* 10:1568–1577. https://doi.org/10.1109/TII.2014.2302583

28. Dimitrov D V (2016) Medical Internet of Things and big data in healthcare. *Healthcare Informatics Research* 22:156–163.

29. Zhao W, Wang C, Nakahira Y (2012) Medical application on Internet of Things. In: IET Conference Publications, Beijing, China, pp. 660–665.

30. Aceto G, Botta A, De Donato W, Pescape A (2012) Cloud monitoring: Definitions, issues and future directions. In: 2012 1st IEEE International Conference on Cloud Networking, CLOUDNET, 2012–Proceedings, pp. 63–67.

31. Islam M, Hasan M, Wang X, et al (2018) A Systematic Review on Healthcare Analytics: Application and Theoretical Perspective of Data Mining. *Healthcare* 6:54. https://doi.org/10.3390/healthcare6020054

32. Weiskopf NG, Weng C (2013) Methods and dimensions of electronic health record data quality assessment: Enabling reuse for clinical research. *Journal of American Medical Informatics Association* 20:144–151. https://doi.org/10.1136/amiajnl-2011-000681

33. Bennett J, Rokas O, Chen L (2017) Healthcare in the Smart Home: A Study of Past. *Present and Future Sustainability* 9:840. https://doi.org/10.3390/su9050840

34. Postolache G, Girão PS, Postolache O (2013) Requirements and barriers to pervasive health adoption. In: *Smart Sensors, Measurement and Instrumentation*. Springer International Publishing, Switzerland, pp. 315–359.

35. Jovanov E, Milenkovic A (2011) Body area networks for ubiquitous healthcare applications: Opportunities and challenges. *Journal of Medical Systems*. Springer, Switzerland, pp. 1245–1254.

36. Solanas A, Patsakis C, Conti M, et al (2014) Smart health: A context-aware health paradigm within smart cities. *IEEE Communications Magazine* 52:74–81. https://doi.org/10.1109/MCOM.2014.6871673

37. Kvedar JC, Fogel AL, Elenko E, Zohar D (2016) Digital medicine's March on chronic disease. *Nature Biotechnology* 34:239–246.

38. Appelboom G, Camacho E, Abraham ME, et al (2014) Smart wearable body sensors for patient self-assessment and monitoring. *Archives of Public Health* 72:28. https://doi.org/10.1186/2049-3258-72-28

39. Dash S, Shakyawar SK, Sharma M, Kaushik S (2019) Big data in healthcare: Management, analysis and future prospects. *Journal of Big Data* 6:1–25. https://doi.org/10.1186/s40537-019-0217-0

40. Ullman-Cullere MH, Mathew JP (2011) Emerging landscape of genomics in the electronic health record for personalized medicine. *Human Mutation* 32:512–516. https://doi.org/10.1002/humu.21456

41. Ohno-Machado L, Kim J, Gabriel RA, et al (2018) Genomics and electronic health record systems. *Human Molecular Genetics* 27:R48–R55. https://doi.org/10.1093/hmg/ddy104

42. Wang L, McLeod HL, Weinshilboum RM (2011) Genomics and Drug Response. *New England Journal of Medicine* 364:1144–1153. https://doi.org/10.1056/NEJMra1010600

43. Muhammed T, Mehmood R, Albeshri A, Katib I (2018) UbeHealth: A personalized ubiquitous cloud and edge-enabled networked healthcare system for smart cities. *IEEE Access* 6:32258–32285.

44. Yeole AS, Kalbande DR (2016) Use of Internet of Things (IoT) in healthcare: A survey. In: ACM International Conference Proceeding Series. Association for Computing Machinery, pp. 71–76.

45. Laplante PA, Laplante NL (2015) A structured approach for describing healthcare applications for the Internet of Things. In: IEEE World Forum on Internet of Things, WF-IoT 2015 – Proceedings. Institute of Electrical and Electronics Engineers, Inc., pp. 621–625.

46. Alemdar H, Ersoy C (2010) Wireless sensor networks for healthcare: A survey. *Computer Networks* 54:2688–2710. https://doi.org/10.1016/j.comnet.2010.05.003

47. Ramesh D, Suraj P, Saini L (2016) Big data analytics in healthcare: A survey approach. In: International Conference on Microelectronics, Computing and Communication, MicroCom 2016. Institute of Electrical and Electronics Engineers, Inc.

48. Taylor RH (2006) A perspective on medical robotics. *Procedures of IEEE* 94:1652–1664.

49. Harmon RR, Castro-Leon EG, Bhide S (2015) Smart cities and the Internet of Things. In: Portland International Conference on Management of Engineering and Technology. Portland State University, Portland, Oregon, pp. 485–494.

50. Ai Y, Peng M, Zhang K (2018) Edge computing technologies for Internet of Things: A primer. *Digital Communications Networks* 4:77–86. https://doi.org/10.1016/j.dcan.2017.07.001

51. Zribi M, Boujelbene Y (2016) Neural networks in the medical decision making. *International Journal of Computer Science and Information Security* 14:70–74.

52. Jozefowicz R, Zaremba W, Sutskever I (2015) An empirical exploration of recurrent network architectures. *Proceedings of the 32nd International Conference on Machine Learning* 37:2342–2350.

53. Hochreiter S, Schmidhuber J (1997) Long short-term memory. *Neural Computing* 9:1735–1780. https://doi.org/10.1162/neco.1997.9.8.1735

54. Steele R, Lo A (2013) Telehealth and ubiquitous computing for bandwidth-constrained rural and remote areas. In: *Personal and Ubiquitous Computing*. Springer, Switzerland, pp. 533–543.

55. Paksuniemi M, Sorvoja H, Alasaarela E, Myllylä R (2005) Wireless sensor and data transmission needs and technologies for patient monitoring in the operating room and intensive care unit. In: Annual International Conference of the IEEE Engineering in Medicine and Biology – Proceedings. pp. 5182–5185.

56. Tawalbeh LA, Basalamah A, Mehmood R, Tawalbeh H (2016) Greener and smarter phones for future cities: Characterizing the impact of GPS signal strength on power consumption. *IEEE Access* 4:858–868. https://doi.org/10.1109/ACCESS.2016.2532745

57. Ferreira L, Putnik G, Cunha M, et al (2013) Cloudlet architecture for dashboard in cloud and ubiquitous manufacturing. In: *Procedia CIRP*. Elsevier B.V., Netherlands, pp. 366–371.

58. Nguyen TTT, Armitage G (2008) A survey of techniques for internet traffic classification using machine learning. *IEEE Communication Survey Tutorials* 10:56–76.

59. Schipper R, Silvius A (2018) Characteristics of Smart Sustainable City Development: Implications for Project Management. *Smart Cities* 1:75–97. https://doi.org/10.3390/smartcities1010005

60. Liu D, Huang R, Wosinski M (2016) Development of smart cities: Educational perspective. In: *Lecture Notes in Educational Technology*. Springer International Publishing, Switzerland, pp. 3–14.

61. Nam T, Pardo TA (2011) Conceptualizing Smart City with Dimensions of Technology, People, and Institutions. In: Proceedings of the 12th Annual International Conference on Digital Government Research. pp. 282–291.

62. Sahoo PK, Thakkar HK, Lee MY (2017) A cardiac early warning system with multi-channel SCG and ECG monitoring for mobile health. *Sensors (Switzerland)* 17:711–739. https://doi.org/10.3390/s17040711

63. Ota K, Dao MS, Mezaris V, De Natale FGB (2017) Deep learning for mobile multimedia: A survey. *ACM Transactions on Multimedia, Computing, and Communication Applications* 13:1–22.

64. Yu D, Deng L, Jang I, et al (2011) Deep learning and its applications to signal and information processing. *IEEE Signal Process Magazine* 28:145–154. https://doi.org/10.1109/MSP.2010.939038

65. Marblestone AH, Wayne G, Kording KP (2016) Toward an integration of deep learning and neuroscience. *Frontiers in Computational Neuroscience* 10:95–135. https://doi.org/10.3389/fncom.2016.00094

66. Zhu Z (2012) An efficient authentication scheme for telecare medicine information systems. *Journal of Medical Systems*. Springer, Switzerland, pp. 3833–3838.

67. Bibri SE, Krogstie J (2017) The core enabling technologies of big data analytics and context-aware computing for smart sustainable cities: a review and synthesis. *Journal of Big Data* 4:1–50. https://doi.org/10.1186/s40537-017-0091-6

68. Fabrizio MD, Lee BR, Chan DY, et al (2000) Effect of time delay on surgical performance during telesurgical manipulation. *Journal of Endourology* 14:133–138. https://doi.org/10.1089/end.2000.14.133

69. CS Allen, R. Burnett, J. Charles, F. Cucinotta, R. Fullerton, JR Goodman, AD Griffith, JJ Kosmo, M, Perchonok, J. Railsback, S. Rajulu, D. Stilwell, G. Thomas TT (2003) *Guidelines and Capabilities for Designing Human Missions*, NASA/Johnson Space Center.

70. Haidegger T, Sándor J, Benyó Z (2011) Surgery in space: The future of robotic telesurgery. *Surgical Endoscopy* 25:681–690. https://doi.org/10.1007/s00464-010-1243-3

71. Eadie LH, Seifalian AM, Davidson BR (2003) Telemedicine in surgery. *British Journal of Surgery* 90:647–658.

72. Rayman R, Croome K, Galbraith N, et al (2006) Long-distance robotic telesurgery: A feasibility study for care in remote environments. *International Journal of Medical Robotics* 2:216–24. https://doi.org/10.1002/rcs.99

73. Vaughan TM, Wolpaw JR (2006) The Third International Meeting on Brain-Computer Interface Technology: Making a difference. *IEEE Transactions on Neural Systems and Rehabilitation Engineering* 14:126–7.

74. Mak JN, Wolpaw JR (2009) Clinical Applications of Brain—Computer Interfaces: Current State and Future Prospects. *IEEE Review on Biomedical Engineering* 2:187–199. https://doi.org/10.1109/RBME.2009.2035356

75. Sellers EW, Donchin E (2006) A P300-based brain-computer interface: Initial tests by ALS patients. *Clinical Neurophysiology* 117:538–548. https://doi.org/10.1016/j.clinph.2005.06.027

76. Vaughan TM, McFarland DJ, Schalk G, et al (2006) The Wadsworth BCI research and development program: At home with BCI. *IEEE Transactions on Neural Systems and Rehabilitation Engineering.* pp. 229–233.

77. Bundy DT, Zellmer E, Gaona CM, et al (2014) Characterization of the effects of the human dura on macro- and micro-electrocorticographic recordings. *Journal of Neural Engineering* 11:16006–16028. https://doi.org/10.1088/1741-2560/11/1/016006.

78. Leuthardt EC, Miller KJ, Schalk G, et al (2006) Electrocorticography-based brain computer interface – The Seattle experience. *IEEE Transactions on Neural Systems and Rehabilitation Engineering.* pp. 194–198.

79. Gunduz A, Sanchez JC, Carney PR, Principe JC (2009) Mapping broadband electrocorticographic recordings to two-dimensional hand trajectories in humans. Motor control features. *Neural Networks* 22:1257–1270. https://doi.org/10.1016/j.neunet.2009.06.036.

80. Pistohl T, Ball T, Schulze-Bonhage A, et al (2008) Prediction of arm movement trajectories from ECoG-recordings in humans. *Journal of Neuroscience Methods* 167:105–114. https://doi.org/10.1016/j.jneumeth.2007.10.001.

81. Sharma Lavanya, Garg P K (2019) Smart E-healthcare with Internet of Things: Current trends challenges, solutions and technologies. In: *From Visual Surveillance to Internet of Things*, Chapman Hall/CRC, Vol.1, p. 215.

82. Sitaram R, Caria A, Veit R, et al (2007) FMRI brain-computer interface: A tool for neuroscientific research and treatment. *Computational Intelligence and Neuroscience* Vol. 2007. https://doi.org/10.1155/2007/25487.

83. Coyle SM, Ward TE, Markham CM (2007) Brain-computer interface using a simplified functional near-infrared spectroscopy system. *Journal of Neural Engineering* 4:219–26. https://doi.org/10.1088/1741-2560/4/3/007.

84. Cavalcanti A, Shirinzadeh B, Zhang M, Kretly LC (2008) Nanorobot hardware architecture for medical defense. *Sensors* 8:2932–2958. https://doi.org/10.3390/s8052932

85. Zhang M, Tao W, Pianetta PA (2007) Dynamics modelling of biolistic gene guns. *Physics in Medicine and Biology* 52:1485–1493. https://doi.org/10.1088/0031-9155/52/5/017

86. Gallo M, Favila A, Glossman-Mitnik D (2007) DFT studies of functionalized carbon nanotubes and fullerenes as nanovectors for drug delivery of antitubercular compounds. *Chemical Physics Letters* 447:105–109. https://doi.org/10.1016/j.cplett.2007.08.098

87. Hilder T, Hill J (2007) Modelling the encapsulation of the anticancer drug cisplatin into carbon nanotubes. *Nanotechnology* 18:275704.

88. Turing AM (1990) The chemical basis of morphogenesis. *Bulletin of Mathematical Biology* 52:153–197. https://doi.org/10.1007/BF02459572

89. Kaiser F (1996) External signals and internal oscillation dynamics: Biophysical aspects and modelling approaches for interactions of weak electromagnetic fields at the cellular level. In: *Bioelectrochemistry and Bioenergetics.* Elsevier Science, South Africa, pp. 3–18.

90. Mesquita M V., Vasconcellos ÁR, Luzzi R, Mascarenhas S (2004) Systems biology: An information-theoretic-based thermo-statistical approach. *Brazilian Journal of Physics. Sociedade Brasileira de Fisica*, pp. 459–488.
91. Jokanović V (2012) *Nanomedicine, the Greatest Challenge of 21st Century*. Datastatus, Belgrade, Serbia.
92. Jokanovic V (2005) Structures and substructures in spray pyrolysis process: Nanodesigning, Finely dispersed particles, Micro-, Nano-, and Atto-Engineering. In: *Surfactant Science Series*. Taylor and Francis.
93. Jokanović V, Spasić AM, Uskoković D (2004) Designing of nanostructured hollow TiO2 spheres obtained by ultrasonic spray pyrolysis. *Journal of Colloid and Interface Science* 278:342–352. https://doi.org/10.1016/j.jcis.2004.06.008
94. Jokanović V, Janaćković D, Uskoković D (1999) Influence of aerosol formation mechanism by an ultrasonic field on particle size distribution of ceramic powders. *Ultrason Sonochem* 6:157–169. https://doi.org/10.1016/S1350-4177(99)00007-3
95. Spasic AM, Jokanovic V (1995) Stability of the Secondary Droplet-Film Structure in Polydispersed Systems. *Journal of Colloid and Interface Science* 170:229–240. https://doi.org/10.1006/jcis.1995.1092
96. Spasic AM, Jokanovic V, Krstic DN (1997) A theory of electroviscoelasticity: A new approach for quantifying the behavior of liquid-liquid interfaces under applied fields. *Journal of Colloid and Interface Science* 186:434–446. https://doi.org/10.1006/jcis.1996.4616
97. Jokanovic V (2016) *Bridge Between Nanophysics and Alternative Medicine; A New Energetic Approach to the Human Cell Treatment and Their Healing*. Lambert House Publishing, Saarbrücken, Germany.
98. Sharma L, Lohan N (March 2019) Internet of Things with object detection, in *Handbook of Research on Big Data and the IoT*, IGI Global, pp. 89–100 DOI: 10.4018/978-1-5225-7432-3.ch006.

5

Portable Smart Home Device for Personalized Interior Display

Aamna Shahab

Amity University
Noida, India

Neetu Mittal

Amity University
Noida, India

CONTENTS

5.1   Introduction 73
5.2   Smart Home Challenges 74
    5.2.1   Adaption 74
    5.2.2   High Cost 75
    5.2.3   Universal Standards 75
    5.2.4   Privacy, Authentication, and Security 75
    5.2.5   Integration of Data 75
    5.2.6   Storage of Data 75
    5.2.7   Networking 75
5.3   Literature Review 76
5.4   Proposed Methodology 77
5.5   Flowchart 77
5.6   Workings of Proposed Device 78
5.7   Results and Discussion 80
5.8   Conclusion 80
References 81

KEYWORDS: *smart walls, display, device, smart-home, IoT*

5.1 Introduction

Internet of Things (IoT) has become huge in the use of future technologies and is considered the backbone of faster communication and industry products. IoT is a series of interrelated programming devices, digital devices, items, and the power to transmit data across a channel without the need for human-to-computer contact. IoT is equipped with an Internet Protocol (IP) address and is able to transmit data over a network. It mainly deals with machine learning and artificial intelligence for utilization of application as well as an embedded perspective.

Smart homes are described as those homes or houses that are capable of simplifying the lives of the people living in it. It can be a change in appliances, environment, interior, light, or climate. Different types of smart home devices have recently been launched on the market. Generally, smart home services haven't been embraced yet, even with a long history and rising interest. There are a variety of factors for avoiding smart home delivery. The biggest obstacle is the lack of resources to construct a smart home infrastructure [1]. Edwards and Grinter [2] argued that problems and social implications in the implementation and delivery of ideal smart home services have been ignored or performed without taking into account the attributes of users or their environment. Most of the methods are focused on experimenting or relying completely on technology. Technical or engineering viewpoints of smart homes are not able to perceive the real needs of potential consumers from a smart home.

In the 1990s, the phase of home automation began while using broadband internet for household functions. In the 2000s, the home network phase came into action while using smartphones and applications for remote monitoring and control functions. Similarly, in the 2010s, smart homes arrived while having IoT and artificial intelligence for the function of context-awareness. This way, the smart home concept has been introduced.

The number of people choosing to incorporate modern and smart technology into their homes has increased rapidly. In this chapter, the proposed device is based on the smart home interior section. With the introduction of new technologies for domestic settings, smart homes have gained significant research and commercial interest from the universal technological sector. Smart home devices allow users to develop their own smart home by integrating sensors and actuators. In this work, a device has been proposed that turns any wall into a display that can change the image/color/pattern/texture of the wall. The wall may change on the basis of the user's wish. It will eventually help in making a smart home with smarter wall interiors.

The conventional smart home control terminal has multiple control schemes. If the device has been used as a smart home controller, software and hardware needs to be built and this will take up a lot of time and resources. If the device is being used as a smart home interface, it does not illustrate the functionality of a smart home port that is powerful and convenient. The proposed device will be used in changing the appearance of walls at home, making the interiors smarter. In other words, a simple wall can be made attractive just by installing the proposed device.

5.2 Smart Home Challenges

While working on smart homes, it was observed that there are many challenges with the process of building a smart home. Those challenges mainly include adaptation to a new environment, high cost of intelligence, standards, privacy and security, data integration, data storage, and networking.

5.2.1 Adaption

Owning a smart home means learning how to use your home, which helps you to adapt to a range of technology around you, such as security systems and many other detectors that also monitor your movements. It's going to involve reading instructions and learning how to go about it [3].

5.2.2 High Cost

While smart homes have several assets that make people's lives simpler, these smart assets are priced higher. The expense of a smart home is high, as some of the hardware is quite new. Moreover, most home automation is only a few of the innovations that are prevalent in a new house, and certain things may also be expensive [3].

5.2.3 Universal Standards

Standardization is very important for the environment of IoT because it spreads globally. Difficulties relate to which model to use, which will provide a reliable structure, and how to make the service more efficient.

5.2.4 Privacy, Authentication, and Security

The data of the user should be kept securely. The link should be made by offering privacy and authentication because it is a must-have in a device in order to protect the smart home network from an intruder. For example, hackers can access the network system, so for such reasons the proposed device must use proper authentication. The proposed application and methods must therefore ensure that the person signing up to their account is the person themselves and not the attacker who is hiding. The server must therefore only give authentic users access, and password protection and two-factor authentication must be enabled in the application itself as the security of a smart home is important.

5.2.5 Integration of Data

The main challenge with IoT is to manipulate applications of IoT into the environment. A smart home is equipped with interconnected, smarter, controllable devices [4]. The Android application is developed and integrated with the smart home device such that it can respond to the user's choice through the application and gets integrated on the wall.

5.2.6 Storage of Data

When IoT implementations are rising, the volume of data produced is immense. Smart homes or automated homes consist of integrated home system intelligent buildings or smart domestics integrated with common devices that control features of the home [4]. It is a broad database that will fix this problem with artificial intelligence algorithms used to produce sense data from repetitive data.

5.2.7 Networking

The layout of the network should be generated in such a way that it can be self-organized by each device connected to it. It's just a network that should be able to coordinate itself. Smart home services policymakers, designers, and developers develop strategies after the analysis of expert views and public attitudes. They not only use energy more efficiently with optimal cost but also provide safety, comfort, and convenience to inhabitants [5].

5.3 Literature Review

IoT is a global neural network used to universally connect various devices and frameworks. A smart home system is the most intelligent technique among IoT concepts. Initially, smart home technology was used for lighting and heating effects, but the technological advancement makes it possible for any of the electrical components within the home. Ricquebourg et al. [6] presented the concept of a smart home with network infrastructures to the habitat and inhabitants. Further smart home augments ubiquitous computing concepts with improved functionality, communications, and mindfulness. Smart homes are proved as a highly advanced automatic system for temperature control, plantation, security, lighting, and so on [7]. Edwards et al. [8] observed the realistic, social, and technical challenges of smart homes to become a reality. Nakamura et al. [9] proposed an ultra-tiny all-in-one sensing hardware platform: SenStick for iOS, Android, and PC. It helps to allow the estimation of context and recognition of activity effortlessly and proficiently with IoT to identify much information from the real world.

To monitor the activity of the person, cameras, sensors, sounds, and power consumption have been used. Further, the technology upgrade model and the aging characteristic variables were implemented to develop an advanced model to improve the elderly's quality of life. Many factors such as computer self-efficacy, subjective norm, perceived reliability, perceived physical condition, perceived usefulness, and attitude were taken into consideration to enhanced human quality of living [10]. Marra et al. [11] present an application of usage control IoT (UCIoT) with a smart home application by implementing a strategy for safety and to save energy. A new model extending the theory of planned behavior was proposed by Yang, Lee, and Zo. Privacy, trust, and mobility risk factors are included for partial least-squares analysis to test hypotheses and models [12].

A rather high cost of setting up a fully functional smart home is the problem with the technology learning curve, security/privacy, and a sedentary lifestyle [13]. Many smart home details with smart networks can be classified into wired and wireless systems with diverse technologies. In a smart home, controllers play an important role in managing systems, challenges, and appliances/smart devices [14]. Sensor and smart objects supply real-world information with the help of the internet along with radio-frequency identification (RFID), sensor networks, and 6LoWPAN [15] for the enormous supply of networks. It helps to transform raw data into meaningful inferences with semantic value as well as semantic logic to make the system intelligent. The service-oriented architecture (SOA) and component technology approach has been proposed by Lia and Yub. It helps to recognize the dynamic semantic integration with its software architecture [16]. A wide range of smart features such as smart kitchen, smart rooms, better security, proper ventilation, and energy saving have been discussed by Jiang et al. [17] for influential harmonic interaction with smart monitoring and online remote-control facility.

An incremental synchronous learning (ISL) technique [18] based on fuzzy logic has been implemented that provides online life-long learning in a nonintrusive mode. Further, intelligent dormitory (iDorm) is used to act as a test-bed for intelligent colonized environments based on the average behavior of users. A home automation system with IoT enables monitoring and control of the home appliances remotely via any method (mobiles or computers) with LAN servers [19].

Given today's hectic life schedule, there is a need for a relaxed and safe lifestyle, simultaneously. Secure home automation is valuable to protect it from theft, gas leakage, trace pass protection, and intruders. The secure wireless system for the smart home is a dynamic model for everyone's life and is acceptable, because of its flexible, portable model with the optimal cost of installation charges. These types of models are the blessing for working people to reduce workload, old age people to provide security, and handicapped people to reduce worries about dependency [20]. Computation overhead and automation with learning human behavior are the major concerns with the smart home concept [21]. The problem in security rises only due to network issues in the home with the internet. To solve this overhead, an internet connectivity module has been proposed that may be attached to the main source unit of the home and can be accessed through the internet. Another concept of Google cloud services has been given by Vasicek et al. The present data and information anytime and anywhere of a smart home are presented for the Android application [22]. The multimodal application for home automation can be operated by a voice recognition technique via Google Assistant [23] or by a web-based application.

5.4 Proposed Methodology

The proposed device will be beneficial for the smart home industry with environment savings. Wallpapers are sold in rolls and wallpaper paste is used to stick them onto the walls. Many wallpapers are of poor quality and most of them use decorative printing with a woven (fabric) or nonwoven (paper) backing.

Groundwood sheets are made by cutting down an entire tree, removing the bark, and pressing the tree with a revolving tread. Wood pulp sheets are also used to make the wallpaper; a roll of paper from the paper mill weighs about one ton. Then, a further process of cutting it is done in subrolls. As millions of trees are being cut down each year just to make wallpaper, the proposed device will avoid all that paper waste and save trees and save the environment. The smart device will have laser projection and distance measure technology, which is used to do the measurement of the wall. It is the perfect tool to test distance measurements. The laser distance meter is used to precisely determine the distance of the object or the span without contact by means of a laser. The basic measurement theory is based on the calculation of the transit time of laser pulses between the laser distance meter and the target to be measured with respect to the speed of light. In addition, this concept allows very wide distances to be calculated within the kilometer range. In addition, the wall's height and width will be precisely calculated with the inbuilt laser measuring in the proposed device. With the help of this smart device, people will be able to change their wall color in a fraction of seconds. The proposed device is completely technology-based with no use of paper. It saves millions of trees for a smarter city and a better home to keep the city clean, green, and flourishing in a smart way.

5.5 Flowchart

In the proposed work, a database has been created and it is best suited with the Android application. The wallpapers will be available for selection by the user including all types of colors and patterns. The user will also have the choice to select an image of their own from their mobile gallery. Thus, the application will then be integrated with the proposed

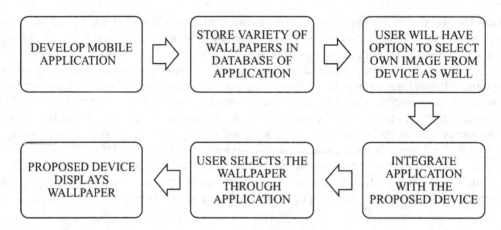

FIGURE 5.1
Flowchart of proposed methodology.

device such that it responds to the commands given by the application. The user may select the choice of wallpaper and the proposed device will successfully display the wallpaper with the help of major edge detection and object detection techniques once attached to the wall. The flowchart of the proposed methodology has been shown in Figure 5.1.

5.6 Workings of Proposed Device

The proposed device will be used to display the user's choice of color on the wall. It will be made of a high-quality metallic globe or a sleek cuboidal structure from which the laser measuring tool will be used to measure the wall's height and width for a precise display of color/images. The Android/iOS mobile applications will be developed for the users to make it easier for them to change the settings on the go. The proposed device will be charged using a USB-C Type charging cable with a Type C adapter included connected to a power source. The charging will last depending on the usage. It will have a 4000 mAh battery installed into it. Best usage will be if it's connected to a power source consecutively.

The creation of a database of a user's choice has been done and the choices have been added to the database to display wallpapers. The user can finally choose from a variety of options: 1,000+ options of wallpapers according to their mood or choice or wish. It will include solid colors, textures, patterns, and images.

Then, once selected, the wallpaper will be displayed on the wall to the user. An option to randomly change the wallpaper or fix it permanently until changed will be provided through the remote or app installed in the smartphone.

Figure 5.2 shows the device in the bottom-left corner is projecting a display in the form of flip-style transitioning tiles. The following steps are shown here for the workings of the proposed device:

1. The tiles will move right as the object is detected, placed, and analyzed according to the proposed algorithm. Only two options, top or right, are possible. It will then move right to start the process.

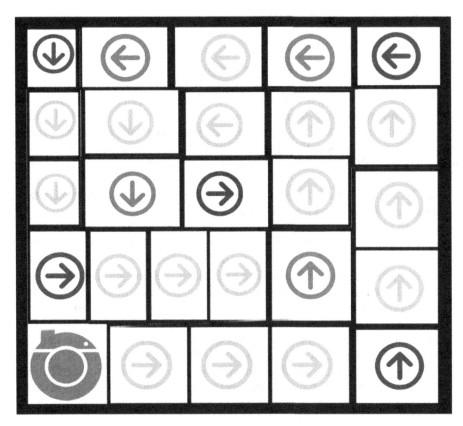

FIGURE 5.2
Workings of the smart device.

2. As soon as it detects an edge, it will analyze again with the help of the algorithm and will move to the left.

3. The tiles will keep detecting the edges and analyzing the wall until it finds an object according to the algorithm. Once it finds the device, it will follow two new rules.

   a. The tiles after detecting the object will not move backward or forward, rather, it will detect whether there is space left or right to move. When one cycle is completed and the dark arrow is above the object, it will move to its left because it is the only way possible.

   b. Once the cycle of processing tiles is on its way after object detection, it will detect the preloaded tiles. It will also detect the places where the tile has already been put. This will be a crucial part in the algorithm because the user does not want to recur the picture they chose.

4. In case of a solid color, the detection of tiles again will not be necessary because the purpose will only be to fill the wall with color.

5. Once completed, it will stop and display the whole image, thus, the whole calculation of the wall will be completed and the picture/color/texture will be shown on the whole wall.

5.7 Results and Discussion

The proposed methodology will make any boring room into a spectacular room within seconds; a bezel-less display that can occupy the whole wall and make it look different each day. Think how amazing it would be to be able to control the look of the walls with just a simple application on a device as small as your smartphone. It will change the way smart interiors work. The flipping tiles display will give a futuristic and modern look to it, which really makes the home a smart home. The best-quality adaptors and laser technologies will be used in the proposed device to make every measurement precise.

This work has taken an analytical look at important factors for the acceptance and deployment of smart home services. Research findings show that there is a need for interconnectivity and reliability together with an acceptable degree of automation. In addition, because there are variations in the choice of variables according to the characteristics of customers, it has been established that the design of the service that considers these characteristics are important. If these factors are taken into account, smart home services that have not been allowed in the past will spread and the market will grow. The resulted outcome of the proposed work is a smart device that may be able to make any type of simple wall at home into a completely different wall. People use wallpapers and spend a lot of money on painting their wall; they may get bored with the wall color but they settle for it because of its permanency. In this device's case, the device will not only be a one-time investment, it will be the future of the smart home environment. A user will purchase this device once and they will have the power to control their wall color with just a click on their smartphone or remote. Both options will be there for the users to make it easily accessible for all.

5.8 Conclusion

A variety of research programs have also been initiated as technology growth progresses. Today, the smart home is more than just a remote-operated central measurement system like a computer. Obviously, the way people live with smart homes will become more successful and enjoyable. The smart home will be protected all the time from home automation, so users have a lot of time to concentrate on other things. Thus, with the popularity of smart homes, the smart device that is discussed in this chapter will lead to changing the smart home environment. The change of wall patterns will definitely be very useful for people in the near future.

The proposed device needs the power to run smartphones, smart televisions, and so on. Continuous energy consumption is a necessity of the device. The proposed device uses the edge detection algorithm so one device always covers one wall each. Users have to buy different devices if they wish to change the colors of multiple walls. These limitations make the device expensive. Smart home technology, however, is a good choice for people who care about safety and comfort but also about saving energy. Smart homes are expected to become more popular as more and more new technologies are explored.

References

1. V. Ricquebourg, D. Menga, D. Durand, B. Marhic, L. Delahoche, and C. Loge, "The smart home concept: Our immediate future," in 2006 1ST IEEE International Conference on E-Learning in Industrial Electronics, pp. 23–28, IEEE, Hammamet, Tunisia, 2006.
2. W. K. Edwards and R. E. Grinter, "At home with ubiquitous computing: Seven challenges," in *Ubicomp 2001: Ubiquitous Computing*, pp. 256–272, Springer, Berlin, Germany, 2001.
3. Paul Lin, "Disadvantages of a Smart Home" [Online], Available: http://www.ehow.co.uk/list_7631272_disadvantages-smarthome.html [2012, October 19].
4. Heetae Yang, Wonji Lee, and Hwansoo Lee, "IoT smart home adoption: The importance of proper level automation," *Hindawi Journal of Sensors*, vol. 2, pp. 1–11, 2018.
5. N. Balta-Ozkan, R. Davidson, M. Bicket, and L. Whitmarsh, "Social barriers to the adoption of smart homes," *Energy Policy*, vol. 63, pp. 363–374, 2013.
6. Jackie Craven, "What Is a Smart House?" [Online], Available: http://architecture.about.com/od/buildyourhous1/g/smarthouse.htm [2012, October 18].
7. V. Ricquebourg, D. Menga, D. Durand, B. Marhic, L. Delahoche, and C. Loge, "The smart home concept: Our immediate future," in *2006 1ST IEEE Int. Conference on E-Learning in Industrial Electronics*, pp. 23–28, IEEE, Hammamet, Tunisia, 2006.
8. W. K. Edwards and R. E. Grinter, "At home with ubiquitous computing: Seven challenges," *Ubiquitous Computing,* pp. 256–272, Springer, Berlin, 2001.
9. Y. Nakamura, Y. Arakawa, T. Kanehira, M. Fujiwara, and K. Yasumoto, "Sen stick: Comprehensive sensing platform with an ultra tiny all-in-one sensor board for IoT research," *Journal of Sensors*, vol. 2017, Article ID 6308302, 16 pages, 2017.
10. A. Leeraphong, B. Papasratorn, and V. Chongsuphajaisiddhi, "A study on factors influencing elderly intention to use smart home in Thailand: A pilot study," in *The 10th International Conference on e-Business*, Bangkok, Thailand, 2015.
11. La Marra, F. Martinelli, P. Mori, and A. Saracino, "Implementing usage control in internet of things: a smart home use case," in *2017 IEEE Trustcom/BigDataSE/ICESS*, pp. 1056–1063, IEEE, Sydney, NSW, Australia, 2017.
12. H. Yang, H. Lee, and H. Zo, "User acceptance of smart home services: An extension of the theory of planned behavior," *Industrial Management & Data Systems*, vol. 117, no. 1, pp. 68–89, 2017.
13. P. Lin, "Disadvantages of a Smart Home" [Online], Available: http://www.ehow.co.uk/list_7631272_disadvantages-smarthome.html [2012, October 19].
14. M. Sripan, X. Lin, P. Petchlorlean, and M. Ketcham, "Research and thinking of smart home technology," International Conference on Systems and Electronic Engineering (ICSEE'2012), Phuket, Thailand, 61–63, 2012.
15. G. Tripathi, D. Singh, and A. J. Jara, "A survey of Internet-of-Things: Future vision, architecture, challenges and service," IEEE World Forum on Internet of Things (WF-IoT), 287–292, 2014.
16. B. Lia and J. Yub, "Research and application on the smart home based on component technologies and Internet of Things," *Advanced in Control Engineering and Information Science*, 15, 2087–2092, 2011.
17. L. Jiang, D.-Y. Llu, and B. Yang, "Smart home research," Proceedings of the Third International Conference on Machine Learning and Cybernetics, Lanzhou, China, 659–663, 2004.
18. H. Hagras, V. Callaghan, G. Clarke, M. Colley, A. Pounds-Cornish, A. Holmes, and H. Duman, "Incremental synchronous learning for embedded-agents operating in ubiquitous computing environments, the international series," *Frontiers in Artificial Intelligence and Application*, pp. 25–54, Dec 2002.
19. K. Agarwal, A. Agarwal, and G. Misra, "Review and performance analysis on wireless smart home and home automation using IoT," 2019 Third International conference on I-SMAC (IoT in Social, Mobile, Analytics and Cloud) (I-SMAC), Palladam, India, 2019, pp. 629–633.

20. V. D. Vaidya and P. Vishwakarma, "A Comparative analysis on smart home system to control, monitor and secure home, based on technologies like GSM, IOT, Bluetooth and PIC microcontroller with ZigBee modulation," 2018 International Conference on Smart City and Emerging Technology (ICSCET), Mumbai, India, 2018, pp. 1–4.

21. T. Chaurasia and P. K. Jain, "Enhanced smart home automation system based on Internet of Things," 2019 Third International Conference on I-SMAC (IoT in Social, Mobile, Analytics and Cloud) (I-SMAC), Palladam, India, 2019, pp. 709–713.

22. D. Vasicek, J. Jalowiczor, L. Sevcik, and M. Voznak, "IoT Smart Home Concept," 2018 26th Telecommunications Forum (TELFOR), Belgrade, Serbia, 2018, pp. 1–4.

23. S. K. Vishwakarma, P. Upadhyaya, B. Kumari, and A. K. Mishra, "Smart energy efficient home automation system using IoT," 2019 4th International Conference on Internet of Things: Smart Innovation and Usages (IoT-SIU), Ghaziabad, India, 2019, pp. 1–4.

6

Importance of Augmented Reality and Virtual Reality in Our Daily Life

Vallidevi Krishnamurthy

Department of Computer Science and Engineering, SSN College of Engineering, Anna University
Chennai, India

D. Venkata Vara Prasad

SSN College of Engineering, Anna University
Chennai, India

Ganesh Kumar

Department of Computer Science and Engineering, SRM University
Chennai, India

B. Surendiran

Department of Computer Science and Engineering, NIT Puducherry
Puducherry, India

Arjith Natarajan

Department of CSE, SSN College of Engineering, Anna University
Chennai, India

Akshaya Natarajan

Department of CSE, SSN College of Engineering, Anna University
Chennai, India

Dattuluri Rushitaa

Department of ECE, SSN College of Engineering, Anna University
Chennai, India

CONTENTS

6.1 Introduction 84
6.2 Literature Survey 84
6.3 Applications 85
    6.3.1 Augmented Reality and Its Application 86
    6.3.2 Virtual Reality and Its Application 86
6.4 Research Method 87
    6.4.1 Premedical Diagnosis System 87
        6.4.1.1 Data Collection Module 87
        6.4.1.2 3D Model Building 88
        6.4.1.3 Medical Data Correlator 88
        6.4.1.4 Technologies and Its Definitions 89

        6.4.2   Smart Education System for Deaf-Mute Children 89
        6.4.3   e-Learning-Based Virtual Car Driving System 90
6.5   Results and Discussion 91
6.6   Conclusion 93
References...93

6.1 Introduction

The fundamental value added by augmented reality (AR) is that it brings factors of the digital world into a person's understanding of the real world. Using AR, one can augment any object into the real world. There are many current operations that implement AR and many more that are still trying to implement their application using AR in their respective fields. The first application that was developed using AR in the 1990s was used for pilot training [1] and since then, its utilization has been incorporated in a variety of fields. The significance of AR is observed when it is used for those training purposes that are generally difficult to do in real life, such as pilot training, medical diagnosis, medical experiments, army training, and automobile industries. AR in conjunction with technologies like Internet of Things (IoT) and virtual reality (VR) has evolved to an extent that makes artificial intelligence sound like a task that can be easily accomplished. This chapter explains a model that saves the time taken to perform preliminary examinations in medical diagnosis.

   The preliminary process of examination is eliminated by digitally transporting the patient's details to the doctor and, hence, the doctor can evaluate them when they are available. The doctor can further suggest the required tests and diagnosis for the respective patient. AR could be used for medical education through which student interaction in classes could be increased and there could be more practical discussions in the class. This will trigger the interest of the students. VR takes the person to that place and makes them learn new things in the environment that is needed for the learning process [2, 3, 4]. In VR, a whole new environment is created according to the demand. On the other hand, in AR, images are superimposed into the real world rather than creating a completely new environment. AR complements reality, rather than completely restoring it. The virtual objects project information that the user can't directly observe with one's own senses. AR not only increases our learning curve but also improves our brain's productivity. It changes the way one thinks, works, and how one learns. Instead of having just one angle of any concept, multiple angles of the same concept can be obtained.

   This chapter also explains how VR could be used in our life with an e-learning interface to learn to drive a car. To achieve this, a VIRECAR is built, which is a virtual reality car simulator that leverages the aforementioned technology to provide a coherent and easy-to-use environment using the Google Cardboard, Leap Motion, and the Trinus VR applications, which provide an interface between the desktop and the head-mounted device.

6.2 Literature Survey

AR technology is being utilized for the interactive environment in education using AR and three-dimensional (3D) visualization, which are explained by White et al. [5, 6]. AR was used in kinetic fusion technology with a kinetic camera to develop 3D models in real time [7]. The pros and cons of AR in the educational environment are discussed in [8, 9]. Agarwal and Thakur discuss the evolution and the recent practices of AR in daily life in [10]. Research articles, namely, Lee et al. [11] and Ng and Komiya [12], discuss the importance of the virtual environment in e-learning through the structural equation and modeling approach for explaining the enhancement in learning outcomes through desktop VR. Quantitative analysis of education through social learning outcomes was explained in [13]. There are many day-to-day applications in which artificial intelligence is being realized through IoT and are even explained in detail in [14]. Sergey et al. [5] discusses collective encompassment for education using AR and 3D visualization. Saidin et al. [8] reviews the importance of the virtual environment in e-learning. Agarwal and Thakur [10] confer about recent practices of AR in daily life. The e-learning and e-learning-based improvement of the skill set of the user is examined in [9, 15, 16]. Bouras [17] explains the applications of AR.

A special issue on the recent advances in intelligent robotic systems have five different chapters [18] that direct the readers toward the different domains, such as the lane detection system in autonomous driving of vehicles, mobile-controlled robots with speaking facilities, and so on. The different types of virtual realities and the working principle are discussed in detail by Gandhi and Patel [19]. Zhao et al. [20] discussed in detail aiding people with visual impairment using VR techniques like haptic and auditory cane technologies. Parvinen et al. [21] discusses the applications of minitrack using AR and VR, a combination of both. Deshmukh et al. [22] discusses four methods of creating 3D video modules using AR, the four methods being Smartphone/Computer, Unity, Vuforia, and Server. Bottino et al. [23] discusses in detail Holo-Defibrillation, which integrates virtual and real-life workplaces using augmented reality and BLSD concepts. Gaikwad et al. [24] discusses in detail the implementation of mixed reality technology by using AR and VR and its various aspects. Stone [25] defines the initial stages and results of a UK research, which consigns the development of "natural" or "intuitive" interfaces by combining telepresence and VR technologies using advanced human interfaces.

6.3 Applications

Two technologies and their applications are discussed in this chapter. The first technology, AR, is discussed with two applications, namely, the Premedical Diagnosis System and the smart education system for deaf and mute people. In the Premedical Diagnosis System, the doctors could carry out a discussion with their seniors for confirming the diagnosis procedure. All the medical documents could be sent digitally and a 3D image of the patient could help the doctor in the remote location to ascertain their findings. Similarly, the same technology could also be used for an education purpose. The doctors could understand the inner working of all the organs by having an augmented view of those organs. Apart from that, even the deaf and mute children in their biology classes could touch and feel every organ with their vision and have a better understanding of the concepts. The second technology that is discussed in this chapter is VR. The e-learning-based virtual car driving system (VIRECAR) is the application that is implemented and the experimental results are also tabulated.

6.3.1 Augmented Reality and Its Application

In order to evaluate where the virtual objects are to be incognito in the environment, the following approaches are considered:

  a. **Marker-Based Approach:** In this approach [26], the pictures and the corresponding picture descriptors to be detected are provided beforehand. The markers that are used can be QR codes or black and white square mirrors.

  b. **Marker-Less Approach:** In a marker-less approach [27], an AR application acknowledges things that were indirectly provided to the application beforehand. This situation is much more difficult to execute because the recognition algorithm running in your AR application has to identify patterns, colors, or some other features that may exist in camera frames.

The advancement of technology in the field of medicine has grown to an extent that makes diagnosis very simple and efficient. Doctors can use AR as a visualization technique and training aid for surgery [7]. The input data of the patient can be either images, or metadata about the heartbeat, and so on, which will be transported to the doctor, along with the patient's 3D hologram. Thus, by using AR in this field, it gives the doctor a complete vision, such as an X-ray of the patient. The goal is to make sure the diagnosis process is accelerated. When the image is being transmitted, there are many chances of additional noise being added to the image due to transportation. In that case, the convolutional neural network (CNN)-based denoising algorithm discussed in [28] could be implemented to overcome the problem. A context-driven visualization tool with AR is discussed in [29]. A review of research work carried out in the last decade for AR-based technology in the manufacturing industry is discussed in [30].

6.3.2 Virtual Reality and Its Application

The e-learning-based virtual car driving system (VIRECAR) is explained in Section 6.4.3. The car driving system provides road safety measures that could help learners to avoid accidents. The VIRECAR is a VR car simulator aimed at educating learners to drive a car with an objective to simplify the learning process and provide an immersive experience for the user. To achieve this, the system environment is built on Unity3D with inputs given as gestures of the hand and touch through electrical sensors. The environment is visualized through a mobile device using Google Cardboard. The input to the environment is given through the Leap Motion device, which tracks the hand gestures, and the pedal input is through the Makey Makey chipboard that translates the touch inputs into keyboard inputs. The Leap Motion device, unlike the Kinect, does not restore a whole depth map, but returns only a set of important hand points and some hand pose aspects. To simulate holding the steering wheel and to handle the gear stick, the hand angle and orientation data is used. Upon making a similar hand shape to holding, the actions will be allowed and thus performed. A chip processor is used to translate touch inputs as pedal inputs to the virtual environment. The developed application runs on a desktop to utilize the better computational powers compared to a mobile device. This results in faster input recognition and translation to actions in the virtual environment.

6.4 Research Method

The three applications of the Premed Diagnosis System, the Smart Education System, and the e-learning-based driving system are explained in this section with the respective diagrams that are needed. Among those, the VR-based e-learning system was implemented and the system was analyzed by the feedback mechanism.

6.4.1 Premedical Diagnosis System

A system that aims to simplify the doctor/patient preliminary examinations is shown Figure 6.1 is the system that is newly proposed in this chapter. The idea is to digitally transport the patient to the doctor's room as a simple simplified 3D object, with all necessary details to facilitate the findings. In addition, without just transporting a digital object, the system will impart interactivity to these objects where in, at the doctor's side, it gets rendered as AR models superimposed in the environment. Thus, the simulation of a patient's appointment could be done with this system.

6.4.1.1 Data Collection Module

The first module of the system comprises of collection of patient data. This is done at the clinical premise. Patient data includes preliminary medical examination data like temperature, breathing level, and blood pressure.

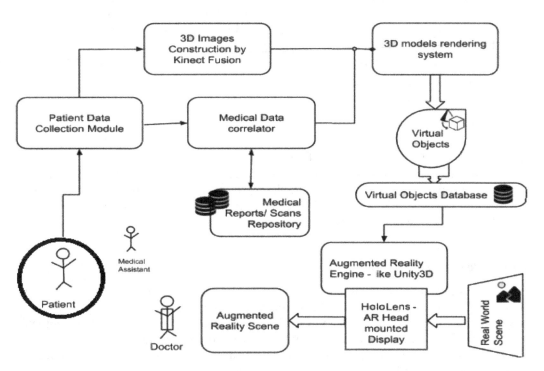

FIGURE 6.1
Premedical diagnosis system.

The collection and gathering shall be conducted by an assistant who uses the respective devices to capture these data. The image of the patient is then captured using Kinect cameras that develop a 3D image of the patient using appropriate depths and coloring.

6.4.1.2 3D Model Building

The videos are to be recorded, featuring the patient with the help of Kinect cameras. These are special cameras with sensors to detect the depth of the patient dynamically. Images and videos are captured via depth cameras and they appear to be as 2D images. These images when fed into Kinect Fusion, will churn out 3D modeling of the scene captured along with objects.

a. **Conversion:** The conversion of 2D images can be performed by Kinect APIs. Although the modeling of the 2D image into 3D models can be done in real time using Kinect Fusion [7], such an approach is traded for more accurate and detailed models by processing it separately. Although the process takes a lot of time, the needed quality of the 3D images that are rendered is achieved. The images captured as photographs are then overlaid onto the 3D objects to improve the originality of the objects. The same process is applied to any particular part of body, under examination.

b. **Exclusion:** The subject of interest at hand is only the patient and their vitals; any other objects present in the surroundings can be ignored. Thus, removal of the other objects is done in this component of the system. Selective capturing of images is not possible using Kinect cameras, hence the approach used is to remove other unnecessary objects from the scene. This additional processing can be achieved through any image/graphic processing libraries like OpenCV, OpenGL, and so on. The sequence of the steps would be:

- Detect unnecessary surfaces
- Select them iteratively
- Remove

The approach may vary for each patient.

c. **Order of Processing:** It is ideal to process the video in a particular order. 3D models are constructed first and then the background objects are removed from the video. However, this reversal may not work due to the presence of the objects in the surrounding area vital for depth sensing.

6.4.1.3 Medical Data Correlator

The patient's data includes their appearance; in most cases, the patient comes in with complaints and no particulars. In all of the medical check-ups, the complaint of the particular patient forms the core of the data collector. The complaint as narrated by the patient and recorded by the medical assistant is the vital information to any decision; general notes/observations about the mental state of the patient are also included. The data collected includes vital signs and basic checkups/examination.

6.4.1.4 Technologies and Its Definitions

The intention of the proposed system is to use some of the existing software technologies to make the preliminary diagnosis process effortless and uncomplicated. Some of the technologies that are used in the system are noticeably defined here. This section is in reference to the readers who do not have a clear idea about the definitions of certain technologies.

a. **Kinect Fusion:** Kinect Fusion [7] is a recent and extensively-accessible product sensor platform that consolidates a composed light-based depth sensor. Original generation framework-free capture of a handheld camera while concurrently aligning the substantial display in great-design assures advanced capabilities for augmented and mixed reality utilization. An accurate approach with study of what may be the early structure that allows real-time, heavy vitric restoration of objects using a handheld Kinect extent sensor can be found in [7]. Users can easily pick up and move Kinect gear to bring about a frequently amending, smooth, fully infused 3D surface structurization.

b. **Unity 3D Kit:** Unity can be used to primarily create 3D and 2D games for computers. It can be defined as a navigating-platform game engine used to create simulations. Unity can be used together with AR to create gaming applications that superimpose things into the current world. Pokémon Go is one example of a game that uses AR. In order to build the application, the SDK (Software Development Kit) of Unity, called Vuforia, is utilized. It uses computer vision technology to identify objects, registers their position, and orients them. Vuforia is a free technology and is an ideal solution that serves the purpose.

c. **HoloLens:** As one of the early augmented reality head gears accessible today in the market, the Microsoft HoloLens is prone to have a deep impact on the advancement of AR applications [31]. The HoloLens is a seated exhibit unit connected to a flexible, soft inner headgear, which can tilt HoloLens up and down, as well as back and forth.

6.4.2 Smart Education System for Deaf-Mute Children

A new era of technology called EduAR comprises of AR with holograms that can be deployed in the field of education. AR sums to the reality that is ordinarily seen rather than renewing the reality. The final goal of EduAR is to create an acceptable and innate immersion such that it becomes extremely easy to understand and interpret what has to be learnt. Compared to previous years, education today has improved and expanded to an extent that it becomes hard to follow and keep track of everything that is being taught. This is where EduAR is helpful. One of the unique features of EduAR is the ability to ease the learning of deaf-mute students. Using their vision and EduAR, these students can understand concepts as easily as any other student.

Consider a scenario of a biology class. Using EduAR, holographic images of the brain are used to explain the minute and intricate parts, which in reality is difficult for the teachers to describe just based on textbooks. As a result, EduAR helps the student understand how a brain works visually, thereby helping them to perform better during operations. It also enables medical students to gain information and perception about the human anatomy by means of interacting with a virtual environment in which no patients are put at risk. This, in further, can be extended to different streams in a way that is usually difficult for a student to interpret.

Teaching and learning has to be much more than a simple process of knowledge transfer by memorizing. EduAR improves the student's learning experience, thereby developing the interests of an individual. Many labs that have 3D models of brains or hearts do not really give much information on the deeper layers of the brain, which will be one the major advantages of using EduAR. Also, with EduAR, dynamic labeling will be an asset. Teachers can modify or add labels of parts as and when required rather than buying a new 3D model every time. Thus, EduAR focuses on transforming the overall education experience.

In the research article [32], a directing system for helping technicians on difficult electronic equipment has been explained with AR concepts. A lot of training has been carried out effectively for the technicians with more ease using the AR concept.

6.4.3 e-Learning-Based Virtual Car Driving System

Simulations of real-world scenarios can be achieved with a high value of realism using the concept of VR. This characteristic of VR environments gives an advantage toward e-learning where the solution to real-world problems can be learned virtually. Gesture recognition is another technology that has seen a steady increase in popularity as a method of human-computer interaction. Specific gestures can be translated to perform specific tasks. With hand gesture detection devices like Leap Motion, gesture detection to communicate with an environment has become simplistic and usable. Combining such technologies with the learning process provides lucrative methodologies, which can be leveraged to simplify the process of learning. After implementing the VIRECAR virtual simulator system, it was analyzed with feedback from a sample of 12 licensed drivers and 12 new learners in driving.

The learning experience obtained from VIRECAR is explained in three stages in this chapter: The first stage is considered as the Pre-Class Content in e-learning, the second stage is considered as the In-Class Content, and the third stage is considered as the Post-Class Content, where these three stages of e-learning are already explained in [13, 14].

1. In the *first stage–Basics of Driving*, the user is required to understand the road and safety regulations prescribed by the Road Transport Office and are also required to understand the basic functionalities of the car. Toward the completion of this phase, the learners are required to undertake a test evaluating their competency in the basics of driving a car.

2. In the *second stage–Learning through VIRECAR*, VIRECAR is used to understand the workings of a car and getting used to the driving environment. At this stage, the concept of an instructor is introduced. The instructor at this stage is present at regular intervals evaluating the learning process undertaken by the learner and feedbacks are provided as and when necessary.

3. The *third stage–Actual Driving*, which can also be described as a post-class exercise, is to drive an actual car based on the results obtained from VIRECAR. In this phase, the instructor is present full-time, which allows them to give a feedback.

The learner at this stage is expected to drive a car with the experience and feedback obtained from the second stage and the knowledge of the rules and regulations obtained from the first stage. The above three steps occurring for the first time constitute the first iteration of the learning process. In the forthcoming iterations, the learner is not required to go through the first stage again, since the requirement to proceed to the second stage is to master the concepts in the first stage. Thus, a concept of back-propagation is used here.

Based on the feedback obtained from the third stage of the VIRECAR e-learning process, the learner might have to gain more experience from the virtual environment before gaining that experience in the real world. Essentially, the learner is expected to experience each aspect of driving a car including changing gears, using the pedals for acceleration, brake, and clutch, to steer the wheel, and so on. This allows for a safe environment for the learner to effectively experience the learning process described in this chapter aimed at learning to drive a car properly.

6.5 Results and Discussion

To analyze the VIRECAR simulator system that is described in this chapter, the system was tested with a sample of 12 licensed drivers and thus the efficiency of the VIRECAR was evaluated by their feedback. They were introduced to the whole system as described in Figure. 6.2. Furthermore, they were asked to try the simulator to answer certain questions that were deemed vital toward evaluating VIRECAR.

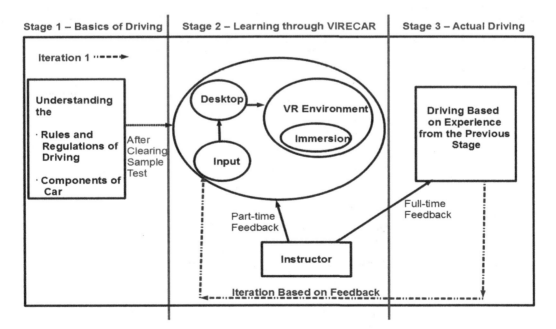

FIGURE 6.2
e-Learning Process in VIRECAR.

TABLE 6.1

Driver Details–Used for Sample Testing of the Proposed Work

Driver's Age in Range	Count	Driver's Gender
20 to 25	4	3 Male and 1 Female
26 to 30	5	2 Male and 3 Female
31 to 40	3	2 Male and 1 Female

Some of the questions that were put forward include:

a. How close to reality was it?
b. How helpful was it in understanding the driving scenario?
c. How useful was the system in learning rules and regulations?
d. If you had not driven an actual car, would you prefer to learn using VIRECAR?
e. Do you think you will be able to rectify any mistakes through VIRECAR?

Table 6.1 shows the details of the drivers who were considered for the testing purpose of the proposed system. These drivers had already obtained their license and knew how to drive. Such skilled drivers of different age groups and gender were considered to test the system and feedback is shown in Table 6.2.

Table 6.3 shows consolidated data that was obtained from the testers of VIRECAR. The drivers gave an average score of 7.833 and 8.167 to the questions regarding driving scenario and understanding the rules and regulations. This gives us the view that stage one of VIRECAR must be made more stringent and some of the elements from stage one must also be implemented in stage two to provide a sense of continuity.

TABLE 6.2

Feedback for the Questions by the Different Test Drivers of VIRECAR

Question\Driver Details	20 to 25 Age Group				26 to 30 Age Group					31 to 40 Age Group		
	1	2	3	4	5	6	7	8	9	10	11	12
Q1	7	8	9	6	7	7	8	6	7	7	8	7
Q2	8	8	8	7	7	9	7	7	9	8	7	9
Q3	9	8	9	7	9	8	9	7	8	9	7	8
Q4	8	9	10	7	9	8	9	8	9	9	9	9
Q5	Y	Y	Y	N	Y	Y	Y	Y	Y	Y	Y	N

TABLE 6.3

Mean Value of the Feedback Acquired from 12 Test Drivers of VIRECAR

Question	Average Rating
Q1	7.250
Q2	7.833
Q3	8.167
Q4	8.667
Q5	10–Yes; 2–No

This same system was given to a driving school and 12 new female driving learners were given training using this system. Those novice learners were happy to use this system. Those learners were all above 35 years of age.

6.6 Conclusion

In spite of the fact that AR and VR sounds appealing, there are several challenges in implementing the system on a practical aspect. They fall in two categories: technical and social. Considering the technical point of view, one requires a lot of components to make the system function properly. Object recognition is the first step in any AR system. If objects in the real world and virtual world are not aligned with each other, the illusion of two coexisting worlds is affected. Hence, the quality of the components is an important factor to be taken care of. Problems like inaccurate sensor readings and poor pattern recognition can greatly affect the accuracy of the system. Considering the social aspect, AR is still at its nascent stage and remains widely unknown to the general public. Similarly, VR also has a problem in implementation as it needs more components and new technologies to be learnt.

There are many more applications for both AR and VR to be used more effectively in our day-to-day lives. One such interesting application is the neonatal care training system that could be developed with these new technologies. In spite of many implementation issues, these technologies have their own benefits of not risking the public during the initial learning process.

References

1. T. P. Caudell, D. W. Mizell, "Augmented reality: an application of heads-up display technology to manual manufacturing processes," Proceedings of the Twenty-Fifth Hawaii International Conference on System Sciences, Kauai, 1992, pp. 659–669.
2. J. Hayes, "Virtual reality enters the real world," *Journal of Engineering and Technology*, 3(14), 2008, pp. 60–62.
3. L. Sharma, N. Lohan, "Performance analysis of moving object detection using BGS techniques," *International Journal of Spatio-Temporal Data Science*, Inderscience, February, 1(1), 2019, pp. 22–53. (ISSN: 2399-1275) doi: 10.1504/IJSTDS.2019.097607.
4. L. Sharma, A. Singh, D. K. Yadav, "Fisher's linear discriminant ratio based threshold for moving human detection in thermal video," *Infrared Physics & Technology*, Elsevier, 78, March 2016, pp. 118–128, (ISSN: 1350-4495, SCI impact factor: 2.31).
5. J. White, D. C. Schmidt, M. Golparvar-Fard, "Applications of Augmented Reality," *Proceedings of the IEEE* 102(2), 2014, pp. 120–123.
6. S. Sannikov, F. Zhdanov, P. Chebotarev, P. Rabinovich, "Interactive Educational Content Based on Augmented Reality and 3D Visualization," 4th International Young Scientists Conference on Computational Science, Athens, Greece, 2015, pp. 720–729.
7. R. A. Newcombe, S. Izadi, O. Hilliges, D. Molyneaux, D. Kim, A. J. Davison, P. Kohli, J. Shotton, S. Hodges, A. Fitzgibbon, "KinectFusion: Real-Time Dense Surface Mapping and Tracking," IEEE International Symposium on Mixed and Augmented Reality 2011 Science and Technology Proceedings, Basel, Switzerland, 26–29 October, 2011.

8. N. F. Saidin, N. D. Abd Halim, N. Yahaya, "A Review of Research on Augmented Reality in Education: Advantages and Applications," *International Education Studies* 13, 2015, pp. 1913–9039.

9. K. N. Senthil, "Enhancement of skills through e-learning: Prospects and problems," *The Online Journal of Distance Education and e-Learning*, 4(3), 2016, pp. 24–32.

10. C. Agarwal, N. Thakur, "The evolution and future scope of augmented reality," *International Journal of Computer Science Issues*, 11(6), No 1, November 2014.

11. E A-L. Lee, K. W. Wong, C. C. Fung, "How does desktop virtual reality enhance learning outcomes? A structural equation modeling approach," *Elsevier Computers and Education*, 55(4), 2010, pp. 1424–1442.

12. K. Hui Ng, R. Komiya, "Multimedia textbook for virtual education environment," *Engineering Science & Education Journal*, 11(2), pp. 73–79.

13. D. Georgios, "Investigating the educational value of social learning networks: A quantitative analysis," *Interactive Technology and Smart Education*, 13(4), 2016, pp. 305–322.

14. A. Ghosh, D. Chakraborty, A. Law, "Artificial intelligence in Internet of things," *CAAI Transactions on Intelligence Technology*, 3(4), 2018, pp. 208–218.

15. U. Vladimir, *"Smart Education and Smart e-Learning,"* Springer Publishing Company Incorporated, Switzerland, 2015.

16. R. Gleadow, "Design for learning–a case study of blended learning in a science unit," *F1000 Research*, 4, 2015, p. 898.

17. C. Bouras, "A e-Learning through distributed virtual environments," *Journal of Network and Computer Applications*, 24, 2001, pp. 175–199.

18. W. Yuan, M. Yang, H. Li, C. Wang, B. Wang, "End-to-end learning for high-precision lane keeping via multi-state model," *CAAI Transactions on Intelligence Technology*, 3(4), 2018, pp.185–190.

19. R. D. Gandhi, D. S. Patel, "Virtual reality and opportunities," *International Research Journal of Engineering and Technology* 05(01), 2018.

20. Y. Zhao, C. L. Bennett, H. Benko, E. Cutrell, C. Holz, M. R. Morris, M. Sinclair, "Enabling People with Visual Impairments to Navigate Virtual Reality with a Haptic and Auditory Cane Simulation," CHI '18: Conference on Human Factors in Computing Systems, Montreal, Canada, 2018.

21. P. Parvinen, J. Hamari, E. Pöyry, "Introduction to Minitrack: Mixed, Augmented and Virtual Reality," 51st Hawaii International Conference on System Sciences, Waikoloa Village, 2018.

22. S. S. Deshmukh, C. M. Joshi, R. S. Patel, Dr. Y. B. Gurav, "3D object tracking and manipulation in augmented reality," Proceedings of the 3rd International Conference on Current Issues in Education (ICCIE 2018), Indonesia, 2018.

23. A. Bottino, P. Ingrassia, F. Lamberti, F. Salvetti, F. Strada, A. Vitillo, "Holo-BLSD: An augmented reality self-directed learning and evaluation system for effective basic life support defibrillation training," IMSH Conference, Los Angeles, CA, 2018.

24. D. Gaikwad, A. Chikane, S. Kulkarni, A. Nhavkar, "Augmented reality based platform to share virtual worlds," *International Research Journal of Engineering and Technology* 05(01), 2018.

25. R. J. Stone, "Advanced human-system interfaces for telerobotics using virtual reality and telepresence technologies," Fifth International Conference on Advanced Robotics: Robots in Unstructured Environments, Pisa, Italy, 1991.

26. M. Nguyen, A. Yeap, "StereoTag: A novel stereogram-marker-based approach for Augmented Reality," 2016 23rd International Conference on Pattern Recognition (ICPR), Cancun, Mexico, 2016, pp. 1059–1064.

27. Y. Genc, S. Riedel, F. Souvannavong, C. Akinlar, N. Navab, "Marker-less tracking for AR: a learning-based approach," Proceedings. International Symposium on Mixed and Augmented Reality, 2002, pp. 295–304.

28. C. Tian, Y. Xu, L. Fei, J. Wang, J. Wen, N. Luo, "Enhanced CNN for image de-noising," *CAAI Transactions on Intelligence Technology*, 4(1), 2019, pp. 17–23.

29. E. Mendez, D. Kalkofen, D. Schmalstieg, "Interactive context-driven visualization tools for augmented reality," IEEE/ACM International Symposium on Mixed and Augmented Reality, Santa Barbara, CA, 2006, pp. 209–218. doi:10.1109/ISMAR.2006.297816.

30. E. Bottani, G. Vignali, "Augmented reality technology in the manufacturing industry: A review of the last decade," *IISE Transactions*, 51(3), 2019, pp. 284–310.

31. M. Garon, P. O. Boulet, J. P. Doironz, L. Beaulieu, J. F. Lalonde, "Real-Time High Resolution 3D Data on the HoloLens," 2016 IEEE International Symposium on Mixed and Augmented Reality (ISMAR-Adjunct), Merida, Mexico, 2016, pp. 189–191.

32. A. F. Abate, M. Nappi, F. Narducci, S. Ricciardi, "Mixed reality system for industrial environment: An evaluation study," Special Issue on Recent Advances in Intelligent Robotic Systems, *CAAI Transactions on Intelligence Technology*, 2(4), 2017, pp. 182–193.

Part 3

7

Internet of Things and Artificial Intelligence

Shailja Gupta

Department of Computer Science Technology, Manav Rachna University
Faridaba, India

Mayank Khattar

Department of Computer Science Technology, Manav Rachna University
Faridaba, India

CONTENTS

7.1 Introduction to Artificial Intelligence 100
7.2 Introduction to Internet of Things 101
7.3 Requirements of AI for IoT 102
7.4 Functional View of AI-Enabled IoT 103
7.5 Smart Solutions for AI-Enabled IoT Devices 104
7.6 Preventive Measures by AI-Enabled IoT 104
7.7 Key Changes Attained Using AI-Enabled IoT 105
7.8 Benefits of AI-Enabled IoT 105
7.9 Real-World Application Based on IoT and AI 106
    7.9.1 Self-Driving Cars 106
        7.9.1.1 Workings 106
        7.9.1.2 Advantages of this System 108
        7.9.1.3 Disadvantages of this System 108
        7.9.1.4 Proposed Model 108
    7.9.2 Classroom Attendance Monitoring System 109
        7.9.2.1 Architectures of Past Attendance Monitoring Systems 109
        7.9.2.2 Architecture of Facial Recognition-Based System 110
        7.9.2.3 Advantages of this System 111
        7.9.2.4 Disadvantages of this System 111
        7.9.2.5 Proposed Model 111
    7.9.3 Smart Home Management Systems 112
        7.9.3.1 System Architecture 112
        7.9.3.2 Advantages of Smart Home Management Systems 115
        7.9.3.3 Disadvantages of Smart Home Management Systems 115
        7.9.3.4 Proposed Work 116
7.10 Conclusion 116
References 116

KEYWORDS: *artificial intelligence, internet of everything, machine learning*

7.1 Introduction to Artificial Intelligence

Artificial intelligence (AI) is a computational tool that is compared as a substitute for intelligence shared by humans. It provides an ability to the machine to perform tasks that are naturally performed by intelligent beings. AI has found its place in the day-to-day life of homes, healthcare, manufacturing industries, banking, retail sectors, and research laboratories [1]. It is the course that researches into understanding and imitation of human intelligence, intelligent behavior, and the law of intelligent behavior. Its main task is to build an intelligent information processing theory, and then design some computer systems that can demonstrate some of the similar acts of human intelligence. AI capability is human intelligence-related behavior performed by intelligent machines, such as judgments, reasoning, proof, identification, perception, understanding, communication, design, thinking, learning, problem solving, and other thinking activities. The various domains that AI covers and where Internet of Things (IoT) can be easily applied include:

1. **AI in healthcare:** This is applied in assisting patients to schedule appointments, in billing process, feedback, and follow up appointments. Chatbots in the healthcare industry aid patients through virtual assistance by providing a platform where the patient can easily post questions based on the information fed regarding the symptom. Patients can also get prescriptions and suggestion from the chatbots. Such support is made available in the healthcare industry by IBM Watson, which understands the questions asked by a patient in their natural language and responds to them accordingly. It is further useful to the healthcare research industry to mine the data of the patients and build a hypothesis that can be helped to train the machine better and improve the quality and efficiency of the guidance provided to the patients [2].

2. **AI in business:** AI has been applied to the machine in the form of robotics to automate the repeated task that requires a huge labor force. With a machine learning algorithm analyzing the data continuously, the error rate in the production has also been reduced. This has also led to serving the customers better by analyzing the feedback provided. This has been achieved by incorporating chatbots on websites, which give automated replies to their queries [3].

3. **AI in education**: AI has helped the educator to understand students better by analyzing performance, using an automated grading system, and providing feedback according to the type of the learner. The AI tutor helps students in keeping them on track by providing support when required by the student. Chatbots in the field of education help students with a guide to provide solutions for the queries anywhere, anytime [4].

4. **AI in finance:** AI in financial services has been providing users with smart solutions or smart financial advice. Some financial application like Turbo Tax and Intuit's Mint collect user data, build user profiles, and provide them with financial advice. Some of the programs like IBM Watson are being used by customers to take better decisions while buying properties [5].

5. **AI in law:** A major challenge faced by humans is going through a large number of documents to find specific information. Automating the process with the help of

AI in terms of providing chatbots can assist people in finding answers to the queries asked in minutes rather than days. These chatbots are trained using taxonomy associated with the database [6].

6. **AI in manufacturing:** Robotic hands are incorporated into the workflow in the manufacturing process. As technology has advanced, use of AI in the robotic arm and machine has given precision that was never achieved by the human without intelligent machines [7].

7. **AI in banking:** Chatbots have been found to be useful in the banking sector to help customers to make better decisions in choosing services such as loan requirements, identifying investment opportunities, setting credit limits, and more. Chatbots have also equipped the customer with the knowledge of services [8].

8. **Machine learning platforms:** These platforms provide algorithm implementations, application programming interfaces (APIs), development and training toolkits, data, as well as computing power to design, train, and deploy models into applications, processes, and other machines. Used in a wide range of enterprise applications, such as prediction or classification.

9. **Virtual agents:** Every customer, at one point or the other, must deal with customer service. According to the Consumer Reports National Research Centre, while almost 88 percent of the customers they surveyed have resorted to customer service in some way, most of them were dissatisfied with their experience. A whopping 75 percent found customer service rude, around 74 percent were disconnected and were unable to reach a representative again, and about 64 percent felt their queries were ignored [9].

10. **Natural language generation:** This is using AI to produce any form of natural language from a data set, i.e., written or spoken language. Natural language generation deals with interaction of humans to machine or vice versa because it is related to natural language understanding [10].

7.2 Introduction to Internet of Things

IoT is considered as machines trying to read human data and perform analysis to generate some predictions or meaningful information from the acquired data. It is considered as a connection between sensors, people, and data. It is based on a network of sensors, machine-to-machine communication, and cloud computing. It is useful to detect anomalies by identifying some patterns and generate information like air quality, humidity, body information, and so on. It also helps in achieving automation of smart devices [1]. For example, consider a smart home where the home senses the presence of the owner and unlocks the door lock that is controlled by an app, switching the light bulbs on, on the arrival of the owner, automatically turn on the air-conditioning 20 minutes before the arrival of the home owner, playing music according to the mood, or recording your favorite shows that can be watched later [11].

IoT is a new reality and can be found almost everywhere and in everything in today's world. It is technology built into your watches keeping track of your day-to-day activities that affect your health and in smart television apps that keep track of your preference and work in the backend to recommend to you suggestions based on your behavior and usage. Here are some more examples:

1. **Driverless car:** AI plays a crucial role in the execution of the idea of driverless cars. These cars are equipped with internet and cloud architecture that keep track of all the road activities, potholes, signal, turns, and speed breakers. It analyzes its surroundings and based on it, take smart decisions that are directed to the controller responsible for taking decisions while driving. These cars are not a myth or a dream but very much in a prototype stage currently [12, 13].

2. **Amazon Go:** An online shopping experience has been provided by Amazon in its online store where the layout is laid out just like any shopping store. The products are placed on the counter and the customer can pick a product from the counter. The product that the customer has purchased is put into their cart and the money is deducted from the Amazon wallet when the customer leaves the store. This online IOT-enabled store gives its user a normal supermarket-like experience where no cashier is available. The users can walk into the store and IOT sensors do all the other work to make the customer experience joyful [14].

3. **Wearables:** IoT is embedded now into the wearable devices. Smartwatches keep a track of your day-to-day activities and provide suggestions accordingly. The data is stored on the cloud and the sensors are responsible for storing and communicating the data. The sensors are smart enough to provide precise information to users when required [15].

4. **Smart home:** An IoT-enabled home is a new reality of today where security to entertainment has become a smooth experience for its user. Some of the smart features of the IOT-enabled home include Smart Lock where using fingerprints one can access their home. Smart lights can be turned on and off from anywhere in the world when you are not in your home and wish to not let anyone know about it. Smart controllers that can enable your heating system/air conditioning 10 minutes before you reach your home. Smart devices can be connected to everything in your home today to give its users a paradise kind of an experience [16].

5. **Smart hotel rooms:** Keeping customers as priority, some hotels have integrated IoT in their hotel rooms. IOT-enabled locks allow users to use an app installed on their phone to open the room lock, giving its customer privacy as priority. Smart lights, heating, and air conditioning are some of the current common solutions. IOT-enabled check in and searching for hotels have become a new reality in the hotel business [17].

7.3 Requirements of AI for IoT

With machines getting smarter day by day, AI plays a role in creating systems that can be trained to learn and imitate everyday tasks of intelligent beings using past experiences and without physical involvement. Intelligent devices or IoT are considered as networks of smart devices that have the ability to collect data and exchange it with other devices when connected to the internet. These massive amounts of collected data, being the requirement of AI algorithms, are fed to the algorithms to convert raw information present as data to useful results that can further be implemented by the intelligent devices (IoT devices).

IoT and AI are considered as a powerful combination because without AI analytics, the data produced by IoT devices would have restricted or little value. Similarly, without the presence of IoT generated data, AI systems would face issues to be proved as relevant in generating solutions for industries. Therefore, a combination of both will help industries by providing intelligent solutions from the massive data available on a day-to-day basis. It will help to provide new business models, create new business propositions, generate revenue streams, and provide improved services for industries [18].

7.4 Functional View of AI-Enabled IoT

All the AI-enabled IoT devices that are implanted into day-to-day use machines generate a huge amount of data using internet connectivity, which is transferred to AI models to provide solutions [19]. All the services related to IoT must go through five steps: create, communicate, aggregate, analyze, and act, as shown in Figure 7.1. The sensors generate the data in the "create" step, which is communicated via internet connectivity in the "communicate" step. The data is collected at the "aggregate" step to provide IoT with the precise value at the "analyze" step. The penultimate analysis is carried out at the "act" step.

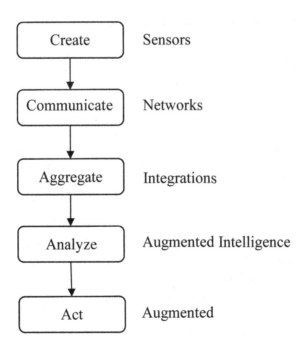

FIGURE 7.1
AI and IoT functional view.

7.5 Smart Solutions for AI-Enabled IoT Devices

The data obtained from the sensors are examined and analyzed by AI and informed decisions are made by businesses. AI in smart solutions helps provide insights to the data. Fields like natural language processing and computer vision are capable of extracting information from human speech, text, and visual content respectively. Smart sensors using machine learning are now intelligent enough to extract a pattern from the data and detect anomalies from the parameters like humidity, temperature, air quality, pressure, and sound with high precision. Business models that used traditional approaches like threshold values are now interested in machine learning approaches that provide improved accuracy for operational prediction to decrease down time and enhance risk management. Machine learning analytics have greatly helped businesses in researching new products and spawning new services [20]. The AI-enabled IoT has succeeded in attaining the following agile solutions:

1. Obtaining, analyzing, and managing useful and meaningful information from data

2. Ensuring quick and precise results

3. Accurate personalization with confidentiality and information privacy

4. Maintaining security check against cyberattack

7.6 Preventive Measures by AI-Enabled IoT

The most common challenges that are faced by the industry using AI-enabled IoT devices are accessibility of the data and applying analytics on it. To solve real-time challenges that can halt the production line, like breakdown of a part, changing a piece of machinery needs to be predicted before such event occurs. For this, businesses today need to have a clear understanding as to how to understand the analytics and apply them proactively to predict events. The IOT data generated using sensors is massive and is changed continuously, which makes it difficult to handle and manage with traditional analytics tools. With AI using unsupervised learning, machine learning can identify the pattern (abnormal from normal) and can alert businesses about this abnormality beforehand so that advanced measures or steps can be taken to avoid misfunctions. AI also helps in finding inside information that was otherwise difficult to observe or sometimes not visible using traditional models. The combination of two powerful concepts, AI and IoT, has led to the creation of smart sensors that consider real-time data to make the predictive, prescriptive, and adaptive analyzes.

1. **Predictive analysis:** It helps in determining the time duration when a machine can experience a breakdown. This analysis will help industries to prevent the failure of a machine by implementing preventive methods [21].

2. **Prescriptive analysis:** It provides immediate suggestions or preventive measures that can be helpful in preventing the mishappenings or disasters [22].

3. **Adaptive or autonomous analysis:** Constant or regular data feeds from IoT-enabled devices can help the organizations take periodic actions automatically without the involvement of any humans [23].

7.7 Key Changes Attained Using AI-Enabled IoT

Following are some of the key changes that occurred with the combination of AI and IoT as AI-enabled IoT in day-to-day activities.

1. **Greater revenue:** The combination of AI and IoT has proved to be beneficial in terms of high revenues for many industries. IoT sensor developers, data providers, and gadget manufacturers are considered to be on the winning side.

2. **Safety standards:** All types of failure can be kept under strict check using real-time monitoring, which provides efficient safety and security solutions. It also helps in minimizing the risk of loss of lives and assets damage.

3. **Reduced costs:** Smart devices like smart electricity meters, smart sensors, and sensor-enabled applications reduce the cost of operation for business and household solutions.

4. **Customer experience:** Smart sensors provide solutions to improve customer experience. These sensors have the ability to learn user preferences and modify their values accordingly.

7.8 Benefits of AI-Enabled IoT

AI and IoT together leads to a large number of benefits for consumers and industries such as intelligent automation, improved personalized experience, and more [19]. Combining these two streams benefits the common person and specialists alike. While IoT deals with devices interacting using the internet, AI makes the devices learn from their data and experience. Following are some of the popular benefits attained from combining both of these technologies:

1. **Operational efficiency:** AI in IoT is able to detect patterns from a large amount of data that are not deceptive on simple machines. It can detect the features and modify them according to operational conditions to ensure enhanced results. This also helps to find time-consuming and redundant processes that then can be fine-tuned to achieve accuracy better than the state-of-the-art methods defined.

2. **Risk management:** Combining AI with IoT in business solutions helps in identifying the risks involved and helps in automating these risks so a prompt response can be achieved, and efficiency can be increased. For example, risks like cyber threats, financial loss, and employee safety can be handled with AI-powered IoT.

3. **Better products and services:** Natural language process enables the machine to understand human language and makes it easy for these IoT-enabled devices to communicate with humans. Therefore, by analyzing the data, AI-enabled IoT devices can be considered as helpful in creating new products and services along with enhancing the existing ones for various business models, enabling industries to grow rapidly.

4. **IOT scalability:** IoT devices range from low-end sensors to high-end computers and mobile devices. These sensors are sufficient to collect a large amount of data and convert the collected data to a scalable form before transferring it to any other device. This scaling and analyzing of data allow a large range of devices to be connected together.

5. **Reduced unplanned downtime:** In manufacturing sectors, the breakdown of any equipment can lead to a halt in production, which can increase the time duration of the production. The AI-enabled IoT devices can ensure the proper maintenance of these equipment by providing an advanced alert for the failure of an equipment, and maintenance procedures can then be scheduled in an organized time interval.

7.9 Real-World Application Based on IoT and AI

IoT has played a wide role in collecting data from real-life applications while AI has provided automation by analyzing the available data. Some examples of a successful merger of both technologies are self-driving cars, classroom attendance monitoring systems, and smart home management systems.

7.9.1 Self-Driving Cars

Since the mid-1980s, several organizations all over the world have been researching and designing self-driving cars. These cars are also known as automated cars and driverless cars [21]. In recent years, the buzz surrounding driverless cars has grown rapidly, with many major technology companies getting behind the project [24]. A self-driving car is said to be a vehicle completely capable of judging the environment and do an effortless navigation without human interference.

7.9.1.1 Workings

To accomplish such a complex task, a vehicle requires some extra bundled components, which usually include a Global Positioning System (GPS) unit, navigation system based on inertia, and a wide range of sensors like laser rangefinders, radar technology, and video-based processing systems [25]. In Figure 7.2, the basic architecture of incorporation of such an automation system in self-driving cars is represented. In this architecture, there are two classes of subsystem: the Perception and Decision-Making systems are presented by different colors. Here, the Perception subsystem is in charge of calculating the state of the car and generating an inner (self-driving) environmental interpretation that utilizes the on-board sensor data. In the decision-making subsystem, in view of the present state of the vehicle, internal representations of the atmosphere and the traffic laws, passenger health, and comfort shall function from its original role to the final purpose defined by the customer [21].

In the sense of the static maps of the region, the Localizer Subsystem (Figure 7.2) calculates the status of the car (position, linear velocities, angular velocities, etc.). Such static maps (Figure 7.2) are automatically computed before autonomous usage, normally

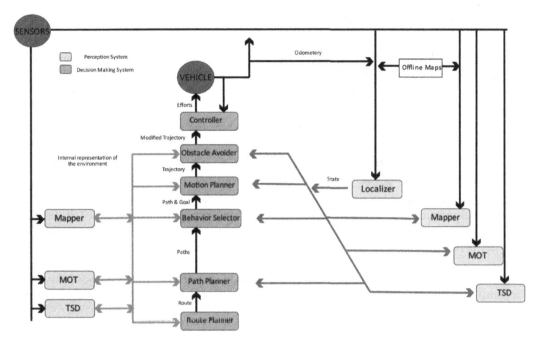

FIGURE 7.2
Hierarchical architecture of self-driving cars.

using the sensors of the car itself, although manual annotations are necessary. The Mapper subsystem collects the offline maps and the condition of the car as an input and produces an online map as an output. The MOT, i.e. Moving Objects Tracker (represented in Figure 7.2) collects offline charts, the status of the self-driving automobile, and defines and monitors the nearest barriers to travel (e.g., other cars and pedestrians) and measures the location and distance. The subsystem Traffic Signalization Detector or TSD (Figure 7.2) is responsible for traffic signal identification and acknowledgment. It provides the final goal specified by the driver in the offline maps; the path planner subsystem in the offline maps calculates a route, W, from the present state of the car to the target.

The Behavior Selection subsystem selects the current actions, including lane management, intersection handling, traffic light handling, and so forth. The Behavior Selection subsystem identifies the goal that takes into consideration existing driving actions in order for the decision-making horizon to prevent accidents with static and changing obstacles. The Motion Planner subsystem computes the route, T, from the present state of the auto drive to the current target, which follows the direction specified by the Behavior Selector, fulfils the moves and complex limitations of the car, and offers comfort to passengers. In order to prevent collisions, the Hazard Avoider subsystem must obtain the route determined from the motion planner. The controller subsystem would obtain, ultimately updated by the obstacle avoider subsystem, the monitoring planner trajectory and will also calculate and deliver effort orders to the steering wheel actuator, the throttle, and the brakes to ensure the car executes the Revised Trajectory as effectively as physically feasible.

7.9.1.2 Advantages of this System

1. **Quick assessment:** The extremely complicated technologies behind driving cars are capable of making hundreds of measurements in a second from the on-board device [26]. Things involve how far you are from objects, current pace of the other cars, action, and position of the cars on the planet.

2. **Less prone to accidents:** Self-driving cars rarely take part in accidents and have a high congestion reduction potential.

3. **Reducing infrastructure need:** They would eradicate any need for traffic signals because self-driving cars can interact with each other.

4. **Least manual assistance:** Self-driving vehicles may not need a driver. In densely developed cities, these cars may mitigate parking problems. For instance, if there were no parking available it would circulate around the facility until the passenger is ready to leave [27].

Other ways to relax and be entertained could include self-driving autos without the need for complex tools. However, modern architecture options are not restricted to the interior, and vehicles will soon be oblivious of today's cars.

7.9.1.3 Disadvantages of this System

1. **Cost-ineffective:** Self-driving vehicles are fascinating because they are packed with the technologies of the space age, but all this equipment is astronomically costly at present. Although good programming will render impossible stuff, there is also an unlikely probability that anything may happen.

2. **Error prone:** Even if a self-driving vehicle works flawlessly at first, it is possible for the technology that powers cars to be modified by an automotive manufacturer with an error string of codes.

3. **Increased rate of energy emission:** Although several businesses are looking at self-driving vehicles that utilize fuel-efficient or electric technologies, if our exposure to self-driving cars meets our pledge to renewable energy, we could be looking at even more emissions.

4. **Breach in privacy:** While businesses researching self-driving vehicles say all benefits and no cons, having a self-driving vehicle implies that a third party will have the ability to monitor the actions. Although several businesses are expected to do this as a consequence of customer outrage, there is also a huge lack of privacy. Since your vehicle will be accessing or connecting with data centers, your location will be easily open to individuals or organizations who might break through the network.

7.9.1.4 Proposed Model

We propose a solution to reduce Vehicle Miles Traveled (VMT), which is an industry standard to measure the aggregate miles traveled by vehicles in a given year. It is a general notion that a VMT increase leads to a significant increase in emissions. So, we suggest that autonomous vehicle technology is paired with ride- and car-sharing services. These

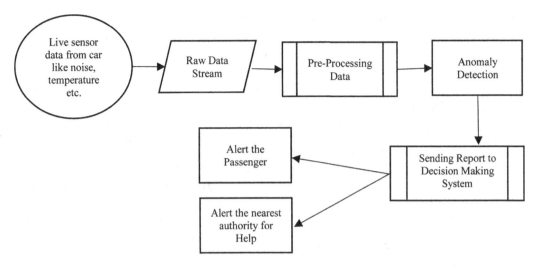

FIGURE 7.3
Flowchart for proposed upgrade in self-driving cars.

services can be offered by public or private organizations. Safety systems like infrared sensors and microphones can be installed in the cars for any sorts of malfunctions or other problems for live monitoring or automated detection for such issues (Figure 7.3). This can significantly reduce the number of cars on the road, which in turn will not just reduce emissions but also reduce traffic in congested areas with a significant drop in travel cost.

7.9.2 Classroom Attendance Monitoring System

Attendance plays a crucial part in assessing the academic success of children and young adults in schools and universities. Manual monitoring of attendance is impractical for the following factors:

1. Manual monitoring consumes more time and this time is deducted from the limited time span provided in lectures as per the timetable.
2. The problem of impersonation by applying proxies of other students who are not physically present in the lecture.

7.9.2.1 Architectures of Past Attendance Monitoring Systems

In order to address this issue of attendance, several attendance management solutions have been implemented in recent years. Jain et al. [28] created a desktop-based program that encourages students to participate by selecting the checkbox in front of their name, and then pressing the Register button to show their attendance. In 2013, a Bluetooth-enabled attendance program has been introduced by Bhalla et al. [29]. An application program installed on a smartphone helped in recording attendance with a Bluetooth link and the attendance message was sent to the teacher. Works of Mahat et al. [30] propose a system for employee attendance based on fingerprints. The program checks the input-provided fingerprint data with the ones stored in the database either online or offline.

7.9.2.2 Architecture of Facial Recognition-Based System

An attendance monitoring system proposed by Bhattacharya et al. [31] is developed by combining interchangeable components of other mentioned systems to create a compact system for monitoring student attendance utilizing Face Recognition technology.

This particular system has incorporated the power of AI using facial representation as one of the core technologies for the recognition algorithm used in this system. The face picture obtained during the quality assurance needs to be depicted in the form of a feature component for further analysis. These preprocessed feature components have high dimensionality so they can't be directly fed to the classifier for further processing. This is where the role of low-dimensional functionality of convolutional neural networks (CNNs) comes into play in gaining the essential low dimensional facial representation from such high-dimensional feature components without any extra steps required. So, to summarize the flow of the system, we can say the facial recognition system is provided with the image and the system fetches the image's data representation and does the face extraction. This face extraction can be done by several methods like checking the similarities in face color and facial proportions or selecting some proportions of an image and comparing with it shapes or forms of similar kind to create a face from those puzzle-like pieces. One of such method is the Viola–Jones method that uses outline masks of several sizes and angles and detects the most accurate one by superimposing them on the image. The dimension or the boundary of the original image is cropped into a smaller image. This cropped image is still high dimensional and it is tough to extract features from it directly and hence it can't be provided to classifiers directly. So, we use CNNs, which provide high accuracy over image recognition tasks. CNNs are a type of feed-forward neural networks built up from multiple layers. The pipeline of the system is in Figure 7.4. The basic operation of Convolution is to preserve the spatial relationship between pixels by learning image features using small squares of input image. The convolutional layer

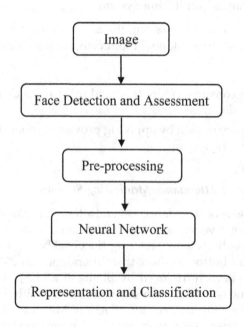

FIGURE 7.4
Pipeline of the system.

acts as the core layer of a CNN. Next, the Pooling layer reduces the dimensionality of the outputs of convolutional operation as well as converges and generalizes them using average or max functions for further processing. To rectify the outputs from the convolution operation, we have to use a rectified linear unit (ReLU), which is a nonlinear operation. The ReLU layer works as max function that gives output X for input X greater than zero, but zero for the value lesser than zero. It is applied elementwise per pixel. The last layer is the Fully Connected Layer that feeds the features to a classifier that uses a Softmax activation function. The sum of output probabilities from the Fully Connected Layer is 1. Softmax classifiers give you probabilities for each class label so that we can interpret those probabilities and do a further operation of marking the attendance of the identified student.

7.9.2.3 Advantages of this System

There are several benefits of this approach, such as:

1. **Increased protection:** Facial Recognition technology gives a very high accuracy in terms of classifying the facial features of a student. If the identification of someone fails, it can report that case to the authorities to take appropriate actions.
2. **Saves time:** The method of identifying a face requires a second or less, and this is extremely helpful in saving the unnecessary wastage of time taken in the manual alternative.
3. **Ease of incorporation:** Facial recognition technology can be very readily incorporated in the system as only the changing of the data set, considering the data set features on which it is trained on remains in the same format, and the retraining of the model is done before the actual deployment.

7.9.2.4 Disadvantages of this System

Nonetheless, there are still certain drawbacks to this method:

1. **Privacy concerns:** While facial recognition does also offer advantages, there is still a great deal of research to be done before it is applied equally and in line with human rights in the area of privacy.
2. **Positioning of the camera system:** Although the shift angles less than 30 degrees are generally accepted and handled by most of the systems, a major shift in the position of the camera or just a shift in design would eventually contribute to a mistake.
3. **Data storage capabilities:** Technology needs large data sets to "read" and produce reliable outcomes. And these data sets require powerful data storage [32].

7.9.2.5 Proposed Model

We propose that this system should also be extended to Emotion Recognition (Figure 7.5). This can help educational institutions to understand if the student is feeling happy, sad, exhausted, energetic, and so on before the class and this data can also be used as a performance measure of the teachers. Also, this can help reveal some of those students who are constantly unhappy or depressed so that the educational system can support/help them.

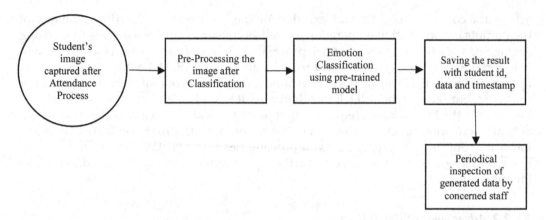

FIGURE 7.5
Flowchart for extension of attendance monitoring system.

7.9.3 Smart Home Management Systems

Smart home and AI technology are evolving exponentially, and numerous smart home devices integrated with AI have increased the quality of life for occupants. In recent years, the growth of smart home technology has led to the move from a conventional home to a modern internet-connected environment [32]. A smart home is a dwelling fitted with devices such as cameras, wired and wireless networks, actuators, and control structures.

7.9.3.1 System Architecture

Smart home systems capture and analyze data from the environment at home. They also relay knowledge to consumers and improve the ability for handling various domestic structures. AI technology is also used by smart home devices. For ease of interpretation, we have identified six core clusters of AI functions in smart homes.

1. **Behavior detection:** Detection of the user's actions in real time. These actions can be anything based on real-life scenarios. For instance, a person walks into a room and lights automatically gets turned on. Here, the behavior of the person can be detected by the sensors and classified as walking into a room and further actions such as turning on the lights can be taken.

2. **Data processing:** The processing system is required for the intelligence system to compute the data taken in raw form from the sensors and giving out results as the commands or just information to output devices.

3. **Speech recognition:** This is a major part in smart home systems as voice-enabled systems are much more interactive and easier to understand by general users. This cluster includes speech processing tasks like Speech to Text, etc.

4. **Image recognition:** This is also used as one of the smaller components of behavior detection and also independently used in facial recognition tasks. It uses a hardware component, such as a camera, and provides the image data to the system for further analysis.

5. **Decision-making:** This is the most important cluster of AI as it gains the processed data from every other cluster and decides future actions.

6. **Prediction-making:** This cluster uses the ability to predict the outcomes from taking action and whether or not the decision has to be corrected. It works synchronously with the decision-making cluster.

For a real-life example of how the architecture is going to work, consider person X living in his smart home. Since there can be infinite possibilities of how a person can interact with his own home, consider a few generalized ones such as presence of the person in the home, walking into a room, walking out of a room, and as in giving general possible commands to the AI. For the presence detection, depending upon the number of cameras installed, we might have to change approaches. If there are enough cameras to cover every single room completely, we can do person detection using face detection as we discussed earlier and if there aren't enough cameras, we might not be able to track the location of X in respect to the entire home but if we can tell X is present in a room then for sure X is in the home. Walking in and out of a room can be done in multiple ways; again, it varies on the hardware sensors installed in the home, but a few possible methods are again using infrared sensors on the doors or just using presence detection in a room. The commands given to the AI by X are going to be in natural language, that is human language, and we need to use the Natural Language processing to make the AI understand what X wants. Natural Language commands have to be passed from the microphones to the system and the system will convert the audio to text form and apply further processing like tokenization, information retrieval, etc. Now, in all the aforementioned possible generalized scenarios, we can say there are some sensors, audio devices, video devices, or even smartphones installed or present in the environment and these devices act as input for the overall system. These devices give raw inputs to three of the aforementioned modules: Data Processing, Speech Recognition, and Image Recognition. More precisely, the sensors give data directly to Data Processing, the audio devices give data to the Speech Recognition module, which does audio analysis, and video devices or cameras output to the Image Recognition module. Since the modules are abstractly classified, we can't say what kind of the process they are supposed to run as it varies from system to system and different purpose or end-targets. The behavior detection system also works in the same loop because the outputs of the aforementioned modules are passed to classify the user action. After classifying the action, the AI fetches the required data to perform those actions if the actions are in scope of the system. The scope varies again from system to system and has to be defined manually as of now. Decision-making and prediction-making modules work simultaneously and handle the scopes and actions performed by the system. For instance, if a person walks into the room, lights automatically turn on. The person is detected by the image recognition module and sends the results to the behavior module, which classifies the action present in the room and forwards it to decision-making, which in turn decides that lights must be turned on.

Intelligent homes and consumers have various types of engagement. There are essentially two forms of interaction styles:

1. **Individual interaction with intelligent devices:** In this interaction scheme, the users give the instructions separately to each of the home automation devices, and the AI embedded in each device benefits the specific device itself. Smart home energy management, medical care, and protection support this model. Figure 7.6 shows a model for self-embedded AI devices. This type of interaction scheme can be interconnected to each other or can be decentralized. In context of smart home management, this scheme would be most likely centralized because the modules

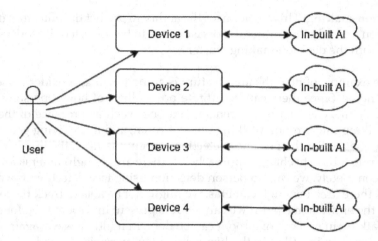

FIGURE 7.6
Individual interaction with intelligent devices.

we previously discussed need each other's results to function, but in a decentralized approach, it can be implemented as giving each device its own set of modules. We can imagine this type of scheme in real life as an AI-enabled television that tunes its settings based on the voice commands or maybe display settings by judging the light intensities in the environment.

2. **Interaction with intelligent devices using an AI-enabled device:** In this interaction scheme, the users provide the instructions to the AI, which internally controls each of the individual units. Smart home systems work on this design mostly as it provides the necessary centralization of all the required modules. This Implementation Scheme is represented in Figure 7.7. This can also be easily implemented because the other one requires more hardware devices, which can be costly considering all of them are IoT and AI enabled. In this type of scheme,

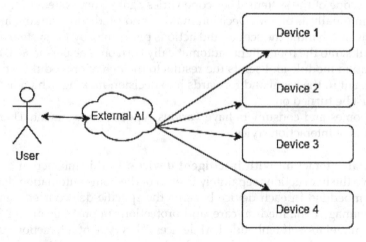

FIGURE 7.7
Users give direction to the AI and the AI controls each unit.

one can even control the entire system using their smartphone application or just a single IoT device that consists of a microphone and a speaker. This scheme is very well known in the industry as the Google Home, Amazon's Alexa, and many more products that work on this scheme.

7.9.3.2 Advantages of Smart Home Management Systems

There are many benefits of smart homes:

1. **Smart home surveillance:** The protection of your home is the most critical part of any home. Regardless of how many locks you have on your home, there's still a chance of burglars getting into your building. And there's the extra trap or the danger of losing your keys. In the case of certain family members who sometimes lose their keys or fail to lock any of the essential doors of your home, it's also a brilliant idea to add a smart home surveillance device.

2. **Energy conservation:** Energy conservation is likely to be the primary concern of any household member. With compact devices and too many technological tools, there is a large rise in electricity use. Not just that, managing the illumination in your home is going to be a lot simpler because the presence detection system can automatically turn on/off the electrical devices based on the presence of the user in that room and since lighting consumes the highest amount of electricity, a person can save money with this kind of home setup. This is a huge asset of the building.

3. **Timely updates for the maintenance of home appliances:** If the machines and equipment need to be serviced to preserve their efficiency, they must be identified in advance. Nevertheless, tracking is not always fast. A person must depend on the smart home network in that situation. This system will also inform a person if any equipment or tool is required to be updated. It is really easy for smart home solutions to tailor the home appliances and equipment to suit a person's needs.

4. **Simplicity of use:** Along with all these amenities and advantages, the simplicity of use is another important advantage [33]. The smart home automation is based on the simplest user interface possible: voice commands. The user just needs to ask the system what to do in their own natural language and the action will be taken by the system.

7.9.3.3 Disadvantages of Smart Home Management Systems

There are still some smart homes pitfalls as discussed here:

1. **Costly:** The greatest challenge, con, or downside of a smart home device is the expense. There are quite a number of companies offering smart home services, but they are all quite costly. It is something that only a handful can manage to do. You will need a decent investment and a strong income to build this device.

2. **Need of constant internet connectivity:** The main prerequisite of the smart home program is the internet. You won't be able to take care of this without a decent and fast internet link. If there is no network connectivity for any reason, there is no other way you can access and manage your device.

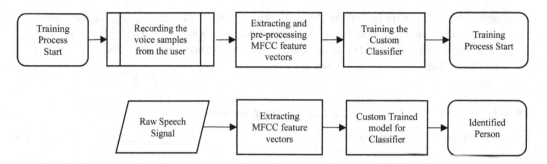

FIGURE 7.8
Flowchart for a voice-distinction module in smart home automation systems.

3. **Servicing and maintenance:** If there is an issue with the smart home system, you can't always call a handyman or someone equivalent to fix or handle a malfunction. You're going to have to rely on the professionals.

7.9.3.4 Proposed Work

We propose to add voice distinction of multiple users to this system. Currently, most applications can only detect one voice and if multiple voices are heard then it can't clearly convert it into a meaningful command. This functionality can be added as a module that works in the way specified in Figure 7.8. However, this can be a future aspect where a set of voices can be trained to the system to distinguish between several users.

7.10 Conclusion

In this chapter, we have discussed AI and IoT along with their applications in multiple industries. We have further elaborated the functional view of embedding both of these concepts together along with requirements and solutions offered by AI-enabled IoT. Some of the preventive measures and benefits of AI-enabled IOT are also a part of this chapter. Toward the end, we have elaborated the concept of self-driven cars, classroom attendance monitoring systems, and smart home management systems where AI can be integrated into IoT to provide smart solutions in these applications. We have further discussed a framework in these applications that will be implemented in the near future.

References

1. Perera, S. (2019). The power of combining AI and IoT. https://towardsdatascience.com/the-power-of-combining-ai-and-IoT-4db98ac9f252/
2. Lee, K. Y., & Kim, J. (2016). Artificial intelligence technology trends and IBM Watson references in the medical field. *Korean Medical Education Review*, 18(2), 51–57.

3. Ivanov, S. H., & Webster, C. (2017). Adoption of robots, artificial intelligence and service automation by travel, tourism and hospitality companies–a cost-benefit analysis. Prepared for the International Scientific Conference "Contemporary Tourism–Traditions and Innovations," Sofia University, Bulgaria, 19–21 October.

4. Dillenbourg, P. (November 1994). The role of artificial intelligence techniques in training software. In Proceedings of LEARNTEC, Karlsruhe, Germany. https://edtechnology.co.uk/latest-news/learntec-event-looks-at-the-future-of-learning-and-digital-trends/

5. Bahrammirzaee, A. (2010). A comparative survey of artificial intelligence applications in finance: Artificial neural networks, expert system and hybrid intelligent systems. *Neural Computing and Applications*, 19(8), 1165–1195.

6. Bench-Capon, T. J., & Dunne, P. E. (2007). Argumentation in artificial intelligence. *Artificial Intelligence*, 171(10–15), 619–641.

7. O'Grady, R., Christensen, A. L., Pinciroli, C., & Dorigo, M. (May 10–14, 2010). Robots autonomously self-assemble into dedicated morphologies to solve different tasks. In: Proceedings of the 9th International Conference on Autonomous Agents and Multiagent Systems: Volume 1, Toronto, Canada, 1517–1518.

8. Pau, L. F., & Gianotti, C. (1990). Applications of artificial intelligence in banking, financial services and economics. In: *Economic and Financial Knowledge-Based Processing*, 22–46. Springer, Berlin.

9. Fishwick, P. A. (December 13–16, 2009). An introduction to OpenSimulator and virtual environment agent-based M&S applications. In: Proceedings of the 2009 Winter Simulation Conference (WSC), Austin, TX, 177–183.

10. Gatt, A., & Krahmer, E. (2018). Survey of the state of the art in natural language generation: Core tasks, applications and evaluation. *Journal of Artificial Intelligence Research*, 61, 65–170.

11. Sekar, A. (2018). 5 Best examples of IoT applications in the real world. https://analyticstraining.com/5-best-examples-IoT-applications-real-world/

12. Rathod, S. D. (2013). An autonomous driverless car: An idea to overcome the urban road challenges. *Journal of Information Engineering and Applications*, 3(13), 34–38.

13. Jones, L. (2017). Driverless cars: When and where? *Engineering & Technology*, 12(2), 36–40.

14. Wankhede, K., Wukkadada, B., & Nadar, V. (July 11–12, 2018). Just walk-out technology and its challenges: A case of Amazon Go. In: 2018 International Conference on Inventive Research in Computing Applications (ICIRCA), Coimbatore, India, 254–257.

15. Luxton, D. D., June, J. D., Sano, A., & Bickmore, T. (2016). Intelligent mobile, wearable, and ambient technologies for behavioral health care. In: *Artificial Intelligence in Behavioral and Mental Health Care*, 137–162. Academic Press.

16. Bregman, D. (2010). Smart home intelligence–the eHome that learns. *International Journal of Smart Home*, 4(4), 35–46.

17. Leung, R. (2019). Smart hospitality: Taiwan hotel stakeholder perspectives. *Tourism Review*, 74, 50–62.

18. Emeakaroha, V. C., Cafferkey, N., Healy, P., & Morrison, J. P. (August 24–26, 2015). A cloud-based IoT data gathering and processing platform. In: 2015 3rd International Conference on Future Internet of Things and Cloud, Rome, Italy, 50–57.

19. Vinugayathri. AI and IoT Blended–What It Is and Why It Matters? https://www.clariontech.com/blog/ai-and-IoT-blended-what-it-is-and-why-it-matters/

20. Boveiri, H. R., Khayami, R., Elhoseny, M., & Gunasekaran, M. (2019). An efficient Swarm-Intelligence approach for task scheduling in cloud-based internet of things applications. *Journal of Ambient Intelligence and Humanized Computing*, 10(9), 3469–3479.

21. Badue, C., Guidolini, R., Carneiro, R. V., Azevedo, P., Cardoso, V.., Forechi, A., ... & Veronese, L. (2019). "Self-driving cars: A survey" (paper, Cornell University, Ithaca, NY). https://arxiv.org/abs/1901.04407

22. Yang, L., Yang, S. H., & Plotnick, L. (2013). How the internet of things technology enhances emergency response operations. *Technological Forecasting and Social Change*, 80(9), 1854–1867.

23. Kopetz, H. (2011). Internet of Things. In *Real-Time Systems*, 307–323. Springer, Boston, MA.

24. D'Allegro, J. (2020). How Google's self-driving car will change everything. https://www.investopedia.com/articles/investing/052014/how-googles-selfdriving-car-will-change-everything.asp/
25. Rayej, S. (2014). How do self-driving cars work? https://robohub.org/how-do-self-driving-cars-work/
26. Prince, A. (2009) Unbelievable benefits and drawbacks of the self-driving car. https://www.lifehack.org/articles/technology/unbelievable-benefits-and-drawbacks-the-self-driving-car.html/
27. Duffer, R. (2014). Chicago Tribune: Self-driving car drops off driver, finds parking spot https://www.chicagotribune.com/autos/ct-xpm-2014-05-13-chi-selfdriving-car-drops-off-driver-finds-parking-spot-20140513-story.html/
28. Jain, S. K., Joshi, U., & Sharma, B. K. (2011). Attendance management system (master's project report, Rajasthan Technical University, Kota, India).
29. Bhalla, V., Singla, T., Gahlot, A., & Gupta, V. (2013). Bluetooth based attendance management system. *International Journal of Innovations in Engineering and Technology (IJIET)*, 3(1), 227–233.
30. Mahat, S. S., & Mundhe, S. D. (2015). Proposed Framework: College attendance management system with mobile phone detector. *International Journal of Research in IT and Management*, 5(11), 72–82.
31. Bhattacharya, S., Nainala, G. S., Das, P., and Routray, A. (2018). Smart attendance monitoring system (SAMS): A face recognition based attendance system for classroom environment. In: 2018 IEEE 18th International Conference on Advanced Learning Technologies (ICALT), Mumbai, India, 358–360.
32. Dash Magazine (2019). The Threats and Benefits of Facial Recognition: What Should We Know? https://becominghuman.ai/the-threats-and-benefits-of-facial-recognition-what-should-we-know-17008f69ae74/
33. Guo, X., Shen, Z., Zhang, Y., & Wu, T. (2019). Review on the application of artificial intelligence in smart homes. *Smart Cities*, 2(3), 402–420.

8

Convergence of Artificial Intelligence of Things: Concepts, Designing, and Applications

Divya Upadhyay

Computer Science & Engineering, Delhi Technical Campus
Greater Noida, India

Shanu Sharma

Computer Science & Engineering, Amity University
Noida, India

CONTENTS

8.1 Introduction 119
8.2 Architecture of IoT 121
8.3 Overview of Artificial Intelligence and Machine Learning Technology 122
    8.3.1 Machine Learning Algorithms and Methodology 124
    8.3.2 Types of Machine Learning Algorithms 124
    8.3.3 Artificial Neural Networks and Deep Learning 127
8.4 Artificial Intelligence of Things: Overview and Architecture 128
8.5 AIoT-Enabled Applications 130
    8.5.1 Smart Transportation: Intelligent and Dynamic Traffic Light System
        Using AIoT 130
    8.5.2 Smart Healthcare Management Using AIoT 133
    8.5.3 Smart Home: Energy Efficient AIoT-Based Smart Air Conditioning
        System Using AIoT 135
    8.5.4 AIoT-Enabled Water Quality Monitoring and Ground Water Level
        Prediction 137
    8.5.5 Air Quality Monitoring System Using AIoT 138
8.6 Conclusion 140
References 140

8.1 Introduction

Two powerful informatics technologies that are presently undergoing speedy evolutionary development are Internet of Things (IoT) and artificial intelligence (AI). Both technologies are unique on their own, and the point where they intersect makes them even more exciting. Various IoT and AI applications are independently fascinating, but according to research and industry experts, their combined claims hold even more potential and attraction [1]. When AI and IoT are combined, they form Artificial Intelligence of

Things (AIoT). IoT devices will act as the digital nervous system, while AI will be the brain of the system.

Professor Andrew Ng stated in NIPS 2017 that "AI is the new electricity" [2], which was expanded as "If AI is the new electricity, Data is the new coal and IoT is the new coal-mine" [3] by A. Kapoor in 2019.

AI is considered best with a large number of information streams, whereas IoT devices are considered as ideal sources for supplying the required data. IoT technology provides us with the opportunity for monitoring and manipulating the physical environment using connected IoT devices. Enormous IoT-based applications can be possible, which can be used for assisting us in daily life such as vehicle tracking, drone-based patrolling, intelligent parking, smart building, society or cities, and many more. Use of these applications provides us with a better way of connectivity as well as ease of accessibility on one side. In contrast, an exponential amount of data is also generated, in which 90% of the generated information is never apprehended. The 10% of captured data is highly time-dependent and loses its importance and value within a few milliseconds [4]. Monitoring of these data manually is both a cumbersome task as well as a costly process. Hence, a necessity for an intelligent and efficient analysis of information is felt. The need opened a way for AI-enabled models and tools to do precise data analysis with least human involvement and intervention.

Both IoT and AI are trending technologies in today's era. The convergence of AI and IoT (AIoT) is said to be the main lead for the Industry 4.0 revolution [5]. AIoT aims at improving the different industry and service sectors by enabling AI techniques into various infrastructure components. It can provide a viable solution to solve existing problems at different levels of operations ranging from device, software, and platform level, all connected to IoT networks [6]. Multiple challenges are involved while converging AI with IoT. For developing an AIoT-based system, a balanced architecture is essential for providing an excellent balance to cost of processing the data at various points. By analyzing the behavior of IoT devices with massive data and application of AI techniques to optimize the process, some of the challenges include [7]:

- Storage of real-time data generated by events.
- Executing statistical and analytical queries over stored data.
- Applying various AI-enabled analytic tools to make predictions and gain insights over generated data.

Hence, the key motivation of this chapter is to focus on the balanced architecture of AIoT in addition with various AI techniques and models that can be applied on different operational points of IoT devices for optimization of different IoT-based systems. This chapter starts with a brief discussion on the architecture of IoT. Introduction of AI and its relationship with machine learning is given in the next section, along with the brief introduction of some of the basic and advanced machine learning as well as deep learning techniques. The use of AI in the IoT spectrum, starting from augmenting the intelligence in sensors to analyzing the captured data in a real time or offline approach is described supported by AIoT architecture. This chapter aims to provide in-depth knowledge about the development of the AIoT-based system to the reader. Targeting this detailed architecture of AIoT-enabled intelligent applications in various sectors like transportation, healthcare, and smart homes, etc., is presented in further sections to get in-depth knowledge about the development of the AIoT-based system.

8.2 Architecture of IoT

Before moving toward the architecture of AIoT, let us draw attention toward IoT, revolutionizing the world. IoT was termed by "Kevin Ashton" in 1999 during a presentation to P&G [8]. IoT is making a vast network of connected devices over the internet. These devices can also have the capability to interact with each other in the system. The automation is derived to the next level with this revolution in which machines will interconnect and communicate with each other, also making their own decisions without any human interventions.

Things in IoT can be any built-in sensor or devices having the capability of assembling, collecting, and transferring data without any human intervention over the internet. By connecting machines, each of them will enhance its knowledge and improve learning capabilities from the experience of other interconnected devices, similar to humans. In other words, like humans, IoT is trying to develop an interdependence such as contribute, interact, and collaborate with things [7, 9]. To understand the concepts of IoT, consider an example: visualize a smart room where a room temperature sensor is installed to gather data. This sensor further sends the collected information over the internet, which is then utilized by various sensor-enabled devices in that room to adjust and regulate their temperatures accordingly—such as fridge sensors that can gather the outside temperature and then regulate its temperature. Similarly, smart air conditioners can also regulate its temperature accordingly. This is how IoT devices contribute, interact, and collaborates during the whole process. A general conceptualization of IoT applications in different fields is presented in Figure 8.1.

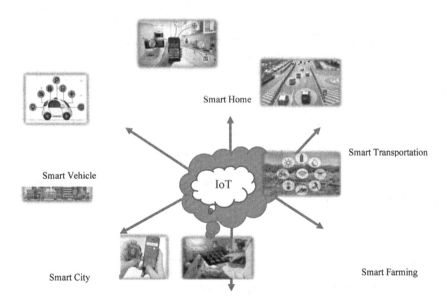

FIGURE 8.1
IoT applications in different sectors.

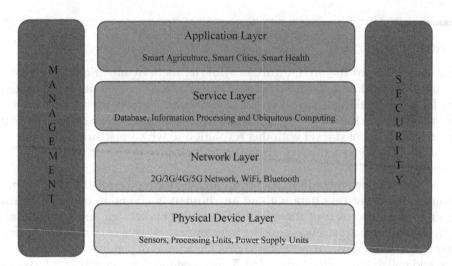

FIGURE 8.2
IoT reference architecture.

Similar to Open Systems Interconnection (OSI) reference architecture, the IoT model also comprises six layers, which includes four layers horizontally and two layers vertically [9]. Management and security services are implemented for all the layers simultaneously. Figure 8.2 represents the IoT reference model.

At physical devices layers, various sensing and controlling devices are connected to acquire data. This layer is also called a perception layer. Different existing hardware deployed at this layer includes sensors, radio-frequency identification (RFID), processing units such as Raspberry Pi, etc. The second layer is the network layer to provide all networking-related supports and data transfers over wired or wireless mediums. It provides supports to all the generations of networks along with Wi-Fi, Bluetooth, and so on. The networks layer also supports both transmission medium and technologies. It passes the data for further processing and storage to the layer above it. The third layer in IoT architecture is the service layer. It provides services such as storage of data in the database, preprocessing and analyzing the information gathered from the lower layers, and passes that information to the upper layer, the application level layer [10]. Finally, the last and the top most layer in the IoT architecture is an application layer. It is also called the user interface layer. It directly deals with the user by using various applications, websites, or graphic user interfaces (GUIs) and provides multiple services smart agriculture [11], smart homes, intelligent health management systems, and so on.

8.3 Overview of Artificial Intelligence and Machine Learning Technology

AI, which is also known as machine intelligence, is the field of mimicking the human's cognitive abilities like learning, problem solving, and perception and simulating it on the machines. The term "artificial intelligence" was founded in 1955 and was based on the principles of human intelligence. AI can be defined in a way through which machines can easily simulate it [12]. Initially, the reasoning-based machines were considered as intelligent, but over the last few decades, there has been continuous evolution in the field of AI. Now, AI models are based on cross-disciplinary approaches that include mathematics, psychology, computer science, linguistics, and many more. Thus, AI-empowered machines are providing benefits to different industries [12, 13]. Today, we can see AI-empowered machines everywhere. These intelligent systems are affecting the way we are living, working, and entertaining. AI technology can be seen in endless applications, such as voice-based personal assistant systems, like Alexa or Siri, autonomous or intelligent driving assistant technology, smartwatches or bands, and many more [10, 14].

In the last decade, we saw a revolution in digital technology, such as in the field of computing power and hardware technology. Today, everything is digitized, or if not, we can say it is in the middle of the process of digitization. Whether it is online payment systems, online shopping or billing, online learning, or online medical assistance, digitization is now ruling every sector ranging from healthcare, retail, banking, to different industries. Digitization is providing us with the ease of accessibility, but in parallel, it is also creating a lot of data.

We are drowning in information and starving for knowledge.

John Naisbitt

The data that is getting generated and stored daily cannot be considered as waste because it contains a lot of hidden patterns and knowledge that can be used for making future use of our technology in a more intelligent way. This is where the importance and role of machine learning as well as advanced deep learning technique comes from [15].

Machine learning is also considered as a subclass of AI, or it can also be considered as the branch of AI dealing with the thought of making machines intelligent by enabling them to learn from experiences and to make decisions without or minimal human intervention [15]. The term "machine learning" was named by Arthur Samuel, a trailblazer in the field of AI in 1959 [16]. It's the technology of making machines to act without being explicitly programmed. Until now, a lot of machine learning algorithms have been developed and have already provided us with a range of intelligent applications such as voice recognition, object recognition, license plate recognition, face recognition, fingerprint recognition, self-driving cars, and many more.

In today's world, machine learning is the most powerful technology. It's like a magical tool for converting data into meaningful information. It is so pervasive today that we are using it daily without even knowing it. AI and advanced machine learning techniques have high demand in different sectors. Some of the application areas of them include:

- **Health Sector:** AI has shown its impact on the healthcare sector by automating its essential processes. Now, a personalized medicine recommendation system and health assistant systems are available on a click. Advanced use of AI can be seen in the form of robotic surgery, where robots are used to assist doctors in operations.

- **Manufacturing:** Here, data of various factories are now analyzed using AI-based techniques to make a forecast about the production and profits.

- **Retail:** A lot of work has been done in the retail sector for providing a personalized experience to the consumer and still advanced AI techniques are in action for optimizing the consumer's experience, e.g., using virtual shopping

- **Banking:** AI-based systems are already functional in the banking sector for finding fraudulent transactions to detecting loan defaulters, etc.

- **Education Sector, Finance, and many more.**

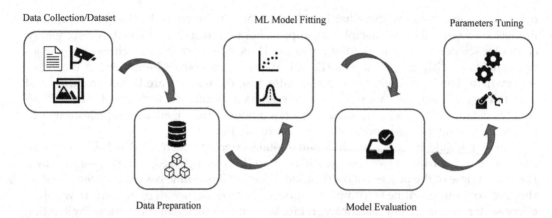

Data Collection/Dataset   ML Model Fitting   Parameters Tuning

Data Preparation   Model Evaluation

FIGURE 8.3
General process flow of machine learning algorithms.

8.3.1 Machine Learning Algorithms and Methodology

As previously mentioned, machine learning (ML) techniques and algorithms are based on a general concept of developing a mathematical model on some sample data, i.e., training data [17]. General working flow of machine learning algorithms is presented in Figure 8.3.

- **Data Collection:** The first and the critical step for any ML techniques is to gather a huge scale of information and data for the given application. ML algorithms usually work on a large amount of quality data. Hence, a good collection of data that contains all required variations for the efficient development of the application is essential.
- **Data Preparation/Feature Extraction:** A data preprocessing and feature extraction step is required for presenting the data in an optimal format, extracting the meaningful parameters from that data and to perform dimensionality reduction in the case of extracting optimal features.
- **Model Fitting/Training:** In this step, the data set is divided into two parts—testing and training set—and the ML model is then processed and trained on the training data set.
- **Evaluation:** The trained ML model is again verified and tested on the testing dataset to find its accuracy.
- **Tuning:** In this step, the hyperparameters of the ML model are then optimized to maximize the performance of the trained model.

A tuned model with good accuracy can then be deployed in related applications for real-time or offline data analysis.

8.3.2 Types of Machine Learning Algorithms

As previously discussed, all ML algorithms are based on the process of learning the model using the training data set. Based on the model's learning technology, a broad classification of ML algorithms is usually done in three categories: supervised, unsupervised, and reinforcement learning [16], as shown in Figure 8.4.

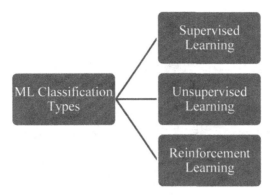

FIGURE 8.4
Machine learning algorithm types.

a. **Supervised Learning:** This is also a class of ML techniques and algorithms where the data set used for training the model is provided with labels, i.e., previous input and output pairs. The model trained in this way can easily imitate the exact things that were shown to them, so to make a good model, it's essential to feed reliable and unbiased labeled data examples to it [15]. The working of supervised ML models can be understood with a simple examination of the classification of mangoes and apples with their images presented in Figure 8.5. Further, based on the type of outputs, supervised learning techniques can be used to perform the following two types of task:

- **Classification:** Here, ML techniques classifies the given data into different classes by applying a rule for differentiating them. These algorithms have discrete output variable—i.e., 0 or 1, Mango or Apple—and can be useful for tasks like object or image tagging, or fake videos detection.

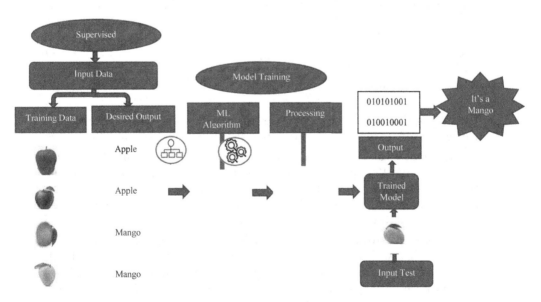

FIGURE 8.5
An example of workings of supervised machine learning techniques.

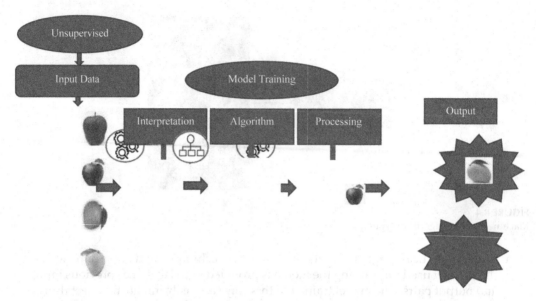

FIGURE 8.6
Workings of unsupervised machine learning techniques.

- **Regression:** In this task, the value of output variable is continuous, not discrete. This constant number provides the ability of prediction based on the given data. The technique is useful for applications like stock prediction, weather forecasting, or profit prediction based on given historical data.

b. **Unsupervised Learning:** This class of ML techniques are applicable for unstructured data, where the output label is not provided with the data, and the model has to learn by itself from the properties of the given training data [17]. The workings of this system can be understood using Figure 8.6. Here, the trained model will use the categories apples and mangoes differently based on their different features such as shape, color, etc. Based on the working concept of supervised learning algorithms, it can be used to perform the following tasks on data:

  - **Clustering:** This is a process of assigning the data into different groups, i.e., clusters based on the various properties of available patterns in data.

  - **Association:** It can be understood as the process of establishing the relationship between different parameters of the data set. One of the leading applications of association is market basket analysis, in which a customer's purchasing history is analyzed to find the relationship among purchased items to provide a better future recommendation to customers.

c. **Reinforcement Learning:** This is a reward-based learning approach, in which positive and negative feedbacks are used to train the model. It is similar to human learning behavior, as humans also learn by their mistakes and positive and negative feedback [16]. This learning approach requires noisy and data-rich environments for better learning. It is a simplified approach for gaming technology, which helps the games to play at superhuman levels.

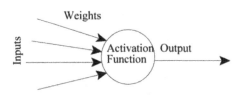

FIGURE 8.7
Neuron in an ANN.

8.3.3 Artificial Neural Networks and Deep Learning

Artificial neural networks (ANNs) is the software implementation of a human brain. It is mainly influenced by the functioning, structure, and learning ability of any human brain. It acquires its processing capability, learns it, and uses it for classification. A human brain has thousand millions of neurons that work in combination with each other. All these neurons inside the brain are complex and connected to each other in an interconnected connection structure called the neural network. Learning in terms of a human brain is the repeated activation of a neural connection, which thus keeps strengthening the connections. So, the neural network's responsibility is to make sure we get a desired output only for a particular input [8]. The feedback obtained in the process is helpful in further increasing the strength of the network at every step. The major elements of any ANN are as follows:

- **Processing Elements:** An ANN is a simplified computation model similar to the brain of a human, which comprises of a processing unit as shown in Figure 8.7, which performs very similar functions to that of a neuron in a brain [18].
- **Topology:** The organization and arrangement of all the processing elements in a neural network with their input and output and relative interconnection is simply called a topology of the neural network.
- **Learning Algorithms:** Categories of ANNs
  - Feed forward
  - Feed back and
  - Competitive learning
- **Deep Networks:** The word deep here is used to refer to the existence of a high number of layers in a network. Every neural network that is used to represent a deep neural network will consist of at least three layers: hidden, input, and output layer.

  The first layer is the input layer of the neural network that is used to provide input features to process the data for model building. The only job of this layer is to forward these parameters to other layers without actually performing any computational task over these [14]. Hidden layers are used to perform all the necessary computations that are required for model building. Thus, it takes the input values from the first layer and then passes the result of the computations made to the next layer. The output layer is used to display the output after getting the ultimate answer to the problem from the previous layer.

  Deep learning is also a subclass of machine learning with numerous neural network layers that can be trained to perform various task such as image and speech recognition by processing and learning through a huge amount of data. Broadly, Figure 8.8 explains the relationship between AI, machine learning, and deep learning techniques [19].

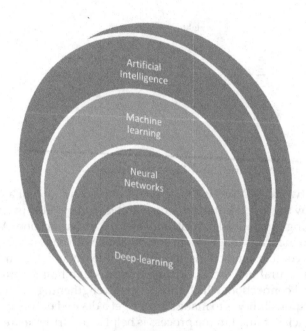

FIGURE 8.8
Connection between various models based on artificial intelligence, machine learning, and deep learning.

8.4 Artificial Intelligence of Things: Overview and Architecture

AIoT is said to be the convergence of AI and IoT. It is the technology of providing an intelligent infrastructure for IoT so that various IoT operations, data management techniques, human–machine interaction, and so on, can be handled more efficiently. IoT provides the features of connectivity and data exchange; however, one of the major issues with IoT technology is the exponential growth in IoT data due to extensive use of IoT devices [3]. This IoT data can be transformed into meaningful data using AI techniques, which can then be further used for taking some important decisions. In this way, these two powerful technologies—AI and IoT—can be proved mutually beneficial to both types of technologies [5].

In today's world, all applications are expected to be intelligent and smart. For example, a smartphone that reminds someone about important meetings without setting the alarm, an intelligent washing machine understanding the type of clothes without setting a particular mode, a smart home, an intelligent car, and so on. For years, AI has been trying to make various appliances intelligent by providing them with the power of analyzing, training, and self-learning from the experience or data set. IoT and AI place a specific role in different industrial product building and processes ranging from water purifying to rocket launching techniques.

IoT technology provides us with the opportunity for monitoring and manipulating the physical environment using connected IoT devices. Enormous IoT-based applications can be possible, which can be used for assisting us in daily life such as vehicle tracking, drone-based patrolling, intelligent parking, smart building, society or cities, and many more. Use of these applications provides us with a better way of connectivity as well as ease of accessibility on one side. In contrast, on the other hand, an exponential amount of data is also generated. This data cannot be considered as waste, as it contains important information about the user's usage-related issues and performance issues of existing applications. Further, this data in an intelligent way can be used for creating a better human–machine interface and more efficient and smart applications [20, 21].

Here, the role of AI and advanced ML techniques come together, because most of these applications need sophisticated AI capabilities for processing the different types of data that include image, video, or audio, in a central location. Whereas, in some applications, data cannot be sent to the server or central location for processing due to the responsiveness required. In this case, the AI techniques need to be implemented at appropriate points to handle the process intelligently. However, the AI and ML techniques are generally computationally expensive and need more power for implementation, which is somehow not possible in the case of real-time processing of data [22]. So, while developing an AIoT-based system, a balanced architecture is very important for providing a good balance to the cost of processing the data at various points. An example of such a balanced architecture is presented in Figure 8.9, where the combination of AI and IoT can be seen at different operational points. The architecture presents that data from the environment is gathered through either normal IoT sensors or AI-enabled IoT sensors. The internal AI-enabled sensors have an in-built AI chip for providing intelligent operation effect of these sensors. These sensors can interact with each other through internal communication

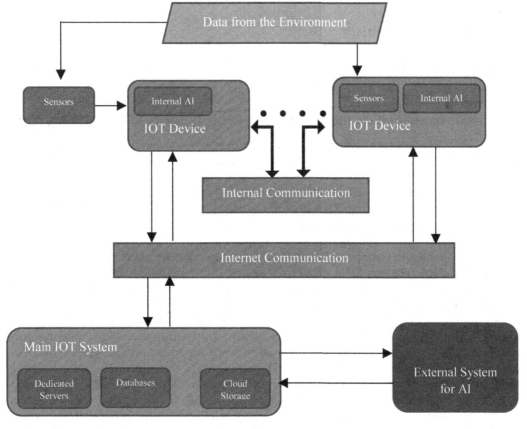

FIGURE 8.9
An example of a balanced architecture for AIoT systems.

Further, the main IoT system is used to store the data gathered from these devices, where the dedicated servers and databases can be used to store the data. Gathered data can also be stored using cloud storage services. For analysis and pattern analysis of the data, AI techniques can be applied externally on these gathered data sets for further improvement of the AIoT-based system.

8.5 AIoT-Enabled Applications

It is time to provide a detailed discussion on some of the industrial applications where the convergence of IoT and AI is possible. A few of the application areas where AI and IoT can be clubbed together are:

- Intelligent transport
- Monitoring and controlling applications
- Medical diagnosis system
- System robotic
- Agriculture industry
- Warehouse optimization

The list goes on and on. Some proposed system using AIoT technology in different sectors are discussed in further sections.

8.5.1 Smart Transportation: Intelligent and Dynamic Traffic Light System Using AIoT

Imagine an intelligent transport system that includes GPS-enabled buses or trains, as well as sensor-enabled waiting areas for travelers to count the number of travelers waiting for a particular transport medium [23]. The system will provide the waiting time for the next coming bus or train to the users as well as adjusting the stopping duration based on the number of passengers waiting. This type of transport system will not only help the traveler and transportation companies, but it would also help in making travel safe and maintain a healthy ecosystem [24–26].

IoT-based intelligent transport systems involve connecting various vehicles, waiting for areas with the internet to build a smart system, and universal mobile accessible advanced technology. Establishing communication using IoT between vehicles is the new era of communication where AI techniques can be used for data analysis accomplishment and assisting in managing the traffic system intelligently and efficiently [23]. This AIoT-based intelligent transportation system can be applied in automating roadways, railways, airways, and docks to enhance the customer experience for transporting goods with real-time monitoring tracking and delivering. The basic aim of these technologies is to make the transport system efficient, smart, safe, and environmentally sustainable. AIoT can help in creating an organized, clean, and hassle-free structure for managing transportation [27–29]. An underlying architecture for AIoT-based intelligent transport systems and communication and information management technology for operational transportation can be understood using Figures 8.10 and 8.11, respectively.

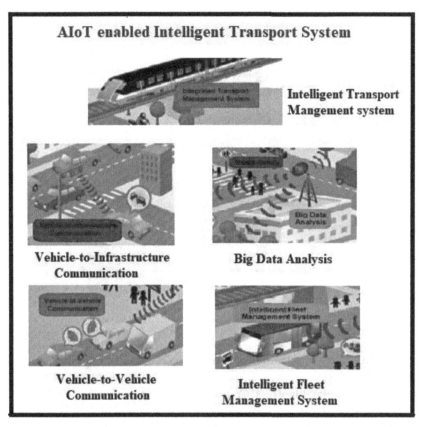

FIGURE 8.10
AIoT-enabled intelligent transport system.

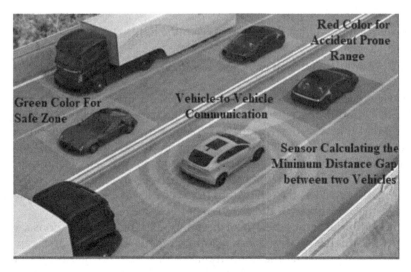

FIGURE 8.11
Communication and information management technology for operational transportation.

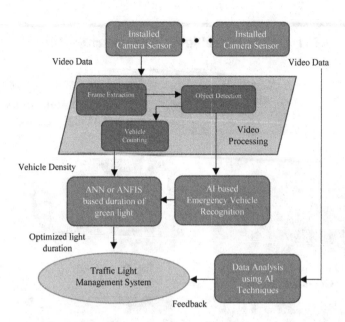

FIGURE 8.12
Working flow of smart traffic light system.

Most importantly, increasing traffic conditions, ever-growing pollution, and a high rate of accidents are the major factors to adopt an intelligent transport system for countries around the world and consequently trim-down these critical issues.

A smart system for managing traffic lights intelligently using AIoT technology is proposed and discussed here. The working architecture of the proposed intelligent model is also presented in Figure 8.12. Here, the objective of the system is:

- To design an intelligent and automated traffic light management system that is capable of controlling the traffic light dynamically based on the density of the vehicles in different lanes.
- The system should adjust the duration of traffic lights according to the density of a particular lane.
- Traffic light adjustment if an emergency vehicle is found in the lane.

As per the system, the highly-dense lane should have a green light for a long duration. The density detection of the particular lane will be based on video processing technology. First, the real-time video is captured using specific camera sensors installed at the intersection. The captured videos are then stored on the cloud, where this video will be processed in real time to extract frames. Further, image processing techniques like background elimination and image segmentation will be applied to detect the total number of vehicles. The density, such as the total strength of vehicles in a particular lane, can then be used for automatic adjustment of the duration of the lights.

As this automation of light adjustment needs a quick real-time response, we need to implement AI techniques that are less computationally expensive and can be implemented on chips. For adjusting the lights dynamically, adaptive neuro-fuzzy or a neural network implication system-based trained model can be stored for real-time classification of detected vehicles density to adjust the lights.

The system can also be enhanced by detecting an ambulance in a lane using object detection and recognition technology. Based on this, if an ambulance is found in any lane, it should be given priority, and the system should turn on the green lights of that lane.

The real-time implementation of the system in today's era is very much possible, and due to the boom in AIoT technology, a lot on AI-inbuilt devices are available on the market like AI accelerators, artificial eyes, etc.

Further, captured traffic light and video data can be processed offline for surveillance purposes or detecting and predicting the future trend using AI techniques like regression analysis, etc. This analysis will help the system to modify it as per the new complex real-time situations.

8.5.2 Smart Healthcare Management Using AIoT

AI and healthcare management systems are closely related; expert systems designed to assist medical practitioners in diagnosis and providing a guideline for medications. In the healthcare industry, wearable devices and smartphones allow the patient to gather information, receive a possible diagnosis based on the symptoms, and monitor metrics such as blood pressure, heart rate, etc. In healthcare enterprises, various AI-based machine learning software is implemented, including hospitals and clinics [30]. These software also offer mobile applications and IoT devices such as inhalers.

Various enterprises claim to design the software for healthcare management systems such as Microsoft Azure [31], Medidata, etc. Microsoft Azure claims to developed an IoT instrument that improves and tracks the well-being of the patient. Microsoft Azure deployed machine learning models, trained on a variety of health and medical data sets including blood pressure readings, personal patience goals, admit/discharge summaries, and patient-generated data including assessment-based depression indicators [32, 33, 34]. The software helps the doctors and medical practitioners to predict the potential risk, readmission, and remedies for the patients.

The software claims the analytics' capability to:

- Monitor and manage in-verto diagnostic devices remotely as a fixed asset.
- Predict potential downtime for any IVD devices deployed at customer end.
- Recommend the best IVD device for customer requirements.
- Provide analysis and data visualization for best decision making.
- Connection for future maintenance.

The next enterprise that claims to design healthcare software is Medidata [35]. It offers a mobile-based healthcare (m-health) management system grounded on cloud technologies. It collects the patient's data to analyze the condition and quality of life with diseases like cancer. It also applies machine learning models and performs predictive analytics. Medidata also claims that healthcare industries can integrate this application with IoT sensors and other activity trackers [36].

Medidata concludes that the machine learning models applied on the software trained on different types of cancer-related datasets, types of nutrition and fitness activities, related factors, and potential therapies that could help in-patient treatment, among others. The model will train the software to differentiate between the various data point and its related treatments that can or cannot improve the cancer patient's quality of life [37–40]. This Medidata software will then be able to predict suitable treatment for cancer-suffering patients. Medidata Patient Cloud software aggregates data collected from portable and moveable devices such

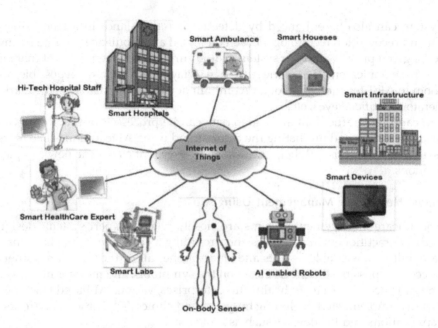

FIGURE 8.13
Structure of an IoT-enabled healthcare management system.

as wearables, sensors, smartphones, tablets, and mobile applications to create more patient-focused datasets. Figure 8.13 presents the basic structure and interconnection between various smart applications to support IoT-enabled healthcare management systems.

A smart IoT-based healthcare management system involves numerous participants, such as patients, doctors, hospitals, sensors, AI-based modeling software, and research institutions. It also includes multiple dimensions, including sickness and disease monitoring and prevention, analysis, diagnosis and treatment, smart hospital management, medical decision-making, and healthcare research. Network techniques, for example, mobile internet, IoT, big data, cloud computing, microelectronics, AI, and 5G, along with recent technologies, establish the cornerstone for smart healthcare management systems. Smart healthcare industries are widely using these technologies in all aspects. From the patient's perspectives, various wearable devices are used to monitor their health, seek online medical assistance using the virtual assistant system, and use remote hospitals to implement remote healthcare services. On the other hand, from the doctor's perspective, various intelligent clinical decision-support systems help to analyze, assist, and monitor diagnosis. Figure 8.14 represents an underlying architecture and flowchart for an AIoT-based healthcare management system.

Scientific researchers are using machine learning as well as deep learning-based tools and techniques instead of manually screening drugs, and for finding suitable subjects using big data tools. AI-enabled surgical robots and machine learning tools perform more precise surgeries. In hospitals, AIoT-enabled RFID techniques help in managing supply chain and personnel material using the integrated management platform for collecting and assisting in decision-making. A mobile healthcare assistant system will enhance the patient's experience. These technologies will reduce risks and make medical procedures cheap; it will also improve the utilization of medical resources efficiently and promote cooperation and exchange to various other regions. It will enhance telemedicine and self-service healthcare and eventually make personalized healthcare facilities ubiquitous.

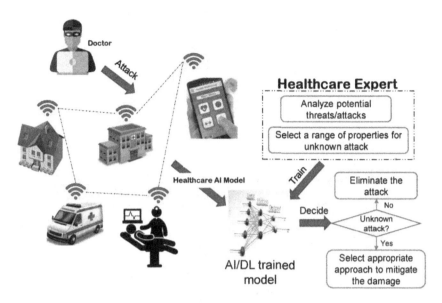

FIGURE 8.14
Underlying architecture and flowchart of an AIoT based healthcare management system.

An underlying network layer architecture for an AIoT-based healthcare management system is present in Figure 8.15. The architecture consists of four layers similar to the OSI reference model: Physical, Network, Decision Support, and Application Layers. Each and every layer has its defined roles. The physical layer is responsible for the collection of data from various sensors that are connected to the patients. The network layer accesses the data from the local storage and utilizes the simple mail transfer protocol (SMTP) to transmit the data to the concerned medical practitioner. After processing the data, the network layer transfers the control to the next highest layer, the decision support layer. In this layer, decision regarding the patient's health is made based upon the analysis of various medical activities: body temperature variations, room environment variations, etc. Based on the review, an advisory message will be transmitted to the application layer for further processing. The application layer then sends the data to the doctors and advisory to the caretakers.

8.5.3 Smart Home: Energy Efficient AIoT-Based Smart Air Conditioning System Using AIoT

A smart home is using technology to automate the home to provide security, accessibility, convenience, and comfort to inhabitants [41]. Visualize a home where you can control each device present in your home by simply a tap on your smartphone. A camera at your door is installed, which can recognize the person standing outside (if a family member or known) and can provide you with the details of the person based on the stored data. If you forget to switch off your air conditioning or TV before going out of your home, you can simply switch them off using your smartphone. AIoT technology has provided us with the ease of developing this smart home [42]. The development of an AIoT-based energy-efficient smart air conditioning system is discussed in the next section.

One of the major difficulties that the world is going to face is the usage of energy. According to a BBC report by Richard Gray, the world population burns more than 10 lakhs watthours of energy everyday while traveling its path. The burnt energy is equivalent to

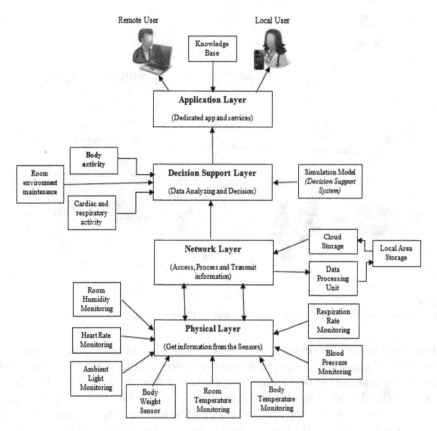

FIGURE 8.15
Network layer architecture for an AIoT-based healthcare management system.

what people will use if 7.5 thousand million boil more than 70 water kettles in an hour. Since the increase of population and industrialization, humanity's need for consumption of power has increased to an unrivalled level. The architecture for a smart air conditioning (AC) system is described here, in which the automation and smart mode of AC can provide energy efficiency. Further, the usage data of AC by different users can be stored on the cloud and analyzed using AI techniques for pattern finding and to give feedback to various brands associated with AC technology.

Currently, ACs are provided with a wireless interface, where the users can control the AC's temperature only if they are configured on the same network. But this restricts the AC's control to either be on the same network or in the same room. Here, a framework is presented that can work on existing AC systems provided with an infrared (IR) receiver. This framework will have various abilities, such as to control the AC system and record the operational parameters. The system is designed to interact only through Wi-Fi-direct and Bluetooth mode; the mobile application in the framework is designed to control the hardware and send the control signals to the server. The central server, in turn, records the control data and transmit it to the server running inside the hardware, which in turn transmits the data to the AC system. The server can record the operational data of various users, and upon the activation of smart mode, it can use the data accumulated from various users having similar AC systems to change the AC parameters. Further, the system

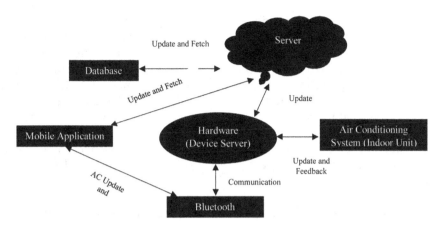

FIGURE 8.16
The architecture of the proposed smart AC system.

can be designed to cover the human error of forgetting to turn things off as the mobile application can be used to turn the AC off even if the person is not within reach of the AC system. This framework, which is presented in Figure 8.16, can be used by the implementing industries or the individual user to analyze the usage pattern, power consumption, most popular choice of AC, etc. The mobile application developed for operating a smart AC will behave as a remote control for the AC. It can be used to send the signal to the central server and receive the operational data from the central server. The mobile application can be designed in the following way to control multiple devices:

- **Signup:** This page, as the name suggests, can be used to register a user to the system. Upon entering the details, an API call can be made to the endpoint and the user is pushed to the home page.

- **Login:** Login page, where the user can enter credentials, then a call can be made to the main server and after a successful authentication, the user is connected to servers with a token and pushed to the home page.

- **Register page:** This page can register a user's AC to the app. First, the app tries to connect the phone to Pi using Bluetooth, then the app sends the credential of the local network to Pi, after which Pi comes to the network and then after a few handshakes between the servers, Pi is registered to control an AC and the AC is registered on the app.

- **Home page:** This page can be designed to show the user a list of all their registered ACs on the server. User can select an AC and navigate to the AC page, or user can register a new AC that will route the user to the register page. User can also edit their ACs or delete them.

- **Control page:** This page can contain all the buttons that are used to control the AC, like temperature up and down, different modes, and many others. Upon a pressing a button, the app makes a call to the Pi server to generate the frequency desired.

8.5.4 AIoT-Enabled Water Quality Monitoring and Ground Water Level Prediction

Water quality is a very grave concern in today's era, and that's because it can impact global public health and the environment. The most widely used sources of freshwater are ground and surface water. According to a WHO report, it is estimated that about 1.1 thousand million people had no clean drinking water in 2005. The period 2005–2015 was considered to be an international decade focused on the slogan "Water for Life" [43, 44]. Efficient use of natural resources is important for the existence of the human race and living creatures. Water pollution is a very major issue as almost close to 70% of surface and shallow water is polluted due to various contaminated, organic/inorganic pollutants, amongst other biological factors. Most of these sources have been declared unfit for consumption by humans.

With the availability of lost-cost sensors and AI techniques, a model can be developed that can solve the water scarcity problem, or if not solve then reduce it. The models can be developed to:

- Predict water quality, which can help in predicting and classifying if the water is impure or not.
- Predict underground water levels, which will help in predicting the underground water levels for an area while keeping specific parameters in mind.

The model can be developed using the following parameters, which represent the water quality standards to label the water as "Pure" [45].

- $6.5 < PH < 8.5$
- $0 < CONDUCTIVITY$ measured in (u-hos/cm) < 2250)
- TOTAL COLIFORM measured in (MPN/100 ml) Mean < 5000
- D.O. (mg/l) > = 4
- $25 < Temp < 40$
- < B.O.D. measured in (mg/l) < 3
- $0 < FECAL COLIFORM$ measured in (MPN/100 ml) < 2500
- $0 < NITRATE AND NITRITE ANN$ measured in (mg/l) < 20

Turbidity is the measure of the haziness of a fluid that can be caused by a large number of tiny particles. When water quality testing a field where turbidity is considered a necessary factor or parameter, pH is used to measure the acidity or basic nature of any solution. Conductivity is used to measure the ability of a solution to conduct electrical current. A solution only conducts electric current when ions exist in an aqueous solution [45]. The movement of these electrical charges decides the flow of charge through the solution. Many prediction models have been used to predict the quality of water such as ANN, support vector machine (SVM), adaptive network-based fuzzy inference system (ANFIS), radial basis function ANN (RBF-ANN), linear regression, and multi-layer perceptron ANN (MLP-ANN) [46].

8.5.5 Air Quality Monitoring System Using AIoT

Over the years, the problem of air pollution in India has become a critical one. In 2019, a survey conducted by WHO revealed that 21 of the 30 most polluted cities in the world were present in India [47]. Air pollution in Delhi has been categorized as hazardous to the health of individuals.

There is no system currently in use in India that is being used to predict the level of ambient air pollutants. The government has air stations that monitor the AQI and several organizations within that are working toward finding solutions to this problem [48, 49]. The efforts to tackle the problem of air pollution should be preemptive and hence call for the need to use intelligent systems that can aid human efforts in fighting this menace.

Here, a prototype model is presented to build a model that can predict the levels of ambient air pollutants in the atmosphere. At the local level, with easy access to advanced IoT technologies, it will be possible to monitor air pollution levels at home and further detect any gas leaks at home. A prototype model will be built, which can collect data in real time on the number of various gases present in the atmosphere. IoT-enabled devices are on the rise in this era of smart technology. Smart home systems that can detect and monitor pollutants in the ambient air thus become a necessity. A prototype model that can collect real-time data and monitor the level of pollutants in the atmosphere can be developed using the following components:

- **Arduino Uno R3 Microcontroller:** This will be programmed to operate the sensors connected to it. It has input/output pins that can be interfaced to various devices. The Uno has an analog-digital converter that helps take readings through sensors.
- **MQ 7 Gas Sensor:** This sensor is used to monitor carbon monoxide (CO) in the air from levels of 10–10,000 ppm.
- **MQ 135 Gas Sensor:** Used to monitor ammonia (NH_3), nitrogen oxides (NOx), and carbon dioxide (CO_2).
- **MQ 2 Gas Sensor:** Used to detect methane, butane, and smoke.

The cost-effectiveness and benefits of this model make it a necessary tool that should be present in every person's home. In residential areas close to industries, smart devices can alert people of the dangers and invest in air purifiers and people seeking to buy homes choose wisely. The workings of the prototype are presented in Figure 8.17.

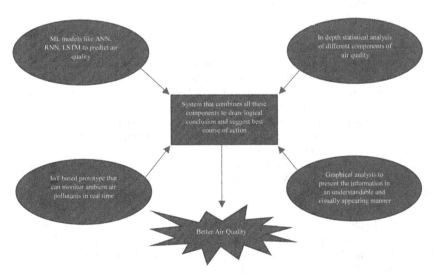

FIGURE 8.17
Prototype for proposed air quality monitoring.

8.6 Conclusion

This chapter discusses the convergence of AI and IoT to form AIoT. AI and IoT are considered as two different and independent techniques that have an important influence on several industry sectors. While IoT is considered as the digital nerve supporting flow of data, AI is said to be the brain of the overall system that makes and controls decisions. This lethal grouping and combination of IoT and AI presents a new generation of AIoT that brings smartly connected, also intelligent systems capable of healing and correcting themselves. The proposed work discusses various AIoT applications in healthcare, transportation, smart homes, and agriculture. It aims to convert smart IoT application to an intelligent AI-enabled application. It aims to convert a smart IoT application to an intelligent AI-enabled application. Various prototypes for AIoT applications are discussed to provide a clear and promising framework for developing intelligent transportation management systems, intelligent healthcare management systems, intelligent homes, and other intelligent applications. It also discusses in detail various AI, machine learning, and deep learning models used to design the discussed intelligent systems. The world is likely to see more advanced AI developers come around to reduce computations enough for economic use, which will ensure that AIoT will lead the way in smart and intelligent transport, intelligent homes, and almost any other field. In the future, AIoT will be unavoidable and an obvious choice.

References

1. C. Stracener, Q. Samelson, J. Mackie, and M. Ihaza, The Internet of Things Grows Artificial Intelligence and Data Sciences, *IT Professional*, vol. 21, no. 3, pp. 55–62, May–June 2019.
2. Andrew Ng, Machine learning Yearning. Available at: https://www.mlyearning.org/ [Accessed on April 15, 2020].
3. A. Kapoor, Principles and Foundations of IoT and AI, *Hands-On Artificial Intelligence for IoT: Expert Machine Learning and Deep-Learning Techniques for Developing Smarter IoT Systems*, Packt Publishing, January 2019.
4. Samuel Greengard, *The Internet of Things*, Cambridge, MA: MIT Press, 2015, p. 232.
5. M.S.V.Janakiram,WhyAIoTIsEmergingastheFutureofIndustry4.0.[online]Availableat:https://www.forbes.com/sites/janakirammsv/2019/08/12/why-aiot-is-emerging-as-the-future-of-industry-40/#c4e350b619be [Accessed April 16, 2020].
6. Klaus Schwab, *The Fourth Industrial Revolution*, Penguin (January 3, 2017).
7. Cuno Pfister, *Getting Started with the Internet of Things: Connecting Sensors and Microcontrollers to the Cloud (Make: Projects)* O'Reilly Media (June 5, 2011).
8. Postscapes, Internet of Things (IoT) History [online]. Available at: https://www.postscapes.com/iot-history/ [Accessed on May 5, 2020].
9. Daniel Kellmereit, Daniel Obodovski, *The Silent Intelligence–The Internet of Things*, DND Ventures LLC (September 20, 2013).
10. R. Milton, D. Hay, S. Gray, B. Buyuklieva, and A. Hudson-Smith, Smart IoT and Soft AI, Living in the Internet of Things: Cybersecurity of the IoT – 2018, London, UK, March 28–29, 2018, pp. 1–6.
11. D. Upadhyay, A. K. Dubey, and P. S. Thilagam, Application of Non-Linear Gaussian Regression based Adaptive Clock Synchronization Technique for Wireless Sensor Network in Agriculture, *IEEE Sensors Journal*, vol. 18, no. 10, pp. 4328–4335, 20
12. Russell Stuart, *Artificial Intelligence: A Modern Approach*, 3rd edition, Prentice Hall. (November 30, 2009).

13. Jeff Heaton, Artificial Intelligence for Humans, *Volume 1: Fundamental Algorithms*, CreateSpace Independent Publishing Platform (November 26, 2013).

14. Kevin Warwick, *Artificial Intelligence: The Basics*, Routledge (October 13, 2011)

15. Ethem Alpaydin, *Machine Learning: The New AI*, MIT Press (October 7, 2016).

16. Christopher M. Bishop, *Pattern Recognition and Machine Learning*, Corr. 2nd printing 2011 edition, Springer (February 15, 2010).

17. S. Ben-David and S. Shalev-Shwartz, *Understanding Machine Learning: From Theory to Algorithms*, Cambridge University Press (May 19, 2014).

18. Ian Goodfellow, Yoshua Bengio, and Aaron Courville, *Deep Learning*. MIT Press. 2016.

19. Lavanya Sharma and P.K. Garg, (Eds.). (2019). *From Visual Surveillance to Internet of Things*. New York, NY: Chapman and Hall/CRC, https://doi.org/10.1201/9780429297922

20. Lavanya Sharma and Nirvikar Lohan, Performance Analysis of Moving Object Detection using BGS Techniques in Visual Surveillance, *International Journal of Spatiotemporal Data Science*, vol. 1, Inderscience, pp. 22–53, January 2019.

21. K. L. Loh, 1.2 Fertilizing AIoT from Roots to Leaves, 2020 IEEE International Solid-State Circuits Conference (ISSCC), San Francisco, CA, 2020, pp. 15–21, doi: 10.1109/ISSCC19947.2020.9062950.

22. H. HaddadPajouh, R. Khayami, A. Dehghantanha et al., AI4SAFE-IoT: An AI-Powered Secure Architecture for Edge Layer of Internet of Things, *Neural Computing & Applications*, (2020). https://doi.org/10.1007/s00521-020-04772-3

23. J. Ma, S. Feng, X. Li, X. Zhang, and D. Zhang, Research on the Internet of Things Architecture for Intelligent Passenger Transportation Services and its Application, 2019 4th International Conference on Electromechanical Control Technology and Transportation (ICECTT), Guilin, China, 2019, pp. 194–197.

24. Y. Liu, Big Data Technology and Its Analysis of Application in Urban Intelligent Transportation System, 2018 International Conference on Intelligent Transportation, Big Data & Smart City (ICITBS), Xiamen, China, 2018, pp. 17–19.

25. P. S. Saarika, K. Sandhya, and T. Sudha, Smart Transportation System using IoT, 2017 International Conference on Smart Technologies for Smart Nation (SmartTechCon), Bangalore, India, 2017, pp. 1104–1107.

26. HERE Mobility, An Introduction to Smart Transport [online]. 2020. Available at: https://mobility.here.com/learn/smart-transportation/introduction-smart-transport [Accessed on May 5, 2020].

27. L. Zhu, F. R. Yu, Y. Wang, B. Ning, and T. Tang, Big Data Analytics in Intelligent Transportation Systems: A Survey, in *IEEE Transactions on Intelligent Transportation Systems*, vol. 20, no. 1, pp. 383–398, Jan. 2019.

28. Qiong Wang, Haofeng Zhang, Minxian Li, and Chunxia Zhao, Transportation Monitoring Framework Based on Dynamic Environment Intelligent Perception, 2011 International Conference on Remote Sensing, Environment and Transportation Engineering, Nanjing, China, 2011, pp. 1852–1855.

29. F. Zantalis, G. Koulouras, S. Karabetsos, and D. Kandris, "A Review of Machine Learning and IoT in Smart Transportation," *Future Internet*, vol. 11, no. 4, p. 94, 2019.

30. Lavanya Sharma and Nirvikar Lohan, Performance Analysis of Moving Object Detection using BGS Techniques, *International Journal of Spatio-Temporal Data Science, Inderscience*, February, 2019.

31. Microsoft Azure, Azure for Health Cloud [online]. 2020. Available at: https://azure.microsoft.com/en-in/industries/healthcare/ [Accessed on May 5, 2020].

32. W. Liu, E. K. Park, S. S. Zhu, and U. Krieger, Smart and Connected e-Health R&D platform, 2015 17th International Conference on E-health Networking, Application & Services (HealthCom), Boston, MA, 2015, pp. 677–679.

33. F. Casino, C. Patsakis, E. Batista, O. Postolache, A. Martínez-Ballesté, and A. Solanas, Smart Healthcare in the IoT Era: A Context-Aware Recommendation Example, 2018 International Symposium in Sensing and Instrumentation in IoT Era (ISSI), Shanghai, 2018, pp. 1–4.

34. Z. Zhang, T. He, M. Zhu, Q. Shi, and C. Lee, Smart Triboelectric Socks for Enabling Artificial Intelligence of Things (AIoT) Based Smart Home and Healthcare, 2020 IEEE 33rd International Conference on Micro Electro Mechanical Systems (MEMS), Vancouver, BC, Canada, 2020, pp. 80–83, doi: 10.1109/MEMS46641.2020.9056149.

35. A. Pang, M. Markovski, and A. Micik, Top 10 Life Sciences Software Vendors, Market Size and Market Forecast 2018–2023. [online] Apps Run the World. 2020. Available at: https://www. appsruntheworld.com/top-10-life-sciences-software-vendors-and-market-forecast/ [Accessed on May 5, 2020].

36. W. Chang et al., An AI Edge Computing Based Wearable Assistive Device for Visually Impaired People Zebra-Crossing Walking, 2020 IEEE International Conference on Consumer Electronics (ICCE), Las Vegas, NV, 2020, pp. 1–2, doi: 10.1109/ICCE46568.2020.9043132.

37. Lavanya Sharma, Introduction: From Visual Surveillance to Internet of Things, *From Visual Surveillance to Internet of Things*, Vol. 1, Chapman Hall/CRC, p. 14, 2019.

38. Lavanya Sharma and P. K. Garg, Block based Adaptive Learning Rate for Moving Person Detection in Video Surveillance, *From Visual Surveillance to Internet of Things*, Vol. 1, Chapman Hall/CRC, p. 201, 2019.

39. Lavanya Sharma and P. K. Garg, Smart E-healthcare with Internet of Things: Current Trends Challenges, Solutions and Technologies, *From Visual Surveillance to Internet of Things*, Vol. 1, Chapman Hall/CRC, p. 215, 2019.

40. Lavanya Sharma, P. K. Garg, and Naman Agarwal, A Foresight on e-healthcare Trailblazers, *From Visual Surveillance to Internet of Things*, Vol. 1, Chapman Hall/CRC, p. 235, 2019.

41. N. M. Kumar, S. Goel, and P. K. Mallick, Smart Cities in India: Features, Policies, Current Status, and Challenges, 2018 Technologies for Smart-City Energy Security and Power (ICSESP), Bhubaneswar, India, 2018, pp. 1–4.

42. E. Mardacany, Smart Cities Characteristics: Importance of Built Environments Components, IET Conference on Future Intelligent Cities, London, UK, 2014, pp. 1–6.

43. Drinking water report released by WHO on 14 June 2019. Available at: https://www.who.int/news-room/fact-sheets/detail/drinking-water [Accessed on January 10, 2020].

44. W. Chang et al., iCAP: An IoT-based Intelligent Liquid Waste Barrels Monitoring System, 2019 11th Computer Science and Electronic Engineering (CEEC), Colchester, UK, 2019, pp. 156–159, doi: 10.1109/CEEC47804.2019.8974314.

45. R. P. N. Budiarti, A. Tjahjono, M. Hariadi, and M. H. Purnomo, Development of IoT for Automated Water Quality Monitoring System, 2019 International Conference on Computer Science, Information Technology, and Electrical Engineering (ICOMITEE), Jember, Indonesia, 2019, pp. 211–216.

46. K. Gopavanitha and S. Nagaraju, A Low Cost System for Real Time Water Quality Monitoring and Controlling using IoT, 2017 International Conference on Energy, Communication, Data Analytics and Soft Computing (ICECDS), Chennai, India, 2017, pp. 3227–3229.

47. G. M. G. Nandigala Venkat Anurag, Y. Burra, and S. Sharanya, Air Quality Index Prediction with Meteorological Data Using Feature Based Weighted Xgboost, *International Journal of Innovative Technology and Exploring Engineering vol.* 8, no, 11S, pp. 1026–1029, September 2019.

48. Ping-Wei Soh et al., Adaptive Deep-learning-Based Air Quality Prediction Model Using the Most Relevant Spatial-Temporal Relations, *IEEE Access*, vol. 6, pp. 38186–38199, 2018.

49. W. Han, Y. Gu, Y. Zhang, and L. Zheng, Data Driven Quantitative Trust Model for the Internet of Agricultural Things, 2014 International Conference on the Internet of Things (IOT), Cambridge, MA, 2014, pp. 31–36, doi: 10.1109/IOT.2014.7030111.

9

Internet of Things and Image Processing

Xiao Yuan Yu

College of Automation Science and Technology, South China University of Technology
Guangzhou, China

Wei Xie

College of Automation Science and Technology, South China University of Technology
Guangzhou, China

CONTENTS

9.1   Introduction...144
9.2   Image Processing and IoT..144
    9.2.1   Relationship..144
    9.2.2   Applications of Image Processing under IoT................................145
        9.2.2.1   Application in Industrial System......................................145
        9.2.2.2   Application in Agriculture..146
        9.2.2.3   Application in Traffic and Vehicle...................................147
        9.2.2.4   Application in Medical Systems.......................................147
        9.2.2.5   Application in Public Security..148
9.3   Applications of Facial Image Processing and IoT in Public Security.......148
    9.3.1   Face Super-Resolution and Deblurring...149
        9.3.1.1   Design Network...149
        9.3.1.2   Training Network...153
        9.3.1.3   Prediction Model...155
    9.3.2   Standard Face Generation and Face Recognition...........................155
        9.3.2.1   Constructed Training Data Set..156
        9.3.2.2   Constructed Network Model...158
        9.3.2.3   Training Model...161
        9.3.2.4   Model Prediction...162
    9.3.3   Face Recognition Architecture Based on Edge Computing and Cloud
        Coordination...163
        9.3.3.1   Edge Node Deployment...163
        9.3.3.2   Design of Local Face Recognition Model and Data Transmission........164
        9.3.3.3   Cloud Model Designing and Training..............................166
        9.3.3.4   Tasks Feedback..168
9.4   Conclusion 168
Acknowledgments..168
References...169

9.1 Introduction

The definition of Internet of Things (IoT) is that microdevices that are equipped with microcontrollers and transceivers by using battery power are integrated into the global internet and are called smart objects. And then, the smart services denote the services that are provided by smart objects [1]. IoT can realize the effective connection between thing-to-thing, thing-to-people, and people-to-people at any time and place, which is more convenient to share information on cross-platforms. IoT has been applied to many practical applications, which makes cities smarter.

Image processing denotes the procedure for operating image files by using mathematical algorithms [2]. More importantly, pictures with image processing are generally digital images. Therefore, image processing is generally considered as digital-image processing (DIP). However, in some instances, the captured images are always blurry or uncomfortable to the human eye. Thus, it is necessary that the algorithms for processing images are used to make these low-quality images clearer and brighter. DIP uses different computer algorithms to process the information of the digital images. In other words, DIP has an obvious advantage that the results processed by DIP methods are always satisfied for the needs of human visual psychology of applications [2]. Meanwhile, methods of DIP can be used to help humans explain the real-world objectively and rapidly.

In addition, methods of pattern recognition with DIP can be used to help humans understand images that are hardly recognized by just using the human eye. Using technology of pattern recognition is beneficial to retrieve, match, and identify various objects quickly and accurately. Recently, DIP has been widely utilized to image classification (determining which type of observed object) [3], pattern recognition (recognizing known or unknown categories of the object) [4], object feature extraction (judging and extracting features that can be used for further processing information) [5], information analysis with different scales, and three-dimensional (3D) image processing [6].

Recently, image processing, especially DIP combined with deep learning theory, has spread to various applications. Therefore, this chapter will introduce the relationships and applications based on image processing and IoT. First, we will simply introduce the relationship and applications of image processing and IoT. And then, we will discuss the related algorithms and applications of IoT combined with technologies of facial image processing in the field of public security (FoPS).

9.2 Image Processing and IoT

9.2.1 Relationship

IoT can achieve the effective connection of thing-to-thing, thing-to-people, and people-to-people at any time and place. The sensors and devices seamlessly communicate by IoT in an intelligent environment, which can achieve cross-platform information sharing conveniently [7, 8]. IoT can connect multiple types of information, and digital images are an important part of the information in IoT. As shown in Figure 9.1, the relationship between image processing and IoT, the image sensor, which is constructed by CCD or CMOS, is used to capture image data and is one part of the network of IoT [9]. Supporting the IoT

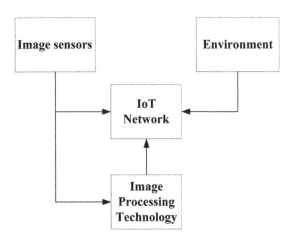

FIGURE 9.1
Relationship between IoT and image processing.

network as a person, the image sensor is equivalent to human eyes, which is used to capture changed images from the outside world. Meanwhile, the processor equipped with DIP technology is equivalent to the visual processing area of the human brain, which is used to process and enhance these images. And then, the processor transforms the processed result to other locations of the IoT network, which can make responses for the task. Therefore, the IoT network loaded with DIP technology can obtain more accurate information and faster response of tasks.

9.2.2 Applications of Image Processing under IoT

IoT is an important trend of research and has broad prospects of application. Combining image processing and the framework of the IoT network has been widely used in many aspects, such as urban construction and live productions. In the real world, the applications of the IoT network include emergency systems based on rescue vehicles, traffic monitoring, path tracking based on GPS, agricultural monitoring, criminal tracking, community service, monitoring systems, security systems for identity verification and authorization, electronic medical, smart industrial systems, and medical systems [10]. Figure 9.2 shows the relevant application scenarios by combing IoT and image processing. We will introduce application scenarios of image processing in IoT as follows.

9.2.2.1 Application in Industrial System

The combination of IoT and industrial applications is mainly applied by mechanical equipment monitoring and environmental monitoring in an intelligent factory. The important role of image processing in IoT is mainly reflected in the detection of production material and information monitoring of equipment. For example, [11] introduces the framework of detecting the 3D surface of a steel billet. A camera is used to perform 3D scanning by continuously capturing multiple images in the smart industry. Meanwhile, the depth information of the billet is checked and extracted from various angles using a green line laser. For equipment information monitoring, [12] designed an automatic reading device of an industrial meter based on online optical character recognition (OCR). The results of

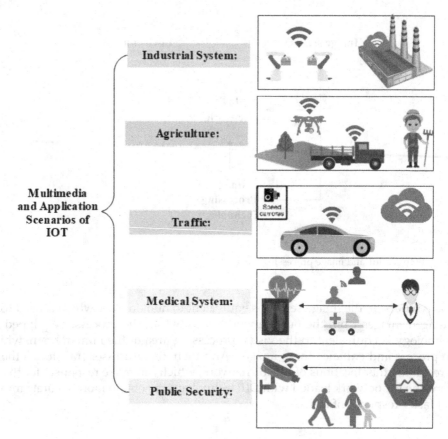

FIGURE 9.2
Multimedia communication types in IoT and related application scenarios of IoT.

industrial instruments were extracted from the monitoring images, which were uploaded to the cloud by devices. And then, this data is processed and provided centrally to authorize users on PCs and smartphones.

9.2.2.2 Application in Agriculture

The integration between agriculture and IoT is reflected in agricultural planting and animal husbandry. In agricultural planting, sensors, cameras, and satellites are used to promote the digital development of crops. In animal husbandry, data is collected by using ear tags, wearable devices, and cameras. And then, the data of animals is used to analyze and determine the status of livestock and poultry, which can manage the health, feeding, location, and estrus period of livestock and poultry. In the problem of plant monitoring, Kapoor et al. [13] added image-processing techniques (such as histogram analysis of leaf images of crops) into the IoT framework, which can determine whether environmental factors or human factors would hinder the growth of crops. Liao et al. [14] proposed the IoT system to monitor the growth of *Phalaenopsis* in greenhouses. This system used canny algorithm to detect edge and seed area growth to predict the leaves' area, which can monitor the growth status of plants and provide referenced information for cultivation strategies of *Phalaenopsis*. In [15], planting problems of crops in greenhouses are described, and then contact and noncontact monitoring methods of plant conditions are introduced.

Furthermore, plant monitoring promotes the implementation of automated irrigation. Tran et al. [16] used image-processing technology to analyze the growth of plants, and then the monitored results are sent to the back-end controller, while it can achieve automatic irrigation and maintenance of plants. [17] proposed a closed-loop irrigation system by analyzing the satellite images, which can achieve water calculation of irrigation and automatic irrigation by adjusting the irrigation plan in time according to the spatial and temporal changes of vegetation. Besides, image processing is also a meaningful aspect in protecting natural animals. Elias et al. [18] designed the "Where's the bear" (WTB) system to identify animals in the monitoring system of wildlife. The WTB system is designed by combining the technology of edge computing and the technology of image processing. The purpose of edge computing is used to save bandwidth for transforming information and obtain better processing accuracy of the WTB system. WTB uses TensorFlow to identify and classify the bear image in the monitoring screen and analyzes the image structure through OpenCV. The results show that carrying the image recognition algorithm on the edge notes where the image is obtained can save bandwidth and reduce the task response delay extremely.

9.2.2.3 Application in Traffic and Vehicle

In this type of application, IoT mainly advances the traffic environment, maintains traffic safety, and upgrades the utilization rate of public resources by closely combining people, cars, roads, and other things. And then, the application of image processing technology in this aspect mainly focuses on vehicle monitoring and traffic monitoring. George et al. [19] proposed an adaptive neuro-fuzzy inference system (ANFIS) by combining the technology of image processing, which has better performance in traffic light management and monitoring system. Here, analysis technology of the spot based on machine vision is used to detect the position of the vehicle, and Otsu image-processing technology is used to enhance the night images that are obtained based on feeble lighting conditions. For ANFIS, the traffic lights can be controlled after the captured images are processed on the cloud server.

In addition, [20] proposed a method to detect obstacle and plan paths based on image processing, which included converting video to fixed-rate image frames. By merging multiple image frames in the video stream, Cai et al. [21] used neural network and vehicle tracking technology to find free parking spaces, which can help the driver save time looking for empty parking spaces. In addition, Chen et al. [22] designed a video surveillance system based on fog computing by using unmanned aerial vehicle (UAV) cameras to monitor traffic systems in urban areas. The author proposes a tracking algorithm that extracts the interesting frames and transmits them to the fog node, which can satisfy the requirements of minimum calculation and delay. The tracking algorithm uses Bayesian estimation and probabilistic Monte Carlo simulation.

9.2.2.4 Application in Medical Systems

By combining IoT, the medical system can get higher accuracy of processing and collecting information. The role of image processing in medical IoT is mainly reflected in facial information processing and surgical assistance. [23] proposed an effective recognition technique of a blood vessel to extract lesion locations from retinal images based on region-based features. Zhang et al. [24] proposed an upgraded method for locating and authenticating the eye iris. This system is modeled by evaluating the quality of the captured images based on the intensity of the image, clarity of image, and completeness of the eye iris. [24] evaluated the image clarity by using the block variance method, and the integrity of the image is determined according to the position of the pupil in the image. After estimating the center range and extracting the pupil radius and pupil area, this method can reduce the delay of iris recognition. Yin et al. [25] proposed an enhanced system for detecting various diseases of the eye. The proposed automatic method uses a fundus camera to collect data on the retina image. In addition, [26] proposed a facial recognition-authentication system based on the retina. The author improves the retinal model by using adaptation truncation, lighting classification, and lighting estimation. In surgical assistance, [27] proposed an automatically detected tool of X-ray images for surgical assistance based on computer vision. The success rate of the system can be achieved by 91% due to using the method of block detection, matching method of geometric model, principal component analysis (PCA), and so on.

9.2.2.5 Application in Public Security

The role of IoT in public security is also extremely significant. The system of traditional public security depends on manual warning, while the system of intelligent public security uses agile apparatus to curtail the staff cost. In intelligent public security systems, the main application scenarios include building access, danger alarm, security monitoring, and video surveillance. The intelligent public security system can address and accumulate the captured images, and then analyze images and make feedback to the tasks. [28] proposed a system of natural language processing that combines an ontology and video monitoring method based on image analysis for content-based visual data retrieval. Meanwhile, principal component analysis and support vector machines are used to detect face area, and then obtain the result of classification. This method is used to guarantee passenger safety in public transportation systems. In addition, Basri et al. [29] proposed a residential monitoring system with IoT. In the specified monitoring range, passive infrared (PIR) sensors are used to detect suspicious movement and the important images are captured by using Pi cameras. In the FoPS, face recognition is an important security measure. Wang et al. [30] proposed face detection technology and face degeneration technology based on deep neural networks (DNNs) within video streaming to protect privacy and security of personal information.

Therefore, facial image-processing technology is very important for IoT in public security. In Section 9.3, several application algorithms are introduced by combining facial image-processing technology and IoT.

9.3 Applications of Facial Image Processing and IoT in Public Security

In the FoPS, the IoT framework with image acquisition sensors and DIP technologies is used for early warning and handling of public security incidents. These image processing technologies include low-quality face restoration, generation of face standardization and face recognition, and so on.

In general, the IoT framework for public security generally uses image acquisition tools such as surveillance cameras to identify, troubleshoot, and lock the faces of target suspects. However, in this application, we need to solve problems as follows. First, to restore the face image from the monitoring picture, the main problem is how to restore the low-resolution and low-quality blurry face images. Second, for facial recognition with a single sample, the main problem is how to solve the standardization of face image. Third, for face recognition with big data under the IoT framework, the main problem is how to solve the transmission efficiency and task feedback efficiency of huge monitored data.

Recently, DIP with deep learning has stronger capabilities for processing different types of image and can obtain more accurate processing results [31]. Therefore, in this section, we would mainly introduce some applications of IoT and learning-based image processing technology corresponding to the three problems to be solved.

9.3.1 Face Super-Resolution and Deblurring

In the FoPS, the captured facial images of surveillance videos are usually blurry and low-resolution (B-LR). To find out information about the person, we need to restore the B-LR facial image. When the resolution of the B-LR image is too low (the image resolution is 16×16, or even 8×8), it is easy to obtain unacceptable results when restoring by using the deblurring method [32] and the reconstruction method [33, 34], respectively. It is noted that the resorted face image would tend to be blurry and over-smooth due to the above method ignoring the conditional dependence between super-resolution pixels of the face image [35]. Meanwhile, when we need to restore the facial image with higher magnification, the aforementioned methods are also incapable to obtain effective restoration results. Furthermore, most of the existing methods focus on obtaining a visually pleasing image from the B-LR face image during reconstruction. However, the aim of the face restored method is not only to obtain the pleasing facial image but also to keep the same identity of the face during restoration.

Therefore, we proposed a consistent identity generative adversarial network (Con-IDGAN), which is designed to learn the relative map $M : \{b \rightarrow f\}, s.t. Id(b) = Id(f)$ between a B-LR image b and a corresponding sharp image f, where $Id(\cdot)$ denotes the identity-information of the face. The essential flow of the proposed method is show in Figure 9.3. The detail is introduced as follows.

9.3.1.1 Design Network

According to the above explanation, the reconstruction results of B-LR face images need to achieve two purposes, including pleasant visual effects and consistent identity information. Therefore, this section proposes an end-to-end network to reconstruct the high-resolution (HR) face image from the B-LR face image. The overall architecture of the network is constructed by using the training mechanism of generative adversarial networks (GAN), which mainly includes a super-resolution generative network (SR-Gnet), discriminative network (Dnet), and a facial identity evaluation network (ID-Evalnet). In detail, the SR-Gnet is used to generate HR face images. The Dnet is used to discriminate the authenticity of the generated images, which is used to training network. Meanwhile, the ID-Evalnet is used to extract face information, which can be used to further constrain the correctness of the generated face image. The specific network structure is as follows.

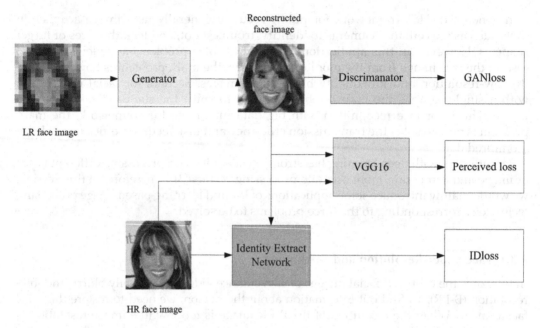

FIGURE 9.3
Overall structure of the proposed face restoration method.

9.3.1.1.1 Super-Resolution Generator Network

As shown in Figure 9.4, our SR-Gnet applies the multibranches framework to reconstruct the super-resolution images with upsampled factor ×16. Here is the introduction of the SR-Gnet concisely. First, as the input image I_{in}, we would get three interpolation results of I_{in}, such as the image with upsampled factor ×2($I_{in(×2)}$), ×4($I_{in(×4)}$), ×8($I_{in(×8)}$), respectively. And then, each interpolation result is used as the input of each branch in SR-Gnet. For instance, the image $I_{in(×2)}$ is applied to the first branch for producing the SR image with an upscaled factor ×4($I_{SR(×4)}$). Finally, the SR image I_{SR} with an upscaled factor ×16 can be obtained. It is noted that the SFT network [36] is used as the backbone network on each layer. However, according to the SFT network, the proposed method has added a salient edge extracted network (2ENet) and a degeneration kernel predicted network (DKPNet). This is because that the degeneration kernel can be estimated more accurately by using the salient edge of image during iterative estimating framework, and the degeneration kernel is good for restoring a blurry image. In general, combining the 2ENet and BKPNet into the SR-Gnet can effectively boost the face construction, which achieves a good visual fidelity of a hallucinated HR face image.

9.3.1.1.2 Salient Edge Extracted Network

As shown in Figure 9.5, these 2ENets are built based on the standard U-net [37]. Since the input of each 2ENet is different, the structure is designed according to the size of the input. For instance, the structure of the first 2ENet whose input size is 32×32 has only two convolution layers with a rectified linear unit (ReLU) and two deconvolution layers with a ReLU. And then, the third 2ENet whose input is 128×128 owns the same structure of a standard U-net, as shown in Figure 9.5. In this way, the edge can be extracted from the

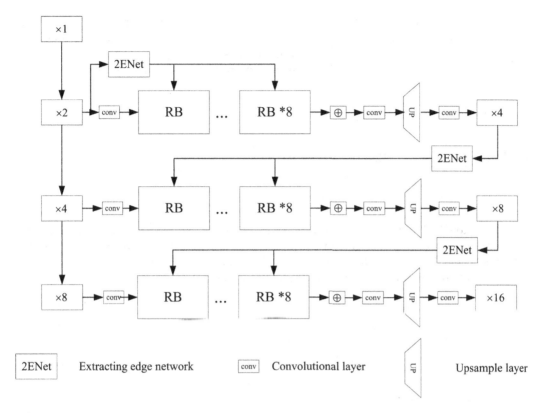

FIGURE 9.4
Structure of SR-Gnet.

image with different scales. It is noted that each 2ENet should be trained before training the whole model.

9.3.1.1.3 *Degeneration Kernel Predicted Network*

A BKPNet is inspired by the estimation of blind kernel in a typical image degradation domain. According to [38], the blind low-resolution image b can be obtained by

$$b = (k \otimes I_m) \downarrow + n, \tag{9.1}$$

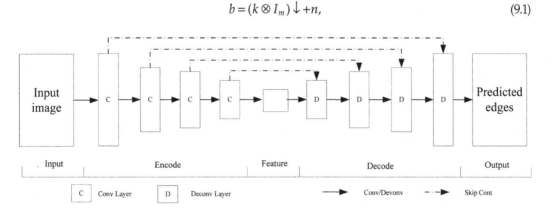

FIGURE 9.5
Structure of a 2ENet.

where k, I_m, and n denote the blind kernel, the clear high-resolution image, and additive noise, respectively. $\otimes$ and $(\ )\downarrow$ denote the blurring operator and downsampling operator, respectively. In literature, n is set as the Gaussian noise.

By writing blurring operator and downsampling operator as matrix multiplication, the model (9.1) is rewritten as

$$b = KI_m + n, \tag{9.2}$$

According to the model (9.2), we can get the clear HR image I_m by

$$I_m = K^{-1}(b + n'), \tag{9.3}$$

According to [38, 39], the kernel K and noise n should be expressed at first. And further, the clear high-resolution image can be obtained. Therefore, as shown in Figure 9.6, the extracted edges E are used to fit the noise at first and the degeneration kernel at second. And then, the result of DKPNet can be obtained by the input feature Fe_{in} as

$$\begin{cases} n' = Conv1(E), \\ K^{-1} = Conv2(E), \\ Fe_{tmp} = Fe_{in} + n', \\ Fe_{out} = K^{-1} \otimes Fe_{tmp}, \end{cases} \tag{9.4}$$

where Conv1 and Conv2 denote the layers with convolutions and Leaky_Relu activation function. In this way, the feature of the image can be extracted after using several residual blocks with DKPNet.

Finally, the algorithm of this section is constructed by using the residual network [40] as the backbone, which replaces the convolution of a residual module to the two degenerate kernel prediction modules. By this way, the depth feature map of the image can be extract. Then, combining multiple residual modules, the network depth can be deepened and the accuracy of image restoration can be improved.

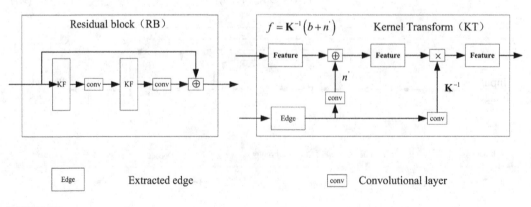

FIGURE 9.6
Structure of DKPNet.

TABLE 9.1

Network Architecture of Dnet

Layer Name	Kernel Size	Stride Value	Output Size
I^{SR} and I^{HR}	-	-	$3 \times 256 \times 256$
Conv, LeakyRelu	3×3	2	$64 \times 128 \times 128$
Conv, BN, LeakyRelu	3×3	2	$128 \times 64 \times 64$
Conv, BN, LeakyRelu	3×3	2	$256 \times 32 \times 32$
Conv, BN, LeakyRelu	3×3	1	$512 \times 32 \times 32$
Conv	3×3	1	$512 \times 1 \times 1$

9.3.1.1.4 Discrimination Network

In this section, the Dnet is used to discriminate that the super-resolution image I^{SR} is considered as fake, and the high-resolution image I^{HR} is considered as true. The network architecture of Dnet is based on the WGAN-GP [41], which includes five convolution layers and one sigmoid and FC layer, as described in Table 9.1. After going through the Dnet, the channel of feature-map is changed from 3 to 512 and the final output is the mean value of the output of the last layer. This mean value is used to discriminate that the input is an SR image or HR image. Thus, by this way, the Dnet can help SR-Gnet to generate the facial image with high quality. Meanwhile, we introduce the ID-Evalnet in the following subsection, which can promote the SR-Gnet to generate the feasible face image with the consistent-identity of the ground truth.

9.3.1.1.5 Facial Identity Evaluation Network

In this study, the pretrained MTCNN [42] and VGGFace2 [43] are used as the main models of ID-Evalnet. The MTCNN is the multi-task convolution neural network to distinguish the face area in the image, which can reduce the interference from the background. And then, VGGFace2 is a face recognition network that is based on the backbone of inception network. The VGGFace2 network has been trained as the facial classifier with nearly 10,000 identities, which can be used to draw the latent feature of face image. Here, these are the main processes. First, the location information of face and facial area A^{HR} in the HR image is detected by the MTCNN. Second, we use the extracted location information to extract the face area A^{SR} in the SR image. At last, the identity information of A^{HR} and A^{SR}, which are extracted by VGGFace2 respectively, are used as identity loss between the SR image and HR image by calculating the similarity score of this information. It is noted that the output of the last second layer of VGGFace2 is used as the identity information of the facial image. The parameters in VGGFace2 are fixed during training.

9.3.1.2 Training Network

In this method, the high-resolution images in the portrait image database are blurred and low-quality processed by the method in [44]. And then, the high-resolution images and B-LR images are used to construct the training database. To further optimize the model, we designed the following loss function.

9.3.1.2.1 Reconstructed Loss Function

The mean squared error (MSE) loss is used to reconstruct the SR face image by calculating the pixel-wise change between the ground-truth image and SR image of SR-Gnet. Due to the SR-Gnet aiming to generate the SR image with a different upscaling factor, we also use the MSE loss to optimize the model based on the HR images and SR images with three upsampled factors, including ×4, ×8, and ×16. Thus, the different upscaling factor version of MSE loss is defined by

$$L_{duf-mse} = \sum_{j\in\{\times4,\times8,\times16\}} w_j \left\| I_j^{HR} - I_j^{SR} \right\|_F^2 \tag{9.5}$$

where the ground-truth HR images I_j^{HR} is generated by downsampling the ground-truth HR image I^{HR} with the factor j. w_j is the j-th weight parameter to control the effect of the j-th branch. It is noted that the quality of the SR image with a low factor affects generated results with a high factor. Thus, we give more weight to control the branch with fewer factors.

9.3.1.2.2 *Perceptual Loss Function*

Although the reconstructed results can get higher peak signal-to-noise ratio (PSNR) values by using the above MSE loss function, the generated result cannot obtain a good visualizing quality. According to [45], perceptual loss function is constructed by the VGG16 network and can advance the visualizing effect of the SR image. Therefore, the perceptual loss between the SR image and the HR image is defined as

$$L_{per} = \frac{1}{C_k H_k W_k} \left\| \phi_k \left(I^{SR} \right) - \phi_k \left(I^{HR} \right) \right\|_2^2 , \tag{9.6}$$

where ϕ_k denotes the output of the k-th convolution layer of the VGG16 [46], and C_k, H_k, and W_k denote the channel, length, and width of the output ϕ_j. The perceptual loss is used for constructing the generated SR image, which has a similar content with that of the HR image.

9.3.1.2.3 *Adversarial Loss Function*

It is well known that adversarial loss can promote the prior distribution of the generated SR face image, which can be similar to prior distribution of the HR face images. In general, the proposed generated network would be trained to learn a map that has a similar distribution of ground-truth image data and the output can fool with the discriminator network. Meanwhile, the discriminator network would be trained to ensure that the result from the generative network is identified as fake and the ground-truth image is identified as truth. Thus, the proposed SR-Gnet is denoted as the generated network, which generates the multilevel SR images from the LR face image.

According to WGAN-GP [41], the proposed SR-Gnet and Dnet are trained by using the adversarial loss function

$$\begin{cases} L_G = \min_G - E_{x\sim P_{SR}} \left[D\big(G(x)\big) \right], \\ L_D = \max E_{x\sim P_{SR}} \left[D(x) \right] - E_{x\sim P_{GT}} \left[D\big(G(x)\big) \right], \end{cases} \tag{9.7}$$

where P_{SR} and P_{GT} denote the distribution of generated image data and ground-truth image data, respectively. x is the LR image input.

9.3.1.2.4 Consistent-Identity Loss Function

As mentioned in the introduction, it is key that the restored face image should have the same identity as the LR face image. Although perceptual loss can promote the visualizing effect of the generated image, it cannot ensure that the information of the generated face image is right. Therefore, the ID-Evalnet based on MTCNN and VGGface2 is used to train the proposed network by comparing higher-level features of the SR facial image and ground-truth face image. The consistent-identity loss can be denoted as

$$L_{id} = 1 - \frac{V\left(A^{SR}\right)V\left(A^{HR}\right)}{\left\|V\left(A^{SR}\right)\right\|_2 \left\|V\left(A^{HR}\right)\right\|_2}, \tag{9.8}$$

where $V()$ denotes the network of VGGface2 without the last layer, and $\| \ \|_2$ denotes the L_2 norm.

Therefore, according to (9.5–9.8), the full loss function for training the whole model is written as

$$L_{all} = \lambda_1 L_{duf-mse} + \lambda_2 L_{per} + \lambda_3 L_G + \lambda_4 L_{id}, \tag{9.9}$$

where $\lambda_1, \lambda_2, \lambda_3,$ and λ_4 denote the weighted parameter to balance each subfunction.

9.3.1.3 Prediction Model

The low-quality face image is extracted from the video surveillance, which is denoted as the input of the model. After high-resolution generation and deblurring by the proposed model, a clearer face image is finally obtained. Specifically, the identity information of the generated high-resolution face image is persistent with the identity information of the real facial image. The generated clear face image lays the foundation for related applications such as face feature extraction and face recognition.

9.3.2 Standard Face Generation and Face Recognition

After calculating the super-resolution facial image by using the algorithm of Section 9.3.2, we can recover low-quality blurred faces and obtain high-resolution face images. However, these face images also have various nonlimiting factors, including facial expression, facial pose, shooting lighting factors, and so on. Thus, the key issue is how to generate a standard positive facial image from a super-resolution facial image, which is good for feature extraction and recognition of facial images in the subsequent operations. Therefore, we introduce a standard face generation method (SFGM) based on the generative adversarial mechanism (GAM) and attention mechanism (AM). This method designs the model of the network based on the related deep-learning model to obtain the standard positive face images, which can be used for face recognition in the single-sample facial database.

According to the paper in [47], the design of the SFGM mainly includes the following steps: design step of the training data set, designing and training step of the model, and prediction step. First, the design step of the training data set is mainly to construct face codes (FCs) with various nonlimiting factors for each face image by using the relevant annotation data of the RaFD data set and the IAIR face data set. It is noted that nonlimiting factors include facial expressions factors, facial pose factors, shooting lighting factors, and so on. Meanwhile, FCs and facial images are the input of the SFGM. Second, the designing

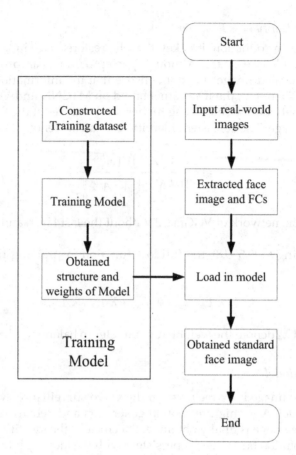

FIGURE 9.7
The flowchart of the SFGM.

and training step of the model is mainly to use the relevant principles of the GAM and AM to design the corresponding network structure, and obtain weights of the network model after using the constructed facial data set to train the proposed SFGM. Third, the prediction step is mainly to use the pretrained model to deal with the facial images that are obtained from the real world, and then the predicted results can be obtained. As shown in Figure 9.7, that is the flowchart of the SFGM. In the next section, details of the proposed method will be introduced.

9.3.2.1 Constructed Training Data Set

In general, the current face data sets are used for recognition tasks. However, these data sets cannot satisfy the requirement of unified information encoding. Therefore, it is necessary to integrate the existing database to construct a suitable database for the SFGM. As shown in Figure 9.8, there is the flowchart of constructing the face images and FCs.

Specifically, we collect the face data set of the RaFD face data set and the IAIR face data set. And then, we construct FCs with various nonlimiting factors for each face image, where nonlimiting factors include facial expression factors, facial pose factors, and shooting lighting factors. The encoded facial image constitutes an information unit $U = \{L_u, E_u, A_u\}$, including 8-bit illumination coding L_u, 8-bit expression coding E_u, and 19-bit gesture coding A_u.

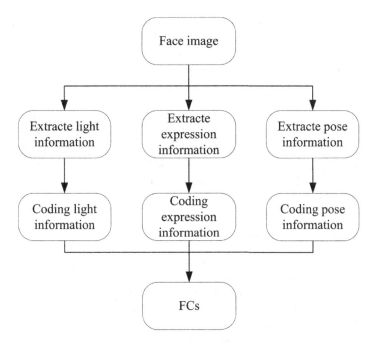

FIGURE 9.8
The flowchart of generating the training data set.

Furthermore, during the processing data, the facial information of the face data set needs to be encoded, which is divided into two types of nonlimiting face images and standard front natural face images. Therefore, specific steps are shown as follows.

9.3.2.1.1 Facial Information Coding

For different face data in the data set, a face code with a variety of nonlimiting factors is constructed for each face image, where the nonlimiting factors include facial expression factors, facial pose factors and shooting lighting factors, and so on. The rules for encoding face images are as follows:

At first, the facial expression factors are divided into eight situations, including happy, angry, sad, contempt, disappointment, fear, surprise, and natural. Thus, the expressional code of the face image is defined as $E_u = (E_{u1}, E_{u2}, ..., E_{u8})$, where E_{ul} denotes the l-th expression, and $l = 0, 1, 2, ..., 8$, whose value is set between 0 and 1. It is noted that $E_u = (0, 0, ..., 1)$ is denoted as the natural expression.

Second, face lighting factors are divided into eight situations, including positive lighting, light from the left, light from the right, and a combination of these three light forms. In more detail, all situations of face lighting factors define as positive lighting, light from the left, light from the right, light from the left and front, light from the right and front, light from the left and right, no lighting, and light from right-left-front. Thus, the lighting code of the face image is defined as $L_u = (L_{u1}, L_{u2}, ..., L_{u8})$, where L_{un} denotes the n-th lighting, and $n = 0, 1, 2, ..., 8$ and its value is set between 0 and 1. It is noted that $L_u = (0, 0, ..., 1)$ is denoted as the front lighting.

Third, the face pose factors are divided into 19 cases, including 9 poses for the left face at intervals of 10°, 9 poses for the right face at intervals of 10°, and the positive face pose. Thus, the lighting code of the face image is defined as $A_u = (A_{u1}, A_{u2}, ..., A_{um}, ..., A_{u19})$, where denotes the m-th facial pose, and $m = 0, 1, 2,...,19$ and its value is set between 0 and 1. It is noted that $A_u = (0,0,...,1)$ is denoted as the front lighting.

At last, the face information encoding is integrated into unified information encoding $U = \{L_u, E_u, A_u\}$, which is one-dimensional information with 35-bits.

9.3.2.1.2 Face Data Classification

We will classify the encoded face data set into nonlimiting face images and standard frontal natural clear face images. In detail, the face images with the unified coding information $U_0 = (L_u(0,0,...,1), E_u(0,0,...,1), A_u(0,0,...,1),)$ are used as the standard frontal natural clear face images that are used as the target of the proposed model. Other face images of the encoded face data set are defined as nonlimiting facial images, which are the input images of the proposed model.

9.3.2.2 Constructed Network Model

According to the purpose of the study, the network model includes three subnetworks, including the image generator subnetwork (IGsN) that generates a standard face, the model discriminator subnetwork (MDsN) that discriminates the generated results, and the image reduction subnetwork (IRsN) that restores the generated results. First, the image generator subnetwork and AM are used to generate the standard face of the input face image. And then, the model discriminator subnetwork is used to discriminate the generated image and the ground-truth image. Finally, after constructing an image reduction subnetwork, it is used to restore the generated image. The restoration result is compared with the input image, which can be used to optimize and constrain the network model.

9.3.2.2.1 Designed Network

Supposed the input image is Y, the corresponding original unified information code is defined as U_y. Meanwhile, the generated standard face image is defined as I_o whose corresponding FC is defined as $\overline{U_0}$, and the corresponding standard face image in the database is defined as I whose corresponding FC is defined as U_0.

In the image generator subnetwork, its inputs are image Y and $\overline{U_0}$. In this model, two encode-decode networks G_c, G_f, and one encode-decoder are designed. And then, the color information C and attention information F of the input image can be obtained by using the above networks G_c and G_f, respectively. Further, the charged face image I_i can be generated. In order to further constrain the correctness of the generated standard-face image, the identity information extracted by VGGface2 [43] is used to generate the standard face image. It is noted that the output of the last second layer of VGGFace2 is used as the identity information of the facial image. The detail is shown as

$$\begin{cases} C = G_c(Y, U_0) \quad F = G_f(Y, U_0) \\ I_i = (1 - F) \odot C + F \odot Y \\ I_o = De(En(I_i), VGG(Y)) \end{cases} \tag{9.10}$$

where $\odot$ denotes element-wise multiplication of matrix, $VGG(\cdot)$ denotes the VGGface2, $En(\cdot)$ denotes the encoder, and the $De(\cdot)$ denotes the decoder.

Therefore, the encode-decode networks G_c is designed to focus on the color information and texture information of face image. Meanwhile, encode-decode networks G_f is designed to focus on the areas of the face that need to be changed. In addition, the encode-decoder network is designed to keep the identity information of generated face image, which is similar to the input face image.

In the model discriminator subnetwork, its input is the image I_o, which is generated from IGsN. Similar to paper [47], we also use two deep convolution networks, including image discrimination subnetwork D_I and coding information discrimination subnetwork D_U. The subnetwork D_I is used to discriminate that the generated standard face image I_o is considered as fake and the corresponding standard face image I of the database is considered as true. Meanwhile, the subnetwork D_U is used to discriminate that the FCs $\overline{U}_0$ of generated standard face image I_o is considered as fake, and the FCs U_0 of corresponding standard face image I of the database is considered as true.

In the image reduction subnetwork, its inputs include the generated standard face image I_o and the corresponding original FCs U_y of the input image Y. The structure of IRsN is consistent with that of the IGsN. The result of the network IRsN is denoted as $\overline{Y}$. By comparing the restoration result with the input image Y, the whole network can be trained by the cyclic optimization.

9.3.2.2.2 Process of the Whole Network

According to the above network structure, the specific processing flow of the network model based on the generating confrontation mechanism and the attention mechanism is as follows.

First, the image Y and the FCs U_0 of the corresponding standard face image I are used as the input of the IGsN, which can generate the standard face image I_o.

Second, in order to discriminate against the real-world image and generated image, we use the image discrimination subnetwork D_I to discriminate the generated image I_o and corresponding standard face image I (real-world image) in the data set. Meanwhile, the FCs $\overline{U}_0$ of the generated image I_o and the FCs U_0 of the standard face image I are used as the input of the coding information discrimination subnetwork D_U. Based on the previously optimized method, the IGsN and the MDsN can be achieved as common progress.

Finally, in order to accomplish the goal that the network model can be optimized cyclically, the IRsN is designed, which can restore the generated standard face image to the restored facial image by using the FCs U_y of the original input image Y. After comparing the restored result with the input image Y, the whole model can be optimized by using some loss function. At last, the network can achieve to remove the nonlimited factors of face images.

9.3.2.2.3 Architecture of the Whole Network

As shown in Figure 9.9, the architecture of the designed network includes the IGsN that generates a standard face, MDsN that discriminates the generated results, and IRsN that restores the generated results, where the parameters of the IGsN and the IRsN are shared with each other. The structure of the IGsN is shown in Figure 9.10 and the structure of MDsN is shown in Figure 9.11. The related parameters are shown as follows.

On one hand, the parameters of the IGsN and the IRsN are consistent. Here, each subnetwork includes the generated network of color information and the generated network of attention. In detail, the generated network of color information, which generates the image of color information with 3 channels, includes 8 convolution layers and 7 deconvolution layers, where the size of the kernel and the step in each layer are established as 5 and 1, respectively. Meanwhile, the generated network of attention, which generates the attention image with 1 channel, includes 8 convolution layers and 7 deconvolution

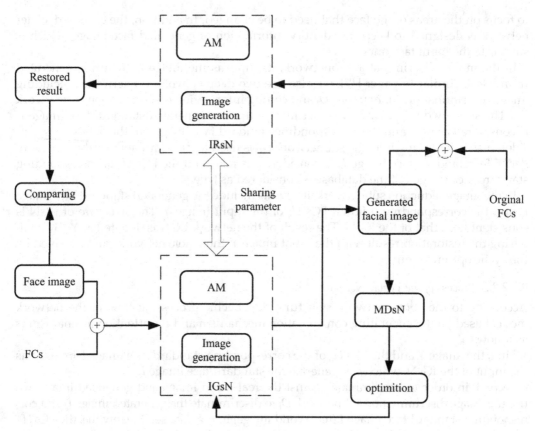

FIGURE 9.9
Architecture of the designed network.

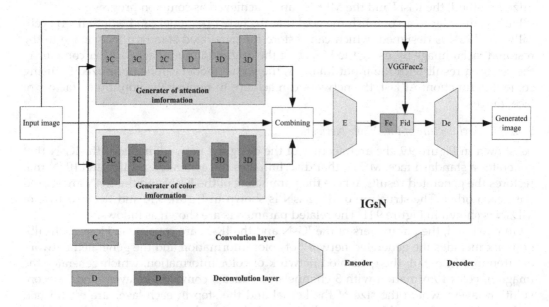

FIGURE 9.10
Structure of the IGsN.

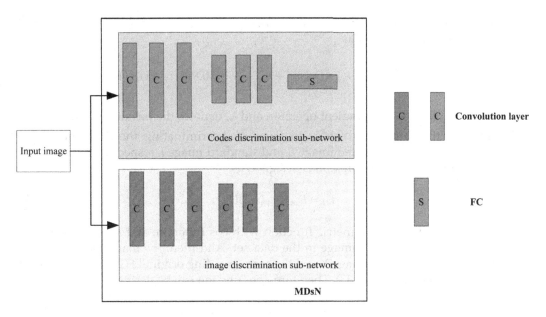

FIGURE 9.11
Structure of the MDsN.

layers, where the size of the kernel and the step in each layer are established as 5 and 1, respectively.

On the other hand, the MDsN includes the image discrimination subnetwork and coding information discrimination subnetwork. In detail, the image discrimination subnetwork includes 6 convolution layers, where the size of the kernel and the step in each layer are established as 5 and 1, respectively. Meanwhile, the coding information discrimination subnetwork, which generates one-dimensional FCs with N-bits, includes 6 convolution layers, where the kernel size and the step of each layer are established as 5 and 1, respectively.

9.3.2.3 Training Model

Taking images with various unrestricted factors as an input of the designed model, the model can achieve convergence after optimizing the label similarity and output of the IGsN, MDsN, and IRsN. In detail, the loss functions of the model are designed as follows.

1. Optimize the difference between the standard-facial image I_o generated by the IGsN and the corresponding standard facial image I in the database. Thus, we establish the image loss function as

$$L_I = \frac{1}{H \times W} \left\| D_I(I_o) - D_I(I) \right\|_2^2 \tag{9.11}$$

where H and W denote the height and width of the input image, respectively. $D_I(I_o)$ and $D_I(I)$ denote the discriminated results of I_o and I by using the image discrimination subnetwork D_I, respectively. Meanwhile, considering the effectiveness of gradient loss, a gradient-based penalty term is aggregated into the image loss function (9.11), which can advance the quality of the generated image. The image loss function is set as

$$L_I = \frac{1}{H \times W} \left\| D_I(I_o) - D_I(I) \right\|_2^2 + \lambda_I \frac{1}{H \times W} \left\| \nabla D_I(I_o) - \nabla D_I(I) \right\|_1 \tag{9.12}$$

where $\nabla(\cdot)$ denotes the gradient operator, and λ_I denotes the penalty weight.

2. Optimize the difference of FCs. In favor of discriminating the different FCs extracted from the generated image I_o and standard image I, respectively, the conditional expression loss function is designed as

$$L_U = F_{\cos}\left(D_U(I_o), U_0\right) \tag{9.13}$$

where $F_{\cos}(\cdot)$ denotes the metric function with cos function, and U_0 denotes the FCs of the standard face image in the data set. And then, the mapping relationship between the input image Y and the corresponding original FCs U_y, should be added into the function (9.13). Therefore, the function can be designed as

$$L_U = F_{\cos}\left(D_U(I_o), U_0\right) + F_{\cos}\left(D_U(Y), U_y\right) \tag{9.14}$$

where $D_U(I_o)$ and $D_U(Y)$ denote the discriminated results of image I_o and Y by using coding information discrimination D_U, respectively.

3. Optimize the difference between the original image and the result of the IRsN. The image I_o generated by the input generator is restored by using the original FCs U_y, which is used to compare the result of the IRsN with the original image Y. Thus, the restored loss function is designed as

$$L_r = \frac{1}{H \times W} \left\| G\left(G(I_o, U_y)\right) - Y \right\|_1 \tag{9.15}$$

Therefore, according to functions (9.12), (9.14) and (9.15), the whole loss function is shown as

$$L = \lambda_1 L_I + \lambda_2 L_U + \lambda_3 L_r + \lambda_4 L_{adv} \tag{9.16}$$

where λ_1, λ_2, λ_3, and λ_4 denote the weight for balancing each subfunction, and L_{adv} denotes the adversarial loss function according to WGAN-GP [41].

By optimizing the function (9.16), the network model can accomplish to the convergence. And then, the generator structure and weights for generating standard faces can be obtained.

9.3.2.4 Model Prediction

After extracting the face form the actual image as the input of the model, we can obtain a more standard face image by controlling the FCs. First, the face image is detected from the natural image by using the MTCNN method. And then, the standard face image can be generated from the detected face image by using the trained model and FCs. In addition, it can be predicted that we can change other structures of the face, such as controlling other expressions, or other face poses by setting different FCs.

9.3.3 Face Recognition Architecture Based on Edge Computing and Cloud Coordination

In the FoPS, a large number of face images are extracted from monitoring data support for training better deep learning networks. However, huge monitoring data also brings some problems, such as the effectiveness of data transmission and training problems of the deep model. Thus, designing the reasonable architecture of a deep learning network is a feasible method to solve these issues. When designing a network based on edge points and clouds, it is important to increase the response speed of face recognition in the subsystem of edge points and improve the accuracy of overall face recognition in the cloud.

Edge computing is used to process data by using the platforms such as network calculation in the edge point, which is set close to the data sources [48–50]. Edge computing is contributed to construct the IoT system. For example, the smartphone can be used as the edge point between the user and the cloud. By making the process-data units near the generation-data units, edge computing can improve the system effectiveness, dwindle the response time of the task, and upgrade the allocation bandwidth.

Therefore, inspired by the methods in [51, 52], we propose the architecture of face recognition based on edge computing and cloud coordination. First, in each edge point, the local model is trained by using local data and edge computing technology. Each local model in the edge point is trained to respond to the regional face recognition tasks. And then, the few discriminated results and a local model of each edge point are transmitted to the cloud. Finally, all local models are utilized to train an advanced face recognition model with higher accuracy by using cloud coordination. It is noted that multiple edge points should be deployed according to the requirements of tasks and each edge point should implement a data front for capturing images and a lightweight server for processing data.

First, in detail, local data is used to train the edge-node face recognition model in each edge node. Second, few data and trained local models of face recognition are transmitted from multiple edge nodes to the cloud server. Third, the uploaded data and local model are used to train and learn a global model of face recognition by using the form of cloud coordination. Finally, for detecting and recognizing the face image, the edge node uses the trained local model to analyze and provide simple feedback on the task. Meanwhile, the cloud server uses the global face recognition model to analyze the suspicious data uploaded from the edge points and returns the result to each edge node. As shown in Figure 9.12, it is the flowchart of the proposed method.

Conferring with the introduction, the proposed architecture of face recognition includes the step for training the model in edge node, the step for transporting data and model, the step for training the global system in the cloud, and the feedback step of tasks. In detail, the training step of the edge node model means that the lightweight deep learning networks in each edge node are designed and trained according to the task. The transmission step of data and model mainly focuses on uploading the corresponding model results of each edge node. Finally, the training step of the global model focuses on training the global model about face recognition by using the uploaded data and local models. The weight of the global face recognition model can be learned by using the cloud coordination. The specific operation steps would be introduced as follows.

9.3.3.1 Edge Node Deployment

In the FoPS, we should design the edge nodes in the key area according to the task demand. It is noted that each edge node should deploy the smart front-point equipment

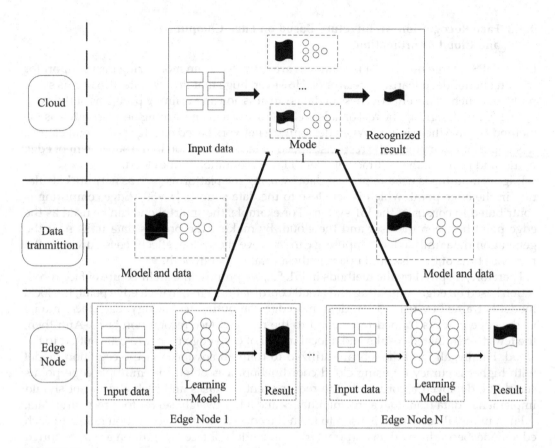

FIGURE 9.12
Architecture of face recognition by edge computing technology and cloud coordination.

that includes a camera and lightweight server. Meanwhile, the principles for selecting edge nodes are shown as follows. On one hand, due to solving the issue of public security, the selected area of edge node would be focused on the key area with high mobility, including community entrances, security point within the community, traffic intersections, railway stations, and so on. In addition, due to making a processing point of data close to the collecting point of data, the lightweight server should be used to process the captured data. For example, the lightweight server can use the local data of the edge node to train the face recognition model. In this way, the time cost of transmitting data can be reduced and the real-time response to data can be advanced.

9.3.3.2 Design of Local Face Recognition Model and Data Transmission

Smart front-point equipment is deployed to obtain the surveillance video in the edge node. And then, the lightweight server is used to respond to the basic task after training the local face recognition model. Furthermore, for the training of face recognition models at edge nodes, we need some steps as follows.

First, the face data is collected from the surveillance video. Furthermore, the obtained corresponding face image data x_i can be obtained from the surveillance video by using the face detection and extraction algorithm [42].

Second, it is supported that there are n edge notes. Meanwhile, the trained data of each edge note is defined as x_i, and the local database of corresponding lightweight sever is defined as $\overline{x}_i$. Thus, we can obtain n local face recognition model after training. For the i-th edge node, the local face recognition model is shown as

$$M_i = Model_i(x_i), \ i = 1,2,3,...,n \tag{9.17}$$

and

$$S_i = match_i\left(M_i, Model_i(\overline{x})\right), \ i = 1,2,3,...,n \tag{9.18}$$

where $Model_i(\cdot)$ denotes the local method for extracting facial feature in the i-th edge node [52], and $match_i(\cdot)$ denotes the matching model of the i-th edge node. Meanwhile, L_i denotes the data features after extracting by the model. And S_i denotes the recognition result of the face image.

Finally, the recognized results of each edge node are used to take feedback for the task of corresponding edge node.

Specifically, for each edge node, the network is a simple deep learning network, as shown in Figure 9.13. The whole network includes three convolution layers with kernel size 3×3, one convolution layer with kernel size 1×1, three pooling layers, and one classification layer. First, the face image is normalized as the standard image with size $3 \times 64 \times 64$. Then, high-dimensional face feature information is obtained after processing by four convolution layers and three pooling layers. Finally, the recognition result of the face image can be obtained after processing by one classification layer.

After training the face recognition network, the uploaded content is few training data and the basic model of each edge node in order to reduce the broadband occupation for uploading data. In detail, the uploaded data includes the trained feature extraction model $Model = [Model_1, Model_2,..., Model_n]$ and few training data $X = [x_1', x_2',..., x_n']$. Meanwhile, the condition for the uploading channel just requires an ordinary bandwidth and a normal transmission rate of internet.

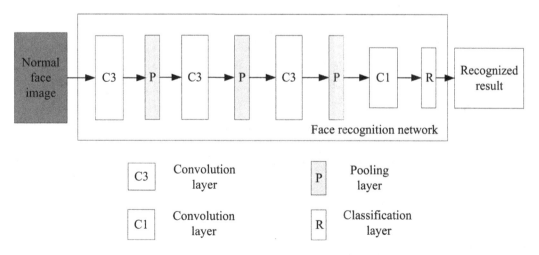

FIGURE 9.13
Face recognition network in edge point.

9.3.3.3 Cloud Model Designing and Training

According to the uploaded data and model, the cloud can construct a global deep learning network by using cloud coordination. After jointly processing the uploaded models, the global face recognition model can be optimized and the accuracy of the global model can be advanced. In detail, the proposed structure is designed as follows.

First, all uploaded local models of edge nodes are combined linearly. It is noted that the local model of each edge node is the trained result by using a huge local face data set. Thus, the structure and parameter of local models do not need to be changed in the cloud. The input feature F for the optimizing model can be obtained by splicing the facial feature, which is processed by each local model. The process is shown as

$$\begin{cases} Loc'_i = Model_i\left(x'_i\right), i = 1, 2, .., n \\ F = \left[Loc'_1, Loc'_2, ..., Loc'_n\right] \end{cases} \tag{9.19}$$

Second, the global model needs to be optimized. According to the task of public security, we optimize the global model based on the papers [51, 53].

1. Build an auto-encoder. As shown in Figure 9.14, an auto-encoder includes the feature coding layer, middle layer, and reconstruction layer. The reconstructive feature can be obtained by using the model

$$\begin{cases} H = \sigma_f\left(w_f F + b_f\right) \\ F' = \sigma_r\left(w_r H + b_r\right) \end{cases} \tag{9.20}$$

where H denotes the output feature of the middle layer, and σ_f and σ_r denote the activation function of the feature coding layer and reconstruction layer, respectively. Meanwhile, $\left\{w_f, b_f\right\}$ and $\left\{w_r, b_r\right\}$ denote the parameters of the feature

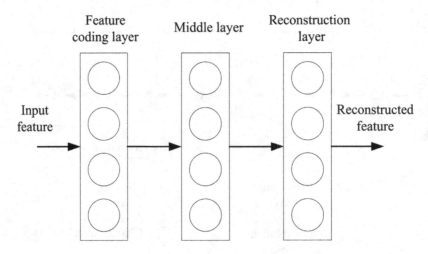

FIGURE 9.14
The basic framework of the auto-encoder.

coding layer and feature reconstruction layer, respectively. Furthermore, the proposed auto-encoder can be constructed by using the following loss function:

$$\min_{w_f, w_r, b_f, b_r} \sum \|F - F'\|_F^2 \tag{9.21}$$

After optimizing the loss function, we can obtain the parameter of the stable auto-encoder.

2. Expanding the auto-encoder. After training the last auto-encoder, a feature coding layer is joined behind the first feature coding layer. And then, a reconstruction layer is joined in front of the corresponding reconstruction layer.

3. The stacked network model by using (2) is trained, and then, we should repeat the previous step (2).

4. After training multi-iteration, we can construct the stacked auto-encoder, as shown in Figure 9.15.

5. We discard the feature reconstruction layers of the trained stacked network, and add a classifier layer (such as a Softmax layer) after the feature encoding network. Finally, the input feature F can be classified. The whole face recognition model is shown in Figure 9.16.

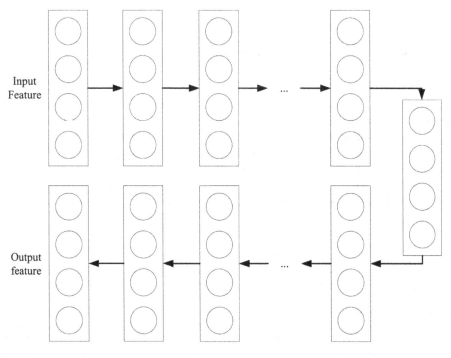

FIGURE 9.15
Trained model of stacked auto-encoder.

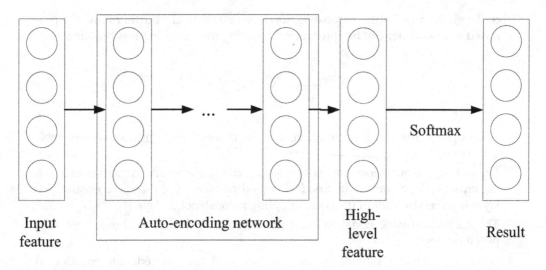

FIGURE 9.16
Global face recognition model in the cloud.

9.3.3.4 Tasks Feedback

After training the global face recognition model, the cloud server can use the global model to analyze the suspicious data that is uploaded from the edge point. And then, the recognition result can be transmitted to the corresponding edge node and respond with the task.

9.4 Conclusion

IoT with an image processing function has been the focus of various researchers, which is a meaningful aspect in constructing smarter cities. At first, we introduced the theory and applications of IoT with image-processing technology. Meanwhile, we discussed three main problems of IoT with facial image in the FoPS, including recovery of low-quality facial images, reconstruction of standard facial image, and respond speed of face recognition in big data. Furthermore, some processing methods are discussed according to these issues in detail. Finally, these methods provide analysis and feasible schemes for solving these problems.

Acknowledgments

This work was supported by Key-Area Research and Development Program of Guangdong Province under the grant 2018B010108001, and National Nature Science Foundation of China under the grant 61973125.

References

1. Zikria, Y. Bin, Yu, H., Afzal, M.K., Rehmani, M.H., and Hahm, O. 2018. Internet of Things (IoT): Operating System, Applications and Protocols Design, and Validation Techniques. *Future Generation Computer Systems*, 88, 699–706.
2. Gonzalez, R. and Woods, R. 1977. *Digital Image Processing*. Upper Saddle River, NJ: Prentice Hall.
3. Chan, T., Jia, K., Gao, S., Lu, J., Zeng, Z., and Ma, Y. 2015. PCANet: A Simple Deep Learning Baseline for Image Classification? *IEEE Transactions on Image Processing*, 24 (12), 5017–5032.
4. He, K., Zhang, X., Ren, S., and Sun, J. 2016. Deep Residual Learning for Image Recognition. In: *2016 IEEE Conference on Computer Vision and Pattern Recognition (CVPR)*. 770–778.
5. Han, J., Zhang, D., Cheng, G., Guo, L., and Ren, J. 2015. Object Detection in Optical Remote Sensing Images Based on Weakly Supervised Learning and High-Level Feature Learning. *IEEE Transactions on Geoscience and Remote Sensing*, 53 (6), 3325–3337.
6. Han, J., Zhang, D., Cheng, G., Guo, L., and Ren, J. 2015. Object Detection in Optical Remote Sensing Images Based on Weakly Supervised Learning and High-Level Feature Learning. *IEEE Transactions on Geoscience and Remote Sensing*, 53 (6), 3325–3337.
7. Atzori, L., Iera, A., and Morabito, G. 2010. The Internet of Things: A Survey. *Computer Networks*, 54 (15), 2787–2805.
8. Daniel Minoli. 2013. Internet of Things Application Examples. In: *Building the Internet of Things with IPv6 and MIPv6*. John Wiley & Sons, 48–96.
9. Dinesh, M and Sudharman, K. 2016. Real Time Intelligent Image Processing System with High Speed Secured Internet of Things: Image Processor with IOT. In: *2016 International Conference on Information Communication and Embedded Systems (ICICES)*. 1–5.
10. Nauman, A., Qadri, Y.A., Amjad, M., Zikria, Y.B., Afzal, M.K., and Kim, S.W. 2020. Multimedia Internet of Things: A Comprehensive Survey. *IEEE Access*, 8, 8202–8250.
11. Hsu, C., Lin, H., Kang, L., Weng, M., Chang, C., and You, T. 2017. 3D Modeling for Steel Billet Images. In: *2017 IEEE International Conference on Consumer Electronics–Taiwan (ICCE-TW)*. 5–6.
12. Kulkarni, P.H., Kute, P.D., and More, V.N. 2016. IoT Based Data Processing for Automated Industrial Meter Reader Using Raspberry Pi. In: *2016 International Conference on Internet of Things and Applications (IOTA)*. 107–111.
13. Kapoor, A., Bhat, S.I., Shidnal, S., and Mehra, A. 2016. Implementation of IoT (Internet of Things) and Image Processing in Smart Agriculture. In: *2016 International Conference on Computation System and Information Technology for Sustainable Solutions (CSITSS)*. 21–26.
14. Liao, M.-S., Chen, S.-F., Chou, C.-Y., Chen, H.-Y., Yeh, S.-H., Chang, Y.-C., and Jiang, J.-A. 2017. On Precisely Relating the Growth of Phalaenopsis Leaves to Greenhouse Environmental Factors by Using an IoT-based Monitoring System. *Computers and Electronics in Agriculture*, 136, 125–139.
15. Sharma, Lavanya, and Lohan, Nirvikar. Performance Analysis of Moving Object Detection Using BGS Techniques in Visual Surveillance. *International Journal of Spatiotemporal Data Science, Inderscience*, Vol. 1, pp. 22–53, January 2019.
16. Tran, H.A.M., Ngo, H.Q.T., Nguyen, T.P., and Nguyen, H. 2018. Design of Green Agriculture System Using Internet of Things and Image Processing Techniques. In: *2018 4th International Conference on Green Technology and Sustainable Development (GTSD)*. 28–32.
17. Klein, L.J., Hamann, H.F., Hinds, N., Guha, S., Sanchez, L., Sams, B., and Dokoozlian, N., 2018r. Closed Loop Controlled Precision Irrigation Sensor Network. *IEEE Internet of Things Journal*, 5 (6), 4580–4588.
18. Elias, A.R., Golubovic, N., Krintz, C., and Wolski, R. 2017. Where's the Bear? Automating Wildlife Image Processing Using IoT and Edge Cloud Systems. In: *2017 IEEE/ACM Second International Conference on Internet-of-Things Design and Implementation (IoTDI)*. 247–258.
19. George, A.M., George, V.I., and George, M.A. 2018. IOT Based Smart Traffic Light Control System. In: *2018 International Conference on Control, Power, Communication and Computing Technologies (ICCPCCT)*. 148–151.

20. Reddy, G.V.P. and Nagaraja, S.R. 2016. Image Based Obstacle Detection and Path Planning for Solar Powered Autonomous Vehicle. In: *2016 International Conference on Robotics and Automation for Humanitarian Applications (RAHA)*. 1–7.

21. Cai, B.Y., Alvarez, R., Sit, M., Duarte, F., and Ratti, C., 2019d. Deep Learning-Based Video System for Accurate and Real-Time Parking Measurement. *IEEE Internet of Things Journal*, 6 (5), 7693–7701.

22. Chen, N., Chen, Y., You, Y., Ling, H., Liang, P., and Zimmermann, R. 2016. Dynamic Urban Surveillance Video Stream Processing Using Fog Computing. In: *2016 IEEE Second International Conference on Multimedia Big Data (BigMM)*. 105–112.

23. Waheed, Z., Akram, M.U., Waheed, A., and Shaukat, A. 2015. Robust extraction of blood vessels for retinal recognition. In: *2015 Second International Conference on Information Security and Cyber Forensics (InfoSec)*. 1–4.

24. Zhang, Z., Li, M., Xia, F., and Ma, J. 2011. An Improved Iris Localization Method for Authentication System. In: 2011 International Conference on Internet of Things and 4th International Conference on Cyber, Physical and Social Computing. 663–666.

25. Yin, F., Lee, B.H., Yow, A.P., Quan, Y., and Wong, D.W.K. 2016. Automatic Ocular Disease Screening and Monitoring Using a Hybrid Cloud System. In: *2016 IEEE International Conference on Internet of Things (iThings) and IEEE Green Computing and Communications (GreenCom) and IEEE Cyber, Physical and Social Computing (CPSCom) and IEEE Smart Data (SmartData)*. 263–268.

26. Cheng, Y., Jiao, L., Li, Z., and Cao, X. 2014. An Improved Retinal Modeling for Illumination Face Recognition. In: *2014 IEEE International Conference on Image Processing (ICIP)*. 244–247.

27. Ma, Y., Dagnino, G., Georgilas, I., and Dogramadzi, S. 2017. Automatic Tool Detection in X-Ray Images for Robotic Assisted Joint Fracture Surgery. In: *2017 IEEE International Conference on Internet of Things (iThings) and IEEE Green Computing and Communications (GreenCom) and IEEE Cyber, Physical and Social Computing (CPSCom) and IEEE Smart Data (SmartData)*. 883–887.

28. QasemiZadeh, B., Shen, J., O'Neill, I., Miller, P., Hanna, P., Stewart, D., and Wang, H. 2009. A Speech Based Approach to Surveillance Video Retrieval. In: 2009 6th IEEE International Conference on Advanced Video and Signal Based Surveillance. 336–339.

29. Basri, A.H.H., Ibrahim, S.N., Malik, N.A., and Asnawi, A.L. 2018. Integrated Surveillance System with Mobile Application. In: *2018 7th International Conference on Computer and Communication Engineering (ICCCE)*. 218–222.

30. Wang, J., Amos, B., Das, A., Pillai, P., Sadeh, N., and Satyanarayanan, M. 2017. A Scalable and Privacy-Aware IoT Service for Live Video Analytics. *In: Proceedings of the 8th ACM on Multimedia Systems Conference*. New York, NY: Association for Computing Machinery, 38–49.

31. Egmont-Petersen, M., De Ridder, D., and Handels, H. 2002. Image Processing with Neural Networks- A Review. *Pattern Recognition*, 35 (10), 2279–2301.

32. Pan, J., Sun, D., Pfister, H., and Yang, M.H. December 2016. Blind image deblurring using dark channel prior. In: *Proceedings of the IEEE Computer Society Conference on Computer Vision and Pattern Recognition*, 1628–1636.

33. Lim, B., Son, S., Kim, H., Nah, S., and Lee, K.M. 2017. Enhanced Deep Residual Networks for Single Image Super-Resolution. In: *2017 IEEE Conference on Computer Vision and Pattern Recognition Workshops (CVPRW)*. 1132–1140.

34. Sharma, Lavanya, and Lohan, Nirvikar. Performance Analysis of Moving Object Detection using BGS Techniques. *International Journal of Spatio-Temporal Data Science, Inderscience*, February, 2019.

35. Xu, X., Sun, D., Pan, J., Zhang, Y., Pfister, H., and Yang, M.H. 2017. Learning to Super-Resolve Blurry Face and Text Images. In: *Proceedings of the IEEE International Conference on Computer Vision*. 251–260.

36. Wang, X., Yu, K., Dong, C., and Change Loy, C. 2018. Recovering Realistic Texture in Image Super-Resolution by Deep Spatial Feature Transform. In: Proceedings of the IEEE Computer Society Conference on Computer Vision and Pattern Recognition. 606–615.

37. Ronneberger, O., Fischer, P., and Brox, T. 2015. U-Net: Convolutional Networks for Biomedical Image Segmentation. In: International Conference on Medical Image Computing and Computer-Assisted Intervention(MICCAI). 234–241.

38. Zhang, L. and Zuo, W. 2017. Image Restoration: From Sparse and Low-Rank Priors to Deep Priors [Lecture Notes]. *IEEE Signal Processing Magazine*, 34 (5), 172–179.

39. Pan, J., Liu, R., Su, Z., and Gu, X., 2013y. Kernel Estimation from Salient Structure for Robust Motion Deblurring. *Signal Processing: Image Communication*, 28 (9), 1156–1170.

40. He, K., Zhang, X., Ren, S., and Sun, J. 2016. Deep Residual Learning for Image Recognition. In: *2016 IEEE Conference on Computer Vision and Pattern Recognition (CVPR)*. 770–778.

41. Gulrajani, I., Ahmed, F., Arjovsky, M., Dumoulin, V., and Courville, A. 2017. Improved Training of Wasserstein GANs. *Advances in Neural Information Processing Systems, 2017-Decem*, 5768–5778.

42. Zhang, K., Zhang, Z., Li, Z., and Qiao, Y. 2016. Joint Face Detection and Alignment Using Multitask Cascaded Convolutional Networks. *IEEE Signal Processing Letters*, 23 (10), 1499–1503.

43. Cao, Q., Shen, L., Xie, W., Parkhi, O.M., and Zisserman, A. 2018. VGGFace2: A Dataset for Recognising Faces Across Pose and Age. In: Proceedings – 13th IEEE International Conference on Automatic Face and Gesture Recognition, FG 2018. IEEE, 67–74.

44. Kupyn, O., Budzan, V., Mykhailych, M., Mishkin, D., and Matas, J. 2018. DeblurGAN: Blind Motion Deblurring Using Conditional Adversarial Networks. In: 2018 IEEE/CVF Conference on Computer Vision and Pattern Recognition. 8183–8192.

45. Johnson, J., Alahi, A., and Fei-Fei, L. 2016. Perceptual Losses for Real-Time Style Transfer and Super-Resolution. *In:* B. Leibe, J. Matas, N. Sebe, and M. Welling, (Eds.). *Computer Vision – ECCV 2016.* Cham: Springer International Publishing, 694–711.

46. Szegedy, C., Ioffe, S., Vanhoucke, V., and Alemi, A. 2016. Inception-v4, Inception-ResNet and the Impact of Residual Connections on Learning. In: AAAI Conference on Artificial Intelligence.

47. Pumarola, A., Agudo, A., Martinez, A.M., Sanfeliu, A., and Moreno-Noguer, F. 2018. GANimation: Anatomically-Aware Facial Animation from a Single Image. *In:* V. Ferrari, M. Hebert, C. Sminchisescu, and Y. Weiss, (Eds.). *Lecture Notes in Computer Science (including subseries Lecture Notes in Artificial Intelligence and Lecture Notes in Bioinformatics).* Cham: Springer International Publishing, 835–851.

48. Sharma, Lavanya. 2019. Introduction: From Visual Surveillance to Internet of Things. *In: From Visual Surveillance to Internet of Things.* Chapman Hall/CRC, Vol. 1, p. 14.

49. Sharma, Shubham, Verma, Shubhankar, Kumar, Mohit, and Sharma, Lavanya. 2019 Use of Motion Capture in 3D Animation: Motion Capture Systems, Challenges, and Recent Trends. In: *1st IEEE International Conference on Machine Learning, Big Data, Cloud and Parallel Computing (Com-IT-Con)*, India, 14–16 February. 309–313.

50. Satyanarayanan, M., Simoens, P., Xiao, Y., Pillai, P., Chen, Z., Ha, K., Hu, W., and Amos, B. 2015. Edge Analytics in the Internet of Things. *IEEE Pervasive Computing*, 14 (2), 24–31.

51. Ding, C., Hu, Z., Karmoshi, S., and Zhu, M. 2017. A Novel Two-stage Learning Pipeline for Deep Neural Networks. *Neural Processing Letters*, 46 (1), 159–169.

52. Sharma, Lavanya, Singh, Annapurna, and Yadav, Dileep Kumar. March 2016. Fisher's Linear Discriminant Ratio based Threshold for Moving Human Detection in Thermal Video. *Infrared Physics and Technology*. Elsevier, 78, 118–128.

53. Sharma, Lavanya, and Lohan, Nirvikar, Internet of Things with Object Detection. *In: Handbook of Research on Big Data and the IoT.* IGI Global, 89–100, March, 2019. DOI: 10.4018/978-1-5225-7432-3.ch006.

10

Internet of Things Enabled by Artificial Intelligence

Rinku Sharma Dixit

Department of Business Analytics and Data Sciences, New Delhi Institute of Management
New Delhi, India

Shailee Lohmor Choudhary

Department of Business Analytics and Data Sciences, New Delhi Institute of Management
New Delhi, India

CONTENTS

10.1	Introduction	174
10.2	Literature Review	175
10.3	Disruptive Technologies: Their Evolution and Growth	176
10.4	Smart Systems	177
	10.4.1 Technology Enablers for Smart Systems	178
10.5	Artificial Intelligence: Putting Intelligence into IoT	179
	10.5.1 The Rise of Connected Things	180
	10.5.2 Major AI Technologies for Enabling IoT	181
10.6	Real-Life Applications of AI in IoT Systems	182
	10.6.1 Smart Homes	182
	10.6.2 Smart City	183
	10.6.3 Smart Health	185
	10.6.3.1 Benefits of Smart Health Systems	186
	10.6.4 Use Cases of Smart Healthcare Systems	186
	10.6.4.1 Smart Continuous Glucose Monitoring and Insulin Pens	186
	10.6.4.2 Connected Inhalers	187
	10.6.4.3 Ingestible Sensors	187
	10.6.4.4 Connected Contact Lenses	187
	10.6.4.5 The Apple Watch App that Monitors Depression	187
	10.6.4.6 Apple's ResearchKit and Parkinson's Disease	188
	10.6.5 Smart Transportation System	188
	10.6.5.1 Advanced Traffic Management System	188
	10.6.5.2 Smart Vehicle Control and Safety System	188
	10.6.5.3 Smart Public Transportation System	189
	10.6.5.4 Commercial Vehicle Operation	189
	10.6.5.5 Guiding Principles of ITS	189
	10.6.5.6 Use Cases of Intelligent Transportation Systems	189
	10.6.6 Smart Environment Monitoring Systems	190
	10.6.6.1 Use Cases of the Smart Environment	190
	10.6.7 Smart Security	191

10.7   Proposed Framework: Smart Connected Restaurant
        Management System 192
10.8   Critical Success Factors for AI-Enabled IoT.. 192
10.9   Conclusion 193
References... 193

KEYWORDS: *internet of things, artificial intelligence, smart objects, smart homes, smart city, smart health, smart transportation system, smart security*

10.1 Introduction

The Internet of Things (IoT) in association with artificial intelligence (AI) is transforming the World of Things into a World of Data [1]. Practically anything can be equipped with a sensor [2] and made smart—from a smart watch that monitors your blood pressure, heart rate, and blood sugar levels to a connected factory that oversees every stage of the production process. The impact of IoT will vary between applications but the basic task of extracting new data and improving existing processes, bringing innovation into products and services, and predicting trends and preferences will be uniformly evident [3, 4]. There is a vast potential in IoT and it is estimated that there will be 20.4 billion IoT devices generating zettabytes of data every year by 2020. But to date, implementation of IoT projects has been pretty difficult and, if implemented, the setup remains underutilized because only a fraction of the generated data is analyzed and put to practical use. To utilize this data, we need AI [1, 2, 5, 6]. Within the broad field of AI, it's machine learning that's poised to make the greatest impact [7–9]. It has the potential to enable fast, intelligent decision-making—either in support of human intelligence, or in place of it. Businesses can delegate mundane or complicated tasks to achieve a level of accuracy and efficiency beyond the capabilities of human workers. But putting decisions in the hands of intelligent machines has profound moral and ethical implications [10]. While AI and machine learning are already making intelligent interventions on behalf of humans— in our voice-activated personal assistants, for example—there's work to be done before machines are given full agency [11]. And before we get there, some far-reaching questions will need to be asked— and answered. This chapter explores the disruptive technologies at work to bring the current technologies, which we use, at our disposal. This chapter further discusses the power of AI to explore IoT to its full potential and presents certain use cases where AI has interfaced with IoT and delivered the expected automation and results. The authors also propose a framework for the Smart Connected Restaurant Management System (SCRMS). The proposed framework can be used for connecting and automating a restaurant or a chain of restaurants and thereby create a Smart Connected Restaurant. The proposed framework, comprising of five layers, has been described in detail in Chapter 12. The proposed framework depicts the components of an SCRMS, which after implementation can help gain insights and control of the restaurant processes and systems.

10.2 Literature Review

The internet has changed from a network of computers to an interconnection of things. The authors are envisioning an "Internet of Everything in a Smart Physical Earth" and have suggested complete architecture and components of IoT systems [1]. The data generated from this huge system can be effectively used with AI. The combination of AI and IoT can lead to not only saving money but smart intelligent systems that can reduce the efforts of humans. But these systems would have ethical and security issues. The authors have suggested that as technology grows, these systems will control each other and may rule the human race. Hence, humans need to be in total control of these developments so that the systems are really of use to the human race.

There are serious ethical concerns with the deployment of IoT systems [10] but the fact is that these systems are being deployed and their use is increasing with every passing day. The intrusion of AI is beyond our control and the impact of intelligent technologies is clearly evident in everything we do or happens around us. The authors suggest that there is a need for responsible AI systems. The design and working of the learning processes must be free from bias. Only then we can expect systems that support humans and not control them [3].

The future of technological coalescence is IoT that will transform objects in the real world to Intelligent Virtual Objects connected to each other and to a central controlling unit [2]. IoT aims at unifying everything in the world under a common infrastructural unit that will keep us informed of the state of all its component things [2]. IoT will be a global network that will allow communication between humans, between humans, and things and among things by allocating unique identifiers in terms of IP addresses to all of its components [3]. These physical systems are being deployed now and some do not even need human intervention for their working. IoT requires coding and networking of objects around us so that it can be detected, traced, and controlled on the internet [4, 12, 13].

IoT has been implemented in almost every domain now. Smart homes integrate IoT in residences to provide better quality of life, comfort, convenience, and security to the residents. The systems in smart homes can be used for monitoring health and other activities [14]. Once the homes and complexes are connected, the next big thing will be to connect the entire city. The largescale deployment of IoT is actually a step toward enabling Smart City Projects [15].

Smart cities can provide services to its citizens as per their demands. The connected devices shall produce a large amount of data that if intelligently analyzed can lead to realization of various intelligent services. The authors in [16] have proposed an AI-based Semantic IoT Architecture for smart cities and also various use cases for the proposed architecture.

In smart cities, IoT offers opportunities for empowering citizens and improving engagement of societies with the governments. This will help the governments in assisting societies and citizens at macro and micro levels and thereby effectively help in providing public services to citizens [17]. Another study evaluates how public and government organizations can adapt their existing structures and processes to adapt to IoT implementation. The authors have presented an integrative framework for public IoT for Smart Government implementations thereby enhancing the understanding of key factors for effective public management via Smart Governance [18].

IoT and AI convergence in devices can result in real-time data streams. Applying analytics over this real -time data can help predict insights and help take control of decisions for future events [7–9, 19–21]. The authors have used an advanced class of machine learning algorithms such as deep learning to analyze learning in IoT.

10.3 Disruptive Technologies: Their Evolution and Growth

The innovations and developments of smart systems are governed and guided mostly by the growth of *Disruptive Technologies*.[1] Most evolving technologies of today are naturally disruptive and when they coalesce, they are even more powerful. The evolution and adoption of the internet marks the first wave of disruptive technologies [2, 5]. The internet, the so-called network of networks, emerged in the United States in the 1970s, but has become popular with the general public since the 1990s. Since then, various technologies have developed around the internet, such that it is difficult to imagine life without the internet today. Since its inception, there has been an exponential growth in the number of internet users worldwide. It was expected that by 2020, more than half of the world's population will have access to the internet. This has become a reality and is evident as we look around. It is quite evident that our dependence on the internet has become an essential part of our day-to-day lives and this dependence is increasing with every passing day and every new technology that is evolving. The internet has become very powerful and it can be used for almost any purpose that depends on information, and it is accessible by every individual who connects to one of its component networks. The internet has completely transformed the way we communicate, do business, interact socially, educate, entertain, and react to events and concerns.

The advent of *Mobile Devices* signified the second wave of disruptive technologies after the first era of fixed connected devices [2]. Smartphones have become one the most successful consumer device ever due to their features of always being connected, instantly on, their intuitive interface, and their form factor. After mobile devices came the disruption of services and markets. The establishment of digital platforms such Amazon, Flipkart, Ola Trivago, etc., led to a wave of disruption in their respective markets. These platforms are unique in a way that they do not own assets but help in connecting the supply and demand channels in innovative ways. They were able to create newer revenue opportunities by lowering the costs of transactions, augmenting the supply chains, and having exponential scalability.

The evolution of *IoT* marked the third wave of disruptive technologies. This wave connected a plethora of things to the internet, creating a situation where the majority of internet addresses were assigned to objects instead of people [1, 2, 9]. IoT primarily has advanced sensors along with wireless communication among the connected physical devices [3]. This large number of sensors leads to a humungous collection of data that can provide intrinsic information about the system for optimal use of the resources and the infrastructure. The concept of IoT and thereby of connected devices is the result of certain developments in the past. The most crucial among them are:

- A constant drop in the prices of sensors, making it an economically viable option for installation at various locations.
- Availability of ubiquitous wireless connectivity across all networks.
- Abundant storage and processing capability of the data produced by connected systems.
- Availability of unlimited IP addresses after IPV6 adoption.

---

[1] Disruptive Technology: Technology that displaces an established technology and disturbs the industry, or an innovative out-of-the box product that creates a completely new industry.

IoT has moved on to create a further disruptive effect that arises due to the fusion of information technology with other technologies. The most promising combination here comes with AI technologies. *IoT* coupled with *AI* can provide a foundation for improved and, eventually, entirely new products and services [1, 11, 14, 16]. Devices coupled with wireless communication and intelligent sensors are termed *Smart Objects* that exhibit newer functions and are capable of adapting behavior to suit their contexts. It is estimated that we will soon witness the emergence of a system that will have smart objects communicating with each other and the intelligent cloud system creating possibilities for newer developments and products.

The next wave of disruptive technologies came with the term *Big Data*. Big data refers to data sets that are very large and cannot be processed by traditional software and hardware systems. Big data is characterized by the 7 Vs—volume, velocity, variety, variability, veracity, visualization, and value—and may exist in forms such as structured, semi-structured, or completely unstructured [22]. The smart systems that were created due to coalition of IoT and other technologies together with social media, are generating vast amounts of data that has now taken the form of big data. This huge data store can be analyzed for predicting and forecasting trends, patterns, and correlations. This data soon took the form of *Open Data*, which is machine readable, nonproprietary in nature and freely available for use and republishing. Companies have started releasing parts of their data that can be used for igniting the creativity of the masses. This will require creating a data infrastructure for sharing and maintenance of data.

The next phase is the development of *Cognitive Systems* that bring together the machine learning and the capabilities for interacting with humans in natural languages and generate insights from the humungous data. These intelligent systems will be able to learn and reason like the human brain and will be able to deal with ambiguous and uncertain circumstances. *Robots, Self-Driving Cars,* and *Drones* are a few examples of such systems that are already around us.

In subsequent sections, we shall be focusing on *Smart Systems* and *Systems Working* on *IoT* and *AI Technologies*.

10.4 Smart Systems

The word "smart," traditionally used to reflect a person's acumen and appearance, is these days used for indicating the intelligence and capabilities of machines. It signifies connected devices sensing and guiding each other and informing the human agent(s) to control and coordinate processes. This connected environment may range from the confines of a home, a building, a complex, a campus, a city, a country, or the entire world. Although the conceptions of the smart world and smart country seem a distant reality today, smart homes, smart buildings, smart campuses, smart industries, and other such smart setups are evolving rapidly. Smart setups are not limited to only scientific or engineering design but solicit a multidisciplinary approach involving but not limited to disciplines of biology, psychology, philosophy, linguistics, mathematics, and computer science [9, 19–21, 23]. The principal aspects of any smart system include:

- **User Centricity:** All processes and the designs of smart systems must be in accordance with the requirements of the main stakeholder, i.e., the anticipated and targeted users.

- **Technical Infrastructure and Connectivity:** Technology must be extensively used and thoroughly connected for seamless exchange and transmission of information and data. The set must be secured and protected against any intrusions and attacks.

- **Sustenance of the Smart System:** The system must be stable and future ready with suitable maintenance and protection.

10.4.1 Technology Enablers for Smart Systems

The smart system needs certain technology enablers for its effective enablement [5]. The key technology enablers for smart system implementation are presented here:

- **The Internet of Things (IoT):** The smart system needs a setup of connected devices, comprising sensors and monitors to monitor smooth functioning of processes and devices so as to predict problems/failures in advance and take corrective actions before any serious malfunctions. The data from these devices can be leveraged to continuously improve services and enhance the quality and services of assets [21, 23, 24].

- **Big Data Analytics:** The large amount of data being generated by the connected devices can be processed with AI tools, technologies, and algorithms to predict and prescribe. These models have become more specialized and are becoming more sophisticated in nature. With the knowledge from historical data, these models can help in effectively monitoring the real-time data and situations and thereafter take proactive decisions for ensuring efficient and safe operations.

- **Cloud Computing:** The cloud provides unlimited online storage, and powerful services such as SaaS, PaaS, IaaS, and recently AaaS. Smart systems cannot sustain without cloud storage, which is a major requirement for its effective implementation and availability of data on the go, meaning anytime, anywhere accessibility to the stored data.

- **Augmented Reality (AR)/Virtual Reality (VR)/Extended Reality (ER):** AR/VR technologies can be used in providing information and experiences to its users virtually. AR is a mixture of a real as well as an imaginary world. Whilst the other technologies are considered as "back-end" technologies working in the background and hidden from view, AR/VR/ER are the interfaces that provide access to all the benefits of a smart system. With these technologies, it is possible to interact with the normal environment in a completely different way such as remote navigation, visual search, virtual tours, remote monitoring and maintenance of devices, and infrastructure components [25].

- **Blockchain:** Blockchain technology, which is a decentralized ledger of all transactions across a peer-to-peer network, assures that participants can confirm transactions without the need for a central certifying authority. This technology empowers smart home transactions by eliminating the middleman and thereby plays a vital role in improving network and data security across all technologies [9].

- **5G Networks:** 5G communication technologies are all set to enhance the carrier bandwidths and correspondingly the network speeds to support seamless transmission of data and provisioning of network services to users in all dynamic and pervasive environments.

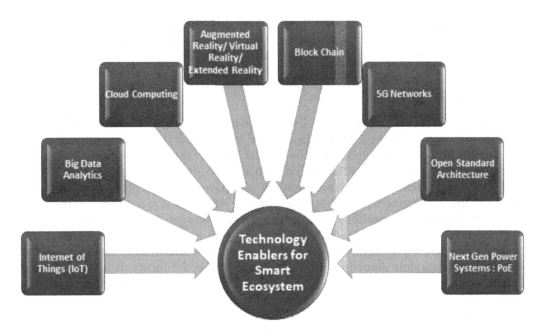

FIGURE 10.1
Technology enablers for smart systems.

- **Open Standard Architecture:** Open standards, as always, have helped in providing seamless and ubiquitous connectivity and interaction across systems and standards. This, therefore, helps in seamless communication, coordination and integration of sensors, actuators, and other connected devices.
- **Next Gen Power Systems-PoE:** Also called as Power over Ethernet (PoE), is the cabling technology that transmits data and power using the standard Ethernet cable. Therefore, a single Ethernet cable can be used to transmit both data and power. This technology is destined to be a game changer for smart systems, wherein a single cable will be deployed to connect the infrastructure components for transmission of data as well as for powering the devices. This will provide the flexibility to install power devices at any location irrespective of the availability of power sources in their vicinity. PoE shifts the monitoring and control of power to the device. Therefore, communication and location-based systems can be effectively deployed above lighting systems for better information and control.

10.5 Artificial Intelligence: Putting Intelligence into IoT

AI was once used in science fiction, mythology, horror, and animated cartoon movies as enabling technology for all paranormal, unnatural, and imaginative scenes. But today, AI has practical applications and is changing the way things happen around us and in our businesses. Developers are exploring and to a great extent have devised ways to combine AI with IoT. It has been proved that the technologies of IoT and AI should be tightly connected as they complement each other. IoT connects and shares data across a network of devices or "things" and organizations that effectively apply analytics are able to gain advantage. This analytical capability is offered by AI [24–33].

10.5.1 The Rise of Connected Things

The concept of a network of smart devices dates back to 1982 when a modified Coca-Cola vending machine at Carnegie Mellon University could report if the newly stocked inventory was cold or not. In 1989, John Romkey created a toaster that could be turned off and on over the internet during the INTEROP conference. This device was considered as the first IoT. Today, we have come a long way, where we now have more connected devices (things) than humans. According to a 2020 Business Insider Report, it is estimated that there will be close to 41 billion IoT devices in 2027 as compared to approx. 8 billion in 2019.

IoT extends across a network of devices ranging from domestic home appliances, vehicles, assembly line equipment, and other things that have electronic equipment, sensors, software, and actuators embedded in them. These connected things in IoT can transmit signals to their environment and be monitored and controlled remotely and, as predicted for the future, will be able to take decisions and actions.

There are numerous IoT around us today such as the home automation systems that on detecting changes in the conditions in the home, adjust the lights or the temperature thermostat. Predictive maintenance systems keep monitoring the equipment and alert the technician as and when the machine needs maintenance. Digital assistants such as Siri and Alexa use speech recognition to interpret commands. All these connected devices and things around us are like data stores that keep generating humongous data of all types and complicacies. This data has huge potential and can generate insights and opportunities for businesses. For deriving these benefits, one needs to understand smart components. A smart component has four layers:

1. **The Physical Layer**: the mechanical and electrical components.
2. **The Smart Layer**: the sensors, the software, the processor, and the storage.
3. **The Connectivity Layer**: the ports, the antennas, and the protocols.
4. **The Analytics Layer**: powered by AI to train and implement the predictive and prescriptive models.

Each layer is amplified by the layer above it, with the Physical at the bottom and Analytics at the top. At the most basic level, the sensors on detecting certain abrupt activities in the Physical components generate alerts for the human attendants. Connectedness creates a sequence of connected activities as devices trigger each other in the network. But the real applicability comes when these connected things store not only data but their experiences and perform the same activity in a better way every consecutive time. This level of sophistication foresees creation of learning devices that learn from their own experiences and from their environments. The devices will become adaptive and learning systems that will improve their performance over time and will be able to take decisions in the specific contexts that they are confronted with. This is where AI will come in action. AI has been around since the 1950s, but the real capabilities and applications of AI are being explored now. The true sense of the term AI is now emerging: creating systems that can emulate human beings through learning and automation, learn from experiences, adapt to their environment, and independently handle tasks without any human intervention.

Such well-trained systems have been developed over time and implemented successfully. Examples include the Chess Playing Programs and Biometric Systems. IoT applications combined with AI are now becoming part of our daily lives in the form of various smart and connected objects around us and they are creating huge volumes of data, provisioning high-speed connections, and delivering highly effective computing. Machine learning, a subdomain of AI, uses statistical techniques and computational and evolutionary algorithms to analyze data to make predictions about health and detect anomalies in sensing equipment. The machine learning algorithms are getting more and more accurate day by day and therefore outperform traditional Business Intelligence Tools making decisions more accurate and faster.

10.5.2 Major AI Technologies for Enabling IoT

There are a number of AI technologies that support the smart system such as machine learning, deep learning, natural language processing, and computer vision/localization. These technologies when used for real-time forecasting and optimization make AI an essential complement to IoT [5]. A brief about the major AI technologies is presented here:

- **Machine Learning:** Machine learning brings the ability to automatically learn and perform better by identifying patterns and detecting anomalies in the data (such as temperature, pressure, humidity, air quality, vibration, and sound) that smart sensors and devices generate. Learning may be *Supervised, Unsupervised, or Reinforcement*. Apart from these, other learning methodologies that may be used by systems are *semi-supervised learning, active learning, inductive learning, deductive learning, transfer learning,* and *nature inspired learning.*
- **Deep Learning (DL):** DL, a subdiscipline of machine learning, has recently been quite popular in IoT applications to the extent that IoT and DL were ranked in the top three strategic technologies by Gartner for 2017. These models bring more precision into the feature extraction process and enhance the accuracy of the results. IoT and DL constitute a chain of data production-consumption, in which IoT generates raw data that is analyzed by DL models and these models produce high-level abstraction and insights that are fed to IoT systems for fine-tuning and improvement of services. The DL models fall into three categories: generative models (works on supervised approaches), discriminative models (works on unsupervised approaches), and hybrid models (incorporates benefits of generative and discriminative models). Areas where DL methods have shown promising results include complex application areas as image recognition systems in smart homes and smart cities, natural language processing systems/voice recognition systems, localization services in agriculture and other such areas, security and privacy services, and IoT Infrastructures [25, 33].
- **Computer Vision/Localization:** In smart systems as smart homes, campuses, malls, and hospitals, computer vison and location aware services can be a great help. Computer vision technology can be seen in gaming consoles that recognize the gestures of the player and in the cameras of smartphones that set focus automatically on the object to be clicked. We can see the impact of this technology on our lives. Ranging from optical sensors in manufacturing for quality assurance, high-resolution intelligent cameras in battlefields for collecting information, and drones and sensors in vehicles are some examples to quote. The computer vision

applications were mostly limited to closed platform applications, but after combining with IoT, the devices are equipped with IP connectivity and thus are creating a new set of applications such as video analytics, 3D imaging, robotics, digital reality (VR and AR), and many more that have and will arise by a combination of these technologies [8, 23, 28].

- **Natural Language Processing (NLP):** NLP refers to the power of speech understanding. It implies implementing voice control over different systems. Hands-free command interfaces can lead to ample advantages for IoT systems. Implementing voice controls in IoT systems provides an intuitive characteristic to the device, thereby making it extremely useful, especially in safety critical applications where working by hands may lead to accidents. For example, a technician working at a height on high-power lines and giving voice commands to the digital tools or passing observations to teams for remote handling of the problem instead of doing it manually. Home assistants such as Alexa have already made their place in smart homes today. Sentiment analysis is being used to a great extent by marketers who analyze emotional reactions. The systems study the speaker's emotional reaction and identify their reactions as agree, conscience, emotions, and openness in natural language. Therefore, emotions speak more than words is being implemented through such capabilities.

10.6 Real-Life Applications of AI in IoT Systems

10.6.1 Smart Homes

Home automation is the new style of living and is not just a luxury anymore. With the adoption of IoT and AI, home automation offers powerful solutions to our everyday tasks and responsibilities. AI is creating solutions to the common problems we face every day, and making life simpler for everyone. Its presence in home automation allows us to control our appliances, secure our homes, and even limit our expenses. The ultimate goal of home automation is to limit the need for human involvement. AI can help achieve this goal. A smart home can be defined as a home that allows remote control and monitoring of connected devices. The devices or things remain connected, communicate with each other, think, act, and react. They can be programmed to remain bound by the owner's rules and work as per their desires and directives. Industry giants such as Google, Apple, and Amazon are focusing on creating smart assistants for smart homes such as Siri, Google Assistant, and Alexa.

Apart from these packaged systems, a smart home also encompasses connectivity of electrical devices and appliances inside homes ranging from basic illumination, air conditioning, washing machines, refrigerators, and so on, to the more critical electrical gizmos such as pumps and fire boards. In a smart home, all such devices remain connected creating IoT frameworks that give information to AI. AI, in turn, gains from that information specific undertakings on the tasks to be accomplished and controls to be enforced that will relieve the involvement of humans.

With this integration of AI and IoT, smart devices can respond to voice commands of the user even remotely or a through a preprogrammed AI command with the help of a voice assistant such as Siri or Alexa. An example of this is the Google Nest thermostat that can control the cooling and warming of the home automatically. It constantly monitors the inhabitants' conduct and within a week learns how warm or cold you like your home throughout the day. When at home, the home will be cooled, and as when go out, the systems will be automatically turned off, thereby saving energy.

AI converts the raw sensor data collected in smart homes from the smart connected devices and interprets it into behavior design of daily routines of the inhabitants. They learn the routine and start predicting the activities. For example, if no one is home, the electrical appliances shall remain turned off and the doors locked.

A smart oven shall constantly screen the temperature of the food that is cooking and as soon as it reaches a specific temperature, the intelligence in the device will reduce the temperature and thereby prevent burning of the food or may inform the cook once the food is ready. This AI and IoT potential is not only limited to new homes, but existing devices that can also be changed over to their smart counterparts. For example, switches changed to smart switches and air conditioners amended to provision its remote access through a smart app or some AI-enabled cloud server [5, 32, 33].

AI enablement in smart homes offers assistance to solve human problems, ranging from creating schedules to searching songs for playing on the music system, or answering nearly every query. But the capabilities of these assistants are still to be unleashed. AI integration on almost every home device and remote response is just the beginning. The future foresees the ability to teach and train the smart assistants as per individual lifestyle and requirements. Other smart home controls that can be particularly useful in the future are:

- **Controlling appliances:** Equipping appliances with sensors for monitoring their state and sending notifications to the user in case of errors or maintenance requirement.

- **Remote monitoring** of the security appliances through a smart device and locking the doors and windows in case of intrusion.

- **Intelligent feedback** from the home automation system, such as the refrigerator. After learning the owner's health and habits, it registers its contents, advises menus, proposes healthy substitutes, and orders replenishments as the contents are consumed.

- **Landscape control:** Maintaining ideal environment for pets, serving food at the optimal time and in correct proportions, and watering the plants.

- **Healthcare monitoring:** Through wireless sensors in the walls that constantly monitor the heart rate and breathing. The benefits of this technology are particularly useful for observing the elderly and babies during their sleep.

10.6.2 Smart City

We are in the age of digitization and connectedness. Once the individual units are digitized, the criteria shall be to digitize the entire city. Such connected cities will be termed as smart cities. We are moving in this direction and some cities are moving toward becoming smart cities. But do we yet have a city that can be categorized as a smart city? [5, 15, 16] The definition of a smart city as per the IEEE Standards Association is:

"As world urbanization continues to grow and the total population expected to double by 2050, there exists an increased demand for intelligent, sustainable environments that reduce environmental impact and offer citizens a high-quality life. A smart city brings together technology, government and society to enable a smart economy, smart mobility, a smart environment, smart people, smart living and smart governance."

The concept behind smart cities needs IoT in place, which can revolutionize the way smart cities function. Some of the areas that offer opportunities in a smart city are presented here:

- **Efficient Water Supply:** IoT can change the manner in which urban communities use water. Implementation of smart meters can help detect leakage thereby reducing water wastage. In addition, they can be used to furnish occupants with continuous access to data regarding their water utilization and water supply.

- **Smart Traffic Management:** Owing to rapid urbanization, there has been a drastic increase in traffic problems. Traffic jams and congestion have become a massive problem and it is getting worse as the number of vehicles on the roads increase. IoT can be used for handling traffic congestion with smart traffic signals that will help in controlling the traffic in a better way. Commuters can collect and share data from their smartphones, vehicles, and road sensors to monitor real-time traffic incidents. If routes are blocked, alerts can be sent to the drivers with redirected routes and alternate paths. This will also ease Public Transport Systems, making them more reliable and efficient.

- **Energy-Efficient Buildings:** IoT provisions construction of energy-efficient building structures. With IoT, the devices can be connected to a smart management application that controls nonstandard heating, cooling, lighting, and fire-safety systems.

- **Smart Parking:** GPS-enabled smart parking systems are the solutions that can provide respite from the prevalent parking problem in urban setups. With the help of data from sensors on smartphones and video monitoring, car drivers can be directed straight to vacant parking spots. The real-time data helps create a virtual parking map that shows the user the nearest vacant parking slot. Moreover, users can make advance parking reservations while on their way to the parking lots. The drivers will receive a notification on their phone to find the parking spot. Such systems are already installed in cities around the world and have been useful in assisting effective utilization of parking spaces.

- **Smart Street Lighting:** IoT devices can be implemented for the maintenance and control of streetlamps in a more cost-effective way. Sensors with the help of a cloud management solution can help in controlling and scheduling the switching operations. Smart lighting solutions can be implemented with sensors to keep track of movement of people and vehicles. With the help of this data, the street lamps can adjust the lighting to either dim, bright, or switch off or on automatically based on the environment.

- **Crime Detection and Prevention:** Smart sensors, video cameras, and other such devices can help the police in solving crimes after they happen, and also detect new crimes before they occur. US states such as Atlanta and Georgia have significantly reduced their crime rates with the help of smart street lights that have crime-detection capabilities. Cities are also using smart patrolling to predict the time and venue of the occurrence of a crime through analysis of gathered data and patterns analysis [27, 30].

- **Emergency Response:** Cities can be provided Emergency-Response-Operators that can activate street lights to guide emergency personnel to the exact location.

Lights may also flash in a specific sequence or change colors, thereby indicating emergency evacuation routes during natural disasters or other emergency situations.

- **Environmental Monitoring:** Sensors can be installed and trained to identify air pollution levels and presence of toxic chemicals in the environment.
- **Warnings and Alerts:** Warnings and alerts can be issued through speaker-equipped devices to warn people of looming dangers. The smart city apps can be designed to automatically send messages about various issues and snags for the benefit of the public at large.
- **Smart Grid:** Smart meters and sensors can be joined to create "ultra-reliable, self-healing" power grids. These can give users more control over their bills and power usage. Self-contained microgrids can be used for making campuses, hospitals, and so on, more robust to handle disasters.
- **Waste Management:** Garbage containers can be fitted with sensors that gather data about the level of waste in the container. As a specific threshold is reached, the sensor shall send an alert to the waste management solution and a notification will reach the mobile app of the truck driver.
- **Smart Buildings:** Buildings equipped with sensors and information systems help improve safety and convenience and at the same time slash water and electricity usage.
- **Digital City Services:** Most of the services are available digitally through a smartphone. These transactions are cost-effective and provide more satisfaction to the consumer because they are hassle free and anytime executable.

These are just some of the IoT-based smart city applications that can ensure vast benefits to citizens and governments.

The realization of the concept of a smart city needs creation of a connected digital platform that allows maintenance of a central pool of information and all systems accessing this pool to share and utilize the data they use, generate, and accumulate. This digital platform will also provide a real-time city view of sensors and systems to give city managers immediate insight and context to take better and timely decisions. The platform shall bring together all the key system components and provide a different dashboard-based view to all department and users.

10.6.3 Smart Health

As healthcare technologies advance, there's an increased engagement and consciousness of consumers when it comes to their health. Healthcare services are getting costlier, the global population is aging, and the number of chronic diseases are on the rise. Therefore, there is a need to make healthcare easier on the pocket and also more accessible.

Medical diagnostic consumes a large part of hospital bills while technology can move routine medical checks to the patient's home, making it home-centric instead of hospital-centric. The right and timely diagnosis will also reduce the need for hospitalization [28, 29, 31, 32, 34]. Thus, the rise in the demand for remote care is the current requirement. The IoT solution equipped with AI termed as smart healthcare systems can allow hospitals these facilities.

10.6.3.1 Benefits of Smart Health Systems

- **Simultaneous reporting and monitoring:** Real-time monitoring via connected devices fitted in the patient's body and storing data on the cloud for the physician to study can be extremely useful in cases of medical urgency such as heart failure, asthma, etc. The health data collected by the IoT device may include blood pressure, blood sugar, oxygen levels, ECGs, etc.

- **Assortment and analysis of data:** The vast amount of speedy data sent through healthcare devices needs cloud storage for effective analysis. AI helps real-time analysis of data on the cloud such that the physician gets the final reports with graphs. All this collected data can also help in deriving insights and aid in decision making by health organizations.

- **Real time alerts and tracking:** Timely alerts are extremely critical when in life-threatening situations. These real-time alerts by medical IoT devices enable smart health systems that help track and monitor, thus helping in immediate and timely handling by the doctor and enhanced accuracy of treatment. The doctors get vital data for real-time tracking of their patients' health.

- **Remote medical assistance:** Remote medical assistance implies providing doctoral support to the patients from a remote location in case of emergency. This also entails provisioning medicines to patients as per their prescriptions and ailments.

- **Medical research:** IoT enabled with AI in healthcare systems can be used for research purposes. Because the system will collect massive amounts of data in the form of medical record of patients, this data can be used for analytical studies and help enable bigger and better medical treatments.

- **Personalized treatments through big data:** Innovative medical technologies like DNA sequencing are being vastly applied. These techniques along with advanced medical imaging and analysis working on the collected data helps in designing a personalized treatment plan for the patients.

- **3D printing:** The use of 3D printing in healthcare for prosthetics and implants will be extremely useful as it will make complete personalization. Surgeons can use 3D printing for practicing a complicated surgery on a model of the body part of the patient.

- **Robotics:** Robots can provide more accuracy than humans for specialized tasks. They can also support people at home, letting them stay safe in their environments.

10.6.4 Use Cases of Smart Healthcare Systems

10.6.4.1 Smart Continuous Glucose Monitoring and Insulin Pens

Smart continuous glucose monitoring (CGM) is a device that helps diabetics to continuously monitor their blood glucose levels for several days at a time, by taking readings at regular intervals. CGMs were approved for the first time by the US FDA in 1999 and are now available as a number of smart CGMs (*Eversense* and *Freestyle Libre*). They send data on blood glucose levels to an app on iPhone, Android, or Apple Watch, allowing the wearer to easily check their information and detect trends. Insulin Pens are another smart device that are currently helping the lives of diabetic patients. Smart insulin pens/pen caps such as *Gocap, InPen,* and *Esysta* can automatically record the time, amount and type of insulin injected in a dose, and recommend the correct type of insulin injection at the right time. These smart devices interact with a smartphone app that can store long-term data, help diabetics calculate their insulin dose, and even allow patients to record their meals and blood sugar levels, to see how their food and insulin intake are affecting their blood sugar.

10.6.4.2 Connected Inhalers

Asthma is a major problem and needs to be addressed like diabetes. Propeller health is the biggest producer of smart inhaler technology. Propeller does not produce the complete inhaler but a sensor that is attached to an inhaler or Bluetooth spirometer. It connects up to an app and helps people with asthma and COPD (Chronic Obstructive Pulmonary Disease, which includes emphysema and chronic bronchitis) understand what might be causing their symptoms, track uses of rescue medication, and also provide allergen forecasts. Using connected inhalers helps in improving adherence to medication. The Propeller sensor generates reports on inhaler use that can be shared with the patient's doctor, and show whether they are using it as often as is prescribed. For patients, this provides motivation and also clarity, showing how the use of their inhaler is directly improving their condition.

10.6.4.3 Ingestible Sensors

Ingestible sensors can help track and improve the regularity of the patients in taking their medication and allowing them to have a more informed consultation with their physician about treatment. A study by WHO suggests 50% of medicines are not taken as directed. Proteus' Digital Health and Otsuka Pharmaceutical Co. created ABILIFY MYCITE—an antipsychotic medication, the first FDA-approved drug with a digital tracking system. They have created pills that dissolve in the stomach and produce a small signal that is picked up by a sensor worn on the body. The data is then relayed to a smartphone app, confirming that the patient has taken their medication as directed.

10.6.4.4 Connected Contact Lenses

Smart contact lenses are an ambitious application of IoT in the healthcare sector. It all started in 2014 when Verily, a subsidiary of Google' parent company Alphabet, in partnership with Alcon, the eyecare division of a pharmaceutical company Novartis, claimed that they had developed a smart contact lens that could measure tear glucose and provide early warning for blood sugar levels dropping or crossing a threshold. The project was criticized by researchers and proved wrong. But other prospective medical applications for smart contact lenses such as for treating presbyopia (long-sightedness due to loss of elasticity in the eye lens) and cataract surgery recovery are in the pipeline. Swiss company Sensimed has developed a noninvasive smart contact lens called Triggerfish, CE-marked and FDA-approved, which automatically records changes in eye dimensions that can lead to glaucoma.

10.6.4.5 The Apple Watch App that Monitors Depression

In 2017, Takeda Pharmaceuticals USA and Cognition Kit Limited, a platform for measuring cognitive health, explored the use of an Apple Watch app for monitoring and assessing patients with Major Depressive Disorder (MDD). The findings from the study had a very high level of compliance with the app, which participants used daily to monitor their mood and cognition. The study demonstrated the potential for wearable devices to assess the effects of depression in real time. The Apple Watch app could also give patients and healthcare professionals greater insight into their condition, and enable more informed conversations.

10.6.4.6 Apple's ResearchKit and Parkinson's Disease

In 2018, Apple added a new Movement Disorder API to its open-source ResearchKit API, which allows Apple Watches to monitor Parkinson's disease symptoms. The symptoms are normally monitored by physicians in clinics through physical diagnostic tests, and patients are encouraged to keep a diary in order to give a broader insight into symptoms over time. The API aims to make that process automatic and continuous. An app on a connected iPhone can present the data in a graph, giving daily and hourly breakdowns, as well as minute-by-minute symptom fluctuation.

Apple's ResearchKit has also been used in a number of different health studies, including an arthritis study carried out in partnership with GSK, and an epilepsy study that used sensors in the Apple Watch to detect the onset and duration of seizures.

10.6.5 Smart Transportation System

Managing transportation is becoming a great challenge in large cities for commuters and traffic officials. The motive is to improve efficiency and reduce pollution and frustration for commuters. The solution to this can possibly be achieved by an Intelligent Transportation System (ITS), which shall include traffic and mobility management, managing movement of vehicles and assisting drivers, enhancing transport infrastructure, and providing improved interfaces for transport systems [25, 28, 29, 32, 33]. ITS helps provide real-time information about traffic and public transportation conditions to all citizens, thereby reducing travel time and making the journey easy and safe. There are four important applications of the ITS, which are discussed here.

10.6.5.1 Advanced Traffic Management System

The advanced traffic management system (ATMS) integrates real-time information from various sources (traffic lights, parking lots, and toll booths) and uses it to manage traffic. ATMS helps to smooth traffic and control pollutants. For controlling traffic, ATMS takes the following steps:

- Real-time adjustments to traffic lights and road signals for shifting traffic away from congested roads.
- Dynamic rates on toll roads to motivate a public transportation system instead of private vehicles.
- Smart management of parking lots as previously described in this chapter.

10.6.5.2 Smart Vehicle Control and Safety System

With sensors installed in vehicles, drivers have access to visual alerts and information about unsafe situations. In a way, smart vehicle control and safety system (SVCSS)-equipped vehicles can be considered the first step toward autonomous vehicles. For safe driving, SVCSS has the ability to:

- Control a vehicle automatically, thereby reducing errors by humans while driving.
- Help in avoiding risky situations or reacting to them effectively.
- Assist in journey overlook, and assistance while parking.

10.6.5.3 Smart Public Transportation System

A smart public transportation system (SPTS) provides information about public transport systems and the journey. It provides a centralized mechanism for making payments in diverse areas, similar to FASTag in practice today. SPTS uses real-time passenger data to improve the safety of people, provide bus arrival notifications, and give priority to buses at various points.

10.6.5.4 Commercial Vehicle Operation

This is similar to SPTS and is used for managing commercial vehicles such as buses, trucks, taxis, and ambulances. It tracks performance and behavior of the driver, manages commercial fleets through GPS tracking, driver's compliance with routes, operating costs, fuel consumption, and so on. The data gathered can help organizations monitor their fleet for reducing costs.

10.6.5.5 Guiding Principles of ITS

1. Collection of traffic data, such as location and speed of vehicles, traffic conditions, and delays through sensors and other distributed devices (GPS devices, road camera, vehicle identifiers) in real time.
2. Data transmission to management center for analysis and forwarding to specific applications.
3. Traffic data analysis after cleaning and customizing the data to reach conclusions and make predictions.
4. Traveler Information such as citizens' data for collection of data and disbursement of information.

10.6.5.6 Use Cases of Intelligent Transportation Systems

10.6.5.6.1 Connected Cars

Connected cars work on a network of sensors, antennas, communication networks, and software to take timely and accurate decisions. The systems are designed to monitor the components such as brakes and engine, tire pressure, and composition of exhaust gas. The future predicts that Vehicle-to-Infrastructure (V2I) may soon help in reserving parking and Vehicle-to-Vehicle (V2V) may support in-vehicle networks while the vehicles are moving, thereby helping vehicles to detect each other and prevent collisions.

10.6.5.6.2 Volvo Uses IoT and AI to Reduce Downtime

Every day, the national highways witness millions of trucks transporting fuel, produce, essential commodities, and electronics. But sudden and unplanned downtimes can lead to increase in the toll on the operator and the customers who have tasks dependent on the delivery. Volvo Trucks and Mack Trucks (subsidiaries of the AB Volvo, the Swedish manufacturer) have used remote diagnostic and preventive maintenance for handling this challenge using IoT, AI, and analytics. Thus, they minimize the costs of service disruptions by proactively servicing the connected components of the vehicles.

The Remote Diagnostics of Volvo Trucks monitors data from each truck detecting fault codes when something goes wrong. The trucks are fitted with thousands of sensors to collect real-time streaming IoT data that provides information about the event, where it happened, and the conditions that existed when the fault occurred. On the same lines, the GuardDog Connect of Mack Trucks allows customers to understand the seriousness of the problem and thus manage repairing remotely by checking the parameter data and fault codes, then rank them on the basis of the severity. If the severity is high then the customer is told about the problem and the action to be taken, otherwise the repair is postponed to a later time.

The technology adopted by Volvo Trucks reduced the diagnostic time by 70% and the repair time by 25%.

10.6.5.6.3 *App Modifies Traffic Lights for Slower Pedestrians*

Launched in April 2018 by Dutch company Dynniq, the Crosswalk app allows pedestrians with restricted mobility sufficient time to cross the road. The system has traffic lights that are fitted with a sensor for scanning the pavements on both sides of the road. If someone using the Crosswalk app is detected, it automatically adjusts the time that the lights remain green. The app has four different time settings, and the light's sensor will select the one suitable for the pedestrian's mobility level and thus ensure that they have sufficient time to cross the road. The app works both with GPS and the software installed in the light. The company is also working for cyclists, notifying the lights when a cyclist is approaching, and also for the visually impaired that activates a sound pattern to let them know if the light is green or red.

10.6.6 Smart Environment Monitoring Systems

Smart cities' infrastructure houses a network of sensors, cameras, wireless devices, and data centers. The setup is utilized by the authorities to provide essential services. Smart cities are also more environmentally friendly because the facilities are built using sustainable materials that lower consumption of energy [25, 28, 29, 32, 33]. Technology can be used to create a pollution monitoring system apart from the other systems previously discussed.

The data collected by sensors can be used for controlling, detecting, and managing unnecessary use and making certain adjustments. Environment sensors such as temperature sensors, humidity sensors, flood sensing units, rainfall sensors, sound/noise sensors, and light sensors gather data about pollution, temperature, rain, levels of gases in the city (pollution), and any other events on a daily basis, which is required for taking appropriate actions by authorities or administrators. Sensors are adopted in many wearable devices to monitor weather conditions.

10.6.6.1 *Use Cases of the Smart Environment*

10.6.6.1.1 *Compact IoT Green Wall Cleans Urban Air*

Certain indoor plants can be used to purify the air in homes. A German startup, Green City Solutions, has designed an innovative solution using IoT. They have created a freestanding plant filter, named CityTree, a 12-foot high green unit that is able to clean the surrounding air of pollutants removing 240 tons of carbon dioxide equivalents in a year. It is a moss culture with vascular plants that can ingest polluting gases such as nitrogen dioxide and ozone, providing a cleansing effect the same as that provided by 275 urban trees, for just 5% of the cost and 1% of the space. It needs energy from solar panels and automated provision of water and nutrients using a built-in tank and minimal maintenance.

Apart from the environmental benefits, the CityTree contains sensors that collect and analyze environmental and climatic data, which is used for remotely regulating and controlling the unit to ensure the health of the plants with the changing weather conditions. CityTree also contains space for displaying visual/digital information. Advertisers can rent space on the unit, and nondigital advertising messages can be spelled with plants of different colors. The units can also include benches, Wi-Fi hotspots, and e-bike charging stations.

10.6.6.1.2 *Protecting Endangered Species, One Footprint at a Time*

Nonprofit research organization WildTrack monitors endangered species to understand how best to protect them and reduce human–wildlife conflict. Traditional methods using radio collars and observational surveys were costly, stressed the animals, and put researchers in danger.

WildTrack wanted to go for a better way. They realized that more information can be derived by monitoring the animals' footprints and coding the expertise of indigenous trackers into sophisticated AI algorithms.

WildTrack's footprint identification technique (FIT) was developed with the help of bushmen trackers in southern Africa. From digital images of footprints tagged with date, time, location, and other information, FIT was able to identify the species, individual, age-class, and gender of an animal. These tracks could be compiled into a collective story that held significant value in conservation efforts.

The only equipment needed in this setup is a digital camera, GPS unit, a scale, and either voice-tag or pen and pencil. Local community members photograph the footprints. The FIT process converts that footprint into a geometric profile and analyzes it for classification. With enough data gathered over a substantial time period, a computer can be trained to accurately identify footprint images and recognize patterns, simulating the methods used by expert trackers. The system is capable of applying these concepts quickly at large scale and coupled with analytics, the whole process effectively gives insights into species populations that WildTrack never had before.

10.6.7 Smart Security

IoT and AI has a huge potential for ensuring public safety and security. Some systems that can be part of smart security systems include:

- **Smart street lights** play a major role in security systems. They can become brighter when movement is detected, thereby indicating traffic, and can be used for indicating the coming of an ambulance or fire truck.
- **Drones:** They be used for assessing risk, preventing ambushes, searching accidents, investigating crime scenes, and studying factors before sending humans to dangerous situations.
- **Crime prevention and predictive policing:** Using big data analysis, we can determine causes of crime and use them to prevent their occurrence in the future. These insights can be extremely useful for government agencies targeting specific localities who can use this information to focus police officer patrols in high risk areas.

- **Emergency apps:** Such apps can be used by people to send alerts such as medical or emergency or crimes. The apps detects the locations, along with audio or video recordings if possible, and notifies the nearest police station.
- **Detecting gun shots:** Acoustic sensors in the entire city fitted on roof tops of high-rise buildings can help detect gunfire accurately. If 10 sensors simultaneously detect the gunshot, the location can be immediately traced. The accuracy rates are as high as 95% for these systems.

10.7 Proposed Framework: Smart Connected Restaurant Management System

After a thorough study of the cases and models of IoT implementation in various real-life applications in this chapter, the authors propose a framework for managing a restaurant or a chain of connected restaurants using IoT, AI, and big data analytics. The proposed framework has been explained in detail in Chapter 12 after explaining the concepts of AI enablement and big data analytics implementation in the two chapters and how these concepts can be incorporated in the proposed SCRMS. The AI module in the proposed framework encompasses the AI services described in this chapter such as machine learning, natural language processing, computer vision, robotic process automation, and scheduling. All these AI services can provide tremendous functionality to the SCRMS and provide smart management and control of processes in the SCRMS.

10.8 Critical Success Factors for AI-Enabled IoT

Apart from establishing the physical infrastructure of the smart system, the following practices are required for ensuring the successful deployment of smart IoT:

1. **Think real-time analytics:** Take immediate action and grab opportunities of real-time analysis of speedy big data even before storing it. Such data handling shall provide the ability to:
   a. **Detect events of interest and trigger suitable action.** Example, quick detection of unusual activity such as threats during a banking transaction in real time.
   b. **Monitoring aggregated information** by the smart devices and taking suitable action.
   c. **Clean and validate the data from the sensors** to detect the source of erroneous data and troubleshoot it.
   d. **Predict and optimize operations in real time.** Information about a delayed train and its impact on the timings of other connected trains can be analyzed and studied so that passengers do not miss their trains for the onward journey.

2. **Deploy intelligence at the point where the application needs it**, maybe in the device, the network, or the cloud. Data is dynamic, in motion, and discrete, so to handle such data analytics needs to be applied in dynamic ways and forms:

    a. **High-performance analytics** works on resting data stored in the cloud or in other storage.

    b. **Streaming analytics** helps analyze large amount of varying data while still in motion. The entire data may not be of use and needs filtering. Moreover, this data only has a transient value so speed is critical, such as alerts about component failure.

    c. **Edge computing** helps a system to immediately act on the data, while still at source, without pausing to carry or store it.

3. **Combining AI Technologies**: AI technologies such as machine learning, NLP, and computer vision must be combined to realize the highest returns from IoT and AI.

4. **Unifying the analytics life cycle**: Streaming, filtering, storing the relevant data, analyzing it, and using the results to improve the system.

10.9 Conclusion

IoT and AI offers tremendous opportunities. But the real challenge for organizations is to build on existing technology, infrastructure, and capabilities. This will lead to generating value from money with minimal implementation time and least complexity. The benefits for those successful will be significant and noticeable.

To exploit the real value of machine learning, enterprises must recognize opportunities for enhancing intelligence within the business or supply chain, accumulate and store all types of data such as internal, external, structured, unstructured, and semi-structured. Organizations must employ and retain the right people with the right skills to apply machine learning and they should be able to integrate machine learning into new as well as existing applications.

References

1. Ghosh, A., Chakraborty, D., Law, A. (2018) Artificial Intelligence in Internet of Things. *CAAI Transactions on Intelligence Technology*, 3(4): 208–218.
2. Madakam, S., Ramaswamy, R., Tripathi, S. (2015) Internet of Things (IoT): A literature review. *Journal of Computer and Communications*. 3: 164–173.
3. Aggarwal, R., Das, M. L. (2012) RFID Security in the Context of Internet of Things. In: Proceedings of First International Conference on Security of Internet of Things, Kerala, India, 51–56.
4. Butler, D. (2004) Computing: Everything, everywhere. *Nature*. 440: 402–405.

5. Sharma, Lavanya, Garg, P.K. (Eds.). (2020) *From Visual Surveillance to Internet of Things.* New York, NY: Chapman and Hall/CRC, DOI: 10.1201/9780429297922

6. Tiwary, A., Mahato, M. (March 2018). Internet of Things (IoT): Research, architectures and applications. *International Journal on Future Revolution in Computer Science & Communication Engineering.* 4(3): 12–20.

7. Wirtz, B. W., Weyerer, J. C., Schichtel, F. T. (2019) An integrative public IoT framework for smart government. *Government Information Quarterly.* 36(2): 333–345.

8. Sharma, Lavanya, Lohan, Nirvikar. (January 2019) Performance analysis of moving object detection using BGS techniques in visual surveillance. *International Journal of Spatiotemporal Data Science,* Inderscience. 1:22–53.

9. Kumar, Anubhav, Jha, Gaurav, Sharma, Lavanya. (July 2019) Challenges, Potential & future of IOT integrated with block chain. *International Journal of Recent Technology and Engineering.* 8(2S7): 530–536.

10. Dixit, R., Choudhary, S. (2020) Artificial intelligence & biased decisions – IS AI safe for the Mankind? *International Journal of Grid and Distributed Computing.* 13(1): 443–450.

11. Mohammadi, M., Al-Fuqaha, A., Sorour, S., Guizani, M. Fourthquarter (2018) Deep Learning for IoT big data and streaming analytics: A survey. *IEEE Communications Surveys & Tutorials.* 20(4): 2923–2960.

12. Gershenfeld, N., Krikorian, R., Cohen, D. (2004) The Internet of Things. *Scientific American.* 291: 76–81.

13. Lombreglia, R. (2010) The Internet of Things. *Boston Globe,* October, 2010.

14. Moniruzzaman, Md., Khezr, S., Yassine, A., Benlamri, R. (2020) Blockchain for smart homes: Review of current trends and research challenges. *Computers and Electrical Engineering.* 83: 106585.

15. Hammi, B., Khatoun, R., Zeadally, S., Fayad, A., Khoukhi, L. (2018) IoT Technologies for smart cities. *IET Networks.* 7(1): 1–13.

16. Guo, K. Lu, Y., Gao, H., Cao, R. (2018) Artificial intelligence-based semantic Internet of Things in a user-centric smart city. *Sensors.* 18: 1341.

17. Sharma, Lavanya, Yadav, Dileep Kumar. (June, 2016) Histogram based adaptive learning rate for background modelling and moving object detection in video surveillance. *International Journal of Telemedicine and Clinical Practices,* Inderscience. (ISSN: 2052-8442, DOI: 10.1504/IJTMCP.2017.082107).

18. Haddadeh, R., Weerakkody, V., Osmani, M., Thakker, D., Kapoor, K. K. (2019) Examining citizens' perceived value of internet of things technologies in facilitating public sector services engagement. *Government Information Quarterly.* 36(2): 310–320.

19. Liu, Yong, Hou, Rongxu. (2010). About the sensing layer in Internet of Things [J]. *Computer Study.* 5:55.

20. Anand, Akshit, Jha, Vikrant, Sharma, Lavanya. (July 2019) An improved local binary patterns histograms techniques for face recognition for real time application. In *International Journal of Recent Technology and Engineering.* 8(2S7), 524–529.

21. Sharma, Lavanya, Lohan, Nirvikar. (February, 2019) Performance Analysis of Moving Object Detection using BGS Techniques. *International Journal of Spatio-Temporal Data Science,* Inderscience. 1, pp. 309–313.

22. Frary, M. (Feb 2020). 5 IoT innovations that will change your life. *Raconteur.* https://www.raconteur.net/technology/iot-innovations-ces

23. Sharma, Shubham, Verma, Shubhankar, Kumar, Mohit, Sharma, Lavanya. (2019). "Use of Motion Capture in 3D Animation: Motion Capture Systems, Challenges, and Recent Trends." In: 1st IEEE International Conference on Machine Learning, Big Data, Cloud and Parallel Computing (Com-IT-Con), India, 14–16 February, pp. 309–313.

24. Lavanya, Sharma. (2019). Introduction: From visual surveillance to Internet of Things. *From Visual Surveillance to Internet of Things,* vol. 1, Chapman Hall/CRC, p. 14.

25. Jha, Gauri, Singh, Pawan, Sharma, Lavanya. (July 2019) Recent advancements of augmented reality in real time applications, *International Journal of Recent Technology and Engineering.* 8(2S7): 538–542.
26. Sharma, Lavanya, Lohan, Nirvikar. (March, 2019). Internet of things with object detection. *Handbook of Research on Big Data and the IoT,* IGI Global, pp. 89–100. DOI: 10.4018/978-1-5225-7432-3.ch006
27. Sharma, Lavanya, Garg, P. K. (2019). Block based adaptive learning Rate for moving person detection in video surveillance. *From Visual Surveillance to Internet of Things,* vol. 1, Chapman Hall/CRC, p. 201.
28. Sharma, Lavanya, Garg, P. K. (2019). Smart E-healthcare with Internet of Things: Current trends challenges, solutions and technologies. *From Visual Surveillance to Internet of Things,* vol. 1, Chapman Hall/CRC, p. 215.
29. Sharma, Lavanya, Garg, P. K., Agarwal, Naman. (2019). A foresight on e-healthcare Trailblazers. *From Visual Surveillance to Internet of Things,* vol. 1, Chapman Hall/CRC, p. 235.
30. Makkar, Suraj, Sharma, Lavanya. (April 12–13, 2019) A face detection using support vector machine: Challenging issues, recent trend, solutions and proposed framework. Third International Conference on Advances in Computing and Data Sciences (ICACDS 2019, Springer), Inderprastha Engineering College, Ghaziabad.
31. Sharma, Lavanya, Garg, P. K. (2019). Future of Internet of Things. *From Visual Surveillance to Internet of Things,* vol. 1, Chapman Hall/CRC, p. 245
32. Sharma, Lavanya, Garg, P. K. (2019) IoT and its applications. *From Visual Surveillance to Internet of Things,* vol. 1, Chapman Hall/CRC, p. 29.
33. Bouwmans, T., Baf, F. E. (2009) Modeling of dynamic backgrounds by type-2 fuzzy Gaussians mixture models. *MASAUM Journal of Basic and Applied Sciences.* 1(2): 265–277.
34. Madakam, S., Ramaswamy, R., Tripathi, S. (2015) Internet of Things (IoT): A literature review. *Journal of Computer and Communications.* 3: 164–173.

11

Cloud Computing and Internet of Things: Towards Smart World for Real-Time Applications

Sugandhi Midha

Computer Science and Engineering Department, Chandigarh University
Mohali, India

CONTENTS

11.1   Research Trends and Interest Trends about the Cloud and IoT.............................197
11.2   Convergence of IoT and Cloud Computing 198
           11.2.1   Drivers for Cloud Computing and IoT Integration.......... 201
           11.2.2   Convergence Approaches 202
                          11.2.2.1   Cloud-Centric IoT 202
                          11.2.2.2   IoT-Centric Cloud 203
11.3   Challenges to Bridge between the Cloud and IoT...203
11.4   Applications of CloudIoT..205
11.5   Implementation of Cloud of Things..206
11.6   Conclusion and Future Scope 211
References..212

KEYWORDS: *Internet of Things, cloud computing, CloudIoT, Cloud of Things convergence, IBM IoT cloud*

11.1 Research Trends and Interest Trends about the Cloud and IoT

Internet of Things (IoT), which has been evolved as a fascinating and unimaginative technology, has not only made technical improvements but also made our day-to-day routine work easier and more sorted beyond our expectations. The impact that IoT has caused on human lives is huge and it is right to label it as "the next internet." IoT is a network of networks of physical objects or things such as devices, buildings, vehicles, and various embedded items equipped with sensors and internet connections that enables them to collect and exchange data. IoT applications in the real world are limitless. Yet, there are many hindrances to avail the full potential of IoT such as limited storage capacity and processing capability of devices and major concerns regarding reliability, performance, privacy, and security [1–8].

In contrast to this, cloud computing (CC) offers almost unlimited storage capacity and processing capability. CC technology is mature enough to solve problems of IoT to a certain level [9, 11, 12, 13, 14]. CC has given numerous benefits in terms of scalability and cost-effectiveness due to its pay-as-you-go utility. Its on-demand approach has set the user free from all infrastructure and platform management techniques by changing an ownership-based approach to a subscription-based approach. IoT and CC are complementary to each other and can bring revolution in the current and future real world. The integration of cloud and IoT is known as *CloudIoT* or *Cloud of Things or Cloud-Enabled IoT* [15].

In the literature, lots of work has been performed in both the areas separately. In the work, I have performed in-depth analysis of the CloudIoT paradigm. By adopting this CloudIoT paradigm, numerous applications are gaining momentum.

After performing rich analysis in this field, I analyzed that both the topics of the cloud and IoT are gaining popularity as depicted in Figure 11.1(a) and (b). In this chapter, I have reviewed the literature of the cloud and IoT, focusing on integrating the cloud and IoT as both together, which can be proved as a promising tool witnessed by the increasing trend of searching the cloud and IoT together as depicted in Figure 11.1(c). These results are obtained from Google Trends.

Inspired by our results in the analysis, I adopt the systematic methodology in my work as depicted in Figure 11.2. In Section 11.2, I have given a brief introduction to IoT and CC to provide the reader with the basic understanding necessary to deal with the integration of the cloud and IoT. I present a detailed view of the drivers for integration of the technologies. I elaborated the role of CC in IoT and convergence techniques of both the technologies. Section 11.3 highlights the challenges and issues that can arise from adopting the integration of the two. Section 11.4 discusses various applications of Cloud of Things. In Section 11.5, I describe the implementation platform and research projects of Cloud of Things. Finally, I close this chapter with concluding remarks and future scope.

11.2 Convergence of IoT and Cloud Computing

Cloud and IoT technologies have seen rapid and independent growth in the real world. These two technologies are independent but still complementary to each other.

Cloud provides various services such as Platform as a Service (PaaS), Infrastructure as a Service (IaaS), Software as a Service (SaaS), and Network as a Service (NaaS). This service business model of CC serves billion of devices connected over the internet. The number of devices connected to the internet have reached billions and are expected to grow rapidly and reach 75.44 billion by 2025 [16, 15, 17, 20].

The IoT vision in reality involves any interconnected devices such as sensors, computers, buildings, home appliances, smart planes, vehicles, real infrastructure devices, or any other device that can have internet connectivity or can be monitored or attached. These interconnected devices require huge amount of data for storage and processing. Large amounts of information sources in IoT produces semi-structure or unstructured data with volume, velocity, and variety as three major characteristics. CC aims at providing an on-demand service.

The cloud features such as ubiquitous computing, on-demand service, resource pooling, scalability, and elasticity support the obstacles of IoT such as reliability, efficiency, storage, and processing capabilities.

So, it's rightly said

IoT is a king, Big Data is a queen and Cloud is a palace [21].

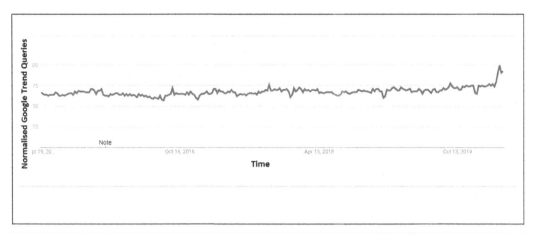

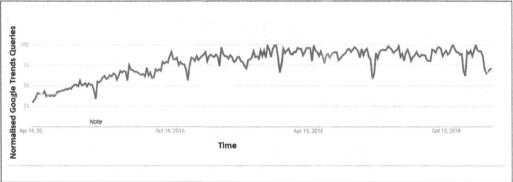

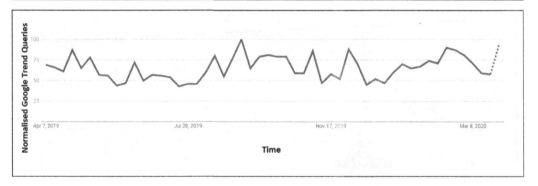

FIGURE 11.1

(a) Term "cloud" search—as per Google Trends (April 2015 to October 2019 report); (b) term "IoT" search—as per Google Trends (April 2015 to October 2019 report); (c) term "Cloud of Things" search—as per Google Trends (2019–2020 report).

Figure 11.3 [22] depicts how IoT generates services for the management of which it is dependent on CC and generated services are consumed by users over the internet.

Not only is IoT benefiting from CC, but CC can also benefit from IoT by exploring its scope in dealing with real-world things in a more distributed and dynamic way. In reality, the cloud serves as an intermediate layer that functions between the objects and applications where it abstracts the complexity and functionality used to implement the latter.

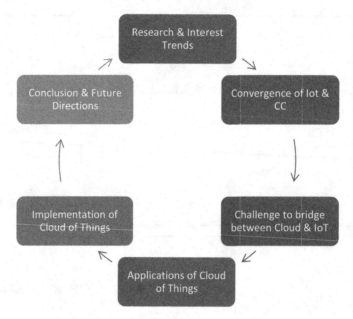

FIGURE 11.2
Research methodology adopted in this chapter.

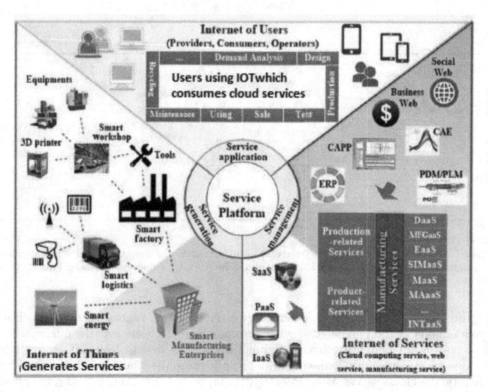

FIGURE 11.3
IoT using cloud computing.

11.2.1 Drivers for Cloud Computing and IoT Integration

There are various aspects of cloud and IoT that makes them a better combination or complementary to each other. These characteristics are listed here:

1. **Displacement:** Where IoT is pervasive, Cloud is centralized. Both the techniques work towards increasing the efficiency of everyday tasks. IoT generates a huge amount of data and CC serves as a path for this data to travel.

2. **Reachability:** The reach of IoT is very limited, whereas CC knows no boundaries; it is far and wide spread.

3. **Storage:** IoT provides none or very limited storage, whereas CC provides virtual storage that is large or never ending.

4. **Role of the Internet:** In the case of IoT, the internet acts as a convergence point, whereas in the case of CC, it serves as a means for delivering services.

5. **Computing Capability:** IoT provides less or no computing capability, whereas CC provides virtually unlimited computing capability. Cloud is a rescue power when IoT finds itself in the demand of processing and computational power. CC allows the developers of IoT to offload processing capabilities to CC services.

6. **Components:** IoT runs on hardware components such as sensors, gateways, and small devices, whereas CC runs on virtual machines that imitate hardware components. CC allows the innovators and developers of IoT to explore the real world without having large infrastructure. CC offers readymade infrastructure to talented and creative innovators where they can just plug and play their devices and services.

7. **Big Data:** IoT generates big data, whereas CC is a means to manage big data.

Due to offerings that a cloud provides in IoT, several new expansions of cloud services have evolved, which are listed in Table 11.1.

The architectural view of the cloud service for IoT is depicted in Figure 11.4.

TABLE 11.1

New Paradigms Evolved by Cloud of Things: Everything as Service

XaaS (Acronym)	X (Expansion)	Description Change
	Things as a Service [23–25]	CC and IoT-based service system
S²aaS [12, 26, 27]	Sensing as a Service	Huge sensor data and related context-capturing techniques and challenges resolved by cloud-based management, storing, archiving, and processing capabilities.
SAaaS [28]	Sensing and Actuation as a Service	Control logics automatically enabled and managed in the cloud
SEaaS [28, 29]	Sensor Event as a Service	Dispatching the services and signals generated back and from the sensor
SenaaS [30]	Sensor as a Service	Performing ubiquitous management of sensors
DBaaS [30]	DataBase as a Service	IOT generates huge data and the cloud manages that data in the database.
DaaS [30]	Data as a Service	Enabling access to ubiquitous data
EaaS [30]	Ethernet as a Service	Providing connectivity over the internet
IPMaaS [30]	Identity and Policy Management as a Service	Providing controlled access over data
VSaaS [31]	Video Surveillance as a Service	Providing complete visual control over data

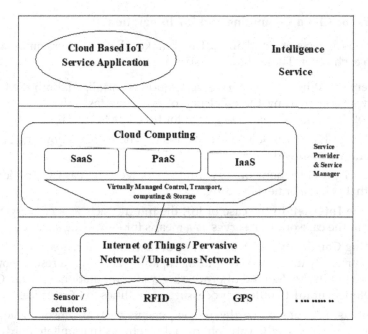

FIGURE 11.4
Cloud service architecture for IoT.

11.2.2 Convergence Approaches

Two convergence approaches of the cloud and IoT exist:

11.2.2.1 Cloud-Centric IoT

Cloud-centric IoT is bringing IoT functionality into the cloud so that cloud can explore the diversions of the real world. It implements processing and computing of IoT data into the cloud and its management into the cloud (Figure 11.5).

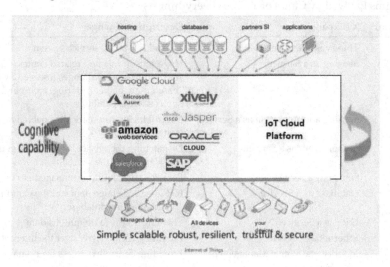

FIGURE 11.5
Cloud-centric IoT.

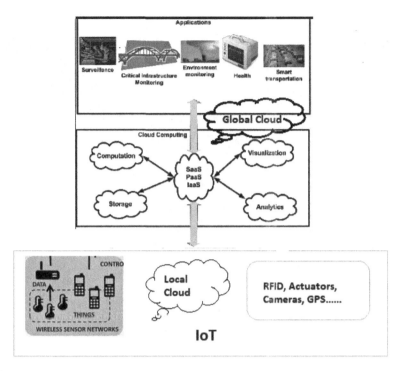

FIGURE 11.6
IoT-centric cloud.

11.2.2.2 IoT-Centric Cloud

The IoT-centric cloud is bringing cloud functionalities into IoT. This paradigm extends CC services with a view in mind to process and store the data closer to users. It supports dense geographical distribution that solves various problems like latency, traffic, hop count, etc. It also supports end-user security. It provides local autonomy when data is coming from the same location.

The IoT-centric cloud scheme consists of two clouds as depicted in Figure 11.6.

- **Local Cloud:** An on-demand cloud created to provide a sufficient amount of storage and appropriate computing and networking capabilities to the users in a particular geographical area over a particular time period. The ultimate goal is to serve users of a certain area.

- **Global Cloud:** Has an illusion of infinite storage and processing capabilities and serves business users.

11.3 Challenges to Bridge between the Cloud and IoT

IoT has changed our life chores to smart chores. As demand for processing power increases, the cloud will rescue IoT. The cloud can offer various services to IoT such as infrastructure, analytics and monitoring capability, and security and privacy, and can smooth interservice and interdevice communication; yet, there exists several challenges on the way to

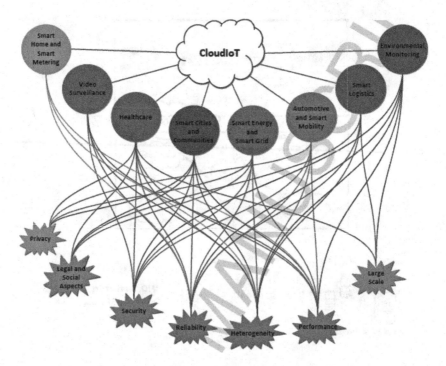

FIGURE 11.7
Application scenarios driven by the CloudIoT paradigm and its related challenges.

integrate the two. Figure 11.7 [32] explains various applications of CloudIoT and major challenges associated with each application.

1. **Heterogeneity:** A big challenge to be tackled while implementing CloudIoT is heterogeneity of devices, OS, and platform. In the case of CC, heterogeneity is not a big concern as the cloud service comes with a proprietary interface. Resource integration is customized in the case of CC based on specific providers. The aspect of a multi-cloud approach has been partially taken into account and solved by cloud brokering. In IoT, on the other hand, all the components are tightly coupled as per specific application. It becomes a challenging issue with the cloud to deal with heterogeneous things. There is a need for an interoperable programming interface to deal with this diversity.

2. **Privacy/Access Control:** Major IoT security challenges are related to authorization and authentication of devices, secure communication, ensuring privacy and integrity, managing vulnerabilities, and so on. The property of IoT of "everywhere, everything" simply implies a threat to privacy and when an IoT application is upgraded to the cloud, an issue of trust arises like lack of knowledge about Service Level Agreements (SLAs), physical location of data, and so on. Multitenancy of clouds brings another security issue. Distribution of data on the cloud raises several other concerns on security such as session hijacking, SQL injection, and virtual machine escape.

3. **Performance:** Quality of Service (QoS) becomes a major issue in CloudIoT as there are delays, jitter, bandwidth issues, high packet loss ratio in the communication.

In the case of IoT, a good amount of performance ratio is required in terms of time due to real-time response. But CloudIoT QoS parameters are highly affected by distributed architecture mostly when multimedia streaming is required.

4. **Reliability:** When applications are deployed in the cloud environment, a number of challenges related to the device not being reachable always exist [33].

5. **Large Scale:** Cloud IoT involves billions of devices that are networked and these devices produce a huge amount of data. These billions of IoT objects connected through the cloud will definitely overstretch the cloud storage. It may sometimes lead to a difficult situation in analyzing the need for the amount of resources required for that particular application.

6. **Legal and Social Aspect:** These challenges are equally important but partly related. For example, both the cloud and IoT services need to conform to different laws.

7. **Big Data:** Billions of devices are networked in CloudIoT and these devices produce vast amount of data. IoT is one of the major sources of big data and cloud facilitates its storage. Ubiquity of devices demands for scalability. It has been observed in studies that no solution exists for the cloud to manage big data.

8. **Sensor Network:** Different objects use different protocols. For example, WirelessHART, Zigbee, and IEEE 1451, for connectivity. The cloud no doubt offers new opportunities for sensor data aggregation. But in contrast to this, lack of mobility of some sensors has caused a big problem in the implementation of CloudIoT freely.

9. **Monitoring:** The three major characteristics of IoT data—volume, velocity and variety—has affected the monitoring requirements of the cloud.

10. **Fog Computing:** Research shows that the adoption of fog computing for edge location has mandate usage of specific algorithms and methodologies.

In addition to these challenges, there could be some generic issues of importance [15]:

- Virtualization of IoT devices
- Portability of services
- Real-time communication
- Interoperability between CloudIoT services and infrastructure
- Accountability services and data hosted and executed across borders

11.4 Applications of CloudIoT

In this section, several applications of CloudIoT is discussed:

1. **Smart Home:** It is a place where we can see the real application of CloudIoT. Objects at home such as TVs, microwaves, phones, ovens, air conditioners, and PCs can be equipped with smart IoT capabilities. These are equipped with sensor and actuators. These actuators communicate with microcontroller and cloud services. A microcontroller enables sensors to analyze and process the sensors

data. Data from a microcontroller is stored and analyzed with the help of cloud services. Web applications in cloud services are used to visualize and monitor the sensor data [12, 17, 19].

2. **Smart Cities:** Cities are concerned with economic growth and energy management efficiency techniques. CloudIoT provides an environment that supports and provides desired information and services. Smart bins, geo-tagging, dynamically annotated maps, and automatic IoT-enabled traffic lights, are a few applications in cities where cloud-based platforms develop and provide IoT plugins that support timeliness, scalability, configurability, and flexibility features.

3. **Healthcare:** Researchers found that CloudIoT can innovate and expand the field of healthcare. It can provide various services in this area such as patient monitoring via sensors, collecting vital patient data through sensors, storing that data on clouds for monitoring, observation, and analyzing. Electronic healthcare (EHC) records help in real time to provide a service to patients at a reduced cost [13, 14, 19, 20].

4. **Video Surveillance:** The cloud efficiently stores, manages, and processes video data coming from video sensors and easily extracts information scenes. CloudIoT has become a wide usage tool for several security applications. The cloud manages the extreme video data by distributing the task among various servers with a view in mind to balance load and fault tolerance [13, 14, 17–20].

5. **Environment Monitoring:** CloudIoT can highly contribute to the environment by deploying sensors for monitoring water levels in lakes, streams, and sewage works; for gas concentration in certain areas; and for lighting conditions.

In our next section, I have used CloudIoT for one such environment application of agriculture information transmission. I have carefully found, observed, and described a number of applications of the CloudIoT paradigm.

11.5 Implementation of Cloud of Things

We have discussed various applications of Cloud of Things in our last section. In all these applications, we can use the cloud for infrastructure, scalability, computing, and other capabilities to avail the benefits of IoT. Various CloudIoT platforms exist:

- ThingWorx 8 IoT Platform
- Microsoft Azure IoT Suite
- Google Cloud's IoT Platform
- IBM Watson IoT Platform
- AWS IoT Platform
- Cisco IoT Cloud Connect
- Salesforce IoT Cloud
- Kaa IoT Platform
- Oracle IoT Platform
- GE Predix IoT Platform
- ThingSpeak IoT Platform

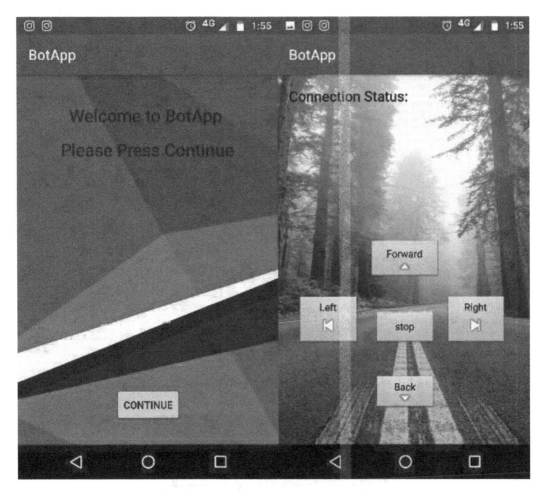

FIGURE 11.8
BotApp—Robo Car.

For my Robo Car project, I have developed an Android app that controls it. This is actually a moisture sensor through which moisture of a particular soil is obtained. The moisture sensor implementation determines the fertility of the soil by obtaining detailed information about soil moisture readings. I have used the IBM Watson cloud platform tool for storing and computing data obtained from the sensor. IBM Watson has recently added a data sensor data service.

Figure 11.8 depicts the moisture sensor app created on an Android phone that controls the Robo Car movements, fetches the data from the sensor, and data is transferred to the IBM Bluemix cloud.

For my Moisture Monitoring System, I'll be using an Android smartphone device in my project implementation. I added another device to the system to represent the gateway layer. I have added a Raspberry Pi device that supports Wi-Fi and is used as a gateway. You can use a different microcontroller or even your own PC to run the code related to the gateway. I have leveraged the IBM Watson IoT Platform to reduce worrying about security, device-management, monitoring, analytics, and visualizations. Figure 11.9 shows the architecture of my Moisture Monitoring System.

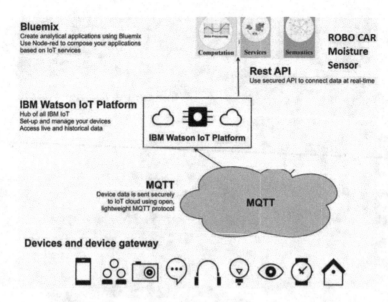

FIGURE 11.9
Moisture monitoring system architecture.

The procedure for this implementation process is as follows:

Step 1. Create an IoT Platform service on IBM IoT Cloud.

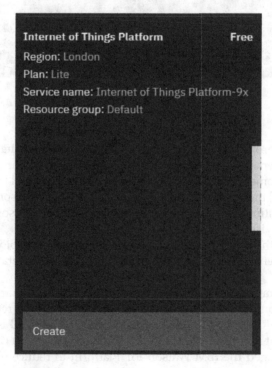

FIGURE 11.10
IBM CloudIoT project region.

Step 2. Create a new gateway device type and register the gateway device.

Device Drilldown - raspi-1

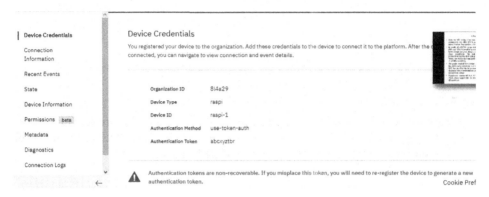

FIGURE 11.11
Gateway device—raspi-1.

Step 3. Create a device type for a smartphone.

Device Drilldown - phone1

FIGURE 11.12
Android phone device—phone1.

Step 4. Configure and connect the gateway to the device.

MQTT protocol is used by the gateway device to communicate with the cloud. To configure the connection to the MQTT broker in the IBM Watson IoT Platform, the following information is required (which I copied when I registered our gateway device–raspi-1):

- Organization ID (the 6-character identifier)
- Device Type (in our case, raspi)
- Device ID for the specific device (for example, I used raspi-1)
- Authentication Token

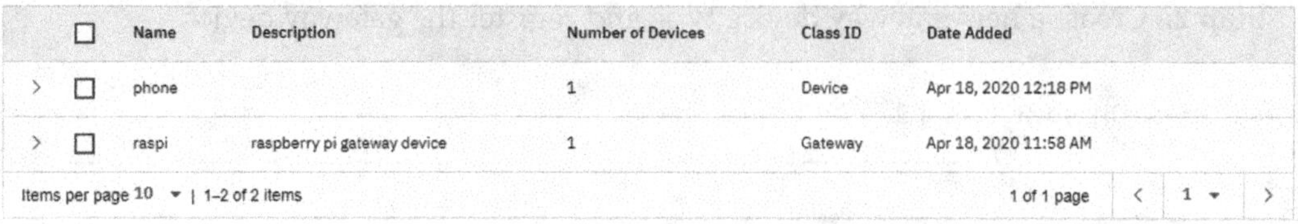

		Name	Description	Number of Devices	Class ID	Date Added
>	☐	phone		1	Device	Apr 18, 2020 12:18 PM
>	☐	raspi	raspberry pi gateway device	1	Gateway	Apr 18, 2020 11:58 AM

Items per page 10 ▾ | 1–2 of 2 items   1 of 1 page < | 1 ▾ | >

FIGURE 11.13
Device credentials.

Step 5. Send gateway events.

After the connection establishment, publishing some data to the broker can be tried. This can be done by sending events to the cloud, or in MQTT terms, we'll be publishing messages to a specific topic in the MQTT broker.

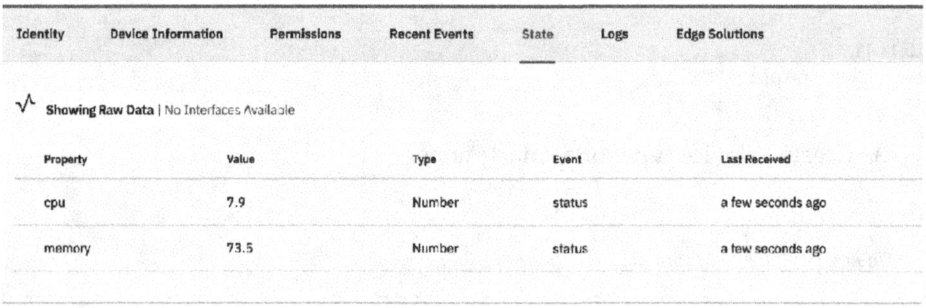

Identity	Device Information	Permissions	Recent Events	State	Logs	Edge Solutions

〜 **Showing Raw Data** | No Interfaces Available

Property	Value	Type	Event	Last Received
cpu	7.9	Number	status	a few seconds ago
memory	73.5	Number	status	a few seconds ago

FIGURE 11.14
Device data publishing.

Step 6. Connect device to the gateway.

Now let's add the smartphone device to the system. As mentioned before, we're going to connect the smartphone to the gateway over the UDP socket.

Step 7. Send device events via the gateway.

Data is coming from the device in the gateway; only publishing the work is left to the MQTT broker in the cloud.

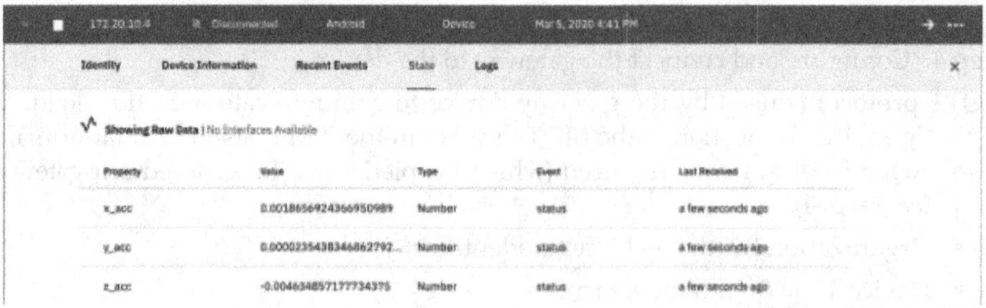

■ 172.20.10.4	R Disconnected	Android	Device	Mar 5, 2020 4:41 PM	→ ···

Identity	Device Information	Recent Events	State	Logs	✕

〜 **Showing Raw Data** | No Interfaces Available

Property	Value	Type	Event	Last Received
x_acc	0.0018656924366950989	Number	status	a few seconds ago
y_acc	0.0000235438346862792...	Number	status	a few seconds ago
z_acc	-0.004634857177734375	Number	status	a few seconds ago

FIGURE 11.15
Device data publishing with the MQTT broker.

Step 8. Visualize the data.

This help in providing a clearer image of the events that actually happened. Let's use the IBM Watson IoT Platform for visualizing the data that is sent to the cloud.

FIGURE 11.16
Data Visualization.

Similarly, the above steps can be applied for any IoT application over the cloud.

11.6 Conclusion and Future Scope

CloudIoT convergence has a series of issues and challenges. Various drivers exist for their integration. As CloudIoT requires a network of networks, as a result there are always issues to implement their integration. Table 11.2 outlines some major challenges pertaining to CloudIoT application.

CloudIoT is an exemplary research area that can bring numerous benefits in the real world. Areas that can be explored in CloudIoT aim at dealing with the heterogeneity of things and clouds. OpenIoT is another area that can be fostered as a research project.

TABLE 11.2

Challenges Pertaining to CloudIoT Application

Applications	Challenges						
	Privacy	Legal & Social Aspects	Large Scale	Security	Reliability	Performance	Hetrogeneity
Smart Home					✓	✓	✓
Smart Cities	✓	✓		✓	✓	✓	✓
Health Care	✓	✓	✓	✓	✓	✓	✓
Video Surveillance					✓	✓	✓
Environmental Monitoring				✓	✓	✓	✓

References

1. Liu, C., Yang, C., Zhang, X., Chen, J. (2014). External integrity verification for outsourced big data in cloud and IoT: A big picture. *Future Generation Computer Systems*, vol. 49C, pp. 58–67.
2. IBM Developer, Build your IoT Skills by developing door management system. Online: [https://developer.ibm.com/tutorials/iot-lp201-build-door-monitoring-system/].
3. Rao, B. P., Saluia, P., Sharma, N., Mittal, A., Sharma, S. V. (2012). Cloud computing for Internet of Things and sensing based applications. In: 2012 Sixth International Conference on Sensing Technology (ICST), IEEE, pp. 374–380.
4. Yun, M., Yuxin, B. (2010). Research on the architecture and key technology of Internet of Things (IoT) applied on smart grid. In: 2010 International Conference on Advances in Energy Engineering (ICAEE), IEEE, pp. 69–72.
5. Kuo, A. M.-H. (2011). Opportunities and challenges of cloud computing to improve health care services. *Journal of Medical Internet research*, vol. 13, no. 3, p. e67.
6. Grozev, N., Buyya, R. (2014). Inter-cloud architectures and application brokering: Taxonomy and survey. *Software: Practice and Experience*, vol. 44, no. 3, 369–390.
7. Kumar, Sanjay, Gupta, Priyanka, Lakra, Sachin, Sharma, Lavanya, (February 14–16, 2019). The Zeitgeist Juncture of "Big Data" and its Future Trends, 1st IEEE International Conference on Machine Learning, Big Data, Cloud and Parallel Computing (Com-IT-Con), Faridabad, India, pp. 309–313.
8. Sharma, Lavanya, Garg, Pradeep K., From Visual Surveillance to Internet of Things, Taylor & Francis, CRC Press (ISSN: 9780429297922).
9. Tao, F. (2014). CCIoT-CMfg: cloud computing and Internet of Things based cloud manufacturing service system, *IEEE Transactions on Industrial Informatics*, vol. 10, no. 2, pp. 1435–1442.

10. Chen, Y., Zhao, S., Zhai, Y. (2014). Construction of intelligent logistics system by RFID of Internet of things based on cloud computing, *Journal of Chemical and Pharmaceutical Research*, vol. 6, no. 7, pp. 1676–1679.

11. Wang, H. Z. (2014). Management of big data in the Internet of Things in agriculture based on cloud computing, *Applied Mechanics and Materials*, vol. 548, pp. 1438–1444.

12. Kantarci, B., Mouftah, H. T. (2014). Mobility-aware trustworthy crowdsourcing in cloud-centric Internet of Things. In: 2014 IEEE Symposium on Computers and Communication (ISCC), IEEE, pp. 1–6.

13. Jha, Gauri, Singh, Pawan, Sharma, Lavanya, (July 2019). Recent advancements of augmented reality in real time applications. *International Journal of Recent Technology and Engineering*, vol. 8, no. 2S7, pp. 538–542, (Indexed in Scopus). DOI: 10.35940/ijrte.B10100.0782S719.

14. Anand, Akshit, Jha, Vikrant, Sharma, Lavanya, (July 2019). An improved local binary patterns histograms techniques for face recognition for real time application, *International Journal of Recent Technology and Engineering*, vol. 8, no. 2S7, pp. 524–529, (Indexed in Scopus). DOI: 10.35940/ijrte.B1098.0782S719. ISSN: 2277-3878.

15. Biswas, Abdur Rahim, Giaffreda, Raffaele, (2014). IoT and Cloud Convergence: Opportunities and Challenges, IEEE World Forum on Internet of Things (WF-IoT).

16. Statista research development 2020. Online: [https://www.statista.com/statistics/471264/iot-number-of-connected-devices-worldwide/].

17. Saraogi, Gunjan, Gupta, Deepa, Sharma, Lavanya, Rana, Ajay, (August 2019). Un-supervised approach for backorder prediction using deep autoencoder. *Recent Patents on Computer Science*, Bentham, vol. 12, (Indexed in Scopus). DOI: 10.2174/2213275912666190819112609.

18. Sharma, Lavanya, Lohan, Nirvikar, (January 2019). Performance analysis of moving object detection using BGS techniques in visual surveillance. *International Journal of Spatiotemporal Data Science*, Inderscience, vol. 1, pp. 22–53.

19. Kumar, Anubhav, Jha, Gaurav, Sharma, Lavanya, (July 2019). Challenges, potential & future of IOT integrated with block chain. *International Journal of Recent Technology and Engineering*, vol. 8, no. 2S7, pp. 530–536, (Indexed in Scopus). DOI: 10.35940/ijrte.B1099.0782S719.

20. Chopra, Ujwal, Thakur, Naman, Sharma, Lavanya, (July 2019). Cloud computing: Elementary threats & embellishing countermeasures for data security. *International Journal of Recent Technology and Engineering*, vol. 8, no. 2S7, pp. 518–523, (Indexed in Scopus). DOI: 10.35940/ijrte.B1097.0782S719.

21. Sherin C. A., Internet of Things with cloud computing and M2M communication. Online: [https://www.slideshare.net/SherinCAbraham/internet-of-things-with-cloud-computing-and-m2m-communication].

22. Tao F., Cheng Y., Xu L., Zhang L., Li B. H., (May 2014). CCIoT-CMfg: cloud computing and Internet of Things-based cloud manufacturing service system, *IEEE Transactions on Industrial Informatics*, vol. 10, no. 2. DOI: 10.1109/TII.2014.2306383.

23. Christophe, B., Boussard, M., Lu, M., Pastor, A., Toubiana, V. (2011). The web of things vision: Things as a service and interaction patterns. *Bell Labs Technical Journal*, vol. 16, no. 1, pp. 55–61.

24. Mitton, N., Papavassiliou, S., Puliafito, A., Trivedi, K. S. (2012). Combining Cloud and sensors in a smart city environment. *EURASIP Journal on Wireless Communications and Networking*, vol. 1, pp. 1–10.

25. Distefano, S., Merlino, G., Puliafito, A. (2012). Enabling the Cloud of Things. In: 2012 Sixth International Conference on Innovative Mobile and Internet Services in Ubiquitous Computing (IMIS), IEEE, pp. 858– 863.

26. Perera, C., Zaslavsky, A., Christen, P., Georgakopoulos, D. (2014). Sensing as a service model for smart cities supported by Internet of Things. *Transactions on Emerging Telecommunications Technologies*, vol. 25, no. 1, pp. 81–93.

27. Kantarci, B., Mouftah, H. (2014). Trustworthy sensing for public safety in cloud-centric Internet of Things. *IEEE Internet of Things Journal*, vol. 1, no. 4, pp. 360–368.

28. Rao, B. P., Saluia, P., Sharma, N., Mittal, A., Sharma, S. V. (2012). Cloud computing for Internet of Things and sensing based applications. In: 2012 Sixth International Conference on Sensing Technology (ICST), IEEE, pp. 374–380.
29. Dash, S. K., Mohapatra, S., Pattnaik, P. K. (2010). A survey on application of wireless sensor network using cloud computing. *International Journal of Computer Science and Engineering Technologies*, vol. 1, no. 4, pp. 50–55.
30. Zaslavsky, A., Perera, C., Georgakopoulos, D. (2013). Sensing as a service and big data, Proceedings of the International Conference on Advances in Cloud Computing (ACC), Bangalore, India.
31. Prati, A., Vezzani, R., Fornaciari, M., Cucchiara, R. (2013). Intelligent video surveillance as a service. In: *Intelligent Multimedia Surveillance*. Springer, pp. 1–16.
32. Botta, Alessio, de Donato, Walter, Persico, Valerio, Pescapé, Antonio (October 2015). Integration of cloud computing and Internet of Things: A survey, *Future Generation Computer Systems*, vol. 56, pp. 684–700.
33. Armbrust, M., Fox, A., Griffith, R., Joseph, A. D., Katz, R., Konwinski, A., Lee, G., Patterson, D., Rabkin, A., Stoica, I., et al., (2010). A view of cloud computing. *Communications of the ACM*, vol. 53, no. 4, 50–58.

12

The Convergence of Internet of Things and Big Data

Shailee Lohmor Choudhary

Department of Business Analytics and Data Sciences, New Delhi Institute of Management
New Delhi, India

Rinku Sharma Dixit

Department of Business Analytics and Data Sciences, New Delhi Institute of Management
New Delhi, India

CONTENTS

12.1   Introduction 215
12.2   Literature Review 216
12.3   Internet of Things 218
12.4   Big Data 219
12.5   Significance of IoT and Big Data 219
12.6   Association: IoT and Big Data 220
12.7   Big Data Analytics 222
12.8   Big Data Tools for IoT 224
12.9   IoT and Big Data: Foundation for a Smart City 226
12.10   Case Study of a Smart World 227
        12.10.1 Smart City: The Barcelona Experience 227
        12.10.2 Smart Connected Restaurant Management System (SCRMS) 229
12.11   Proposed Framework 229
        12.11.1 The Infrastructure Layer 229
        12.11.2 The Network Layer 230
        12.11.3 IoT Gateway 230
        12.11.4 Services Layer 230
        12.11.5 The Provisioning Layer 231
12.12   Conclusion 231
References 232

KEYWORDS: *Internet of Things, big data, big data analytics, smart city, smart factory*

12.1 Introduction

Internet of Things (IoT), known to be a "Technology of the Future," has already been a key driving force for businesses to extract information from the internet about its customers, competitors, government policies, weather, financial predictions, and global markets. IoT with access to the Wi-Fi network delivers one of the fastest communication platforms that can facilitate instant access to diversified data sets, which helps business organizations in critically analyzing hidden patterns within the data set and take timely data-driven decisions. IoT data storage and processing techniques act as a core function in IoT devices and applications. These internet-connected devices collect data from built-in sensors, applications, or websites, and finally share the data with connected devices, other IoT-based applications, and industry-based machines. However, IoT data extracted from various sources and devices is huge in volume and can't be handled with conventional data storage devices and this is where the new terminology of "big data" comes into the spotlight. Big data acts as one of the crucial factors in the timely analysis of the data collected from IoT devices and has thus become a necessity. However, both big data and IoT are based on entirely different concepts and don't share any common features [1–5]. Big data aims to collect and store large volumes of data from multiple data sources whereas IoT is a major source of data generation [6–8]. The two big technologies when combined accelerate the power to make sense out of the data generated for real-time decisions by the industry.

Let's explore the difference between the two technologies and the relationship that binds them together. The authors in this chapter have explained the technologies as IoT and big data. These technologies are different and were developed separately but when they are used together, their capabilities have an additive effect and can create newer solutions and applications. This chapter discusses the methods and tools of big data analytics [9]. These capabilities have been used in various smart setups such as the smart city and a real-time case study of a smart city has been discussed in this chapter. The authors have also presented a theoretical framework that they have proposed for a Smart Connected Restaurant Management System (SCRMS). The proposed framework implements services of artificial intelligence (AI) and big data analytics for deriving the complete benefits of the SCRMS. The framework will be technically implemented in some future work.

12.2 Literature Review

IoT convergence with big data facilitates the storage of a huge amount of data along with the process of streaming this data [6]. The reports generated are largely used by businesses in predictive maintenance and anomaly reduction without the need of any human interventions. Thus, it is the collaborative approach of AI, big data analytics and IoT that helps in timely and proactive action taken by enterprises for example fraud detection in the domains like e-commerce, online payments and so on. Harika [10] shared the description of the major components used in IoT applications and their convergence with big data. The author emphasized that it's almost impossible that IoT demand will decrease in the near future. Moreover, as per the statistical surveys [11–24], the usage of internet services will rise to approximately 6 billion by 2025, which directly enhances IoT and big data applications.

The core elements of big data are volume, variety, velocity, value, veracity, validity, variability, viscosity, virality, and visualization of data [25]. Volume refers to the size of the data. In big data, the data is captured from various sources, thus refers as variety. The data, especially in IoT, is generated with high speed, which is called velocity. The data significance depends on its stakeholder that added the new term of value. With the existence of significant data on social media platforms, uncertainty about the data is referred to as veracity; on the other hand, context of data is referred to as virality. One major V in big data definition is visualization, such as graphical representation of data that makes data easily understandable. Even after the definition of big data extended by various Vs, volume, variety, and velocity remain the set of basic conceptual characteristics. Big data analytics has a significant role to play in IoT data analysis due to storage technologies and the techniques, which highlights big data and IoT as two converging technologies for new domains like smart cities.

IoT data has brought transitional change in the technique used for storing data sets, specifically concepts like NoSQL databases that have completely replaced relational databases in the case of big data storage [11]. Apart from data storage, data integration is a primary step for preparing data, which is performed in three steps: Extract, Transform, and Load (ETL). Existence of direct correlation between IoT data analytics and big data analytics demands incorporation of high-quality techniques for data extracted from IoT devices. Mostly, IoT-big data is unstructured data in the form of images or streaming data with high velocity and large volume that requires techniques like classification, mining, and visualization before deriving predictions. For example, in IoT for smart cities, the data is captured from various sources such as road surveillance, satellite and traffic signals, and so on. Data mining techniques like clustering is used firstly to get insights.

One of the major components for smart cities is the huge amount of data captured from IoT devices that is shared across multiple platforms and applications to gain insight and enable cities to be smarter in terms of predictions derived from the data and used for timely decision making in the planning and development of the city. Ganesh [7] presented a 4-tier architecture for the development of a smart city. Tier-1 handles the data generation from IoT devices, Tier-2 talks about communication technologies, Tier-3 refers to real-time analytics where tools like Hadoop, Hive, HBase, and Spark are used and data is analyzed for effective decision making.

There are various challenges such as data storage, knowledge discovery, computational complexities, visualization, scalability, and information security [12]. Big data analytics researches primarily focus on its convergence with IoT, cloud computing, and quantum computing. The author presented the tools like Hadoop and Spark for big data analytics and summarized all big data platform emphasis on particular applications like batch processing or streaming.

Rahaman et al. [12] presented a 4-tier architecture for developing a smart city where planning and monitoring decisions are derived based on big data analytics. This has been presented by data captured from various sources such as weather, pollution, parking, and vehicle movement, and are analyzed, investigated, and evaluated for urban smart city planning. The proposed system was evaluated on Spark over Hadoop and tested on various data sets on the basis of processing time and system throughput. An IoT-based application for restaurants has been implemented through which customers can find free parking slots, unoccupied tables, order food, and pay their bills (with smartphones). The application allows managers to manage the entire system and monitor the entire work [13]. But they did not implement processes to utilize the power of big data analytics. Rahman [14] proposed a theoretical IoT and big data-based solution that could be used in restaurants. The model allowed customers to place orders through mobiles, sent promotional offers to them, tracked locations of customers, provided real-time sentiment insights and targeted offers, and provided real-time kitchen updates through IoT sensors in kitchen utensils. The framework proposed in this chapter incorporates AI and analytical modules for efficient restaurant management.

12.3 Internet of Things

IoT is a system of billions of interrelated physical devices around the world that are connected via the internet. The term "thing" refers to any device or a person with an assigned IP address to derive, store, and process without the requirement of any human intervention. The advent of IoT has made the world around us smarter and responsive. Increasingly, a large number of organizations are merging their digital and physical universes with IoT to enhance customer satisfaction and have better insights to do more meaningful data-driven decision making. IoT devices are available in smart homes, virtual assistants to smart healthcare, and tracker devices and they make human lives healthier and safer.

Appliances we use in our daily life in our homes, offices, cars, shops, and so on, are all non-internet physical devices. IoT enhances connectivity from digital devices to these non-internet physical devices as most of them remain plugged in to the internet. This gives interconnectivity in a seamless manner by storing and transferring data to central systems for controlling remotely and performing real-time analytics [9, 15–24, 26]. The core player behind the scenes are sensors by which devices and objects gather information from nearby areas. Once connected to an IoT platform, a device's data is stored centrally for analysis.

The smart home concept is a worthy instance of IoT in action, aimed at enhancing quality of life, and the technology helps urban areas in operating smoothly and effectively. From doorbells, smoke detectors, security alarms, air quality monitors, traffic monitors, to crime pattern analyzers, all devices are well connected via the internet to share data with physical devices, IoT applications, and other remotely connected users to make smart cities safer, efficient, and greener. Streetlight data is an example of how smart cities can derive information about traffic and monitor it from a remote location. The platform analyzes "mobility behavior" from the data captured from smartphones, GPS devices, nearby cars, commercial trucks, healthcare devices like fitness bands, and so on, to create location records. Its propriety algorithms also deliver on-demand daily traffic metrics. Another milestone application for the smart city is from Clarity Movement, which provides an air monitoring system by capturing data from various sensor nodes of Clarity for analysis to the centralized cloud-based software platform of the company. Thus, on the basis of IoT hardware devices, AI, and machine learning algorithms, the Clarity platform offers cloud-based analyzed data about air quality [16–24, 26–29].

On a positive note, IoT offers the ability to access data from any remote device at any point of time with a seamless connected device and helps the business's services by automating tasks and reducing human intervention. On the other hand with IoT applications, businesses may need to face the challenge of capturing and processing a huge volume of streaming data from diverse data sources [30]. In the absence of International Standards for IoT devices compatibility, the challenge becomes difficult to address. In the next section, let's understand the role of big data in the context of IoT data handling and processing techniques.

12.4 Big Data

A large amount of data generated from diversified areas such as IoT devices, social media, smartphones, and the internet has given rise to new term "big data." Big data was initially defined as "Data that is so huge, fast and complex that conventional data storage techniques can't process it." In early 2000, the big data terminology gained momentum and in 2001, Gartner analyst Doug Laney expressed big data as three Vs [14–24, 26–30], as listed below:

1. **Volume:** This refers to a large amount of data generated from various sources such as business data, IoT devices, videos, social media, mobiles, industrial equipment, and so on.

2. **Velocity:** This addresses the problem of speed at which the data is generating. Most of the real-time data generated from RFID tags, smart meters, and sensors all play a major role in IoT applications.

3. **Variety:** This refers to both structured and unstructured data. Traditional data types were stored in a tabular form (rows and columns) in relational databases and Excel sheets were termed as structured data. Unstructured or semi-structured data can't be processed with conventional methods including video, emails, audios, text documents, and log details.
   Over the last few years, two additional Vs have emerged:

4. **Veracity:** This talks about accurate or trustful data. Veracity is the most complex dimension of big data as compared to all others because data is derived in varied formats and sources, thus it becomes very difficult to specify how trustworthy the data source, type, and processing is performed. To improve the quality or accuracy of the data, we must address issues like biasness, inconsistencies, and duplicity from data by removing them before processing or deriving insights.

5. **Variability:** Constantly changing behavior of the big data makes it variable. Big data is loaded into your database at an inconsistent speed, thus we must use methods such as anomaly detection or outlier detection to derive meaningful analysis.

Three core dimensions of big data such as volume, velocity, and variety are internally dependent on each other to process big data with machine learning, natural language processing (NLP), and business intelligence [17, 21, 23, 24, 31]. With the exponential growth of data globally and a rise in demand of IoT platforms for smart cities, big data has become a big deal for businesses and industries [32]. With applications in diverse fields such as retail, education, ecommerce, healthcare, automobile, research and development, and many more, companies are investing in big data management and analytics technology.

12.5 Significance of IoT and Big Data

Data is the most consistent connection among the two technologies. Generation of massive data and the potential of revealing insights from massive data has brought the two technologies together. Thus, understanding the relationship between the two is crucial. IoT aims at acquiring data from devices whereas big data aims at storing huge amounts

TABLE 12.1

Differences Between IoT and Big Data Technologies

Based on	Big Data	IoT
Aim	Big data is all about data.	IoT is all about data, devices, and their connectivity.
Time	Streamed data is not processed at the same time. Processing and analysis of the data is done at a later stage (allowed to rest). Widely used for predictive analytics, capacity building, product development, etc.	Streamed data is processed instantly at the same time. Processing and analysis of the data is constantly managed for real-time analysis. Widely used for traffic management, smart homes, etc.
Data Generator	Most of big data generated is through human activity such as social media, log records, online browsing, etc. This refers to static data stored to understand patterns within, predictions, etc.	Most of the IoT data is received from machines, i.e., sensors attached to everyday appliances. This refers to dynamic data captured for real-time decisions.

of data. Originated to address different needs and are based on different concepts, both technologies have different characteristics [33]. Table 12.1 lists the differences between the two technologies:

Both IoT and big data are independent of each other but when combined together they bring value to any system. Both leverage the power of each other in bringing insights into data analytics.

12.6 Association: IoT and Big Data

IoT-connected devices act as generators of a huge amount of data, which places high demand on businesses for better data solutions to manage big data. Thus, businesses are forced to upgrade their current data solutions in terms of technologies, processes, and data security in order to meet requirements. Industries like transportation, health, energy, ecommerce, and many more, are employing IoT and big data together to explore business opportunities, hidden patterns, and align with customers' requirements [9, 34]. The concept of smart homes has resulted in the growth of applications like smart farming, e-health, smart retail, smart water management, smart traffic management, and many more. These applications generate a lot of data that is required by industries to have better insights about their stakeholders. To utilize the huge data generated by IoT devices and bring meaning out of it, this big data needs to be analyzed. The steps followed by IoT and big data during the capturing and processing of data is depicted by the flowchart in Figure 12.1.

To harness the power of big data in processing huge data generated from IoT applications, we need to understand the effect of IoT on big data [35].

1. **Data Storage Technology**: Generation of a high volume of data by IoT applications has already challenged the conventional techniques of data management and storage. To handle a growing load of data, new innovative solutions need to be adopted. Along with advances in technology, many organizations have adopted PaaS (Platform as a Service) to handle scalability issues in big data storage

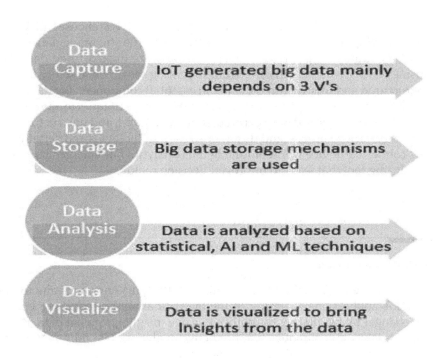

FIGURE 12.1
Steps followed by big data and IoT for capturing and processing data.

infrastructure. IBM Bluemix is cloud-based IoT platform offering PaaS and IaaS (Infrastructure as a Service) platforms to build, monitor, and execute scalable applications with data security features in-built. A new entrant namely Edge Computing offers the ability to preprocess data on premises itself before shifting it on to the cloud.

2. **Security & Privacy**: IoT ecosystem refers to connected devices, thus the devices and appliances that use to operate quietly earlier are now connected to the internet, which on the other hand exponentially increases the risk of security and privacy. Today's world of apps and cloud services has connected our life with the public internet either directly or indirectly. All these IoT devices increase the risk of cyber security as they could become an entry point onto our network. Mostly, these devices spread across our home, campuses, even geographies. The risks associated with IoT devices can't be ignored. Big data solution providers must innovate new techniques that offer high-security data, devices, and develop standards for implementing IoT devices.

3. **Protocols for Big Data Technologies**: IoT devices communicate over Wi-Fi and Bluetooth, thus technologies must provide leak-proof solutions for data transfer. Control mechanisms based on standard protocols are required for dataflow management. MQTT (Message Queuing Telemetry Transport) is a commonly used protocol in IoT projects. Being lightweight, and lower in size and power usage, it minimizes data packets and makes it best suited for IoT applications. Mosquitto is a very popular open source protocol that implements the MQTT protocol.

4. **Big Data Analytics**: The traditional Enterprise Data Warehouse (EDW) and Business Intelligence (BI) tools can't efficiently handle the streaming data received from IoT applications. Specifically, EDWs can't analyze unstructured data. Thus, for businesses to have better insights from streaming sensor data, ability to handle both structured and unstructured data is an essential component. Big data analytics comes into play because it uses advanced analytical techniques to analyze huge, diverse data sets comprised of structured, semi-structured, and unstructured data regardless of varied sources, and different sizes from terabytes and zettabytes. In today's connected-device world of IoT, big data analytics has emerged as an effective analyzing tool that leads to improved decision making.

12.7 Big Data Analytics

Data is of no use if we can't derive meaning out of it. With the enormous amount of data generated by IoT applications, blending of the big data analytics technique became the major game changer by facilitating the ability to drive insights from big data. Businesses uses advanced analytical techniques like predictive analytics, data mining, text mining, natural language processing, artificial neural networks, and statistics to gain a competitive edge, improve productivity, know customer behavior patterns, product reviews, operations optimization, enhance human productivity, anomaly detection, and many more unprecedented insights on a real-time basis with dynamic dashboards [36].

Big data analytics has emerged as a key role player in IoT platforms. Analysis of the data captured from connected devices is one of the most important processes of IoT and industrial units. To gain advantage of IoT, we can use various types of data analytics methods listed here:

- **Predictive Analytics**: Predictive analytics is one advanced analytics technique that uses historical data to predict the future. It collectively uses data mining statistical and predictive modeling techniques to understand patterns and relationships among factors in historical or transactional data to identify risks. Crucial business operational decisions like risk analysis and anomaly detection relies heavily on predictive analytics techniques.

- **Time Series Analytics (Forecasting)**: Prediction problems that involve time as a crucial component are often difficult to handle but it is a necessity for businesses to understand seasonality, cyclicality, trends, and randomness in the data. The major application areas of time series forecasting are forecasting online users (retail), forecasting customer satisfaction (retail), forecasting traffic (smart cities), forecasting spending habits of users (retail), forecasting staff turnover (HR), and many more.

- **Spatial Analytics (Location intelligence)**: A world of connected-devices (IoT) produces data sets of locations that highly impact the problem-solving and decision-making capabilities of businesses. Location-based data refers to information about transportation, education, crime rate, soil type, weather, water reserves, vegetation, construction, traffic, credit card usage, etc. Location-based sensor data brings insights into sensitive domains like planning, product tracking, supply chain management, customer habits, to optimizing operations. One such example of an organization who utilizes geospatial data for positioning emergency responders is Nokia (earlier Space-Time Insight), a Silicon Valley firm that helps logistic companies, public utilities, oil and gas firms about the efficacy of their physical assets in the field. The data captured is of varied types of data format, which is stored in Hadoop or HANA big data platforms for analysis. The central server, such as situation intelligence (SI) of the company, visualizes the data on mapping software from Google. Thus, it helps the companies and government agencies to take timely action in case of big storms or any other natural calamity.

- **Prescriptive Analytics**: In the business domain, prescriptive analytics is not a well-known term as compared to predictive analytics. Although with the rising adoption of IoT and big data collaboration, managers have started to understand that time factor as the value of the decision vanishes if strategies are not put into place within the timeframes. Predictive analytics works on recommending specific actions as per the situation. Thus, predictions we receive from predictive analytics are followed by a set of recommendations and actions for a particular situation.

- **Visualization:** Data is useless in itself unless we analyze and present it into a useful format that can give insight information that will benefit business goals. IoT data mostly talks of sensors and the basic reason for visualizing even a single sensor data aims at monitoring the status, location, and operation, etc. But the ultimate benefit of visualization comes when we combine the IoT data with other organizational data like online data, social media, financial data, marketing data, etc., to discover business patterns and trends. Tools like Grafana, Kibana (OSS), Tableau, and Power BI are used to analyze IoT data.

The actions in Figure 12.2 can be described as recommending traffic diversions, prospective customers, repairing of critical parts, suspicious fraud activity, maintenance of the machinery, optimal resource planning, etc.

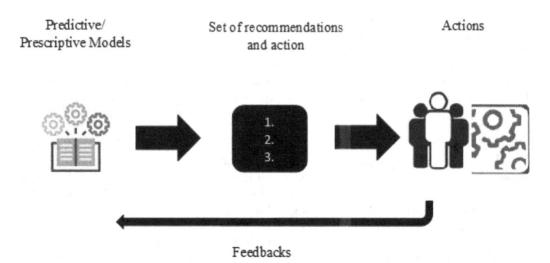

FIGURE 12.2
Steps of predictive and prescriptive analytics.

12.8 Big Data Tools for IoT

In order to deal with machine-generated data from IoT and human-generated data from big data pools in a meaningful manner, specialized tools of big data analytics are used that are categorized in three broad categories based on data-processing requirements [37]:

- **Batch Analysis**: Here, the data is first stored and then analyzed. This works extremely well with a huge data set and balances the high volume by distributing the processing among different machines. Popularly used in data mining and machine learning techniques. Apache Hadoop and Map Reduce are two open source platforms widely used in batch processing.
- **Stream Processing**: Widely used in most of IoT applications with real-time data analytics requirement. Analysis on data is performed simultaneously as the data comes as a never-ending stream of events. It works well with less hardware requirements as compared to batch analysis. It refers to data processing of website visits, customer transactions, or log activities. Apache Steam and Spark are the most popular platforms for stream-based analytics.
- **Interactive Processing**: One of the prominent features of interactive processing is its ability to interact with data and then proceed with data analytics. Apache Drill, Google's Dremel, and D3 (Data Driven Documents) are widely used platforms for interactive processing of big data.

Each category has specialized tools for processing. The Table 12.2 lists the comparative summary of these tools.

On the basis of data-processing specifications, a decision is made for storing and processing the unstructured data and deriving meaningful information for business goals. The entire implementation strategy of an IoT and big data collaborative implementation aims at increasing revenue, enhancing productivity and efficiency, and lowering the cost to business. To achieve an overall business goal, the clearly stated strategy must be put into place to achieve value from the data as per the requirement of the business. Business decisions like real-time analytics, offline analytics, or business intelligence (BI) depend on the business requirement. No all-fit solution is possible because these tools and techniques require substantial cost and technical manpower. Thus, deliberate discussion on outcomes expected from big data analytics is a must. The generic framework used by IoT technology and big data analytics is depicted in Figure 12.3.

Real-time analytics are typically used when speed and fast analysis is crucial, mostly in the case of sensor-based data; on the other hand, data offline analytics can be an option when a quick response is not required. If cost is not a constraint, SAP HANA is very effective real-time analytics architecture; on the other hand, Hadoop and Kafka architecture reduces the cost and delivers a good solution for massive analytics. MongoDB provides memory-level analytics and fits well when the data size is smaller than the memory of a cluster. For example, connected IoT devices such as traffic lights, security cameras, and home devices generate data of varied formats. The low-cost commodity storage databases that can facilitate distributed fault tolerance are Spark, MapReduce, and Splunk.

TABLE 12.2

Comparative Analysis of Big Data Technologies

Data Processing Techniques	Big Data Tools	Features	Benefits
Batch Analysis	Apache Hadoop	Open Source HDFS (Distributed File System) YARN (Resource Management) MapReduce	Complete platform and infrastructure Scalability, reliability Fault tolerant
	Microsoft Dryad	Proprietary Platform Dryad LINQ (Language Integrated Query) DSC (Distributed Storage Catalog)	Fault tolerant Good programmability Complete platform and infrastructure
	Apache Mahout	Open Source Machine Learning Algorithms	Quick analysis of huge dataset Implements classification algorithms, clustering
Stream Processing	Apache Spark	Unified Analytics Engine – Big Data and ML Capable of both Batch & Stream Analysis Work with R, Python, Java Spark SQL Spark MLLib (Machine learning) GraphX	Fast and easy to use Efficient data processing Multiple data source accessibility Machine learning efficacy
	Apache Storm	Steam processing platform Real-time analytics	Efficient Scalable Fault tolerant Easy to use
	Samza	Open Source Distributed Stream Processing Works with Apache Kafka for messaging Works with YARN for resource management	Real-time asynchronous system Distribute streaming analysis
	Flink	Open Source Hybrid Framework for both batch & stream analysis Programmable with Python, R, Java, SQL No own storage system	Event time management State management High throughput, low latency streaming engine
Interactive Processing	Apache Drill	Hadoop and NoSQL platform on SQL Query engine Storage – HDFS Batch processing using MapReduce	Flexible – varied Query languages, sources and data types Fast – process petabytes of data Can explore nested data Effective ad hoc query handling
	Google Dremel	Storage – HDFS Batch processing using MapReduce	Fast execution of group query Process petabytes of data
	D3 (Data Driven Document)	Interactive Processing	Scalability
	Spago BI	Business Intelligence	Advanced functionality for visualization Real time Geospatial analysis

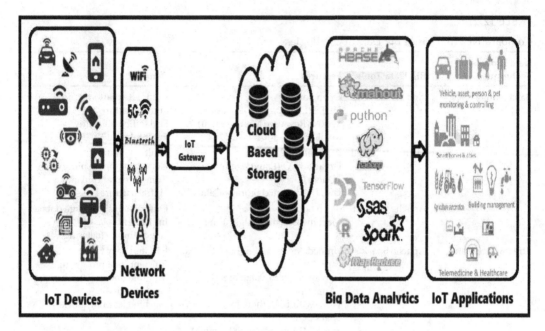

FIGURE 12.3
Framework of big data analytics and IoT.

12.9 IoT and Big Data: Foundation for a Smart City

The expansion of IoT and big data technologies have made businesses realize that Data is a major fuel and crucial business asset. Both together have the potential to facilitate the platform for a smart world to smart cities and finally to smart homes. Smart cities aim to bring more comfortable and secure day-to day living to its residents. The smart city concept is entirely dependent on IoT and big data. In order to create a smart city service, we need to analyze data received from all major stakeholders such as city officials, the private sector, city citizens, along with massive data streams captured from IoT devices and big data platforms [9, 16–24, 26, 38]. The entire process of data analysis is referred to as big data analytics, which enables smart city projects to convert data into meaningful insights for timely decisions.

For smart city conceptualization, both big data and IoT lies at its core of innovative technologies. The insights captured from the data, gathered from connected devices, government agencies, social media platforms, and other data sources, will help the city officials and businesses to optimize their processes for better city administration [16–24]. The summary of different IoT applications for a smart world are listed in Table 12.3.

A smart city platform mainly uses sensors data to monitor city management. The three-step policy for effective transformation of a city to a smart city is:

1. Technology base for network of sensors and connected devices.
2. Deployment of IoT applications for raw data capturing.
3. Usage of tools and technologies of big data analytics for alerts, insights, and action.

TABLE 12.3

IoT Applications for Smart World

Smart World	Smart Cities	Smart Parking	Parking space monitoring
		Structure Health	Historical monuments, buildings, flyovers, structural health monitoring
		Traffic Congestion	Vehicle movements and routes monitoring
		Smart Lighting	Intelligent street lights
		Waste Management	Optimization of trash routes and collection
		Smart Roads	Intelligent highways with optimized routing in case of emergency
		Urban Maps	Monitoring centric and important zones
	Smart Environment	Fire Detection	Monitoring fire alert zones
		Air Pollution	Monitoring pollution emitting cars, factories
		Earthquake Detection	Monitoring tremors and administering
		Soil Quality	Monitoring soil moisture, earth density for understanding land condition
	Smart Water	Sea Pollution	Monitoring sea levels and pollution levels
		Portable Water	Monitoring the quality of tap water in the city
		River Quality	Detecting chemical leakages in river water
	Smart Metering	Smart Grid	Monitoring and management of energy consumption
		Tank Level	Water, oil, and gas levels monitoring in storage tanks
	Smart Retail	Intelligent Shopping	Intelligent applications to recommend customers on the basis of age, buying history, preferences
		Smart Product Management	Automated restocking of products in shelves and warehouses
		Smart Supply Chain	Tracking product and storage condition along supply chain process
	Smart Logistics	Shipment Quality	Administering quality of shipment in terms of strokes, opened container, cold chain management
		Item Locating	Optimized identification of product in warehouses or harbors
	Smart Health	Smart Need Analysis	Monitoring of elderly and disabled people who need assistance
		Patients Surveillance	Keeping check on critical patients' health inside hospitals
	Smart Homes	Energy and Water Usage	Monitoring the consumption of water and energy for cost saving
		Smart Appliances	To avoid accidents and save energy all appliances controlling with auto on/off panel
		Smart Safety	Monitoring of door and window openings

12.10 Case Study of a Smart World

12.10.1 Smart City: The Barcelona Experience

In the 1980s, Barcelona was facing a big challenge in terms of economy collapse as unemployment slashed the industrial dream of the city. The city council decided economic reforms in terms of a new economy based on modern city quality infrastructure, tourism, and industries. Thus, technology took center stage and a strategy to develop Barcelona as a smart city emerged in the 2010s. In 2013, the city council of Barcelona defined a smart city as "a self-sufficient city of productive neighborhoods at human speed, inside a hyper-connected zero emissions metropolitan area." Aiming at economic growth and quality living, the city decided to incorporate new technologies and infrastructure [39, 40]. The strategic plan was shared with all stakeholders, both local and regional, including businesses and universities.

Barcelona invested heavily on IoT and big data for urban systems. Let's explore a few of the high-tech improvements initiated by the city to achieve smart city status:

- **Smart Street Lights:** To achieve energy efficiency and reduce the cost of heat, an LED-based lightning system was put in place that was further aligned with sensors to receive information about humidity, pollution, temperature, noise, people nearby, etc.

- **Waste Disposal:** The concept of smart bins was used to reduce the smell from trash and noise during waste collection by vehicles. The smart bins used a vacuum to suck the waste and forward it to an underground storage system. The entire system helped in understanding the overall waste generated within the city and optimized the process for allocation of manpower and other resources for timely and effective working.

- **City Bicycle System:** Barcelona was one of the first cities to implement a public sharing bicycle concept to reduce the number of cars in the city. Recently, a bicycle app was introduced to check the real-time availability of bicycles at stations.

- **Smart Parking:** The city installed light and metal detectors so that sensors can detect the availability and location of a parking spot. Quick parking allocation and optimization of the pattern of parking allocation helped the authorities in managing urban mobility.

- **Stellar Bus Transit System:** A new bus network was introduced for faster, easier travel and has smart solar panels and screens displaying waiting times, arrival times, and seat information. This system is an example of sustainable mobility and decreasing emissions.

- **Irrigation System:** Data on humidity, velocity of wind, sunlight, temperature, and atmospheric pressure was gathered from various sensors. This helps farmers and gardeners to understand the soil quality and schedule the watering as per the data to avoid over watering. This project helps in saving water to a large extent.

- **Public Network:** In order to receive participation from the grassroot level, citizens play a key role in the development of smart cities, thus a public network of Fab Labs was introduced.

- **Open BCN:** Repository of database, which is available for public information. It provides data about election results, population, public facilities, and pollution to keep citizens informed.

The Barcelona smart city plan aimed at twofold achievement: first, incorporation of new tools and technologies for economic growth and second, overall well-being of its citizens.

The case study of Barcelona has highlighted how big data and IoT contribute to a smart city development initiative. Key findings including technological advancement applied in the crucial domains like pollution, traffic management, parking allocation, soil and waste management, disaster forecasting in manufacturing units, urban mobility, and addressing the city specifically makes an ideal platform for smart city projects. Although it's the data that acts as the driving force behind the scene of any smart city, on the other hand, a good vision strategy of the city council and governance are also major contributors for a successful smart city project.

12.10.2 Smart Connected Restaurant Management System (SCRMS)

Restaurants are facing tremendous competition for quality of food and other services such as dine-in, home delivery, ease to customers, cost, technology, ambience, and so on. IoT-enabled smart solutions can help improve sales, marketing, operations, customer satisfaction, convenience, and loyalty. These systems can help in ensuring overall management of the restaurant from inventory, billing, kitchen management, energy management, customer management, to the growth of the business. A network of smart connected devices can create a continual circle of feedback and enhancement. The basic IoT components, for instance, may be smart sensors in fryers, ovens, and other cooking utensils that notify the chef when the food is cooked and also alert the managers of the quality and hygiene standards maintenance. Sensors in refrigerators can check for spoilt food, alert for depleting food items, monitor perishables, and check expiry notifications of stored items. Similarly, sensors in other components and locations in the restaurants can lead to effective management. With historical data, the system can implement predictive analytics for efficient process management such as ascertaining whether the orders received can be satisfied with the available reserves. Systems coupled with customer data can provide hyperpersonalization leading to customer satisfaction, better stock management, on-demand delivery, preventing food wastage, and optimizing resources. Beacons and Wi-Fi networks can send tailored promotional messages to lure customers [9, 28]. All these and many more applications in the SCRMS can be extremely useful for automating and implementing AI and big data analytics methods and services for incorporating smart solutions and services in SCRMS.

12.11 Proposed Framework

The proposed framework is composed of five layers: Infrastructure Layer, Network Layer, IoT Gateway, Services Layer, and Provisioning Layer. The overall architecture of the theoretical proposed SCRMS is depicted in Figure 12.4.

All these layers are now explained in detail.

12.11.1 The Infrastructure Layer

This is the lowermost layer that houses all the smart components in the SCRMS. These include smart appliances, smart monitoring systems, smart cameras, smart phones, wearables, smart lighting, beacons, etc. The smart devices may be of three types:

1. Sensors that sense the environment for heat, light, humidity, radio frequencies or other parameters.
2. Actuators that act on receiving command.
3. Hybrid that combine sensing and actuating functionalities, most of the devices around us fall into this category.

The data collected is passed on to the Services Layer for further processing.

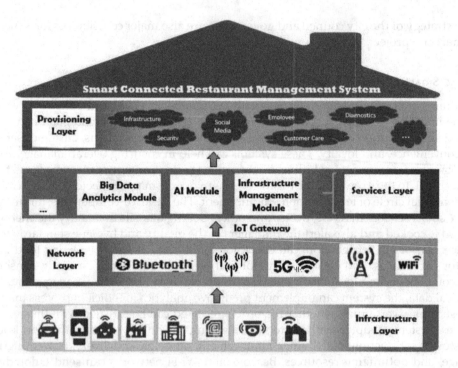

FIGURE 12.4
Proposed framework: Smart connected restaurant management system (SCRMS).

12.11.2 The Network Layer

This layer provides functionality for connecting the components of the Infrastructure Layer. The networking devices functional in this layer include Wi-Fi, 5G, Bluetooth, antennas, radars, and satellites depending on the range of connectivity desired.

12.11.3 IoT Gateway

The IoT Gateway connects the Network Layer to the Cloud Storage where all the data collected from the devices in the Infrastructure Layer is collected and stored for further analysis and for anytime, anywhere access, security, and unlimited storage.

12.11.4 Services Layer

The Services Layer is responsible for management of devices in the Infrastructure and Networking Layer, analysis of collected data, and provision of additional services. It therefore consists of three modules to handle these three types of responsibilities:

1. **Infrastructure Management Module**: This module is used for controlling the accessed devices and collecting the data from those devices. It is the interface for connecting the Infrastructure Layer with the Services Layer. The two main functions of this layer are:
   - Controlling the connectivity of smart devices to the Services Layer.
   - Providing remote management of the devices and other extended services.

2. **AI Module**: This module is responsible for provisioning the AI services for SCRMS. The typical services that may be required to be implemented in this module include:

   - **Machine Learning** for training the systems for effective decision making.
   - **NLP** for providing an interface for user interaction and providing personalization of services.
   - **Computer Vision** for perceiving through cameras and interpreting emergency or other situations and raising alerts.
   - **Robotic Process Automation and Scheduling**: Automation of routine tasks and scheduling of activities.

3. **Big Data Analytics**: This module is for implementing analytics on the SCRMS data. The data collected over time and the real-time and streaming data collected every second will be used for deriving useful insights and taking strategic decisions for extending and improving the restaurant business. Typical services in this module include:

   - **Predictive Analytics**: The data collected over time can be used for providing hyperpersonalized services to the customers and also predict trends for the future based on past events.
   - **Time Series Forecasting**: The real-time data will used for forecasting customer satisfaction, online order traffic, handling beacon data for tailored promotional messages, forecasting spending habits of customers, etc. These forecasts will help take strategic decisions.
   - **Spatial Analytics**: Location-based sensor data will be used for deriving insights from sensitive domains like order tracking, depletion and tracking of reserves, customer habits and reactions and other such optimizing operations.
   - **Prescriptive Analytics**: This service will be used for suggesting and prescribing actions and reactions to specific events, identifying prospective customers, repairing critical parts, flagging suspicious or fraudulent activity, maintenance of the machinery, optimal resource planning, etc.
   - **Visualization**: This service shall provide visualization of the restaurant data such as the online data, data from social media, financial data, marketing data, and so on, to discover business patterns and trends.

12.11.5 The Provisioning Layer

The Provisioning Layer houses the possible applications of the SCRMS. These applications may include infrastructure, social media interface, diagnostics, management decision and reporting, security, customer care, employee forum, and so on.

12.12 Conclusion

The potential of IoT and big data technology has led to the rise of smart city projects. IoT applications provide a connected devices platform that captures data from all devices, networks, and sensors that are embedded in its infrastructure. This machine-generated data is further combined with human-generated data received from social media sites, government data, online surfing data, and so on, and finally processed using big data analytics tools and technologies. Data becomes the most valuable after the processing phase and finally reaches data visualization so that it can bring insights for all stakeholders. The real meaning of the smart city concept comes from the ability to take quick and immediate action by stakeholders to solve issues and work toward a healthier and greener life for its residents. The concept of smart homes has resulted in growth of applications like smart farming, e-health, smart retail, smart water management, smart traffic management, and many more. These applications generate lot of data that is required by industries to have better insights about their stakeholders. To utilize the huge data generated by IoT devices and bring meaning to it, big data needs to be analyzed. The proposed framework for SCRMS can be used for effectively utilizing the methods of AI and big data analytics for deriving insights and trends and taking decisions for future strategies.

References

1. Sharma, Lavanya, Lohan, Nirvikar. (January 2019) Performance analysis of moving object detection using BGS techniques in visual surveillance, *International Journal of Spatiotemporal Data Science*, Inderscience, vol. 1, pp. 22–53.
2. Kumar, Anubhav, Jha, Gaurav, Sharma, Lavanya. (July 2019) Challenges, potential & future of IOT integrated with block chain, *International Journal of Recent Technology and Engineering*, 8(2s7):530–536.
3. Liu, Yong, Hou, Rongxu. (2010) About the sensing layer in Internet of Things [J], *Computer Study*, 5:55.
4. Sharma, Shubham, Verma, Shubhankar, Kumar, Mohit, Sharma, Lavanya. (2019). Use of motion capture in 3D animation: motion capture systems, challenges, and recent trends. In: 1st IEEE International Conference on Machine Learning, Big Data, Cloud and Parallel Computing (Com-IT-Con), India, 14–16 February, pp. 309–313.
5. Sharma, Lavanya, Lohan, Nirvikar. (March, 2019) Internet of Things with object detection, In *Handbook of Research on Big Data and the IoT*, IGI Global, pp. 89–100. (ISBN: 9781522574323, doi: 10.4018/978-1-5225-7432-3.ch006).
6. Dandugudum, M., Naik, S. K., Yamsani, N. Harshavardhan, A., Srikanth, Y. (2019) New challenges and future trends: Big data analytics and artificial intelligence in IoT. *Studia Rosenthaliana (Journal for the Study of Research)*. 11(12): 165–172.
7. Ganesh, E. N. (2017) Development of Smart City Using IOT and Big Data. *International Journal of Computer Techniques*. 4(1): 36–41
8. Rathore, M. M. U., Paul, A., Ahmad, A., Jeon, G. (2017) IoT-based Big Data: From smart city towards next generation super city planning. *International Journal on Semantic Web and Information Systems*. 13(1): 28–46.
9. Sharma, Lavanya, Garg, P.K. (Eds.). (2019) *From Visual Surveillance to Internet of Things*. New York, NY: Chapman and Hall/CRC, https://doi.org/10.1201/9780429297922
10. Sai, P. Y., Harika, P. (2017) Illustration of IOT with Big Data analytics. *Global Journal of Computer Science and Technology*. 17(3): 5–10.
11. Ge, M. et al., (2018) Big data for Internet of Things: A survey. *Future Generation Computer Systems*. 87:604–614. https://doi.org/10.1016/j.future.2018.04.053.
12. Rahaman Sk, Althaf, Rajesh K, Sai, Rani K, Girija. (2018) Challenging tools on research issues in big data analytics. *International Journal of Engineering Development and Research*. 6(1): 637–644.

13. Saeed, H., Shouman, A., Elfar, M., Shabka, M., Majumdar, S. and Horng-Lung, C. (2016) Near-field communication sensors and cloud-based smart restaurant management system. In 2016 IEEE 3rd World Forum on Internet of Things (WF-IoT). 686–691. doi: 10.1109/WF-IoT.2016.7845440.

14. Rahman, M. (2017) "IoT & Big Data Based Applications for Restaurant Questions of Opportunities, Challenges, Benefits & Operations" (technical report, University of Derby, UK). doi: 10.13140/RG.2.2.35231.05287.

15. Kaur, S., Singh, I. (2016) A survey report on Internet of Things applications. *International Journal of Computer Science Trends and Technology*. 4(2) ISSN: 2347-8578.

16. Sharma, Lavanya, Garg, P. K. (2019) Block based adaptive learning rate for moving person detection in video surveillance, In *From Visual Surveillance to Internet of Things*, Chapman Hall/CRC, vol. 1, p. 201.

17. Sharma, Lavanya, Garg, P. K. (2019) Smart E-healthcare with Internet of Things: Current trends challenges, solutions and technologies, In *From Visual Surveillance to Internet of Things*, Chapman Hall/CRC, vol. 1, p. 215.

18. Sharma, Lavanya, Garg, P. K., Agarwal, Naman. (2019) A foresight on e-healthcare Trailblazers, In *From Visual Surveillance to Internet of Things*, Chapman Hall/CRC, vol. 1, p. 235.

19. Sharma, Lavanya, Garg, P. K. (2019) Future of Internet of Things, In *From Visual Surveillance to Internet of Things*, Chapman Hall/CRC, vol. 1, p. 245.

20. Abraham, Sherin C., Internet of Things with cloud computing and M2M Communication, Online: [https://www.slideshare.net/SherinCAbraham/internet-of-things-with-cloud-computing-and-m2m-communication].

21. Jha, Gauri, Singh, Pawan, Sharma, Lavanya. (July 2019) Recent Advancements of augmented reality in real time applications, *International Journal of Recent Technology and Engineering*, 8(2S7):538–542.

22. Distefano, S., Merlino, G., Puliafito, A. (2012) Enabling the cloud of things. In: 2012 Sixth International Conference on Innovative Mobile and Internet Services (IMIS) in Ubiquitous Computing. IEEE, pp. 858–863.

23. Sharma, Lavanya, Singh, Annapurna, Kumar Yadav Dileep. (March, 2016) Fisher's linear discriminant ratio based threshold for moving human detection in thermal video, *Infrared Physics and Technology*, Elsevier. 78: 118–128.

24. Christophe, B., Boussard, M., Lu, M., Pastor, A., Toubiana, V. (2011) The web of things vision: Things as a service and interaction patterns. *Bell Labs Technical Journal* 16(1): 55–61.

25. Bangui, H., Buhnova M. G. B. (2018) Exploring big data clustering algorithms for Internet of Things applications. 2018. In Proceedings of the 3rd International Conference on Internet of Things, Big Data and Security (IoTBDS 2018). 269–276.

26. Mitton, N., Papavassiliou, S., Puliafito, A., Trivedi, K. S. (2012) Combining Cloud and sensors in a smart city environment. *EURASIP Journal on Wireless Communications and Networking*, 2012(1): 1–10.

27. Ahsan, U., Bais, A. (2016) A review on big data analysis and Internet of things (IoT). In Proceedings of 13th International Conference on Mobile Ad Hoc and Sensor Systems, IEEE.

28. Fei, Tao, Ying, Cheng, Lida, Xu, Lin, Zhang, Bo Hu, Li, (May 2014) CCIoT-CMfg: Cloud computing and Internet of Things-Based cloud manufacturing service system, *IEEE Transactions on Industrial Informatics*, 10(2): 1435–1442.

29. Perera, C., Zaslavsky, A., Christen, P., Georgakopoulos, D. (2014) Sensing as a service model for smart cities supported by internet of things. *Transactions on Emerging Telecommunications Technologies*. 25(1): 81–93.

30. Ahmed, E., Yaqoob, I., Abaker, I., Hashem, T., Khan, I., Vasilakos Athanasios V. (2017) The role of big data analytics in Internet of Things. *Computer Networks*. 129: 459–471.

31. Sharma, Lavanya. (2019) Introduction: From visual surveillance to Internet of Things, *From Visual Surveillance to Internet of Things*, Chapman Hall/CRC, vol. 1, p.14.

32. Tyagi, N. (2019) How is big data analytics shaping up Internet of Things(IoT)'s? *Analytic Steps*, November 4. https://www.analyticssteps.com/blogs/how-big-data-analytics-is-shaping-up-internet-of-thingsiots

33. Joseph, T. (2018) Why big data and IoT differs yet is compliant across a common ground. *Zeomag*, November 12. https://www.zeolearn.com/magazine/why-big-data-and-iot-differs

34. Delago, R. (2016) Big data and the Internet of Things: A match made in heaven. *KD Nuggets*. https://www.kdnuggets.com/2016/09/big-data-iot-match-made-heaven.html

35. Goyal, A. (2018) How will the Internet of Things (IoT) impact big data? *Data Diversity*, October 3. https://www.dataversity.net/will-internet-things-iot-impact-big-data/

36. Ahmed, E. et al. (2017) The role of big data analytics in Internet of Things. *Computer Networks*. 29(2): 459–471. http://dx.doi.org/10.1016/j.comnet.2017.06.013

37. Naganuri, S. (2019) 7 Important Big Data Tools for Data Processing. *Techi Expert*, May 13. https://www.techiexpert.com/7-important-big-data-tools-for-data-processing/

38. Sinha, R. (2019) Key benefits of big data for developing smart cities. *Analytics Insight*, December 14. https://www.analyticsinsight.net/key-benefits-big-data-developing-smart-cities/

39. Zigurat Global Institute of Technology. (2019) Smart city series: The Barcelona experience. February 7. https://www.e-zigurat.com/blog/en/smart-city-barcelona-experience/

40. Park, E., Pobil, A. P, Kwon, S. J. (2018) The role of Internet of Things (IoT) in smart cities: technology roadmap-oriented approaches. *Sustainability*. 10: 1388.

13

Moving from Cloud to Fog: An Internet of Things Perspective

Sudhriti Sengupta

Amity Institute of Technology, Amity University
Noida, India

CONTENTS

13.1   Introduction 235
13.2   Cloud Platform 237
    13.2.1   Characteristics of Cloud Computing 239
13.3   The Fog Platform 240
    13.3.1   Fog Computing Features 241
    13.3.2   Fog Architecture 241
    13.3.3   Fog Infrastructure 242
13.4   Fog and the Cloud: An Interplay 244
13.5   IoT: An Overview 245
    13.5.1   IoT Layered Architecture 246
    13.5.2   Application of IoT 247
        13.5.2.1   Consumer IoT 247
        13.5.2.2   Industrial IoT 247
        13.5.2.3   Infrastructure IoT 248
        13.5.2.4   Commercial IoT 248
13.6   Role of Fog Computing in IoT Applications 248
    13.6.1   Challenges in Fog-Enabled IoT 249
13.7   Proposed Framework 250
13.8   Conclusion 250
References 251

KEYWORDS: *cloud platform, fog computing, IoT, mist computing*

13.1 Introduction

The term "Internet of Things (IoT)" was first coined by Kevin Ashton in 1999. IoT is the interconnection of heterogeneous devices whose main purpose is message sharing and communication. IoT has the potential to revolutionize the lifestyle of our society. IoT simply means the ability of objects or "things" around us to be connected with the internet without human meditation. IoT led to the concept of smart cities, which uses technology for daily life routines such as traffic control, healthcare, and fuel control. It is estimated that innovations in IoT will lead to unlimited benefits for our society [1]. For proper utilization of techniques in IoT, there is a requirement of computational power and storage. The cloud computing infrastructure helps us to use IoT processes like storage, analysis, and deployment effectively. This led to merging of cloud computing architecture with IoT applications, leading to the concept of Cloud of Things. Cloud computing is centralized in nature, where all processing and storage takes place in the cloud. This led to a lower bandwidth in transfer of data, less mobility, and lower location awareness. So, to resolve these issues, the concept of fog computing is introduced. Fog computing brings data closer to IoT applications. Many tasks like filtering and aggregation are done in fog infrastructure before sending the data to storage in the cloud. Fog infrastructure acts as a bridge between cloud infrastructure and users' applications, which eliminates the need of a high bandwidth. This increases mobility and improves quality of service (QoS) of user applications in real time [2, 3].

IoT has initiated the revolution of an application-driven human world in terms of operation, management and control of different aspects of life. IoT has been introduced in different parts of life like home automation, vehicle or car automation, automatic healthcare practices, and security automation, to name a few. IoT is a collection of a large number of interconnected devices like actuators and sensors by using the existing internet framework. A huge volume of data is exchanged between devices, server, and sensors at a very high speed. Proper infrastructure should be present to store, control, and analyze these data, which may be collected from heterogeneous sources. The cloud computing framework is often chosen as the storage and processing media of these IoT applications. However, the centralized computational architecture of the cloud hinders the requirement of fast processing and transfer of data to the devices that may be connected anywhere. This issue can be solved by using the concept of fog computing. Fog computing is distributed in nature where multiple nodes are present closer to the application domain. These increase the speed of processing of data. The storage of data can be done in a cloud framework if needed. It is noteworthy that fog computing is supporting cloud infrastructure instead of replacing it. Various applications of IoT can be optimized by using the fog computing framework. However, some challenges of fog computing are also present such as security, resource limitation, irregular network connection, and so on. So, the researchers in this area can work in development of technology such as "mist computing," which will further facilitate the rise of IoT application and domain.

This chapter aims to discuss the architecture, applications, and challenges found in the IoT application domain using cloud and fog infrastructure. It presents the difference between the fog computing paradigm and the cloud computing paradigm. The main input of this chapter is to:

- Discuss the cloud architecture, characteristics and challenges in its usages in IoT application.
- Discuss the concept and features of fog architecture.
- Present an interplay between fog computing and cloud computing. Discuss the role of Fog computing in the cloud computing architecture.
- Discuss IoT architecture and its various application areas.
- Present the involvement of fog in IoT and its challenges.
- Discuss the future scope of evolution in IoT applications by introducing new techniques such as mist computing.

In this chapter, Section 13.2 describes cloud computing architecture characteristics and challenges, Section 13.3 elaborates fog computing architecture, and Section 13.4 describes the interaction between cloud architecture and fog architecture. The IoT paradigm along with its application is defined in Section 13.5. The future of IoT and the introduction of a newer concept is described in Section 13.6. Section 13.7 provides the conclusion to this chapter.

13.2 Cloud Platform

Cloud computing does not need direct involvement of the users [4]. They are essentially data centers available via the internet. Cloud computing is adopted by many companies like IBM, Microsoft, Amazon, and Google for maintaining and deploying software. Cloud computing has impacted organizational and IT infrastructure. Cloud computing offers many services like healthcare, banking, and education. The main purpose of cloud computing is that instead of investing in physical infrastructure, the users can use a provider via the internet that will take care of necessary requirements of the user. The three main services provided by cloud computing are SaaS (Software as a Service), PaaS (Platform as a Service), and IaaS (Infrastructure as a Service). In SaaS, the users do not have to install the software on their computer because they can access it via the internet. In this case, the SaaS users do not have to buy hardware or software or invest in managing complex infrastructure. To use this, only a good internet connection is needed. PaaS provides an interface over which a user can run their own software. The users can create customized software that can run on infrastructure of the cloud. LAMP (Linux, Apache, MySQL, and PHP) is a classic example of using PaaS. Network, storage capacity, operating system, and hardware are the common resources provided in the form of the internet. A virtual platform for hardware and operating system services can be created by IaaS. These can be obtained by using the internet. A virtual platform for hardware and operating system services can be created using IaaS. There are three stages of deployment of cloud computing:

1. Development of the applications to be provided to the user of the cloud as a service.
2. Delivering of the cloud computing service for developing frameworks, platforms, and infrastructure.
3. System for leveraging solutions to users' requirement by providing infrastructure. Some of the common technologies available for cloud users are Amazon Web Service, Google AppEngine, Microsoft Azure, and Salesforce.com.

Some types of cloud services are available via the public network to be used by users having any requirements. This is called the public cloud. A high-security cloud service is provided by the private network to some privileged users. This is called the private cloud. A combination of the private and public cloud is called the hybrid cloud. Reduced maintenance cost, worldwide accessibility, and automated services are some of the services provided by the cloud. A basic infrastructure of the cloud is given in Figure 13.1.

Cloud computing is basically divided into two parts, the cloud and the users. The cloud is available to the users via an internet connection, which may be public or private. The users send some request to the cloud and the cloud processes the request and provides necessary service to the users. Important characteristics of cloud computing include availability, QoS, and reliability. Availability means that it is present for users in real time.

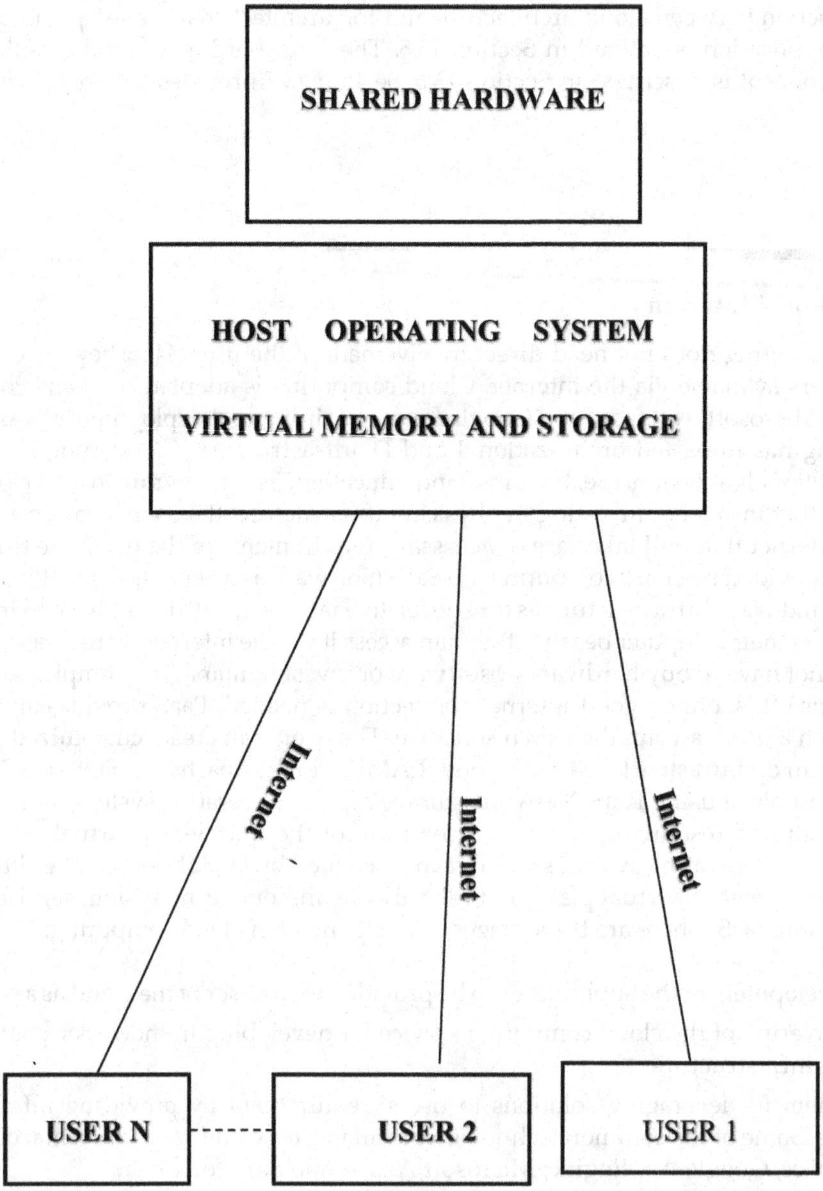

SHARED HARDWARE

HOST   OPERATING   SYSTEM

VIRTUAL MEMORY AND STORAGE

Internet

Internet

Internet

| USER N | - - - - - - | USER 2 | | USER 1 |

FIGURE 13.1
Architecture of cloud computing.

QoS signifies that the user requirement is always satisfied. The ability of incurring no loss while processing and storage is reliability. Economically, cloud computing has reduced the cost for the users. It has been a pioneer in building a "Pay-per-use" frame that enables real usage of resources. It is sustainable in terms of energy consumption, which led to a decrease in carbon footprints. An important technical aspects of cloud computing is virtualization that hides the implementation details and provides flexibility of use. The information storage capability of the cloud should be well dispersed among the users across different platforms and various APIs and other programs should be available for accessing cloud usage [5, 6].

13.2.1 Characteristics of Cloud Computing

The chief characteristics of cloud computing are discussed here:

1. Storage over Internet: Storage of data and information can be deployed using the internet to the servers or other storage units. This leads to high performance and unlimited storage architecture.
2. Use of Service over Internet: Various types of services can be provided to users by utilizing the efficiency of the existing internet framework. Different types of process can be performed on a server via an internet connection. This will eliminate the necessity of installing a program in the user's computer.
3. Energy Utilization: Energy is most efficiently utilized in a cloud computing environment by providing more service for the same amount of energy utilized.
4. Increase Computational Power: Intensive mobile applications have improved the computational capabilities by providing the desired output to users.

There are certain limitations or issues with the cloud computing framework in spite of its huge benefit and applications. Many businesses of different types are already using the cloud service to maintain their business and deploy products. Some of the main concern while using cloud architecture are:

1. **Security and Privacy:** The data of cloud users are stored in a third-party storage, which itself is a threat to the sensitivity of confidential data. So, organizations using cloud computing technologies should ensure that they are using a reliable cloud provider. The cloud providers, in turn, must acknowledge the proper security measures taken to protect the data of their clients. The application developed must take care of data privacy and authentication measures [7].
2. **Performance:** In some cases, latency of using cloud infrastructure is very high.

The services provided by cloud computing have become an integral part of major applications that affect human lifestyle. A reliable, efficient, and effective cloud computing environment should possess the following characteristics: state-of-the-art security measures, provision for real-time and reliable service, availability of service on demand, stability to support a large number of users, multiple backup to support any kind of disaster, and consistent and high-speed performance for clients worldwide. One of the important technologies that uses cloud computing is IoT. IoT tends to make our daily activities easier by making various things interconnected by a network. Many technologies such as cloud computing ensure proper functioning of IoT devices by providing a robust, smart, and self-configuring service. However, the centralized model of cloud computing inhibits the growth of IoT domain applications. Cloud computing undoubtedly plays an important role in the development of IoT applications. But this concept may not be in sync with the distributed concept of IoT. Further, security and privacy issues of cloud computing have worried companies of IoT applications in continuation of cloud architecture in IoT. The cloud computing possesses serious accessibility issues while providing services to end users. Thus, a need to bring "Cloud closer to Users" was in need and hence the distributed concept of fog computing was introduced to mitigate the issues of the cloud.

13.3 The Fog Platform

The "pay-as-you-go" computing also known as cloud computing is a good option to manage confidential data centers for clients using web applications. It has gotten progressively significant due to many related qualities, for example, minimal storage cost, accessibility and availability of information whenever and wherever required, and easy maintenance. Mobile devices can gather personal information from different sensors inside a shorter timeframe and sensor-based information comprises of significant data from users. However, mobile access presents numerous issues, for example, duplication to make information effectively accessible, access to required information, security of information, and artificial intelligence strategies for speedy and effective access to information.

Another choice for cloud computing is fog computing since fog is closer to the ground when contrasted with a cloud. We additionally assert that as opposed to utilizing cloud for registering, fog processing serves another type of use and administration. It revolves around bringing cloud-based administrations closer to IoT customers in an advantageous way. An enormous part of the physical devices in fog figuring conditions, typically named as fog hubs, are geographically dispersed and are heterogeneous. To totally utilize the limits of the fog hubs, tremendous scope applications that are disintegrated into between subordinate application modules can be disseminated or passed on effectively over the hub's subject to their idleness affectability. In this chapter, we have discussed the technique behind fog computing, its architecture, its combination with IOT, and its overview [8].

Fog is closer to the ground than clouds in the same way, technically, it has been possible to bring clouds closer and easily approachable to the ground (where end users and end devices are present) by using fog as a medium. We can clearly see that fog is the distributed medium of cloud computing and is thus more suitable for users as it is not centralized and hence latency and work load are low, comparatively. Fog computing, otherwise called edge computing, was presented in 2012 by Cisco. Fog processing was essentially acquainted to meet constant prerequisites of a huge number of users and gadgets. It must be noted that fog is not a replacement to the traditional cloud but just an alternative to it. Any end devices that have networking, computing, and storage capabilities are termed as fog nodes. Examples can be video surveillance cameras, switches, routers, machines, mobile devices, and servers. The major aim of fog computing is to decrease the work load of data being transported to the cloud for processing and storage. It basically leads to reacting more quickly to events. The main issues related to cloud computing is that it may not always be connected to IoT devices where connectivity is essential. In IoT applications, there may not be enough bandwidth to collect data from "cloud" infrastructures. Cloud computing basically supports centralized system so it might create issues for a system where the application will not get sufficient time to get data to the cloud, analyze it, and get the report back. To reduce these issues, fog computing concepts are preferred in IoT applications. Fog computing places processes and resources in a distributed environment called "edges" while the data remains stored in a "cloud." The main advantage of this system is reduced processing time and usage of resources [9].

13.3.1 Fog Computing Features

There are different features that make fog a critical extension of the cloud. Fog computing essentially extends the objectives of cloud computing by introducing elements of distributed computing. It tends to bring the computation and memory closer to the users, which increases performance of the system. Some important features of fog computing are:

1. **Interoperability:** The main aim of interoperability is to provide a variety of services. This leads to requirement of interaction of fog components.
2. **Geographical Distribution:** Fog computing nodes are distributed over a wide range of area spanning a variety of locations, including both urban areas and rural areas.
3. **Decentralization:** The fog nodes are self-managing and there is no centralized component to control the computing resources.
4. **Location Awareness:** This is the ability to determine the nearest geographical location of a fog node.
5. **Mobile Support:** For communicating directly with mobile devices, fog computing should have proper mobile support.
6. **Low Latency-Fog Nodes:** These are closer to user device, which results in less response time as compared to the cloud.
7. **Heterogeneous Network-Fog Computing:** This includes a variety of devices such as edge routers, servers, and setup boxes. These devices may have different operating system or associated software. Thus, fog nodes are heterogeneous in nature.

The main purpose of fog computing is that it is decentralized and the data centers and processes are distributed via different nodes closer to the users. This leads to real-time interaction, proper utilization of storage space, and low latency while bringing the application closer to the user [10, 11].

13.3.2 Fog Architecture

Distributed computing is an accumulation of homogeneous physical assets that are set up and overseen in a private fashion. Fog augments the cloud to the edge and endpoints. Fog's scattered structure contains heterogeneous resources. The different players in the scattered fog system ranges from server farms center of network, edge of system, and endpoints. The fog foundation empowers appropriated grouping of utilizations that require computing, networking, and capacity of assets of these distinctive components.

The key goal of fog programming architecture is being heterogeneous in nature; fog hubs are arranged into different conditions like core, edge, access system, and endpoints. Fog architecture ought to give smooth assets administration crosswise over different platforms. Fog computing uses "edges" of the network for some operations of the users. Fog architecture is a layered architecture consisting of six layers:

1. **Transport Layer:** Uploads secured data to the cloud for creating and extracting useful services.
2. **Security Layer:** Provides functions like encryption and decryption, privacy and integrity measures.

3. **Temporary Storage Layer:** Used in data distribution, replication, and duplication. Data no longer needs to be stored locally when transmitted to the cloud, instead it is stored in temporary storage.

4. **Preprocessing Layer:** Filtering and analyzing of data is done in this layer to extract meaningful information.

5. **Monitoring Layer:** Provides monitoring of power, resources, response, activities, and service.

6. **Physical and Virtualization Layer:** Includes a variety of components like virtual sensor, virtual nodes, and physical nodes that are controlled depending on their demand and service.

Figure 13.2 depicts the six-layer architecture of fog computing, along with their application domain. The physical layer comprises of sensors of different types and actuators; the monitoring layer performs system and resource consumption monitoring; the preprocessing layer is concerned about analysis, filtering, and formatting of data; the data back-up and storage virtualization layer is the main job of the temporary storage layer; and the transport layer is concerned about the application domain that checks the IoT application, wireless sensor network, and so on.

13.3.3 Fog Infrastructure

The physical entities in fog computing are known as fog infrastructure. These are the connected devices, sensors, and actuators that are located widely and help to connect to fog. These components must provide resources for storage, connection, and computation for optimum efficiency of fog computing. A large number of devices are connected in a fog computing environment, which increase the rate of data consumption and transfer. Although the devices like sensors and actuators consume low bandwidth, the required bandwidth in fog computing is high. This happens due to large numbers of devices connected and transferring data at same time. This led to the requirement of change and upgradation of the existing network system, so that it will support the fog computing environment. Connectivity and mobility are very essential for fog computing.

One of the main purposes of fog computing is supporting IoT-related technology. Many applications use cloud computing for storing data. However, for intermediate processing, fog computing devices are used (Figure 13.3). These devices include storage devices, fog gateway devices, and sensor management devices. There is a high degree of collaboration between these devices to maintain the performance of the fog environment. IoT devices are categorized into two parts: sensing devices and actuators. A sensing device has the capacity to sense its surrounding and actuators works when it is necessary. Sensors are of different types, such as pressure sensors, temperature sensors, chemical sensors, and biosensors. Fog processing devices are any devices that have computational power, memory capacity, and network connectivity. Some common examples of fog processing devices are switches, routers, network controllers, and video surveillance cameras. Fog servers are fog devices that can manage several fog devices belonging to the same application domain. The commercial boards used as IoT gateway devices and fog devices can be used as fog gateway devices and fog devices. These fog gateways support the heterogeneous capability, which is a prerequisite of fog computing. Some of the common boards commercially available on the market include Tessel, Arduino, Edison, and Raspberry Pi [12].

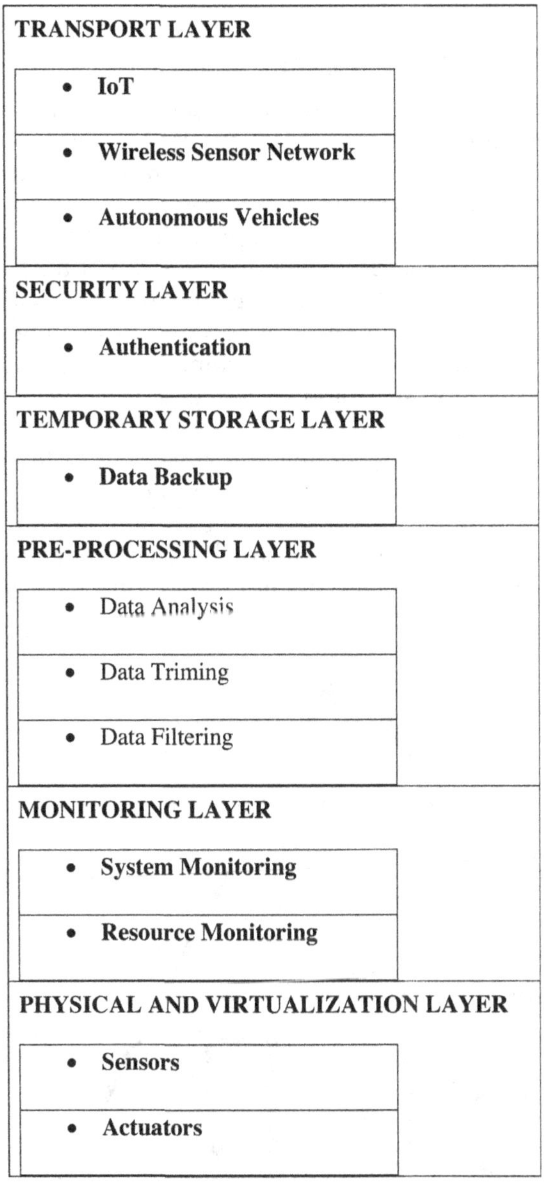

TRANSPORT LAYER

- **IoT**
- **Wireless Sensor Network**
- **Autonomous Vehicles**

SECURITY LAYER

- **Authentication**

TEMPORARY STORAGE LAYER

- **Data Backup**

PRE-PROCESSING LAYER

- Data Analysis
- Data Triming
- Data Filtering

MONITORING LAYER

- **System Monitoring**
- **Resource Monitoring**

PHYSICAL AND VIRTUALIZATION LAYER

- **Sensors**
- **Actuators**

FIGURE 13.2
Layered architecture of Fog.

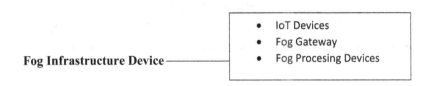

Fog Infrastructure Device
- IoT Devices
- Fog Gateway
- Fog Procesing Devices

FIGURE 13.3
Fog infrastructure device.

13.4 Fog and the Cloud: An Interplay

The main purpose of fog computing is to provide a distributed computing environment between cloud infrastructure and user applications. It brings storage and computing capabilities closer to end devices. Cloud computing is an infrastructure that provides hardware and software services to the users based on the "pay-per-use" model. It combines cluster and grids to form a central access point to support high-level processing. Fog computing adds on to the capacity of the cloud by bringing some of the storage and processing components closer to the user applications. Fog computing is a distributed architecture that provides better performance in terms of speed of processing and security of data. Fog computing is not an alternative to cloud computing. In fact, it provides facilities to the cloud to provide faster processing and accessing of data. The basic architecture of the cloud and fog is given in Figure 13.4.

Cloud computing is used for processing and storage of different user applications. However, if the cloud is directly used in these applications, it will lead in increased processing time and delay in storage access. By using fog infrastructure, we can resolve these issues [13]. Fog provides resources as a bridge between the ultimate cloud storage and user applications. This not only reduces the processing speed but

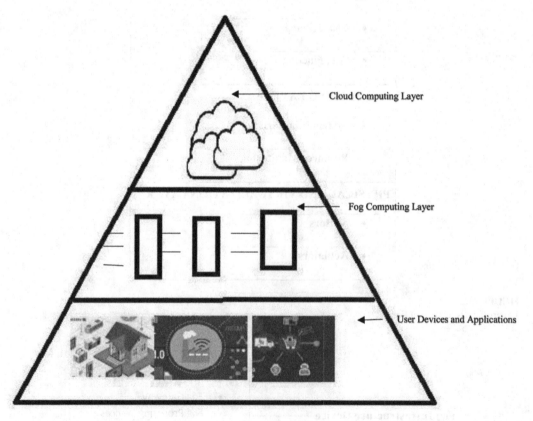

FIGURE 13.4
Merging of cloud and fog architecture.

TABLE 13.1

Comparison of Fog and Cloud Computing

Basis	Fog Computing	Cloud Computing
Response Time	Low	High
Transmission	Device to device	Device to cloud
Computational Focus	Fog functions on the network edge	Data requests are handled in the cloud
Goal	Improve proficiency and performance of the process that is transported to the cloud for handling, examination, and storage	Immensity and powerful provisioning of IT administrations
Operating System Support	Hypervisor virtualization	A hypervisor (VM) on which multiple OSs can run
Ownership	Multiple	Single
Service Price	Utility pricing and payment is made based on the uses	Utility pricing discounted for larger customers
Multitask Support	Yes	Yes

also provides better mobility. In essence, fog improves the cloud computing framework by providing intermediate storage and processing speed, which are in a distributed environment. One of the chief examples of cloud computing is its usage in IoT applications. The number of devices using IoT are increasing, which leads to degradation of performance.

In the case of cloud computing, it is possible that all our important and private data may be hampered at once because they are stored on the same networks, whereas in case of fog computing, losing all the data at one time is not possible as data is dispersed into different networks. Cloud is centralized and contains a large amount of data that can be positioned around the globe, far away from client devices. Fog is scattered and contains several small nodes situated close to client devices. Fog is the layer between the cloud and the devices like computers, laptops, and smartphones. As fog acts as a mediator, it is less time-consuming to transfer the data. When there is no layer, then the cloud needs to communicate directly to the end devices, which takes more time than using fog computing. Cloud computing has low latency but not as compared to fog. Fog computing has low latency when it comes to the network. Cloud computing doesn't provide any reduction in data while transferring data, but fog computing reduces data while sending to the cloud [14, 15]. Cloud computing preserves less bandwidth compare to fog. Table 13.1 compares fog and cloud computing.

13.5 IoT: An Overview

The main goal of IoT is to connect all the devices to internet infrastructure. By using the techniques of IoT, different devices, like washing machines, coffee makers, and air conditioners can also be connected to the internet. IoT enables interconnection of any device used in any service or business by anybody in anytime [16, 17].

13.5.1 IoT Layered Architecture

IoT connects different varieties of devices anytime from any place by using the internet connection. As per some researchers, there are three layers in an IoT architectural framework:

1. Perception layer
2. Network Layer
3. Application Layer

However, it is also common to consider a fourth layer called the support layer, which lies between the network layer and application layer. For this study, we will consider a three-layered architecture of IoT as shown in Figure 13.5.

The figure shows the basic architecture of IoT. The perception layer is the lowest layer in IoT architecture. This layer collects information and data from the devices used in IoT and transforms them into a digital format. This layer can identify objects by addressing a scheme used in many various technologies like radio-frequency identification (RFID) and Bluetooth. The perception layer is also called the recognition layer. The main purpose of the network layer is to provide efficient data transmission between the perception and application layer of IoT architecture. This layer collects information from the perception layer and channels it to the application layer. The network layer is the most developed and important layer of IoT, which has addressing and routing functionality. It creates an integration of heterogeneous and multiple devices to a single cohesive network. The topmost layer of IoT architecture is the application layer. It provides the services according to the user requirement. It provides a link between the users and applications. This layer links various domains to provide high-end application. These are the basic layers in IoT architecture. There are also several essential components of IoT architecture: hardware, middleware, presentation, data acquisition, service, and virtualization [18].

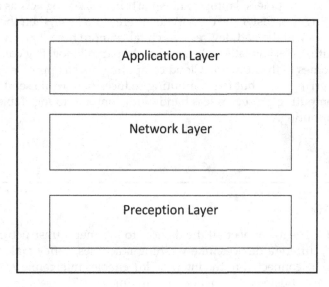

FIGURE 13.5
IoT Layered architecture.

By using the concept of IoT, various devices can be connected with the help of the internet for collection and exchange of data. The basic components of IoT consists of the following items:

1. **Sensors and Actuators:** These are devices used for information gathering from the environment. Actuators have the capacity to manipulate for generation of data. These devices send data to the next stage.
2. **Data Acquisition System (DAS):** The data aggregation and conversion function is performed by DAS. It converts data in analog form from sensors and convert it into digital form.
3. **Edge IT:** To ensure that no resource is lost, the data is transferred to the cloud or any data center. These cloud or data centers act as storage.
4. **Cloud Infrastructure:** In cloud infrastructure, the data is analyzed, processed, and feedback is sent to the edge IT [19].

13.5.2 Application of IoT

Any device with some amount of storage capacity and processing power connected to the internet is a thing in IoT. Smartphones, gadgets, watches, washing machines, and refrigerators having sensors and actuators are examples of such devices. Daily life objects such as door handles, seat of an automobile, and furniture can also be considered as a "thing" if they have sensors and actuators enabling collection and exchanging of data. The application domain of IoT is very large and varied. The various applications of IoT can be categorized into consumer, industrial, commercial, and infrastructure domains [20–23].

13.5.2.1 Consumer IoT

From a consumer point of view, one major domain of consumer application is the smart home, which led to the concept of home automation. This includes lighting, air conditioning, security, and media usage. A smart home is the use of different machines in a home to access the internet. It uses different types of sensors and actuators, which enables connection to the internet that can be controlled, monitored, and analyzed to provide services to the users. The main aim of smart homes is to use IoT technologies to control home devices by a seamless network for enabling controlling of the functions of the devices without human intervention. Different types of devices can be a part of IoT applications. Some of the commonly used devices are thermostats, wireless speaker systems, home security systems, and lighting [24, 25].

13.5.2.2 Industrial IoT

Industrial IoT is interconnected devices merged with a computer's industrial applications. IoT have being integrated with various devices used in manufacturing to enhance sensing and networking capabilities. This integration has led to the new domain of application that ushers the introduction of a cyber-physical system. Various agricultural applications are used for collecting data using different sensors such as pressure sensors, temperature sensors, and humidity sensors. This data can be utilized to automatize farming techniques, minimize wastage and risk and overall reducing human effort for agricultural growth.

13.5.2.3 Infrastructure IoT

Infrastructure IoT is the use of IoT devices to monitor the conditions of infrastructure like bridges, roads, and buildings in urban and rural areas. IoT applications for infrastructure management can be used to monitor changes in structures to decrease risk factors and increase safety measures. One infrastructure IoT usage is environmental monitoring applications. IoT devices can assist in environment disaster management by monitoring atmospheric conditions like temperature, water quality, and movement of wildlife. It is suitable for early warning systems for calamities like cyclones and tsunamis.

13.5.2.4 Commercial IoT

The most widely used application of IoT is in the commercial domain. IoT applications can be used in a variety of fields like medicine and healthcare, transportation, energy saving devices, and water supply. Remotely connected CCTV can be included in an IoT network to catch criminals whenever a crime is happening. Also, automated incident detectors can be used to maintain security of homes or premises in a city. One of the crucial impacts of IoT is in the field of healthcare. Real-time monitoring of patients with life-threatening diseases is possible with IoT applications. IoT tools can be used for collecting and exchanging information and sending them to specialist doctors. These doctors can also diagnosis and prescribe treatment from a faraway place. Some of the benefits of IoT in healthcare and medicines are better treatment, better disease and medicine control, and maintenance of devices. Energy efficiency can be achieved by utilizing devices only when in use. Real-time applications are being developed that will monitor the applications and put them in use only when necessary. For example, sensors in a door can understand when a person is entering a room and then switch on the lights.

13.6 Role of Fog Computing in IoT Applications

IoT devices have the ability for interconnecting a variety of devices from different domains. The conventional centralized cloud in usage of IoT devices may have certain issues such as low bandwidth and high latency. To resolve these issues, an extension of cloud computing is introduced. This extension is called fog computing and it brings the distributed nature of computational architecture by being a middle tier between user application and the cloud storage system. The integration of cloud architecture, fog architecture, and IoT devices will enable better service to the user application, especially IoT applications.

Some of the significant areas where fog computing plays an important role in IoT applications are discussed here:

1. **Automatic Vehicle:** These are vehicles with automatic streaming operations such as vehicle enabled parking. These vehicles can also communicate with vehicles in the neighborhood using the internet. This requires a strict real-time interaction that can be provided by fog computing infrastructure. Cloud computing suffers from low speed due to its centralized architecture. So, fog-enhanced cloud architecture is a better option for autonomous vehicles [23].

2. **Smart Traffic System:** This is the system of routing vehicles and traffic by combining artificial intelligence with sensors and traditional traffic lights. The interaction between these lights and the vehicles can be done by using fog computing infrastructure for better speed and efficiency.

3. **Home Automation or Smart Homes:** A smart home has control and monitoring of gadgets in the home. These gadgets may be of a huge variety like entertainment systems, washing machines, and appliances. Many of these devices are connected to IoT. These devices are heterogeneous and require a large amount of computational and storage power. Fog computing enables the smart home automation system by providing resources and integration [23].

4. **Smart Healthcare:** Real-time monitoring and a quick response are an inevitable part of healthcare and medicine practices. Smart healthcare is the use of technology to enable better treatment of patients. Fog computing ushers the evolution of smart health as it does not suffer latency issue or an unreliable network as in the case of cloud computing. Fog computer architecture will provide distributed computing to enable faster storage and response time [26, 27].

13.6.1 Challenges in Fog-Enabled IoT

IoT has a lot of applications that revolutionize lifestyle and social structure. Development of smart cities is one of the chief applications of IoT, which promises to provide better facilities and lifestyle [23, 28]. However, there are certain challenges in IoT using fog computing:

1. Low Processing Speed
2. Low Network Bandwidth
3. Resource Limitation
4. Security Challenges
5. Irregular Network

Most IoT applications demand real-time analysis and controlling of data. Fog brings the data and process to end users and so we can conclude that fog is suitable for addressing the latency constraints. Also, the fog computing paradigm reduces the data amount required to be stored in the cloud from IoT devices and this will solve the required network bandwidth. Fog computing also allows to reduce complexity of devices and their power consumption. Fog is independent so even if the network is not regular, continuous service will be there [29].

Fog can control and monitor the security of nearby devices and acts as proxy for a device to update software and security measures. Fog computing provides many benefits for different IoT applications, but it also faces certain challenges. One of the chief challenges that IoT applications face is the large amount of data generated by the millions of devices connected to the internet. IoT devices are heterogeneous in nature. They comprise of sensors, hardware, and software from different manufacturers and versions. This leads to the requirement of a common protocol for managing and controlling these varied IoT devices. Due to the decentralized nature of fog computing, there is a large requirement of energy that can be consumed by a large number of fog end devices. As compared to the cloud, fog is more prone to cyberattacks and security measures need to be strong for protection of the data in fog architecture.

Fog computing is a promising technique for enabling IoT applications and devices. Researchers are carrying out work in this area to mitigate the challenges in the fog computing paradigm and integrate it with IoT technologies.

To overcome the challenges in IoT applications, there is a new computing paradigm called "mist computing." Mist computing architecture is at the extreme edge of the network. It contains sensors, microcomputers, and microcontrollers. Mist enables some amount of network capabilities and computational power in the sensors itself. This architecture allows data to be controlled and managed in the sensors itself. These data are feed to the fog architecture and then to the cloud architecture if necessary. The researchers in this field are working for integrating the cloud, fog, and mist computing paradigm, which will benefit the entire computing architecture in different applications, especially in IoT applications.

13.7 Proposed Framework

The main objective of the fog computing environment is to provide low latency and high speed to its application. Managing of the functions and QoS of the fog environment is very crucial in terms of expected a real-time response of the fog computing environment [30]. This chapter proposes a framework for monitoring the resources and job allocations in the fog environment, so that the resources in the fog environment can be optimally utilized. In the proposed model, a centralized managed fog component is introduced for interacting with other nodes present in fog infrastructure. All the components in the fog environment report the current status to the controlling fog node. The current status includes various information such as pending tasks and estimated time to complete the tasks. Depending on this information, the centralized node makes decisions such as:

- To allocate more tasks to a specific node for optimal usage of its computational power.
- To redirect the job of a slow node to another node to have a high response time.

The proposed model shown in Figure 13.6 does not need the common distributing protocol that is necessary in the distributed environment of conventional fog computing.

13.8 Conclusion

We have discussed what fog computing is and also the key features of it. In this chapter, the study of cloud architecture, its services, features, and characteristics is presented. Fog computing is introduced along with its architecture, features, and significances. This chapter also introduces the concept of IoT, its application, and its architecture. This chapter also presents the issues of cloud-based IoT applications. It discusses the interplay between the cloud computing paradigm and the fog computing paradigm. It draws insight in resolving issues in development and deployment of IoT applications in different domains by integrating fog computing with cloud computing architecture. This chapter further draws conclusions on some issues that might be there in IoT applications based purely on

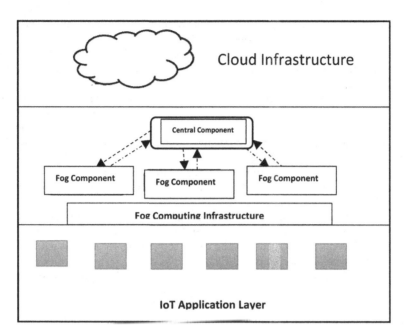

FIGURE 13.6
Proposed framework.

integrated fog and cloud-based architecture. This chapter provides future scope by study-ing and research by introducing a new architecture called mist computing to herald the world toward an IoT-driven application and lifestyle. It also provides researchers in this field to apply the proposed framework in different areas of IoT applications like healthcare and traffic monitoring.

References

1. Kohli, D., and Sengupta, S. 2020. Recent trends of IoT in smart city development. Proceedings of the International Conference on Computer Networks, vol. 49. pp. 376–380.
2. Bonomi, F., Milito, R., Natarajan P., and Zhu J. 2014. Fog computing: A platform for Internet of Things and analytics. *Big Data and Internet of Things: A Roadmap for Smart Environments*, vol. 546, pp. 169–186.
3. Chiang, M., and Zhang, T. 2016. Fog and IoT: An overview of research opportunities. *IEEE Internet of Things Journal*, vol. 3, no. 6, pp. 854–864.
4. Yogi, M., Chandrasekhar, K., and Kumar, G. 2017. Mist computing: Principles, trends and future direction. *International Journal of Computer Science and Engineering*, vol. 4. pp. 19–21.
5. Bardsiri, K. Amid, and Mohsen. H. 2014. QoS metrics for cloud computing services evaluation. *International Journal of Intelligent Systems and Applications*, vol. 6, pp. 27–33.
6. Cusumano, M. 2010. Cloud computing and SaaS as new computing platforms, *Communications of the ACM*, vol. 53, no. 4, pp. 27–29.
7. Sadiku, M., Musa, M., and Momoh, O. 2014.Cloud computing: Opportunities and challenges potentials, *IEEE Potentials*, vol. 33, no. 1, pp. 34–36.
8. Yi, S., Qin, Z., and Li, Q. 2015. Security and privacy issues of fog computing: A survey. *Performance of Target Tracking in Radar Network System Under Deception Attack*, vol. 1, pp. 685–695.

9. Yi, S., Qin, Z., and Li, Q. 2015. A survey of fog computing: Concepts, applications and issues. *Proceedings of the 2015 Workshop on Mobile Big Data*, vol. 1, pp. 37–42.

10. Yousefpour, A., Ishigaki, G., and Jue, J. P. 2017. Fog computing: Towards minimizing delay in the internet of things. IEEE International Conference on Edge Computing (EDGE), Honolulu, Hawaii, pp. 17–24.

11. Hu, P., Dhelim, S., Ning, H., and Qiu, T. 2017. Survey on fog computing: Architecture, key technologies, applications and open issues. *Journal of Network and Computer Applications*, vol. 98, pp. 27–42.

12. Dabhi, A., Raval, T., and Chaudhary, K. 2017. Fog computing: A review and conceptual architecture, issues, applications and its challenges. *International Journal of Advance Research and Innovative Ideas in Education*, vol. 3, pp. 717–722.

13. Roman, R., Lopez, L., and Mambo, M. 2018. Mobile edge computing, fog et al.: A survey and analysis of security threats and challenges. *Future Generation Computer Systems*, vol. 78, pp. 680–698.

14. Shawish, A., and Salama, M. 2014. Cloud computing: Paradigms and technologies. *Inter-Cooperative Collective Intelligence: Techniques and Applications*. vol. 495, pp. 39–67.

15. Zissis, D., and Lekkas, D. 2012. Addressing cloud computing security issues. *Future Generation Computer Systems*, vol. 28, no. 3, pp. 583–592.

16. Lee, I., and Lee, K. 2015. The Internet of Things (IoT): Applications, investments, and challenges for enterprises. *Business Horizon*, vol. 58, pp. 431–440.

17. Kumar, Anubhav, Jha, Gaurav, and Sharma, Lavanya. July 2019. Challenges, potential & future of IOT integrated with block chain, *International Journal of Recent Technology and Engineering*, vol. 8, no. 2S7, pp. 530–536

18. Sharma, Lavanya, and Lohan, Nirvikar. March, 2019. Internet of things with object detection, In: *Handbook of Research on Big Data and the IoT*, IGI Global, pp. 89–100. (ISBN: 9781522574323, DOI: 10.4018/978-1-5225-7432-3.ch006).

19. Misra, G., Kumar, V., Agarwal, A., and Agarwal, K. 2016. Internet of Things (IoT) – A technological analysis and survey on vision, concepts, challenges, innovation directions, technologies, and applications. *American Journal of Electrical and Electronics Engineering*, vol. 4. pp 23–32.

20. Rolf, H. 2010. Internet of Things-New security and privacy challenges. *Computer Law and Security Review*, vol. 26, pp. 23–30.

21. Atzori, L., Iera, A., and Morabito, G. 2010. The Internet of Things: A survey. *Computer Network*, vol. 54, pp. 2787–2805.

22. Sharma, Lavanya, and Garg, P. K. 2019. IoT and its applications, *From Visual Surveillance to Internet of Things*, Chapman Hall/CRC, vol. 1, p. 29.

23. Sharma, Lavanya, and Lohan, Nirvikar. January 2019. Performance analysis of moving object detection using BGS techniques in visual surveillance, *International Journal of Spatiotemporal Data Science, Inderscience*, vol. 1, pp. 22–53.

24. Miorandi, D., Sicari, S., Francesco, D.P., and Chlamtac, I. 2012. Survey internet of things: Vision applications and research challenges. *Ad Hoc Network*, vol. 10, pp. 1497–1516.

25. Rahman, M. 2013. A Survey of intelligent car parking system. *Journal of Applied Research and Technology*. vol. 11. pp. 714–726.

26. Sharma, Lavanya, and Garg, P. K. 2019. Smart E-healthcare with Internet of Things: Current trends challenges, solutions and technologies, *From Visual Surveillance to Internet of Things*, Chapman Hall/CRC, vol. 1, p. 215.

27. Sharma, Lavanya, Garg, P. K., and Agarwal, Naman. 2019. A foresight on e-healthcare Trailblazers, *From Visual Surveillance to Internet of Things*, Chapman Hall/CRC, Vol. 1, p. 235.

28. Sharma, Lavanya, and Garg, P. K. (Eds.). 2019. *From Visual Surveillance to Internet of Things*. New York, NY: Chapman and Hall/CRC, https://doi.org/10.1201/9780429297922

29. Ngu, A., Gutierrez, M., Metsis, V., Nepal, S., and Sheng, Q. 2017. IoT Middleware: A survey on issues and enabling technologies. *IEEE Internet of Things Journal*, vol. 4, no. 1, pp. 1–20

30. Al-khafajiy, M., Webster, L., Baker, T., and Waraich, A. 2018. Towards fog driven IoT healthcare: Challenges and framework of fog computing in healthcare. *Proceedings of the 2nd International Conference on Future Networks and Distributed Systems*. vol. 2. pp. 1–7. doi: 10.1145/3231053.3231062.

Part 4

14

The Architecture of Internet of Things with Applications and Healthcare Working Models

Dr. T. Venkat Narayana Rao

Department of Computer Science and Engineering, Sreenidhi Institute of Science and Technology
Hyderabad, India

Vivek Kapa

Department of Computer Science and Engineering, Sreenidhi Institute of Science and Technology
Hyderabad, India

Vinutha Kapa

Department of Computer Science and Engineering, Sreenidhi Institute of Science and Technology
Hyderabad, India

CONTENTS

14.1 Introduction 256
14.2 Architecture 257
    14.2.1 Sensing Layer 257
    14.2.2 Network Layer..258
    14.2.3 Interface Layer..259
14.3 Tools and Technologies of IoT..259
    14.3.1 Cancer Treatment...259
    14.3.2 Use of Glucose Aldohexose Monitor and Insulin Pens..............259
    14.3.3 Closed-Loop (Automated) Internal Secretion Delivery 259
    14.3.4 Connected Inhalers...260
    14.3.5 Ingestible Sensors 260
    14.3.6 IoT-Based Saline Level Monitoring System...................................261
    14.3.7 Basic System Requirements for and IOT-Based Healthcare
            Environment and Its Workings.. 261
            14.3.7.1 IR Sensors 261
            14.3.7.2 Arduino Microcontroller 261
            14.3.7.3 DC Motor 261
            14.3.7.4 Buzzer... 261
            14.3.7.5 Power Supply Unit.. 262
            14.3.7.6 Database.. 262
            14.3.7.7 Clamp.. 262
            14.3.7.8 Spring 262
            14.3.7.9 Websites 262

        14.3.8   System Architecture and Workings 262
        14.3.9   Heart Attack Detection by Heartbeat Sensing Using IoT 264
14.4   Conclusion 265
References 266

14.1 Introduction

Internet of Things (IoT) is indeed the pool of everyday objects such as sensors, tools, automobiles, homes, and other things integrated into electronic devices, circuitry, software, indicators, and wireless connectivity that supports such objects to amass and share information. IoT allows objects to be remotely sensed and managed through current systems, opening doors to many direct combinations of the virtual world into PC-based structures while triggering enhanced power and precision.

As early as 1982, the creation of a network of sensitive devices was discussed, with an improved Coca-Cola machine at Carnegie Mellon University turning into the key web-connected device. This system was able to track its stock so as to check whether or not freshly charged beverages were chilled. Kevin Ashton, a British citizen, coined the term "Internet of Things" to designate a network wherever the web is linked to the external world by omnipresent sensors.

IoT is able to act when human interference is not evident. Many early IoT implementations have already been introduced in the automotive, transport, and healthcare industries. IoT systems are in the initial stages; however, there have been several new findings in the incorporation of artifacts with detectors onto the network. IoT entails a number of issues such as networks, interactions, frameworks, specifications, and norms. The aim of this article is to manage its entire IoT framework, IoT architecture and stages, and other simplistic terms relevant to and, ultimately, services offered. In IoT, physical and virtual objects have their own personalities and characteristics, and are capable for victimizing cognitive systems and being incorporated as a communication network. In plain terms, IoT can be viewed as a set of unambiguously identifiable external devices. The terms "internet" and "technology" imply a worldwide connected model based on communication, detectors, and data processing applications, which influence the cover version of Information and Computing (ICT). Multiple innovations deal with IoT, such as remote and hence-called networks (WSNs), QR codes, smart detection, radio-frequency identification (RFID) tags, and minimum-energy communication systems. IoT represents the corresponding network age, where all the concrete objects can indeed be viewed and understood via the internet. The definition of IoT varies depending on the diverse incorporating technologies [1–18]. Simple IoT means that things in such IoT can be unambiguously identified throughout the simulated depictions. All items must share information with IoT and, if necessary, system information per predetermined schemes [19, 20].

In 1999, Kevin Ashton specifically projected the concept of IoT, and defined IoT as unequivocally identifiable linked entities via RFID technology. Moreover, the precise meaning of IoT remains within the method of creation, which is open to perceptions drawn. It was generally defined as dynamic international network infrastructure powered by standards and communication protocols with self-configuring capabilities.

14.2 Architecture

A vitally important IoT requirement is that the node objects must be interconnected. IoT system design should ensure IoT activities to fill in the gap between both the external and thus, augmented reality. IoT architecture is composed of several aspects such as connectivity, communication, economic models, and operations including security. The extensibility, measurability, and ability between interdependent systems and their prototypes should also be taken into deliberation with IoT design. As objects may move dynamically and want to move in live time mode with each other, IoT design must be flexible to build devices that move continuously with alternative things and support unambiguous communication of events [21, 22].

14.2.1 Sensing Layer

The architecture of IoT is shown in Figure 14.1. IoT is expected to become a good interconnected physical network that enables constant connection and can be regulated from anywhere. Sensitive systems on barcodes or detectors are ready to mechanically perceive the setting and exchange of information between devices in the sensing layer. Everything can be clearly known and the close environments can also be controlled for various functions and apps. Each IoT item has a digital signature, as well as possibly half-tracked within the digital space. A fundamental distinguishable symbol is called the method of designated distinctive identity to the associated object. The identifiers could contain names and addresses. It could be a 128-bit set unequivocally that is subjected to defining a certain item or entity on a network [21].

The following issues should be taken into account when deciding on the sensing layer of IoT: price, capacity, asset, and power consumption. The objects that may well be fitted with sensing devices are barcode tags and system nodes. Regardless of the enormous variety

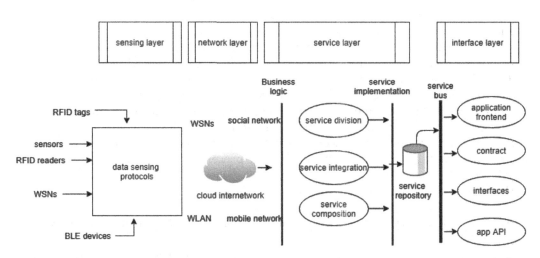

FIGURE 14.1
Architecture of IoT.

of detectors in applications, smart devices should still be built to upgrade the resources required.

- **Deployment:** Sensing stuff can be implemented one-time, or progressively, looking at the needs.
- **Connect:** To build objects that are usable and recoverable, the sensors should be transmissible.
- **Bind:** The objects are arranged as a multi-hop.

14.2.2 Network Layer

An IoT networking layer binds all objects and enables them to have their environment in mind. Through the networking layer, objects can exchange data with associated objects, which is important for smart event management and IoT applications.

A reliable network is essential for exchanging information and delivering resources through a device. The network can collectively automatically explore and map items. Things will be allocated roles to deliver, control, and organize the actions of items automatically and should be willing to turn to any responsibilities whenever necessary. This helps machines to cooperatively carry out tasks.

The following issues will be discussed in the networking layer:

- Network control systems and the control of wired, virtual, cellular networks
- Quality of service (QoS) specifications
- Information systems that look out, procedures
- Protection and privacy

Within these concerns, authentication of information and human confidentiality are important as IoT binds a variety of personal objects that present significant privacy risks. The current network protection systems will provide a foundation for security and privacy in IoT, but a great deal of work still needs to be done.

The service layer provides IoT services and applications. It is an efficient platform whenever the hardware and software systems are reused. The applications within the service layer operate exclusively on the network to efficiently locate new services and to dynamically retrieve information about services. Much of these are carried out using a range of standards established by entirely different groups. A service layer is widely agreed as essential for implementation of IoT. A suitable service layer comprises of minimal collection of programs, application programming interfaces (APIs), and related protocols that support the applications and services required. The most service-oriented operations such as information sharing and handling, knowledge processing, and browsers are at the service layer.

The activities that are carried out at the service layer are:

- **Service discovery:** Locating entities that can promptly deliver the stated service and data.
- **Service composition:** Allows interaction between linked things and defines the relations between subjects for sanctioning the service specified.
- **Service APIs:** Offer the user-needed interface between services [23, 24].

14.2.3 Interface Layer

An equally huge number of devices are associated with IoT; these devices relate to totally different tasks and, thus, do not mean equal expectations forever. For interaction between objects, the issue of compatibility amongst the objects must be resolved. Compatibility involves the process of sharing knowledge. There is a powerful design framework that would like to change the administration and interconnection of items. The interface layer resides within the application front end or API and a single removed node does not affect the entire network [25].

14.3 Tools and Technologies of IoT

14.3.1 Cancer Treatment

In 2018, details from an unusual study of 357 patients seeking care for head and neck cancer were presented at the ASCO Annual Meeting. The test was done using a Bluetooth-enabled weight scale, pressure level cuff, and symptom-tracking app to send symptoms and treatment response notifications to patient physicians every weekday [15–18].

The study reveals the possible edges of technology because it includes patient contact with doctors and tracking the circumstances of patients during an approach that causes minimal conflict with their everyday lives. Some of the changes we continue to see have discouraged people from being confined to their homes or from regularly staying in hospitals. Technology makes interaction along with medical skills way more powerful and helpful, and puts everybody in a more comfortable position [5].

14.3.2 Use of Glucose Aldohexose Monitor and Insulin Pens

Diabetes has sought to be great fodder for the event of successful tools as a disorder that affects around one in ten adults and needs constant monitoring and care administration. A Continuous Aldohexose Monitor (CGM) can be a tool that helps diabetics track their blood sugar levels unceasingly for several days at a time, collecting readings at periodic intervals. A number of strong CGMs have hit the market in the last few years. Smart CGMs such as *Eversense* and *FreeStyle Libre* send insulin-level information to an app on iPhone, Android, or Apple Watch, enabling the user to easily test their data and note patterns. LibreLink software jointly enables caregivers to watch remotely, which could accommodate elderly people with diabetic children or older patients. Another useful instrument currently in the lives of patients with polygenic disorder is the internal secretion pen. They have the ability to mechanically monitor the time, amount, and form of internal secretion injected during every dose and recommend the right type of internal secretion injection at the right moment. The devices are moving with a mobile app that will store semi-permanent information, make it easier for patients with polygenic disorder to measure their internal secretion level, and also allow patients to monitor their diets and insulin levels, but to display their food and internal secretion intake area unit poignantly with their blood glucose [26].

14.3.3 Closed-Loop (Automated) Internal Secretion Delivery

The ASCII text file project OpenAPS, which accounts for the Open Artificial Exocrine Gland Project, is one of the most interesting fields of IoT medicines. OpenAPS can be a kind of fenced-loop intrinsic secretion delivery device that varies from a CGM as well as calculating the amount of aldohexose in the blood of a patient, jointly supplying internal secretion, thus closing the loop.

Automating the delivery of internal secretion provides a range of benefits that will transform the lives of diabetic patients. Through monitoring individual insulin levels and manually changing the amount of internal secretion supplied to their body, the APS helps to maintain sugar within a safe range, avoiding excessive ups and downs. The automated distribution of internal secretion together enables diabetic patient to sleep through the night without a threat of lowering their blood glucose. OpenAPS isn't the only one to have this notion. The primary automated and web-connected closed-loop virtual exocrine gland system was developed in 2013 by Bryan Mazlish, a father with a partner and young son who have a type of polygenic disorder. In 2014, he sponsored SmartLoop Labs to expand and promote the event of an automated internal secretion delivery device that enabled his discovery, called Bigfoot Biomedical, which currently foresees the commercial launch by 2022, pending review and approval by the FDA.

14.3.4 Connected Inhalers

A respiratory disease, like a polygenic illness, is a problem that affects the lives of many people around the world. Because of linked inhalers, good technology is beginning to provide them with numerous perspectives and control of their symptoms and care. A Health Mechanical System is the main manufacturer of successful inhalator technology. Rather than producing full inhalers, a mechanical device has been developed that is connected to the inhaler or Bluetooth monitoring system. This links up to software and people with respiratory disease, and COPD, and perceives what may well be causing their symptoms, monitors rescue drug usage, and provides forecasts [1, 12, 13, 27].

Increased adherence is one of the benefits of using a linked inhaler; in other words, medicine is taken regularly. The mechanical system provides information on the use of the inhaler that is exchanged with the doctor of a patient and demonstrates whether or not it is as normal or as recommended. This offers inspiration and mutual clarification for patients, demonstrating that the use of their inhaler is directly up to their condition.

14.3.5 Ingestible Sensors

Proteus Digital Health and its field of ingestible sensors combine yet another example of successful drugs that will track adherence. The method of Proteus is one attempt to scale back this figure: the company has developed pills that dissolve within the abdomen and turn out to be a little signal that a tool placed on the body is picking up. The information is then forwarded to a mobile device, confirming that the patient took the drug as instructed [1, 12, 13, 15–17, 28].

As with connected inhalers, ingestible sensors will facilitate to trace and improve how frequently patients take their medication, in addition to permitting them to discuss with their medical practitioner concerning treatment. Whereas the thought of taking pills with a device may appear invasive, the system is opt-in on the part of patients, and they can discontinue sharing some types of data, or opt out of the program altogether at any point [27].

14.3.6 IoT-Based Saline Level Monitoring System

IoT assumes a significant job in the wellbeing checking framework. At whatever point saline is taken, the patient should be continually observed by a medical caretaker or any relatives. Most frequently because of carelessness, obliviousness, a busy schedule, and a progressive number of patients, the attendant may neglect to change the saline container when it is consumed. Just after saline completion, the blood surges back to the saline jug because of a contrast in pulse and weight inside the vacant saline jug. This may reverse the blood saline jug from their vein. This outcome in the decrease of hemoglobin levels of patients may likewise prompt a deficiency of red blood cells in the patient's blood, causing tiredness. Therefore, there is a need for building up a saline level checking framework that will diminish the patient's reliance on medical attendants or guardians [21].

To expel the disadvantages of traditional saline level checking frameworks, an IoT-Based Saline Level Monitoring System will fulfill the accompanying goals:

1. Give a practical and programmed saline level observing and controlling the framework, which can be easily executed in any medical clinic.
2. Reduce harm of well-being because of carelessness toward the saline finish.
3. Defeat the disadvantages and give more prominent exactness in a physically controlled saline stream rate framework.
4. Educate the specialist/nurture immediately for tolerant well-being.
5. Naturally, stop the stream subsequent to discharging of saline container

14.3.7 Basic System Requirements for and IOT-Based Healthcare Environment and Its Workings

14.3.7.1 IR Sensors

An infrared sensor (IR sensor) is an electronic gadget that transmits to detect parts of the surroundings. An IR sensor is situated at the base of the saline jug to detect the basic alignment of saline.

14.3.7.2 Arduino Microcontroller

Arduino is an open-source microcontroller pack for building advanced gadgets and intelligent articles that can detect and regulate physical world objects. Arduino microcontroller will be utilized as a handling and programming unit for sending signals to the DC motor, buzzer, and database.

14.3.7.3 DC Motor

A DC motor is a revolving electrical machine that changes over direct flow electrical vitality into mechanical energy. A DC engine will work as indicated by the orders given by the smaller scale controller and cause developments in the spring.

14.3.7.4 Buzzer

A buzzer is a sound-flagging device. A buzzer will notify the attendants, overseers, and specialists when saline arrives at the basic level and for substitution of the saline container.

14.3.7.5 Power Supply Unit

The power supply unit changes over fundamental AC to low-voltage-controlled DC power for the inward parts pertaining to the computer system. It supplies capacity to the remainder of the segments of the anticipated saline level observing framework.

14.3.7.6 Database

The database will store data about the patient's name, constituents, amount of saline taken, room number of the patient, contact details of three next-of-kin of the patient, and contact details of medical attendants and specialists answerable for checking the patient's saline [1].

14.3.7.7 Clamp

The clamp is integrated to the spring, with an extension of the spring, and the brace will move forward and squeeze the intravenous cylinder and halt the turnaround of the stream of blood into the saline container.

14.3.7.8 Spring

The spring is a flexible item that stocks mechanical energy useful for saline functioning. When the spring is extended from its resting point, the pinch connected to the spring will move toward the intravenous cylinder for halting the invert stream of blood into the saline jug or bottle. When a spring is compressed, it will come back to its rest position.

14.3.7.9 Websites

The website will contain forbidden data about the constituents and the amount of the saline taken dependent on the clinical issue. It will likewise contain the means or the guidelines concerning how the saline jug can be supplanted on the off chance that it is completely devoured and would answer the questions of the individuals with regards to taking saline and substitution of the saline jug at home.

14.3.8 System Architecture and Workings

The system architecture is as shown in Figure 14.2 where the explanation of each component is specified. This proposed framework will work for two distinct situations that are clarified here:

1. Saline scopes at the basic level.
2. The nurse neglects to go to the patient to supplant the saline container. In the first situation, in the wake of getting devoured by the patient, saline arrives at the basic level, which is detected by the IR sensors. This detected yield is sent to the miniaturized scale controller that filters the database for recovering the mollified data and the buzzer begins sounding for cautioning the attendants and specialists in the emergency clinics. A period breaking point will be set for the sounding of the buzzer. An alarm message is transmitted to the concerned medical caretakers and specialists related with the patient using the web. In the event that the medical

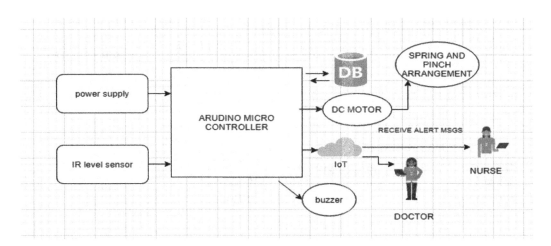

FIGURE 14.2
Architecture of the model.

attendant goes to the patient, at that point they should stop the buzzer and reset the entire framework. In the event that they neglect to do as such, at that point the second situation happens.

The IR sensor position must be as shown in Figure 14.3. In the second scenario, if the medical attendant neglects to go to the patient inside the set time limit, the turnaround stream of blood into the saline container is stopped. For this, a spring-DC engine game plan will be made. The pinch will be appended to the spring, alongside the pressure and extending offspring, and the clip will likewise move in forward and in reverse headings. Again, the IR sensor at the neck of the saline container will detect that the saline is completely devoured and a buzzer will again begin sounding stronger to advise the medical caretaker that the saline is completely expended and there is a necessity for substitution of

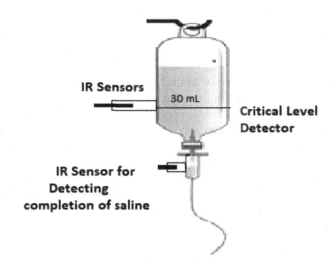

FIGURE 14.3
IR sensor position.

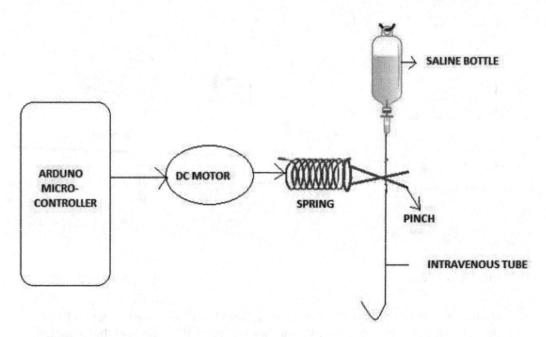

FIGURE 14.4
Mechanism to halt reverse flow of blood.

the saline jug. The guidelines for Arduino will be sent to the DC engine and according to the working of the DC engine, the spring is extended and the brace would move forward and squeeze the intravenous cylinder and stop the turnaround stream of the blood in the saline bottle. The mechanism that is to be followed in order to break the reverse flow of blood is shown in Figure 14.4 [21, 27].

14.3.9 Heart Attack Detection by Heartbeat Sensing Using IoT

With the aid of the detector, this system can discern heartbeats. To all metrics, an expert can set the rate. The machine passes the alarm to servers via Wi-Fi with metrics in the most serious saturation point.

The system uses a pulse beat detector to find and view the current pulse rate on the display screen. The transmission system integrates an AVR group microcontroller interfaced with an LCD panel, and a 12V transformer controls this transmitting circuit. The receiving circuit also includes the AVR family microcontroller and RF benefit, and it has a 12V transformer. The beneficiary circuit also comprises an LED light and a buzzer used to warn the person governing the patient's pulse rate, and turns on the patient's LED light and signal when the patient's pulse level does not drop within the typical pulse set. We are making this mechanism all-inclusive for all emergency rooms at the hospital. The admin can locate in a single place and be prepared to monitor all sufferers.

Components Required

1. **Heartbeat sensor:** The pulse sensor is used to measure the beat speed of the heart in a computerized output. The LED is used to realize the heart rate. The standard pulse range is 78 bpm. This provides an advance indication of prompt yield.

2. **Temperature sensor:** The LM35 detector is used to measure the temperature of the human body. The LM35-structure devices are precision-coordinated circuit temperature detectors with an output voltage directly proportional to Celsius.

3. **Pressure sensor:** The pressure detector is used to measure the diastolic and systolic weight levels of the device. That is calculated in millimeters of mercury (mmHg). The circulatory strain alters from time to time.

4. **Wi-Fi module:** The ESP8266 Wireless Device is an autonomous SOC with a built-in TCP/IP protocol array that can provide any microcontroller access to arrange your Wi-Fi. The ESP8266 is able to facilitate an app or to discharge all Wi-Fi arranging capacities from other device processors.

5. **Atmega 328:** The Atmega 328 is a small-scale controller with 8 bits. It can handle approximate details of the system using 8 bits. It is a narrower-scale controller built on AVR. Its inherent storage would be about 32 KB. It operates from 3.3V up to 5V. Whenever the electric stock is removed from its biased ports, it can save the data.

Points of interest:

- Saves danger of coronary failure as you can check it at home.
- Inexpensive framework.
- Heartbeat and temperature measurement by a single gadget.
- All patients can be investigated by a single individual from a server room.
- This process would additionally comfort the hospital observation system.

14.4 Conclusion

Over the years, IoT has grown swiftly and an enormous range of innovative applications have been introduced. IoT has become a phenomenon for the next internet. The long-awaited IoT breakthrough in healthcare is already underway. IoT building blocks of automation and device-to-device communication continue to be developed with the introduction of the service layer completing the infrastructure. Moreover, the new IoT-based e-Health program not only has a smarter solution to healthcare but also makes the decision-making process efficient. Overall, this approach may tackle a variety of health problems as a mass. Portable IoT sensors will have a big impact on any patient's life, even if they are away from home and the doctor, because they help reduce the fear of risk. Sensory data may be collected in the home or working areas. Since the basis of the current e-Health model is centered on the internet, it will be simpler to integrate outputs to desktops and mobile devices. This chapter has discussed the need for integrating IoT technologies with e-Health applications and wearable devices to enhance patient healthcare. This provides an easy and safe access to electronic medical records of patients. Hence, it can be concluded that IoT promises an inexpensive healthcare and well-organized service system in the future. This can create a more customized and patient-centric service. It further ensures that IoT will empower patients to get superior access to data and personalized attention, thus leading to less visits to hospitals.

References

1. Sharma, Lavanya, and Garg, P.K. (Eds.). 2019. *From Visual Surveillance to Internet of Things.* New York, NY: Chapman and Hall/CRC, https://doi.org/10.1201/9780429297922

2. Sharma, Lavanya, and Lohan, Nirvikar. January 2019. Performance analysis of moving object detection using BGS techniques in visual surveillance. *International Journal of Spatiotemporal Data Science*, Inderscience, vol. 1, pp. 22–53.

3. Kumar, Anubhav, Jha, Gaurav, and Sharma, Lavanya. July 2019. Challenges, potential & future of IOT integrated with block chain. *International Journal of Recent Technology and Engineering*, vol. 8, no. 2S7, pp. 530–536.

4. Liu, Yong, and Hou, Rongxu. 2010. About the sensing layer in Internet of things [J]. *Computer Study*, vol. 5, pp. 55.

5. Tian, S., Yang, W., Michael Le Grange, J., Wang, P., Huang, W. and Ye, Z. 2019. Smart healthcare: Making medical care more intelligent. *Global Health Journal*, vol. 3, no. 3, pp. 63–65.

6. Sharma, Lavanya and Lohan, Nirvikar. February, 2019. Performance analysis of moving object detection using BGS techniques. *International Journal of Spatio-Temporal Data Science*, Inderscience, vol. 1, pp. 22–53.

7. Sharma, Shubham, Verma, Shubhankar, Kumar, Mohit, and Sharma, Lavanya. 2019. Use of Motion Capture in 3D Animation: Motion Capture Systems, Challenges, and Recent Trends. In: 1st IEEE International Conference on Machine Learning, Big Data, Cloud and Parallel Computing (Com-IT-Con), India, 14–16 February, pp. 309–313.

8. Sharma, Lavanya and Lohan, Nirvikar. March, 2019. Internet of things with object detection. In: *Handbook of Research on Big Data and the IoT*, IGI Global, pp. 89–100. DOI: 10.4018/978-1-5225-7432-3.ch006

9. Sharma, Lavanya. 2019. Introduction. In: *From Visual Surveillance to Internet of Things*. Chapman Hall/CRC, vol. 1, p. 14.

10. Sharma, Lavanya and Garg, P. K. 2019. Block based adaptive learning rate for moving person detection in video surveillance. In: *From Visual Surveillance to Internet of Things*. Chapman Hall/CRC, vol. 1, p. 201.

11. Sharma, Lavanya, and Garg, P. K. 2019. Smart E-healthcare with Internet of things: Current trends challenges, solutions and technologies. In: *From Visual Surveillance to Internet of Things*. Chapman Hall/CRC, vol. 1, p. 215.

12. Sharma, Lavanya, Garg, P. K., and Agarwal, Naman. 2019. A foresight on e-healthcare Trailblazers. In: *From Visual Surveillance to Internet of Things*. Chapman Hall/CRC, vol. 1, p. 235

13. Wan, D. 1999. Magic medicine cabinet: A situated portal for consumer healthcare. In: *Lecture Notes in Computer Science (Including subseries Lecture Notes in Artificial Intelligence and Lecture Notes in Bioinformatics)*. Springer Verlag, pp. 352–355.

14. Sharma, Lavanya, and Garg, P. K. 2019. Future of Internet of things. In: *From Visual Surveillance to Internet of Things*. Chapman Hall/CRC, vol. 1, p. 245.

15. Sharma, Lavanya, and Garg, P K. 2019. IoT and its applications. In: *From Visual Surveillance to Internet of Things*. Chapman Hall/CRC, vol.1, p. 29.

16. Jokanovic, V. 2005. Structures and substructures in spray pyrolysis process: Nanodesigning, finely dispersed particles, Micro-, Nano-, and Atto-Engineering. In: *Surfactant Science Series*. Taylor and Francis.

17. Sharma, Lavanya, Singh, Annapurna, and Yadav, Dileep Kumar. March, 2016. Fisher's linear discriminant ratio based threshold for moving human detection in thermal video. In: *Infrared Physics and Technology*. Elsevier, vol. 78, pp. 118–128.

18. Santos, M. Y., Pendão, C., Ferreira, B, Gonçalves, L., Moreira, G., Moreira, A., and Carvalho, J.A. 2015. MyHealth: A cross-domain platform for healthcare, SAC 15: Proceedings of 30th Annual ACM Symposium on Applied Computing, Salamanca, Spain.

19. Shancang, Li., LiDa, Xu., and Shanshan, Zhao. April 26, 2014. *The Internet of Things: A Survey*, Published online: SpringerScience+Business Media.
20. Evans, D. 2011. The Internet of Things How the Next Evolution of the Internet is Changing Everything (White Paper, CISCO), p. 4.
21. Jara, Antonio J., Zamora, Miguel A., and Skarmeta, Antonio F. G. 2010. *An Architecture based on Internet of Things to Support Mobility and Security in Medical Environments*, Murcia, Spain: University of Murcia, Computer Science Faculty.
22. Baker, Stephanie, Atkinson, Ian, and Xiang, Wei. 2017. Internet of Things for Smart Healthcare: Technologies, challenges, and opportunities, *IEEE Access*. DOI: 10.1109/ACCESS.2017.2775180.
23. Al-Fuqaha, Ala, Guizani, Mohsen, Mohammadi, Mehdi, Aledhari, Mohammed, and Ayyash, Moussa. 2015. Internet of things: A survey on enabling technologies protocols and applications. *IEEE Communications Surveys & Tutorials*, IEEE, vol. 17, no. 4, pp. 2347–2376.
24. Saha, Himadri Nath, Paul, Debasmita, Chaudhury, Shreyaasha, Haldar, Siddhartha, and Mukherjee, Ruptirtha. 2017. Internet of Thing based healthcare monitoring system, 8th IEEE Annual Information Technology, Electronics and Mobile Communication Conference (IEMCON).
25. Sharma, Anirvin, Choudhury, Tanupriya and Kumar, Praveen. 2018. Health monitoring & management using IoT devices in a cloud based framework, 2018 International Conference on Advances in Computing and Communication Engineering (ICACCE).
26. Hung, K., Zhang, Y. T. and Tai, B. 2004. Wearable medical devices for telehome healthcare, Engineering in Medicine and Biology Society, *IEMBS'04. 26th Annual International Conference of the IEEE*, vol. 2, pp. 5384–5387.
27. Castillejo, Pedro, Jose-Fernan, Martinez, JesÃžs Rodr, Ãguez-Molina, and Alexandra, Cuerva. 2013. Integration of wearable devices in a wireless sensor network for an E-health application, *Wireless Communications*, IEEE, vol. 20, no. 4, pp. 38–49.
28. Chang-le, Zhong, Zhen, Zhu, and Ren-Gen, Huang, 2018. Study on the IOT architecture and access technology, IEEE 23rd International Conference on Emerging Technologies and Factory Automation (ETFA).

15

Diagnostic of the Malarial Parasite in RBC Images for Automated Diseases Prediction

Karanjot Singh

Amity Institute of Technology, Amity University
Noida, India

Sudhriti Sengupta

Amity Institute of Technology, Amity University
Noida, India

CONTENTS

15.1 Introduction..269
15.2 Proposed Methodology...270
    15.2.1 Input/Read Image..270
    15.2.2 Conversion of Image from the RGB Color Space to the L*a*b* Color Space 270
    15.2.3 Classify the Colors in the a*b* Space Using K-Means Clustering...........272
    15.2.4 Create Images that Segment the H&E Image by Color 273
    15.2.5 Output Image with Malarial Parasite 273
15.3 Implementation 274
15.4 Results and Discussion 274
15.5 Conclusion 276
References..276

KEYWORDS: *malarial parasite, RBC images, segmentation, K-means clustering, structural similarity content*

15.1 Introduction

Malaria is an infection that can be caused by a few different species of the Plasmodium genus, which are single-cell parasites that get spread around by mosquitoes. It is a very dangerous type of infection that can take away a human life. According to data of the World Health Organization (WHO), nearly 438,000 people lost their life due to this disease in 2015 [1]. Once Plasmodium gets into the bloodstream, it starts to infect and destroy mainly the liver cells and the red blood cells (RBCs), which causes a variety of symptoms and sometimes even death. Malaria is a serious global health problem and it affects millions of people. Particularly, it affects young children under the age of five, pregnant women, or patients with HIV/AIDS. The regions where it widely affects humans are Latin America, Sub-Saharan Africa, South Asia, and Southeast Asia.

There are multiple numbers of techniques with which the malarial parasite can be found and detected in the RBCs of a human body. We apply an image-processing technique to an RBC image in a facilities automatizes system [2, 3]. Out of which we have taken a technique called "segmentation" to extract the malarial parasite in the RBC image so that the person with malaria can be detected easily. An efficient segmentation process is very important to carry out classification, which leads to an effective Automated Diagnostics System. Segmentation is a very fast and easy process to detect the malarial parasites present in the RBCs in the human body and this technique can be used in the field of malaria detection [4]. In 2009, Diaz et al. proposed a semi-automated for quantification and classification of erythrocytes infected with malaria parasites in microscopic images [5]. In 2007, a program called Malaria Count was proposed by Sio that was basically an image analysis-based program for the accurate determination of a parasite [6]. In 2009, Sadeghian et al. proposed a framework for white blood cell segmentation in microscopic blood images using digital image processing [7]. A methodology of segmentation of blood images using morphological operators was given by Di Ruberto et al. in 2000 [8]. In 2007, Edward et al. introduced the challenges and potential role of rapid diagnostic tests (RDTs) in the African region, known as Malaria Diagnostic in the community [9]. In 2013, Kamolrat et al. gave a standard operating procedure for malaria slide management [10]. In 2013 [11], Sudhakar et al. gave a methodology for detection of the malaria parasite in blood using image processing [12]. In 2017, Saraswat et al. detected the malarial parasite from RBC images by applying the image-processing technique. They have also provided a review of detection and classification technique of parasitemia in blood images [13–15].

15.2 Proposed Methodology

The proposed system model is implemented by using segmentation techniques, in which there are a total of five steps by which we could segment the image with the malarial parasite in RBC images. Figure 15.1 shows a flowchart of the segmentation technique that we are using to detect the malarial parasite in RBC images [16–22].

15.2.1 Input/Read Image

In this method, we have proposed a color-based segmentation using K-means clustering. For this experimentation we have used the images of Giemsa blood samples from open-source access.

Figure 15.2 depicts a sample input image that might contain malarial parasite traits. The objective is to extract these traits from the test image, which will further help to automatize the malarial detection system efficient.

15.2.2 Conversion of Image from the RGB Color Space to the L*a*b* Color Space

In the second step, we have converted the default red/green/blue (RGB) color space of the image into the L*a*b* color space. The RGB color space model is supposed to tell us about the three primary additive colors of red, green, and blue. A human eye has the color

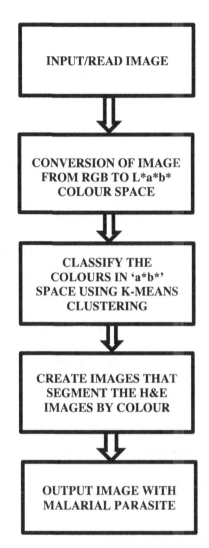

FIGURE 15.1
Flowchart of proposed methodology.

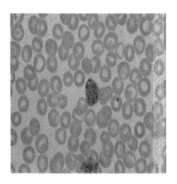

FIGURE 15.2
Input image (Test Case 1).

TABLE 15.1

Color Range and Intensity Value of the L*a*b* Color Space

Axis	Colors	Intensity Values
L* axis	Black, White, Gray	0, 100, 50
a* axis	Cyan to Magenta	−100 to 100
b* axis	Blue to Yellow	−100 to 100

receptors for RGB, therefore every other color can be formed by the combination of these three colors and can be seen by a naked human eye. The possible outcomes for combining or mixing the colors RGB can be represented as a three-dimensional coordinate plane. The three colors of red, green, and blue would have their values on each axis [23].

The L*a*b* color model is a three-axis color system and the L*a*b* colors are absolute, that is, the color is identical. L*a*b stands for L* = Lightness, a* = Red/Green value, and b* = Blue/Yellow value.

The L*a*b* color space is the only way to communicate different colors across different devices.

It is a three-axis system. The first-axis, the L-channel or lightness, consists of white to black and all of the gray colors will be right down the center. The second-axis, the a-axis, goes from a cyan color across to a magenta/red color. The third-axis, the b-axis, consists of blue to yellow colors. The color range and intensity value of the L*a*b* color space is shown in Table 15.1.

By applying the L*a*b* color space method on the input test image in Figure 15.1, we get the image shown in Figure 15.3 as a result.

15.2.3 Classify the Colors in the a*b* Space Using K-Means Clustering

Clustering can be defined as a way to distinguish or separate the objects into groups. K-means clustering defines a location in space for each and every object. It's a process in which the K-means clustering finds the separations such that objects within each cluster are as near as they can be. In the K-means clustering process, it specifically asks you to specify or initialize the number of clusters that are to be partitioned. It also requires a

FIGURE 15.3
Test image in the L*a*b* color space.

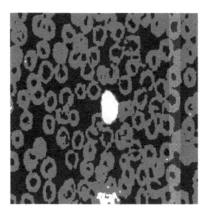

FIGURE 15.4
K-means clustering on test image given by Figure 15.3.

distance metric to find the distance between two objects. The color space a*b* is the color information in the L*a*b* color space. The given data would be converted into data type "single" with the use of *imsegkmeans* [12]. *Imsegkmeans* will be used to cluster the objects into three clusters, so the quantified value of K is 3 (Figure 15.4).

15.2.4 Create Images that Segment the H&E Image by Color

Hematoxylin and Eosin (H&E) is mainly used for displaying cellular and tissue structures. H&E are used by pathologists. They provide a broad and clear image of the microanatomy of the body parts/organs and the tissues in the human body (Figure 15.3).

15.2.5 Output Image with Malarial Parasite

In this step, there are dark blue and light blue objects in the image. They can be distinguished or separated from each other with the help of the "L" layer in the 'L*a*b*' color space. The dark blue objects in the given image are actually the infected cells by malaria

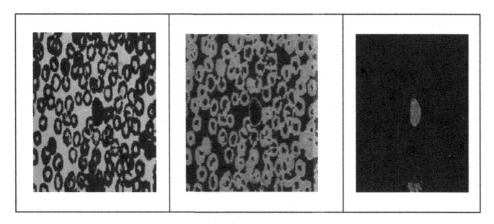

FIGURE 15.5
Three types of clusters formed by the image in Figure 15.3.

FIGURE 15.6
Segmented malarial parasitic traits from the test image.

because "L" holds the brightness values of each color present in the given image. With the help of the global threshold function, the brightness values in this cluster can be extracted as shown in Figure 15.6.

15.3 Implementation

To test the efficiency of the proposed methodology, 10 Giemsa blood sample images were taken from the open-source web portal. The experiments are conducted using MATLAB R2019b on Windows 10, 64-bit OS with Intel® Core™, 1.80 GHz CPU, and 8 GB RAM. To analysis the performance of the proposed methodology, we have used the popular adaptive thresholding on the test images. All the test images are segmented using both the proposed technique and adaptive thresholding technique. The result is given in Table 15.2. In the table, the column a represents the original image. Column 2 depicts segmentation by using the proposed K-means clustering method. Column 3 depicts segmentation by using the adaptive thresholding.

15.4 Results and Discussion

To check the efficiency of the proposed methodology, we have used the popular image segmentation quality parameter called the Structural Similarity Index. Greater value of structural content denotes poor quality of segmentation. It is measured by spatial arrangement of pixels in an image [24]. The following equation shows the concept of the Structural Similarity Index:

$$Structural\ Content = \frac{\sum_{a=1}^{i}\sum_{b=1}^{j}[g(a,b)]^2}{\sum_{a=1}^{i}\sum_{b=1}^{j}[g^s(a,b)]^2} \qquad (15.1)$$

TABLE 15.2

(a) Original Image (b) Segmented Image by K-Means Clustering, and (c) Segmented Image by Adaptive Thresholding

S.NO	Original Image	K-Means Clustering	Adaptive Thresholding
1			
2			
3			
4			
5			
6			
7			
8			
9			
10			
	(a)	(b)	(c)

TABLE 15.3

Quantitative Comparison of the Proposed Method

Image Number	K-Means Clustering	Adaptive Thresholding
1	0.0029	0.8524
2	0.0053	0.8243
3	0.0034	0.8001
4	0.0038	0.8357
5	0.000508	0.5209
6	−0.0012	0.9095
7	−0.00056	0.9526
8	0.0603	0.7807
9	−0.0021	0.6847
10	0.0039	0.7960

where the size of an image is given by i and j, and g and gs denotes the original and segmented image, respectively. An image with lower structural value content is better in terms of segmentation. Table 15.3 shows the structural content of the original image obtained by the proposed method and the segmented image obtained by the adaptive thresholding technique.

It can be observed from Table 15.3 that structural content of the images obtained by applying the proposed image segmentation technique is low as compared to the original image and segmented image obtained by the adaptive thresholding method. On applying the proposed K-means clustering segmentation, we see that the structural content values are 0.0029, 0.0053, 0.0034, [...] and 0.0039. The structural content values of the images obtained by the adaptive threshold technique are 0.8524, 0.8243, 0.8001, [...] and 0.7960. The lower value of the structural content for the proposed techniques signifies that the proposed method is more effective in segmentation of malarial traits from RBC images.

15.5 Conclusion

An automated trait detection is proposed in this method. First, the test image is converted into the L*a*b* color space, then K-means clustering is applied on the a*b* channel of the image. H&E image segmentation is formed and as a result we can have an outline of the image with the malarial parasite. The quality is checked by using structural content of the image and compared with the image obtained by using the adaptive threshold technique.

References

1. WHO, 2019. World Malaria Report 2019. Available at: https://www.who.int/publications-detail/world-malaria-report-2019
2. S. Sengupta, N. Mittal, and M. Modi, 2017. A survey of techniques used in processing and mining of medical images, International Conference on Recent Developments in Science, Engineering and Technology, pp. 139–155, doi 10.1007/978-981-10-8527-7_13.

3. Lavanya Sharma, Annapurna Singh, and Dileep Kumar Yadav, 2016. Fisher's linear discriminant ratio based threshold for moving human detection in thermal video, *Infrared Physics and Technology*, Elsevier, vol. 78, pp. 118–128.
4. P. Rakshit and K. Bhowmik, 2013. Detection of presence of parasites in human RBC in case of diagnosing malaria using image processing, 2013 IEEE Second International Conference on Image Information Processing (ICIIP-2013), Shimla, December 9–11, pp. 329–334. doi: 10.1109/ICIIP.2013.6707610.
5. G. Diaz, A. Gonzalez, E. Romero, 2009. A semi-automatic method for quantification and classification of erythrocytes infected with malaria parasites in microscopic images, *Journal of Biomedical Informatics*, vol. 42, pp. 296–307.
6. W. S. S Sio, et al, 2007. Malaria count: An image analysis-based program for the accurate determination of parasitemia, *Journal of Microbiological Methods*, vol. 68, no. 1, pp. 11–18.
7. F. Sadeghian, Z. Seman, and A. R. Ramli, 2009. A framework for white blood cell segmentation in microscopic blood images using digital image processing, *Biological Procedures Online*, Vol. 11, no. 1, pp. 196–206.
8. C. Di Ruberto, A. Dempster, S. Khan, and B. Jarra, 2000. Segmentation of blood images using morphological operators, Proceedings of 15th International Conference on Pattern Recognition, Barcelona, Spain, Vol. 3, p. 3401.
9. K. Edward, 2007. Malaria diagnosis in the community: Challenges and potential role of rapid diagnostic tests (RDTs) in the African region, *African journal of Health Sciences*, Vol.14, pp. 114–117.
10. S. Kamolrat, 2013. Standard Operating Procedure: Malaria Slide Management, Mahidol Oxford University Research Program. Version 10.2013. https://docplayer.net/75706491-Standard-operating-procedure.html
11. T. Sudhakar, 2013. Detection of malaria parasite in blood using image processing, *International Journal of Engineering and Innovative Technology (IJEIT)*, vol. 2, no.10, pp. 124–126.
12. MATLAB tutorial, 2019. Color-based segmentation using K-means clustering. Available at: https://in.mathworks.com/help/images/color-based-segmentation-using-k-means-clustering.html
13. S. Saraswat, U. Awasthi, and N. Faujdar, 2017. Malarial parasites detection in RBC using image processing, 6th International Conference on Reliability, Infocom Technologies and Optimization (Trends and Future Directions) (ICRITO), Noida, India, pp. 599–603. doi: 10.1109/ICRITO.2017.8342498
14. Lavanya, Sharma, and P. K., Garg (Eds.). 2019. *From Visual Surveillance to Internet of Things*. New York, NY: Chapman and Hall/CRC, https://doi.org/10.1201/9780429297922
15. Lavanya Sharma and P. K. Garg, 2019. Block based Adaptive Learning Rate for Moving Person Detection in Video Surveillance, *From Visual Surveillance to Internet of Things*, Chapman Hall/CRC, vol. 1, p. 201.
16. Image. Test image for experiment. https://www.hsph.harvard.edu/news/features/malaria-parasite-invasion-doorway/
17. Image. Test image for experiment. https://blogs.biomedcentral.com/bugbitten/2018/01/19/vivax-malaria-another-key-red-blood-cell-invasion/
18. Image. Test image for experiment. http://www.bunniklab.org/RESEARCH/index.html
19. Image. Test image for experiment. https://www.sciencemag.org/news/2014/02/origins-malaria-parasite-revealed
20. Image. Test image for experiment. https://newsroom.ucr.edu/2262
21. Image. Test image for experiment. https://medicalxpress.com/news/2012-07-vaccine-vigilance-evolution-more-virulent-malaria.html
22. Image. Test image for experiment. https://www.esanum.com/today/posts/methylene-blue-found-to-kill-malaria-parasites-in-record-time
23. R. C. Gonzalez and R. E. Woods, 2018. *Digital Image Processing*, 4th Edition, Pearson.
24. S. Sengupta, N. Mittal, and M. Modi, 2019. Color space based thresholding for segmentation of skin lesion images. *International Journal of Biomedical Engineering and Technology*. https://www.inderscience.com/info/ingeneral/forthcoming.php?jcode=ijbet/ (Accessed on July 31, 2019).

16

Design of a Multipurpose Android-Controlled Robotic Arm for a Smart City

Satyam Tayal

Thapar Institute of Engineering & Technology
Patiala, India

Harsh Pallav Govind Rao

Thapar Institute of Engineering & Technology
Patiala, India

Suryansh Bhardwaj

Thapar Institute of Engineering & Technology
Patiala, India

Shreyansh Soni

Thapar Institute of Engineering & Technology
Patiala, India

CONTENTS

16.1 Introduction 280
16.2 Literature Review..280
16.3 Schematic Diagram of Proposed System...281
16.4 Hardware Implementation of Robotic Arm..282
    16.4.1 Arduino Uno Microcontroller...282
    16.4.2 Bluetooth Module (HC-05) 283
    16.4.3 Motor Driver (L293D) 283
    16.4.4 Android Application (Arduin Remote Bluetooth-WiFi)......284
    16.4.5 DC Motors...284
16.5 Results and Discussion 284
16.6 Conclusion 285
Acknowledgment...285
References...285

KEYWORDS: *robotic arm, Arduino microcontroller, Bluetooth, motor driver, DC motor, smart city, internet of things*

16.1 Introduction

The word "robot" originated from *robota*, a Czech word that means forced labor. The majority of robots are used to execute dedicated, complex, risky, and continuous manufacturing jobs. In comparison with humans, robots are able to do repetitive work with higher precision and efficiency. Irrespective of the working time, they perform a repetitive task with the same amount of energy [1–3]. A robotic arm is similar to a human arm [4] and can be programmed. This is a mechanical arm able to perform translational or rotational motions in a controlled environment [4–6]. The various links of an arm are connected by joints. Robotic arms are available in a large number of variants. These arms are usually designed for specific tasks to work in varied environments. The automation by robotic arms results in reduction of errors in repetitive jobs [7, 8].

In this work for remote operation, an Android-enabled smartphone is used [9]. The Android smartphone sends commands for stop, backward/forward bending, and right/left rotation. The Android application in the smartphone controls the robotic arm [10]. This has Bluetooth connectivity and sends the control signal to the Bluetooth module. There are two paired Bluetooth modules provided at the receiver and transmitting ends. The Arduino Uno microcontroller [11] compares the incoming signal with the saved information to take matching actions. The objects gripping and arm rotation are achieved by means of DC motors. To control the DC motors, an Arduino Uno microcontroller is used. The L293D motor driver circuit is used to feed the necessary control signals to the DC motor.

The typical applications of robotic arms include drilling, painting, thermal spraying, and welding. Waste management is a tedious problem for modern cities throughout the world. Specialized agencies need to be hired for collection and removal of garbage. In the majority of cases, the disposal of garbage is managed manually. They follow a fixed schedule as per demand of residents. In order to improve trash collection by automatic means, there is a need to employ modern technologies such as Internet of Things (IoT) and sensors [12–14]. Automatic garbage removal by pick and place robots [15–18] may provide such a solution in emerging smart cities. In many developed countries with shortage of labor and aging populations, these robots may play a vital role. This work aims to design a multipurpose triple-axis robotic arm capable of doing numerous tasks such as cleaning of the house, mopping the floor, irrigation of crops, and so on. This can also be utilized in various industrial applications, where handling of objects can be dangerous.

This chapter is organized as follows. The literature review is included in Section 16.2, the circuit diagram and various components/sections and their workings have been illustrated in Sections 16.3 to 16.5, and the conclusion is presented in Section 16.6.

16.2 Literature Review

The robotic arm consists of a mechanical arm with a jaw for pick and place. The robotic arms have variations in solid parts, motion range, types of joints, and sequence of joints and sizes. The robotic arm may be single axis, double axis, or triple axis [19, 20] depending upon the motion in a line, plane, or any point in space. In literature, various design strategies [21–25] for robotic arms have been proposed. The LABVIEW software has been utilized by Oladele et al. [26] to design a microcontroller-based robotic arm. The position of the arm was sensed and its feedback was provided by the accelerometer. The LABVIEW software provides the real-time environment for designing of the pick and place robotic arm. The robotic arm design using the Haptic technique has been proposed by Kumar [27]. The proposed robot was able to work in variety of medical and industrial applications. The robot was designed with four degrees of freedom suitable for heavier loads. The robotic arm can be used in medical applications such as fine eye surgery. For efficient welding, the robotic arm design has been presented by Nair [28]. The robotic arm works on the principle of pick and place with variations in movement angle like human hands. A threaded shaft with spur gears has been utilized with the motors. The prototype aims to carry out spot-welding operations in an effective manner with the minimum power consumptions. The change in movement angle brings more flexibility required for precision welding.

The synchronized robotic arm has been discussed by Omijeh et al. [29] The designed robot was able to do various jobs such as spinning, welding, and gripping. The robotic arm is designed for domestic and industrial application. In the proposed design, pressure sensors have been used to judge the hardness of an object. Thus, suitable action is being taken by the robot for perfect gripping. The pick and place remote-controlled robot design has been proposed by Singh et al. [30]. The working prototype of a robotic arm has been proposed that was able to handle the hazardous objects and bring safety to working people. This robotic arm can be utilized to perform tedious tasks rapidly and safely. In various industries, the application of such robots is highly desired to increase the output. The robot arm with four wheels has been designed for five degrees of freedom. In commonly used existing robotic arms, the complexity of design, flexibility of operations, power consumption, and cost-effectiveness are major issues.

16.3 Schematic Diagram of Proposed System

The schematic diagram of the robotic arm is shown in Figure 16.1. The smartphone is an Android application device. This provides the signal to the microcontroller through the Bluetooth module. The Arduino Uno microcontroller controls the movements of DC motors through an L293D Driver circuit.

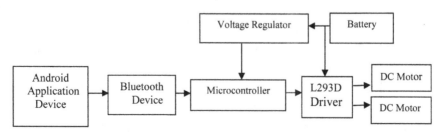

FIGURE 16.1
Schematic diagram of proposed robotic arm.

16.4 Hardware Implementation of Robotic Arm

The designed robotic arm includes the following sections: a microcontroller, a Bluetooth module, a motor driver, an Android application device, DC motors, a voltage regulator, and a battery.

16.4.1 Arduino Uno Microcontroller

The Arduino Uno microcontroller board (Figure 16.2) can be interfaced with other boards. This microcontroller consists of 6 analog and 14 digital input–output pins to interface with various expansion boards.

The microcontroller receives the commands from an Android application device through the Bluetooth module to control the DC motors via the L293D motor driver. The DC motors may be stopped or started as per instructions given by the Android application.

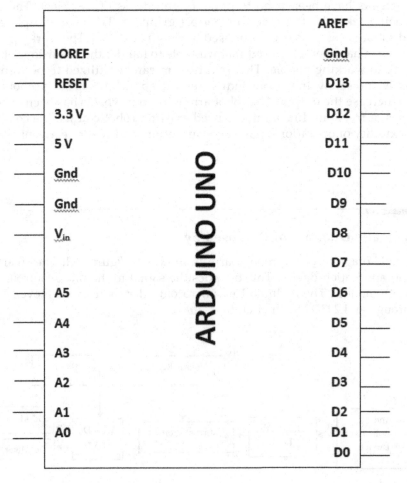

FIGURE 16.2
Arduino Uno microcontroller board.

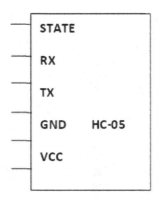

FIGURE 16.3
Bluetooth module HC-05.

16.4.2 Bluetooth Module (HC-05)

The Bluetooth module HC-05 (Figure 16.3) is used for the setup of a wireless serial connection among the circuit and the Android application device. This is made with CMOS technology on a single chip. This can be utilized in a master–slave formation in an easy way. It uses an adaptive frequency hopping (AFH) feature, with a 2.4 GHz radio transceiver and baseband, and 3 Mbps modulation.

16.4.3 Motor Driver (L293D)

In this work, an L293D monolithic integrated motor driver has been used (Figure 16.4). This is a H-bridge, four-channel, high-current and high-voltage driver. This circuit utilizes a DC power supply (maximum 600 mA/channel, 16 Volt) and controls the action of the motors using Arduino code.

This driver circuit utilizes two H-bridge driver circuits. This is an electrical circuit that applies the voltage across motors in both directions. This driver chip is able to drive two DC motors in reverse/forward directions. In order to control the operations of two motors, input logic at pins 10 and 15 and 2 and 7 are used. The logics 10 and 01 rotate the DC motor in anticlockwise and clockwise directions. The logics 11 and 00 will stop the motor.

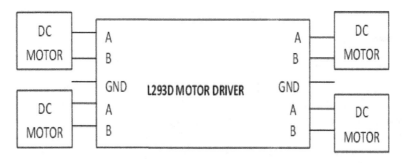

FIGURE 16.4
L293D motor driver.

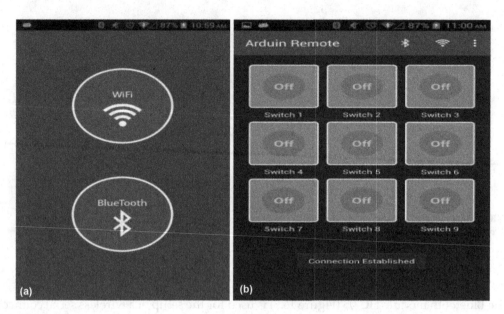

FIGURE 16.5
(a) Arduin remote app homepage; (b) Arduin remote app interface.

16.4.4 Android Application (Arduin Remote Bluetooth-WiFi)

The Arduin Remote Bluetooth-WiFi app as shown in Figure 16.5(a) and (b) is utilized in this work. This includes features such as the ability to control up to seven switches, connect using Wi-Fi or Bluetooth, and the ability to change the switch name.

16.4.5 DC Motors

DC motors are used to carry out the up and down and gripper operations of robotic arm. DC motors operate on direct current and convert electrical energy into mechanical energy. DC motors close/open through a motor driver shield. The current through the motor depends on the pressure in the arm jaws or load at the motor.

The hardware model of a robotic arm from two different angles is shown in Figure 16.6(a) and (b).

16.5 Results and Discussion

The triple-axis robotic arm has been designed with a simple circuit. The existing robotic arms are complex and available at a very high cost. This robotic arm with simple circuitry can effectively carry out the up, down, and gripper operations. The robotic arm can easily move 360° at one place. The DC motors are being turned on/off using the motor driver shield. The pressure exerted by the arm jaw is a function of the DC motor current. Further, there is a scope of forward and backward movement of this robotic arm.

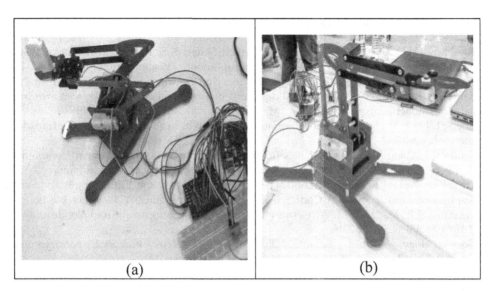

(a) (b)

FIGURE 16.6
(a) and (b) Hardware model of robotic arm.

16.6 Conclusion

This chapter presents the design and hardware implementation of a cost-effective proto-type of a simple robotic arm. The application of a high-torque motor provides an aid to pick up large weights. The multipurpose robotic arm is suitable for various operations in domestic and industrial applications. As the robotic arm is remotely controlled by an Android app, this is ideally suited to carry out versatile operations in hazardous conditions. This robotic arm may also pick up an object such as a bomb from a dense area and place it in a safer location. These pick and place robots can reduce human efforts by providing automatic trash removal in smart urban areas.

Acknowledgment

The authors wish to thank Experiential Learning Centre and Department of Computer Science and Engineering, Thapar Institute of Engineering & Technology (TIET), Patiala, for providing laboratory facilities for execution of this work.

References

1. Mittal R.K., Nagrath I.J. *Robotics and Control*. McGraw Hill, India. 2013.
2. Rahimi H.N., Nazemizadeh M. Dynamic analysis and intelligent control techniques for flexible manipulators: A review. *Advanced Robotics*. 28(2). 63–76. 2014.

3. Miro J.V., White A. S. Modeling and industrial manipulator a case study. *Simulation Practice and Theory*. 9. 293–319. 2002.

4. Tze How D.N., Keat C.W., Anuar A., Mohamed Sahari K.S. Robotic arm control based on human arm motion. International Conference on Robotic, Vision, Signal Processing & Power Applications. Lecture Notes in Electrical Engineering, Springer, Singapore, 291. 81–88. 2014.

5. Jian-Long K. Multi-objective optimal design of motion precision for fork robot arm in LCD panel manufacturing process system. *Microelectronics Reliability*. 99. 19–30. 2019.

6. Zheng J., Liang W., Jiamei J. A novel robotic arm driven by sandwich piezoelectric transducers. *Ultrasonics*. 84. 373–381. 2018.

7. Patidar V., Tiwari R. Survey of robotic arm and parameters. International Conference on Computer Communication and Informatics (ICCCI), Coimbatore, India. 1–6. January 7–9, 2016.

8. Fu S., Bhavsar P. C. Robotic arm control based on internet of things. IEEE Long Island Systems, Applications and Technology Conference (LISAT), Farmingdale, NY. 1–6. May 3, 2019.

9. Prasanna S. B., Madan B. M. Wireless signal transmission using an android mobile and FPGA. *IJARCCE*. 5(5). 605–607. 2016.

10. Google Play. Arduin Remote Bluetooth-WiFi. https://play.google.com/store/apps/details?id=org.beappsmobile.arduinowirelessremote&hl=en_IN.

11. Steven F. B., Daniel J. P. *Atmel AVR Microcontroller Primer: Programming and Interfacing*, Morgan & Claypool Publishers, 2012.

12. Cicerone Laurentiu Popa, George Carutasu, Costel Emil Cotet, Nicoleta Luminita Carutasu, Tiberiu Dobrescu. Smart city platform development for an automated waste collection system. *Sustainability*. 9. 11. 1–15. 2017.

13. Borozdukhin A., Dolinina O., Pechenkin V. Approach to the garbage collection in the "Smart Clean City" project. 4th IEEE International Colloquium on Information Science and Technology (CiSt), Tangier, Morocco, 918–922. October 24–26, 2016.

14. Zhanna Mingaleva, Natalia Vukovic, Irina Volkova, Tatiana Salimova. Waste management in green and smart cities: A case study of Russia. *Sustainability*. 12. 1. 1–17. 2020.

15. Dhayalini K., Mukesh R. Deterioration & non-deterioration wastes separation using pick & place robot. International Conference on Inventive Systems and Control (ICISC). Coimbatore, India, 96–99. January 19–20, 2018.

16. Trincavelli M., Reggente M., Coradeschi S., Loutfi A., Ishida H., Lilienthal A. J. Towards environmental monitoring with mobile robots. IEEE International Conference on Intelligent Robots and Systems, Nice, Italy, 2210–2215. September 22–26, 2008.

17. Shah R., and Pandey A. B. Concept for automated sorting robotic arm. *Procedia Manufacturing*. 20. 400–405. 2018.

18. Salman H., Rahman, M.S., Tarek, M. A. Y., Wang, J. The design and implementation of GPS controlled environment monitoring robotic system based on IoT and ARM. IEEE International Conference on Control and Robotics Engineering (ICCRE), Nanjing, China, 93–98. April 20–23, 2019.

19. Patidar V., Tiwari R. Survey of robotic arm and parameters. International Conference on Computer Communication and Informatics (ICCCI), Coimbatore, India, 1–6. January 7–9, 2016.

20. Anisur Rahman, Alimul Haque Khan, Tofayel Ahmed, Md. Mohsin Sajjad. Design, analysis and implementation of a robotic arm- The animator. *American Journal of Engineering Research (AJER)*. 2. 298–307. 2013.

21. Pawan Shivaji Shinde, Aaditya Manoj Sonawane, Kumar Sunjay Gaikwad, Omkar Vijay Pawar, Suhas Gudhate. Review paper on industrial pick & place robotic arm. *International Journal of Innovations in Engineering Research and Technology*. 218–220. 2018. ISSN: 2394-3696.

22. Sharan, Roneel, Onwubolu, G. *Automating the Process of Work-Piece Recognition and Location for a Pick-and-Place Robot in a SFMS*. 6. 9–17. 2014.

23. Omijeh, Bourdillon, Uhunmwangho, R. Design analysis of a remote controlled "pick and place" robotic vehicle. *International Journal of Engineering Research and Development*. 10. 2278–800. 2014.

24. Kit, Wong Sai, Venkatratnam, Chitturi. Pick and place mobile robot for the disabled through voice commands. 2nd IEEE International Symposium on Robotics and Manufacturing Automation (ROMA). Ipoh, Malaysia, 1–4. September 25–27, 2016

25. Małgorzata Żabińska, Tomasz Sośnicki, Wojciech Turek, Krzysztof Cetnarowicz. Robot task allocation using signal propagation model. *Procedia Computer Science*. 18. 1505–1514. 2013.

26. Jegedele Oladele, Awodele Oludele, Ajayi Ayodele. *Development of a Microcontroller Based on Robotic Arm*, Babcock University, Ilishan-Remo, Nigeria. 2007.

27. Antonio Bicchi, Vijay Kumar. Robotic grasping and contact: A review. Proceedings of IEEE International Conference on Robotics and Automation, San Francisco, CA, 348–353. April 24–28, 2000.

28. Shyam R. Nair. Design of robotic arm for picking and placing an object controlled using LAB view. *International Journal of Scientific and Research Publication*. 2. 5. 2012.

29. Omijeh B.O., Uhunmwangho R., Ehikhamenl M. Design analysis of remote controlled pick and place robotic vehicle. *International Journal of Engineering Research and development*. 10. 5. 57–68. 2014.

30. Puran Singh, Anil Kumar, Mahesh Ashish. Design of robotic arm with gripper and end effector for spot welding. *Universal Journal of Mechanical Engineering*. 3. 92–97. 2013.

17

From Moving Objects Detection to Classification and Recognition: A Review for Smart Environments

Sirine Ammar

Lab. MIRACL, Univ. Sfax
Tunisia

Lab. MIA, Univ. La Rochelle
France

Thierry Bouwmans

Lab. MIA, Univ. La Rochelle
France

Nizar Zaghden

Tunisia, ESC, Univ. Sfax
Tunisia

Mahmoud Neji

Lab. MIRACL, Univ. Sfax
Tunisia

CONTENTS

17.1   Introduction 290
17.2   Background Subtraction Techniques 290
        17.2.1   Mathematical Models 291
        17.2.2   Machine Learning Models 291
                17.2.2.1 Representation Learning 291
                17.2.2.2 Neural Networks Modeling 292
                17.2.2.3 Deep Neural Network Modeling 293
        17.2.3   Signal Processing Models 293
        17.2.4   Solved and Unsolved Challenges 294
17.3   Objects Classification Methods 295
        17.3.1   Conventional Methods 295
        17.3.2   Supervised Deep Learning Methods 296
        17.3.3   Unsupervised Deep Learning Methods 296
        17.3.4   Semi-Supervised Deep Learning Methods 296
17.4   Face Recognition Techniques 297
        17.4.1   Holistic Techniques 297
                17.4.1.1 Linear Techniques 298
                17.4.1.2 Nonlinear Techniques 300
        17.4.2   Hybrid Approach 301

17.4.3   Local Approach 302
17.4.3.1 Local Appearance-Based Techniques 302
17.4.3.2 Key Points-Based Techniques 304
17.5   Conclusion 305
References 305

17.1 Introduction

Smart homes and cities use Internet of Things (IoT) to detect moving objects such as humans and vehicles to optimize home and traffic surveillance. These different tasks involve computer vision algorithms to detect moving objects, to classify them, and to recognize and identify them. To detect moving objects, background subtraction has been increasingly used in different indoor and outdoor environments with multiple challenges and different kinds of moving foreground objects. Once the objects are detected, different objects classification methods can be used to categorize them into different classes such as cars, humans, bodies, and faces. Then, face recognition methods are employed to recognize and identify humans. Considering all of this, we first present a comprehensive review of background subtraction techniques based on mathematical tools, machine learning, and signal processing tools. Solved and unsolved challenges are also investigated showing that progress is still required even if deep learning methods reach quasi-nominal performance on real large-scale data sets. Second, we review the different objects classification methods used to categorize the extracted moving objects. The different existing approaches are classified into different categories of learning, including supervised, unsupervised, and semi-supervised learning. Moreover, we provide an up-to-date review of face recognition methods, covering earlier works as well as more recent advances. These methods are used to recognize humans, and are categorized into three categories: holistic, local, and hybrid methods.

The rest of this chapter is organized as follows. In Section 17.2, we present a comprehensive review on moving objects detection by background subtraction. Section 17.3 reviews classification approaches used to categorize objects extracted from videos. In Section 17.4, we provide a background on face recognition methods classified according to their purpose. Finally, we provide a conclusion and perspectives.

17.2 Background Subtraction Techniques

Moving objects detection methods can be classified into three major categories: consecutive frame difference, optical flow, and background subtraction. Temporal differencing methods [1–3] can be easily implemented but are extremely sensitive to the challenges. Optical flow algorithms are more robust but achieving requirements in real time remains a challenging task since it requires a lot of time. Background subtraction [4, 5], which is the commonly adopted method for moving objects detection, provides a good trade-off between real-time requirements and robustness [6–10]. A wide range of models resulting from mathematical concepts, signal processing, and machine learning techniques have been proposed to model the background, covering crisp models [11–13], statistical models [14–17], fuzzy models [18–20], Dempster–Shafer models [21], subspace learning models [22–26], robust learning models [27–30], neural networks models [31–33], and filter-based models [34–37].

17.2.1 Mathematical Models

Based on mathematical concepts, computing the temporal average [11], the temporal median [12], or the temporal histogram [13] are the most common methods to model a background, which were broadly employed in traffic monitoring in the 1990s. Despite the simplicity of these techniques, they remain very sensitive to the challenging video surveillance situations deriving from illumination variations, camera jitter, and dynamic backgrounds. To take into consideration the inaccuracy, ambiguity, and deficiency in the observed data (i.e., video), statistical models were suggested in 1999 such as single Gaussian (SG) [38], Gaussian mixture model (GMM) [15, 16], and kernel density estimation (KDE) [14]. These statistical techniques using a Gaussian distribution model showed more robustness to dynamic backgrounds [39, 40]. In the literature, more sophisticated statistical models have been provided and can be categorized into those based on another distribution that attenuate the strict Gaussian restriction (i.e., general Gaussian distribution [41], Student's t-distribution [42], Dirichlet distribution [43], Poisson distribution [44]), models based on co-occurrence [45] and confidence [46], free-distribution models [47], and regression models [48]. These models show more robustness to a large variety of challenges over time. The most advanced algorithm in this statistical category is ViBe [47]. Another way of dealing with inaccuracy, ambiguity, and deficiency consists of fuzzy concepts. During 2006 to 2008, several fuzzy approaches such as Type-2 fuzzy sets [19, 49, 50], Sugeno integral [51, 52] and Choquet integral [18, 53, 54] were proposed, which are more robust to dynamic backgrounds [49]. However, the Dempster–Shafer theory has also been employed with success in foreground detection [21].

17.2.2 Machine Learning Models

Background modeling has also been studied through representation learning (or subspace learning), support vector machines (SVMs), and neural networks modeling (regular and deep neural networks).

17.2.2.1 Representation Learning

In 1999, reconstructive subspace learning methods were employed in an unsupervised way to reconstruct the background. One of the most common reconstructive methods is principal component analysis (PCA) [22]. These models are more robust to illumination variations than statistical models [21]. In other methods, discriminative [23–25] and mixed [26] subspace learning models have been employed to improve the results of foreground detection. Nevertheless, each of these conventional subspace models is highly sensitive to outliers, noise, and lack of data. To tackle these weaknesses, since 2009, a robust PCA (RPCA) by decomposition into L+S matrices [27–30] has been broadly employed making them robust not only to illumination variations but also to dynamic backgrounds [55–58]. Nevertheless, they need batch algorithms, which makes them not usable for real-time implementations. To solve this issue, robust subspace tracking [22, 59, 60] as well as dynamic RPCA have been proposed to provide real-time performance of methods based on RPCA. GRASTA [61], incPCP [62], ReProCS [63], and MEROP [64] are the most advanced algorithms in this subspace learning category. Nevertheless, methods based on tensor RPCA [65–68] make it possible to consider spatial and temporal constraints to allow more robustness against noise.

17.2.2.2 Neural Networks Modeling

In 1996, Schofield et al. [33] employed neural networks to model the background and detect foreground objects with a random-access memory (RAM) neural network (NN). This RAM-NN needs a correct representation of the background of the scene and does not require a background maintenance step. Indeed, once RAM-NN is trained with a single passage of background images, this information can no longer be changed. In Jimenez et al. [69], each part of a video frame can be categorized into one of the following groups: static, noisy, or impulsive background group. A multilayer perceptron is designed for classification, which needs a training set from particular parts of each training frame. In a further work, Tavakkoli [70] exploits the concept of novelty detection to design a neural network method. The background is split into blocks in the training phase and each block is associated with a radial basis function neural network (RBFNN). Then, each RBFNN is trained with background samples that match its associated block. RBFNN is used as a detector to generate a close boundary for the specified class. In RBF-NN approaches, the detection of a dynamic object can be considered as a single class issue and the dynamic background is learned. But, a large number of samples is needed for the representation of common background scenarios. In Wang et al. [71], a neural network model called probabilistic adaptive background neural network (ABPNN) is proposed by combining a winner-take-all (WTA) and a hybrid probabilistic network, which contains four layers. In the ABPNN algorithm, each pixel is categorized as background or foreground by its conditional probability of belonging to the background based on a Parzen estimator. The foreground regions are then examined to categorize them as a shadow or a motion region. However, ABPNN requires determining particular initial threshold values for each examined video. In Culibrk et al. [72], the background is modeled using a feed-forward neural network based on an adaptive Bayesian model named background neural network (BNN), which is represented as a general regression neural network (GRNN) and functions as a Bayesian classifier. Despite the architecture is considered as supervised, it can be expanded as an unsupervised architecture in the domain of the background model. The network consists of three subnets: classification, activation, and replacement. The background/foreground characteristics of a pixel are mapped using the classifier subnet based on a probability density function estimation. The network has two summing neurons, one of them calculates the probability that the pixel values belong to the background and the other for estimating whether it belongs to the foreground. However, the principal drawbacks are that the model is with high-complexity and that it needs three nets to determine whether a pixel belongs to the background. In a disruptive study, Maddalena and Petrosino [73–76] presented an approach based on a 2D self-organizing method named Self Organizing Background Subtraction (SOBS) that preserves the spatial coherence of the pixel. This approach can be classified as a pixel-based and nonparametric method and can easily handle multimodality in background pixel distributions. The network neurons weights can automatically model the background and a neural map with weight vectors is used to represent each pixel. The pixel values in the HSV color channel are employed to initialize the weight vectors. After initializing the model, each new pixel value from each new frame is classified as background or foreground by comparing it with its current model. In further studies, SOBS has been improved with methods named Multivalued

SOBS [77], SOBS-CF [78], SC-SOBS [79], 3dSOBS+ [80], Simplified SOM [81], Neural-Fuzzy SOM [82], and MILSOBS [83]. These improvements make SOBS one of the main methods on the CDnet 2012 data set [84] for a long period. SOBS also shows great efficiency for the detection of stopped objects [85–87]. However, one of the major drawbacks of the methods based on SOBS is the necessity to manually adjust the parameters.

17.2.2.3 Deep Neural Network Modeling

Since 2016, DNNs have also been effectively used for background generation [88–92], background subtraction [93–100], foreground detection enhancement [101], ground-truth generation [102], and the learning of deep spatial features [103–107]. More specifically, restricted Boltzmann machines (RBMs) have been used by Guo and Qi [88] and Xu et al. [90] to generate background to further detect moving objects using background subtraction. In a further study, Xu et al. [91, 92] employed deep autoencoder networks to perform similar task while Qu et al. [89] employed context-encoder to initialize the background. Convolutional neural networks (CNNs) have also been used for background subtraction by Braham and Droogenbroeck [95], Bautista et al. [94], and Cinelli [96]. Many enhanced variants of CNNs have been used such as cascaded CNNs [102], deep CNNs [93], structured CNNs [97], and two-stage CNNs [108]. In Zhang et al. [107], robust spatial features are learned using stacked denoising autoencoder (SDAE) and the background is modeled using density analysis, while in Shafiee et al. [109], deep features employed in the GMM [16] are extracted using neural response mixture (NeREM). In another work, Chan [110] presented a scene awareness algorithm based on the deep learning scene recognition model to detect changes in videos, therefore using the appropriate background subtraction technique for the corresponding kind of challenges. In 2020, Ammar et al. [111] presented a deep detector classifier (DeepDC) to segment and categorize moving objects in videos based on both an unsupervised anomaly discovery algorithm called DeepSphere and GANs. DeepSphere is used to determine anomalous cases in spatial and temporal situations to segment foreground objects. In 2019, Ammar et al. [112] suggested to use and validate DeepSphere to detect and then segment moving objects in videos. DeepSphere used both hypersphere learning and deep autoencoders to eliminate anomaly pollution and rebuild normal behaviors. For performance evaluations, DeepSphere is compared with a standard subspace learning technique, RPCA, as well as a deep probabilistic background model (DeepPBM) and has reached more successful results than other existing methods.

17.2.3 Signal Processing Models

The signal processing models take into consideration the temporal history of a pixel as a one-dimensional signal. More specifically, numerous signal processing approaches can be employed: (1) signal estimation techniques (i.e., filters), (2) transform domain models, and (3) sparse signal recovery functions (i.e., compressive sensing).

- **Estimation filter:** In 1990, Karmann et al. [113] developed a method for estimating the background model of a scene based on Kalman filtering. Each pixel that presents a significant deviation from its predicted value is categorized as foreground. Many improvements have been suggested to enhance this method in challenging situations deriving from illumination variations and varying backgrounds [36, 114, 115]. In 1999, Wallflower, a pixel level system, is presented by Toyama et al. [37]

to perform probabilistic predictions of the background pixel values, estimated in the subsequent live frame by applying Wiener filtering. In another study, Chang et al. [34, 116] applied a Chebyshev filter for background modeling. All these filtering methods yield valuable efficiency under slow variations in illumination but they are inefficient in the presence of complex backgrounds.

- **Transform domain models:** In 2005, Wren and Porikli [117] proposed a Waviz algorithm based on fast Fourier transform (FFT) for background modeling using the multimodal backgrounds spectral signatures. These signatures are then employed for detecting scene changes that are incoherent in time. In 2005, Porikli and Wren [118] introduced a Wave-Back method based on the frequency decompositions of pixel's history vector to represent the background. For both the reference and the current frames, the Discrete Cosine Transform (DCT) coefficients are calculated and are compared resulting in a distance map. The distance maps are combined into a same DCT temporal window to be more robust to noise and a subsequent thresholding is applied to extract moving objects. This method can handle situations deriving from waving trees.

- **Sparse signal recovery models:** In 2008, Cevher et al. [119] were the first authors who suggested a background subtraction technique based on a compressive sensing method. They learned and adjusted a compressed background representation with low dimensionality rather than learning the whole background, which is adequate to detect changes. Compressive samples allow estimating the foreground objects directly without the need to reconstruct any intermediate image. However, an auxiliary image is required to simultaneously recover the appearance of objects using compressive measures. To address this limitation, several advances have been presented in the literature [120] and valuable performance is reached using Bayesian compressive sensing methods [121].

17.2.4 Solved and Unsolved Challenges

The challenges included in CDnet 2014 [94], which is a part of the Workshop on Change Detection (CDW 2014), are considered to fairly assess and compare videos. This data set contains all the CDnet 2012 [94] videos plus 22 supplementary ones captured by cameras spanning 5 various categories that integrate additional challenges that have not been solved in the CDnet 2012 data set. The categories are named as follows: "baseline," "dynamic backgrounds," "camera jitter," "shadows," "intermittent object motion," "thermal," "challenging weather," "low frame-rate," "night videos," "PTZ," and "turbulence." In 2015, Jodoin [122] provided valuable observations concerning the solved and unsolved challenges from results reported by the experiments carried out on the CDnet 2014. Current methods of background subtraction can effectively handle the challenges faced in "bad weather" and "baseline" videos. The "thermal," "camera jitter," and "dynamic backgrounds" categories are an accessible challenge for the best background subtraction algorithms. The "low frame-rate," "PTZ," and "night videos" sequences are extremely challenging. In a valuable work, Bouwmans et al. [123] studied the advance achieved during 20 years since the development of the MOG model [16] in 1999 to the current DNNs models designed in 2019. This analysis reveals that the large gap was achieved by DNNs algorithms compared to SuBSENSE with 24.31% and 32.92% using, respectively, Cascaded CNN and FgSegNet-V2. The difference of 1.55% that persists between FgSegNet-V2 and the best algorithm is smaller than the difference of 6.93% between FgSegNet-V2 and

Cascaded CNN. However, it must be noted that the big difference obtained by cascaded CNN and FgSegNet-V2 is generally owing to their supervised appearance, and a necessary limitation of training using labelled samples. Nevertheless, once labeled samples are not available, great efforts must be focused on unsupervised GANs as well as on unsupervised approaches using semantic background subtraction [124, 125] and robust subspace tracking [70, 72, 74, 126, 127] that are always interesting in the background subtraction domain. Moreover, deep learning methods effectively identify the changed areas in images with fixed backgrounds but still suffer from several challenges such as camera jitter and varying backgrounds, even if they offer higher efficiency than standard methods [128]. Moreover, the experiments carried out on the "PTZ" and the "IOM" categories are generally avoided. Furthermore, the F-Measure for these categories is usually low. Therefore, it appears that the DNNs recently assessed meet issues in these categories, maybe due to the difficulties of learning the sleep period of moving objects and handling the constant scene changes. Finally, despite the progression of background subtraction models developed for static cameras for camera jitter and PTZ cameras as with numerous RPCA models [126, 129–133] and deep learning models [134–136], they can only deal with small jitter problems or translation and rotation movements. Therefore, more specific models and algorithms are needed to detect moving objects. Once objects detection is achieved, their classification can be made for further processing modules such as recognition and tracking.

17.3 Objects Classification Methods

In this section, we review the representative studies in object image classification and retrieval applied once the moving objects are detected. These objects can be classified as humans, vehicles, etc.

17.3.1 Conventional Methods

In the study of Zhu et al. [137], color and texture features such as HSV histograms, MB-LBP, and HOG are concatenated and introduced into a Gentle Adboost for feature selection and classification, simultaneously. In [138], an accuracy of 82.7% was obtained using an SVM classifier trained with color and texture features. In 2014, Shruti et al. [139] used Gabor filter coefficients to extract facial features that are fed to the SVM classifier for classification task. In 2013, Zaghden et al. [140] focused on the categorization of ancient documents using the SOM toolbox. The method of fractal dimensions and the points of interest are used to match ancient documents. In 2011, Zaghden et al. [141] proposed an approach to discriminate Arabic and Latin ancient document images based on fractal dimension. In their survey, Ammar et al. [142] provided a review of the different local and global approaches used for people reidentification. They also presented the different objects classification techniques by categorizing them into supervised and unsupervised learning methods. Additionally, the authors proposed a human reidentification system that aggregates color, texture, and shape features as well as some soft-biometric traits by combining local and global representations. In 2018, Ammar et al. [143] proposed an approach for two-person interaction recognition using a Kinect sensor to extract feature vectors based on the distances between a subset of skeleton joints. Each individual is represented by a pentagon with the most representative skeleton joints. Five Euclidean distances are computed using the vertices of two pentagons. An SVM is used for supervised classification.

17.3.2 Supervised Deep Learning Methods

Supervised learning is a learning task that requires labeled training data. There are several supervised learning approaches based on deep learning (DL). The potential capacity of CNNs in image classification has been proven since 1989 when LeCun et al. [144] classified handwritten digits for zip code recognition by achieving only 5% test error. Fully convolutional networks (FCNs) are proposed by Long et al. [145] to segment images. The key innovation of this approach is to train CNN in an end-to-end way for segmentation with input images of arbitrary sizes by converting fully connected layers into convolutional ones to produce spatial feature maps. In 2018, Babaee et al. [146] proposed a background segmentation approach based on deep CNN. The background model is initialized and the pertinent features are extracted from an image-background pair using CNN and fed into a classifier for segmentation. Deep convolutional GANs (DCGANs) are presented by Radford et al. [147] to learn feature representations from object regions to scenes in a hierarchical way for the generator and the discriminator. The discriminators are used to classify images. In 2014, Liu et al. [148] applied CNN to learn certain human-crafted characteristics such as color and Dense-SIFT features and build a bag of words model. SVMs and backpropagation neural networks are used for classification. In 2016, Braham and Van Droogenbroeck [95] proposed a background subtraction method based on CNNs. The background image is generated by computing the temporal median on certain frames. A patch is extracted around the pixel, fed to a CNN, and compared with a threshold to categorize it as foreground or background. However, all these methods are carried out in a supervised way, which needs a great amount of labeled data.

17.3.3 Unsupervised Deep Learning Methods

Unsupervised learning uses information that does not need labeled data, and the objective is to exploit the huge number of unlabeled data and define similarities among objects. In 2016, Li et al. [149] constructed an unsupervised classification method for processing remote sensing images and mapping African land cover based on the stacked autoencoder (SAE). The SAE yields superior performance compared to conventional classifiers. In 2015, Zou et al. [150] proposed a DBN based on feature selection for the classification of remote sensing images. In 2014, Chen et al. [151] presented a hybrid deep CNN for vehicle detection in satellite images. Bidirectional generative adversarial networks (BiGANs) are presented in 2017 by Donahue et al. [152], which extends the conventional GAN by introducing an encoder module that learns to map between latent and data space. The encoder and the generator are adversarially trained. The discriminator is trained to jointly distinguish among data and latent space.

17.3.4 Semi-Supervised Deep Learning Methods

The ever-growing size of recent data sets integrated with the issue of obtaining information labels has made semi-supervised learning one of the major challenges in data analysis. Semi-supervised learning deals with the problem of classification when only a small number of samples are labeled. To tackle these limitations, Ammar et al. [111] considered an extension to GAN, called semi-supervised GAN (SGAN), which allows to learn simultaneously a generative model and a DCGAN discriminator network as a classifier to categorize objects (humans/vehicles) extracted from a VIRAT video data set [153]. They concluded that SGAN increases classification accuracy on restricted data sets using a conventional classifier without generative element. In the study of Rosenberg et al. [154], unlabeled samples taken from its highest-confidence predictions are progressively added to the original small set of labeled samples. The semi-supervised trained model yields similar results to a traditional trained model using a big set of fully labeled samples. In 1999, Joachims [155] proposed an extension to SVMs called transductive SVMs (TSVMs) to classify a text. TSVMs consider a specific test set and try to reduce the misclassifications of these samples. In 2011, Diederik et al. [156] proposed a semi-supervised approach with generative components that generalize small labeled data sets to big unlabeled sets. In their study, rich parametric density estimators are applied, obtained by the combination of probabilistic modeling and DNNs. In 2015, Springenberg et al. [157] proposed a categorical GANs (catGANs) to learn a discriminatively classifier from a not totally labeled or unlabeled data set by combining neural network classifiers with an adversarial generative model. In 2017, a virtual adversarial training (VAT) method [158] was proposed that seeks virtually adversarial samples to smooth the results of the classifier and is adapted to semi-supervised learning. GANs have been shown to yield superior performance in discriminating tasks by using a small number of labeled samples, as presented in the work of Salimans et al. [159]. The authors focused on improving the efficiency of GANs for semi-supervised classification and high-quality image generation. In 2018, two methods are presented in [160] to enhance sequence learning with recurrent networks using unlabeled samples, the neuro-linguistic programming (NLP) language model in which the subsequent element in a sequence is predicted, and a sequence autoencoder in which the sequence is read into a vector and estimated another time. The model is trained on unlabeled samples to output the weights used to train the model in a supervised manner to categorize the data. In 2017, Radford et al. [161] examined a recurrent language neural network, called multiplicative long short-term memory (mLSTM) for a sentiment analysis domain. mLSTM is first trained on Amazon product reviews to guess the following character in the text to extract features in an unsupervised way. This model surpassed the advanced techniques using only a small number of labeled samples.

17.4 Face Recognition Techniques

17.4.1 Holistic Techniques

Holistic approaches process the entire face area as a high-dimensional vector that is fed into a classifier. These approaches do not need to extract face areas or points of interests. However, they consider all pixels of the image with equal importance, which makes them costly in computation. In addition, these approaches generally ignore local information, so they are not very used for face identification. These approaches can be classified into linear and nonlinear techniques according to the method used to represent the subspace.

17.4.1.1 Linear Techniques

- **Eigenface and principal component analysis (PCA):** In Seo et al. [162], locally adaptive regression kernel (LARK) features are extracted to represent a face. A self-similarity measure is calculated among a center and its neighboring pixels on the basis of a geodesic distance. The size of LARK is reduced using PCA, followed by a logistic function to make LARK features approximately binarized. The one-shot similarity measure is applied on the basis of a linear discriminative analysis (LDA) for the image restricted training. In Ghorbel et al. [163], the DoG filter is applied for image processing. The features are extracted using eigenfaces and VLC techniques from the entire face image and matched using the chi-square distance. In 2012, Abdullah et al. [164] optimized the time complexity of eigenfaces without affecting the recognition performance. In 2017, Johannes and Armin [165] have shown that Haar cascade classifiers exceed LBP classifiers in face detection. For face recognition, they demonstrated that eigenfaces are better than Fisherface and LBP histograms. In 2016, Bhuiyan et al. [166] examined the eigenvectors of the covariance matrix of the key images to recognize a face. The features are extracted using eigenfaces and identified using k-nearest neighbors (KNN). Lighting issues are surmounted by root mean square (RMS) contrast stretching. In 2012, a face recognition system based on eigenfaces [167] has been proposed which includes a PCA method to represent the variation among images using some representative characteristics. The work of Abd Rahman et al. [168] was performed using PCA eigenfaces approach to recognize a face in single static, multiple static, and dynamic images. The main idea in [169] was to use only the best eigenfaces that represent the major variance in all facial images, which leads to efficient calculations and speed.

- **Fisherface and linear discriminative analysis (LDA):** Fisher vectors are used by Simonyan et al. [170] to recognize a face. The authors proposed a discriminative reduction in dimensionality due to the high size of Fisher vectors. The Fisherface approach is more effective than the eigenface method. On this basis, Li et al. [171] compared a dual-tree complex wavelet transform (DT-CWT) approach based on LDA with the DTCWT based PCA method. The face recognition efficiencies of the Fisherface and the eigenface are also compared in the DT-CWT area. In Abidin et al. [172], face expressions are recognized on the basis of a neural network using Fisherface. An integral projection method is adopted to segment and locate the face area. Neural network based on the back-propagation algorithm is applied to categorize facial expressions. In Gowda et al. [173], LPQ features are extracted from the face and iris regions and LDA is used for dimensionality reduction in order to achieve efficient computation. Both SVM and KNN are used for classification.

- **Independent component analysis (ICA):** In Bartlett et al. [174], two architectures are proposed to represent facial images using ICA. The spatially local basis vectors are generated by ICA and are considered as a set of independent facial characteristics. In the second architecture, a factorial code is used to generate statistically independent compressed images. The performance of face recognition was evaluated by the KNN classifier and the cosine similarity measure. The authors reported that ICA-based representations outperformed PCA-based representations to recognize a face in sessions and changes in expression. Kong and Bing [175] used both ICA and SVM to recognize a face. Facial features are extracted using an Informax algorithm and classified using a fast least squares SVM (FLS-SVM).

- **Improvements of the PCA, LDA, and ICA techniques:** In order to deal with the large variations in appearance and poor quality caused by approximate alignment of face images, Cui et al. [176] proposed a spatial face region descriptor (SFRD) to recognize a face by partitioning each image into various blocks in spatial domain, then extracting the token-frequency characteristics from all regions by sum pooling the reconstructing coefficients over the patches of each block. whitened principal component analysis (WPCA) is applied to reduce the dimensionality of feature vectors to generate robust face descriptors, which are combined using pairwise-constrained multiple metric learning (PMML). In 2018, Khan et al. [177] proposed to solve complex variations problem in face images by selecting the appropriate features from wavelet sub-bands based on particle swarm optimization (PSO). The LBP-DFT technique is proposed which used LBP features to deal with illumination and expressions variations and discrete Fourier transform (DFT) to solve the issue of translational variance of the discrete wavelet transform (DWT). In Dehai et al. [178], an ameliorated PCA method is introduced FFT, which fuses the amplitude spectrum of one image with the phase spectrum of another image to improve features, followed by the extraction of eigenvectors. Kernel SVM is used as a classifier. In Riddhi et al. [179], a modified PCA method is proposed for face recognition using certain components of the LDA algorithm. Experimental results show that LDA is better than PCA in face recognition. The work presented in Azeem et al. [180] aims to address the problem of partial occlusions in face recognition by using methods based on LDA, PCA, ICA, local nonnegative matrix factorization (LNMF) and nonnegative matrix factorization (NMF). Features extracted from the eyes, nose, or mouth region are used in the recognition phase. In [181], an approach is proposed that combines 2DPCA for face features extraction and SVM for classification.

- **Frequency domain analysis:** In Huang et al. [182], a patch strategy is acquired using 2D-DWT and an integral projection technology is used to extract facial features for face recognition. The overlapped patches are chosen to improve stability and maintain all local information. The classification is made by the nearest neighbor classifier (NNC). In Sufyanu et al. [183], a method called ASDCT is proposed that combines anisotropic diffusion-based normalization technique (AS) and DCT. AS was used for preprocessing and DCT was adapted for feature extraction to address the issue of lighting variations and to improve the decorrelation ability of DCT to enhance face recognition. Performance measurements were evaluated using NNC. In Abdulrahman et al. [184], eigenface and DWT are used for face recognition. A three-level DWT decomposition is applied to the images that are then transmitted to the PCA for dimensionality reduction. In Shanbhag et al. [185], the authors applied spatial differentiation (SD) technique and wavelet transform based feature extraction (WTFE) to preprocess the features by eliminating those that are irrelevant. 2D-SWT is applied with 2D-DWT, which, along with twin pose testing scheme (TPTS), extract pose invariant features that lead to high recognition rates. A binary particle swarm optimization (BPSO) is used to reduce the number of features.

- **Gabor filters:** In 2006, Perlibakas and Vytautas [186] proposed to recognize a face based on both Log-Gabor features and PCA. Their algorithm aims to locate Log-Gabor characteristics with maximal magnitudes at only one scale and different orientations. The cosine similarity measure is used to obtain high recognition performance. In [187], an approach based on 2D face image features is proposed using a subset of uncorrelated and orthogonal Gabor filters. The feature vector is reduced in size using LDA. The face image was enhanced and normalized to tackle variations in illumination. To overcome changes in pose and facial expressions, Ming et al. [188] proposed in 2012 a 3D Gabor patched spectral regression (3D GPSR) method for face recognition that aims to solve least squares issues while using regularization, reduce noise, and exploit the efficiency of the discriminant features. The identification of faces relies heavily on the difference among the test and gallery images. To cope with this limitation, Cament et al. [189] updated the grid to extract Gabor features using a mesh to model the deformations of the faces. A statistical model is calculated on the basis of the scores using Gabor features to achieve high recognition rates across pose.

17.4.1.2 Nonlinear Techniques

- **Robust kernel PCA (RKPCA):** In 2019, Fan et al. [190] proposed an optimization of the kernel PCA algorithm called robust kernel PCA (RKPCA) based on a cost function that needs the reconstructed data point to be near to the original one and to the principal subspace to prevent the implicitness of the feature space. RKPCA remains the only unsupervised method that is robust to issues such as sparse noises and lack of data. In order to deal with the difficult optimization of RKPCA, ADMM+BTLS and PLM+AdSS methods are presented. To overcome the problem of the ORB (oriented-fast and rotated-brief) [191] calculation, Vinay et al. [192] proposed in their approach called ORB-KPCA, an algorithm based on both ORB feature descriptors and KPCA [193]. ORB-KPCA is used for face recognition with threshold-based filtering (TBF) used to filter out wrong matches. Lu et al. [194] have taken into consideration the problem of the nonlinearity of the distribution of face models and the "small sample size" (SSS) and have proposed the kernel direct discriminant analysis (KDDA), which generalizes the direct-LDA (D-LDA). D-LDA is based on SVMs, KPCA, and generalized discriminant analysis (GDA).
- **Gabor-KLDA:** In 2015, Vinay et al. [195] compare the Gabor-LDA (linear) and Gabor-KLDA (nonlinear) to determine which technique is better adapted to face recognition tasks. Both LDA and kernel Fisher analysis (KFA) are used to reduce the dimensionality of facial features filtered by Gabor.
- **Multifeature shape regression (MSR):** In 2018, Yang et al. [196] proposed to improve face recognition performance by adjusting the position of facial parameters using a face alignment algorithm based on multifeature shape regression (MSR). MSR uses gradient, color, and local features to improve the accuracy of the estimation of facial landmarks. A subspace projection optimizations (SPO) method is applied to recognize a face.
- **Fisher discrimination dictionary learning (FDDL):** To address the lack of training images in each class for a linear representation of the variability of the test, Ouanan et al. [197] proposed to extend the FDDL model for face recognition based on the dictionary of occlusion variants. This dictionary is generated by calculating the difference of deep features among two face image pairs of the same individual.

- **Wavelet transform (WT), radon transform (RT), and cellular neural networks:** In Vankayalapati et al. [198], the radon and wavelet transform approaches are combined to extract nonlinear features that are robust to facial expression and illumination changes. Cellular neural networks are also used to extract nonlinear facial features to ameliorate the recognition rate and the calculation speed.

- **2FNN (Two-Feature Neural Network):** In 2010, the 2FNN method was proposed by Devi et al. [199] to recognize a face, which consists of extracting features using PCA and LDA that are merged based on wavelet fusion to enhance the LDA efficiency in case a small number of examples of images is accessible. Neural networks are used for classification.

- **DeepID3:** In 2015, two DNN architectures [200] were proposed, mentioned as DeepID3, for face recognition, which are reconstructed from the stacked convolutions of VGG and the inception layers of GoogLeNet. Supervisory signals are used to decrease the intrapersonal face features variations. DeepID3 reached peak performance on both verification and identification tasks.

- **Convolutional Neural Networks (CNNs):** In 2015, Li et al. [201] proposed a cascade of CNN face detectors with multiple resolutions. A calibration network is also proposed to enhance the quality of bounding boxes.

- **Deep Dense Face Detector (DDFD):** In 2015, Farfade et al. [202] suggested an approach called DDFD by refining the AlexNet model in the context of face detection.

17.4.2 Hybrid Approach

Hybrid approaches simultaneously combine both local and global features for recognizing face images. Methods fusing various features have received a lot of attention, such as the work of Fathima et al. [203] who proposed an approach called HGWLDA that combines both Gabor wavelet and LDA to recognize a face. The global face image is convolved with a Gabor filter bank and different subspace variants of 2D-LDA are used to map the characteristics to a feature space. The KNN classifier is used to recognize a face. To represent the face image, Barkan et al. [204] used over-complete LBP (OCLBP), which is an adjusted variant of the LBP with multiple scales. Faces are recognized based on a matrix-vector multiplication and the LDA technique is combined with within class covariance normalization (WCCN) to reduce large representations and recognize faces. In 2015, Juefei et al. [205] presented a Walsh LBP (WLBP) face recognition technique, which uses one example per subject category to produce face images. In the training phase, a nonlinear subspace is modeled by learning subject-dependent correlation filters, that is, unresistant to the pose variations. In 2013, Simonyan et al. [170] combined both SIFT features and Fisher vectors to recognize a face. The dimensionality of the Fisher vectors is reduced using PCA, which are projected linearly into a subspace of low dimension. In 2015, Sharma et al. [206] presented a method called PCA-ANFIS using both PCA and ANFIS to extract face features under pose variations. The score value obtained by processing training face images by PCA, is used by the ANFIS classifier in the recognition process. The neuro-fuzzy face recognition method gives a superior recognition rate. Face representation based on the genetic algorithm (GA) was known as one of the most successful methods. In 2018, Moussa et al. [207] developed a rapid face recognition system based on GA, DCT, and PCA techniques. GA is used as a feature selection method and is combined with DCT–PCA to extract the most informative face features, remove irrelevant ones, and then reduce the dimensionality. The minimum Euclidian distance is used for the decision. The performance of this system is assessed using various standard data sets. In 2007, Mian et al. [208] presented a multimodal face recognition algorithm using a 3D spherical face representation (SFR) in combination with SIFT features. The eyes, forehead, and nose parts are used to tackle the impacts of facial expressions to improve face recognition. An updated iterative closest point (ICP) algorithm is applied to match these regions and then their matching scores are merged. In 2014, Cho et al. [209] suggested a face recognition algorithm, represented with the local Gabor binary pattern histogram sequence (LGBPHS) and Gabor wavelets; PCA is used to reduce the dimensionality. In 2012, Sing et al. [210] extracted local discriminant features from the face image subregions and global features from the entire image. PCA and Fisher linear discriminant (FLD) are applied to reduce the dimensionality of the combined feature vector. In 2013, Kamencay et al. [211] introduced a face recognition approach called SIFT-PCAKNN. Face images are preprocessed using a graph-based technique. Harris–Laplace and SPCA (SIFT-PCA) local features are extracted to construct the face descriptors. KNN is applied for classification. In 2012, Sun et al. [212] presented a CNN–LSTM–ELM approach to achieve activity recognition with sequential algorithm. It is based on CNN layers, LSTM recurrent layers, and an extreme learning machine (ELM) classifier. This method is more convenient for classifying the extracted features and decreases the execution time. One of the most popular hybrid face recognition approaches, based on the combination of CNN and SAE, is presented in Ding and Tao [213], called multimodal deep face representation (MM-DFR). A facial feature vector of high dimensionality is extracted using CNNs. The size of the features is reduced using three-layer SAE. Experiments on the Labeled Face in the Wild (LFW) [214] and CASIA-Web Face databases [215] indicated that MM-DFR offers superior performance. The idea, proposed in [216], consists of fusing the phase and magnitude of Gabor's representations to extract facial features and then to apply PCA for dimensionality reduction.

17.4.3 Local Approach

Local approaches aim to extract specific features from the face image. These methods are sensitive to issues such as facial expressions, small occlusions, and pose changes. They can be categorized into methods based on local appearance that extract local features from subregions of the face image and methods based on key points that extract features located on the points of interest detected in the face image.

17.4.3.1 Local Appearance-Based Techniques

- **Local binary pattern (LBP) and its variant:** In 2016, LBP and its extensions, pyramid of local binary pattern (PLBP) and rotation invariant local binary pattern (RILBP) were evaluated by Khoi et al. [217] for face retrieval. The Grid LBP technique is used to split the face image into small regions and then the LBP feature vectors are concatenated into a histogram of spatially enhanced features. This system can support the increase in the size of the data set without unexpected fall in mean average precision (MAP). A local-appearance-based method called LBP network (LBPNet) was proposed in [218]. The main contribution was to effectively extract hierarchical data representations. Results showed that LBPNet gave higher accuracy compared to other unsupervised methods using FERET [219] and

LFW [214] data sets. Laure et al. [220] used robust LBP for face features extraction to cope with large variations in expressions, lighting, and poses; KNN is applied for classification. One of the local approaches was the multiscale LBP (MLBP) method proposed in Bonnen et al. [221], an extension of the standard LBP algorithm. Active shape models (ASM) are used to extract features and Procrustes Analysis is applied to preprocess MLBP components. Another variant of LBP is the LTP technique proposed in [222]. The similarities of the face components are fused to encode the differences among the central pixel and its corresponding neighbors into a trinary code using LTP to deal with noise. In Hussain et al. [223], local pattern features are generalized in the local quantized pattern (LQP), using vector quantization and look-up table, which permits them to have deeper surroundings and additional levels of quantization to cope with difficult variations. LQP acquires a part of the adaptability of visual word features and the calculation efficiency of LBP/LTP. Experimental results on FERET [219] and LFW [220] data sets showed that this representation enhanced state of the art by about 3%. Ghorbel et al. [163] used the DoG filter for preprocessing and the uniform local binary pattern (uLBP) to extract local features from face images. In Annalakshmi et al. [224], the spatially enhanced local binary pattern (SLBP) is concatenated with the histogram of oriented gradients (HOG) to allow a robust representation of the face image and then to categorize the human gender with an SVM. The choice of hybrid characteristics yields great precision by fusing features.

- **Histogram of oriented gradients (HOG):** There are a lot of works using HOG features for face recognition. In 2015, Karaaba et al. [225] selected the similar regions of two face images by using a most similar region selection algorithm (MSRS) to deal with misalignment. A distances vector is constructed using a multi-HOG algorithm. Mean of minimum distances (MMD) and multilayer perceptron-based distance (MLPD) functions are used to recognize a face. Combined with MSRS, these techniques give high performance. In Arigbabu et al. [226], the face image is preprocessed using a bi-cubic interpolation resampling technique and noise removal. The shape of the face image is described locally using both a Laplacian edge detector and pyramid HOG (PHOG) descriptor to recognize human gender. An SVM is used for gender classification. Experiments on an LFW data set [214] describe the effectiveness of this method. The work of Leonard et al. [227] showed the efficiency of the correlation filters for face recognition. The best filter is selected according to its robustness to the scale, noise, and rotation changes.

- **Correlation filters:** Advanced face recognition systems provide sufficient efficiency in controlled environments and they are not very effective in uncontrolled situations. Correlation filters have proven their effectiveness in pertinent methods under both controlled and uncontrolled settings. On the basis of this architecture, Napoléan and Alfalou [228] proposed to enhance the efficiency of a correlation approach to deal with illumination changes. The LBP-VLC correlator uses a particular Gaussian function for face image filtering to select the edges. A phase-only filters (POF) filter is used to approve the method. Experiments have shown the good efficiency of LBP-correlation methods under lighting changes. In a similar way, Heflin et al. [229] used an UMACE (unconstrained minimum average correlation energy) filter based on an eye detection pipeline to decrease face misalignment, improving eye location precision. Experiments conducted on LFW [214] and FDHD [230] data sets demonstrated that this algorithm yields a high face recognition accuracy by giving more attention on the eye localization step. Proposed by Zhu et al. [231], a feature correlation filter (FCF) fuses the representations of faces with a correlation method to achieve the correlation on filter instead of pixel values. FCF can effectively decrease the need for storage with only a small number of features and reach significant performance. In 2013, Ouerhani et al. [232] proposed a correlation method to recognize a face based on a segmented composite POF filter, to increase the detection accuracy and reduce the correlation time. The target image is preprocessed and reconstructed on the basis of a spectral phase to achieve discriminant correlation and to tackle noise and face rotation. The comparison of the peak-to-correlation energy (PCE) to a specific threshold reduces the wrong alarm rate.

- **Gabor features:** The complexity of the nonlinear relation between the spaces of heterogeneous face image is one of the drawbacks of heterogeneous face recognition. To address these limitations, Yi et al [233] proposed an unsupervised DL method based on the extraction of local Gabor features at localized facial points. RBMs are used to learn locally shared representations, which are processed by PCA and matched by cosine similarity.

17.4.3.2 Key Points-Based Techniques

- **Scale invariant feature transform (SIFT):** In 2015, a face recognition system was proposed in [234] using the SIFT descriptor combined with the Kepenecki method [235]. The locations of facial landmarks are acquired by Gabor wavelets responses in a dynamic way. A confidence metric based on the posterior probability is presented in a supervised manner to recognize poorly identified faces. The performance of the proposed approach is compared to the Kepenecki method using three public benchmarks, the FERET [229], AR [236], and LFW [214].
- **Speeded-up robust features (SURF):** In 2009, Du et al. [237] applied SURF detectors and descriptors to extract image features for face recognition. A measure of similarity is used that contains the number of matched points, the mean value of the Euclidean distance, and the mean distance proportion of the total matched pairs. In 2015, Vinay et al. [238] adopted two variants of detector-descriptor—the SURF detector with SIFT descriptor, and the SIFT detector with SURF descriptor—to increase the competence of face recognition systems. The fast library for approximate nearest neighbor search (FLANN) distance measure is used to determine the correspondence/miscorrespondence of the feature descriptors match. In 2016, a face recognition technique was proposed by Shah and Anand in [239] using SURF features and an SVM classifier.
- **Binary robust independent elementary features (BRIEF):** In 2011, Calonder et al. [240] adopted a binary descriptor named BRIEF to generate feature descriptors very quickly and with low memory requirements. BRIEF leads to a similar recognition precision with SURF and SIFT, while performing fast. KNN is used with the Hamming distance to match faces.
- **Fast retina keypoint (FREAK):** To address the problems of insufficient memory and computational complexity of descriptors, Alahi et al. [241] suggested a binary key-point descriptor called FREAK, based on the distribution of ganglion cells in

the retina. FREAK is represented by comparing a setting threshold with the difference in intensity between receptive fields pairs.

17.5 Conclusion

In this chapter, we first surveyed the main approaches in the field of moving objects segmentation where background subtraction is used to detect objects of interest. Second, we reviewed the main representative methods used to classify the extracted moving objects. Third, we presented the different approaches used in the area of face recognition in order to recognize humans through their faces. In this context, the importance of moving object detection in video is crucial as it is the first step that is followed by classification and recognition. In summary, deep learning methods are very suitable for smart homes and cities using IoT systems that need to detect moving objects such as humans and vehicles.

References

1. R. Collins et al., A system for video surveillance and monitoring, IEEE T-PAMI (2000).
2. I. Haritaoglu, D. Harwood, L. Davis, W4: Real time surveillance of people and their activities, *IEEE Transactions on Pattern Analysis and Machine Intelligence* 8 (22) (2000) 80–85.
3. L. Zhao, Q. Tong, H. Wang, Study on moving-object-detection arithmetic based on W4 theory, IEEE AIMSEC 2011 (2011) 4387–4390.
4. T. Bouwmans, F. Porikli, B. Horferlin, A. Vacavant, *Handbook on Background Modeling and Foreground Detection for Video Surveillance*, CRC Press, Taylor and Francis Group (2014).
5. T. Bouwmans, N. Aybat, E. Zahzah, *Handbook on Robust Low-Rank and Sparse Matrix Decomposition: Applications in Image and Video Processing*, Taylor and Francis Group (2016).
6. T. Bouwmans, B. Hofer-lin, F. Porikli, A. Vacavant, Traditional Approaches in Background Modeling for VideoSurveillance, *Handbook Background Modeling and Foreground Detection for Video Surveillance*, Taylor and Francis Group (July 2014).
7. T. Bouwmans, B. Hoferlin, F. Porikli, A. Vacavant, Recent Approaches in Background Modeling for Video Surveillance, *Handbook Background Modeling and Foreground Detection for Video Surveillance*, Taylor and Francis Group (July 2014).
8. T. Bouwmans, Traditional and recent approaches in background modeling for foreground detection: An overview, *Computer Science Review* 11 (May 2014) 31–66.
9. T. Bouwmans et al., On the role and the importance of features for background modeling and foreground detection, *Computer Science Review* 28 (2018) 26–91.
10. L. Maddalena, A. Petrosino, Background subtraction for moving object detection in RGBD data: A survey, *MDPI Journal of Imaging* 4 (2018) 71.
11. B. Lee, M. Hedley, Background estimation for video surveillance, IVCNZ (2002), 315–320.
12. P. Graszka, Median mixture model for background-foreground segmentation in video sequences, *WSCG* (2014).
13. S. Roy, A. Ghosh, Real-time Adaptive Histogram Min-Max Bucket (HMMB) Model for Background Subtraction, *IEEE T-CSVT* (2017).
14. A. Elgammal, L. Davis, Non-parametric model for background subtraction, *ECCV* (2000), 751–767.

15. R. Caseiro, P. Martins, J. Batista, Background modelling on tensor field for foreground segmentation, *BMVC* (2010), 1–12.
16. C. Stauffer, E. Grimson, Adaptive background mixture models for real-time tracking, *IEEE Conference on Computer Vision and Pattern Recognition, CVPR* (1999), 246–252.
17. S. Varadarajan, P. Miller, H. Zhou, Spatial mixture of Gaussians for dynamic background modelling, *AVSS* (2013), 63–68.
18. F. E. Baf, T. Bouwmans, B. Vachon, Fuzzy integral for moving object detection, *IEEE International Conference on Fuzzy Systems, FUZZ-IEEE* (2008), 1729–1736.
19. F. E. Baf, T. Bouwmans, B. Vachon, Type-2 fuzzy mixture of Gaussians model: Application to background modeling, *ISVC* (2008), 772–781.
20. F. E. Baf, T. Bouwmans, B. Vachon, Fuzzy statistical modeling of dynamic backgrounds for moving object detection in infrared videos, *IEEE-Workshop OTCBVS* (2009), 60–65.
21. O. Munteanu, T. Bouwmans, E. Zahzah, R. Vasiu, The detection of moving objects in video by background subtraction using Dempster-Shafer theory, *Transactions on Electronics and Communications* 60 (1) (March 2015).
22. N. Oliver, B. Rosario, A. Pentland, A Bayesian computer vision system for modeling human interactions, *International Conference on Vision Systems, ICVS* (January 1999).
23. D. Farcas, T. Bouwmans, Background modeling via a supervised subspace learning, *IVPCV* (2010), 1–7.
24. D. Farcas, C. Marghes, T. Bouwmans, Background subtraction via incremental maximum margin criterion: A discriminative approach, *Machine Vision and Applications* 23 (6) (2012) 1083–1101.
25. C. Marghes, T. Bouwmans, Background modeling via incremental maximum margin criterion, *ACCV* Workshop Subspace (2010).
26. C. Marghes, T. Bouwmans, R. Vasiu, Background modeling and foreground detection via a reconstructive and discriminative subspace learning approach, *IPCV* 2012 (July 2012).
27. E. Candes, X. Li, Y. Ma, J. Wright, Robust principal component analysis? *International Journal of ACM* 58 (3) (May 2011).
28. A. Sobral, T. Bouwmans, E. Zahzah, Double-constrained RPCA based on saliency maps for foreground detection in automated maritime surveillance, *AVSS* (2015).
29. S. Javed, A. Mahmood, T. Bouwmans, S. Jung, Motion-aware graph regularized RPCA for background modeling of complex scenes, scene background modeling contest, *International Conference on Pattern Recognition, ICPR* (December 2016).
30. S. Javed, A. Mahmood, T. Bouwmans, S. Jung, Spatiotemporal low-rank modeling for complex scene background initialization, *IEEE Transactions on Circuits and Systems for Video Technology* (2016).
31. G. Ramirez-Alonso, M. Chacon-Murguia, Self-adaptive SOM-CNN neural system for dynamic object detection in normal and complex scenarios, *Pattern Recognition* (April 2015).
32. J. Ramirez-Quintana, M. Chacon-Murguia, Self-organizing retinotopic maps applied to background modeling for dynamic object segmentation in video sequences, *IJCNN* (2013).
33. A. Schofield, P. Mehta, T. Stonham, A system for counting people in video images using neural networks to identify the background scene, *Pattern Recognition* 29 (1996), 1421–1428.
34. T. Chang, T. Ghandi, M. Trivedi, Vision modules for a multi sensory bridge monitoring approach, *ITSC* (2004), 971–976.
35. G. Cinar, J. Principe, Adaptive background estimation using an information theoretic cost for hidden state estimation, *IJCNN* 2011 (August 2011).
36. S. Messelodi, C. Modena, N. Segata, M. Zanin, A Kalman filter based background updating algorithm robust to sharp illumination changes, *ICIAP* 3617 (2005), 163–170.
37. K. Toyama, J. Krumm, B. Brumiit, B. Meyers, Wallflower: Principles and practice of background maintenance, *IEEE, ICCV* (1999), 261.
38. C. Wren, A. Azarbayejani, Pfinder: Real-time tracking of the human body, *IEEE Transactions on Pattern Analysis and Machine Intelligence* 19 (7) (1997) 780–785.
39. J. Pulgarin-Giraldo, A. Alvarez-Meza, D. Insuasti-Ceballos, T. Bouwmans, G. Castellanos-Dominguez, GMM background modeling using divergence-based weight updating, *Conference Ibero American Congresson Pattern Recognition, CIARP* (2016).

40. B. Garcia-Garcia, F. Gallegos-Funes, A. Rosales-Silva, A Gaussian-Median filter for moving objects segmentation applied for static scenarios, *IntelliSys* (2018) 478–493.
41. T. Elguebaly, N. Bouguila, Finite asymmetric generalized Gaussian mixture models learning for infrared object detection, *Computer Vision and Image Understanding* (2013).
42. D. Mukherjee, J. Wu, Real-time video segmentation using Student's t mixture model, *ANT* (2012), 153–160.
43. T. Haines, T. Xiang, Background subtraction with Dirichlet processes, *European Conference on Computer Vision*, 2012 (October 2012).
44. A. Faro, D. Giordano, C. Spampinato, Adaptive background modeling integrated with luminosity sensors and occlusion processing for reliable vehicle detection, *IEEE Transactions on Intelligent Transportation Systems* 12 (4) (2011) 1398–1412.
45. D. Liang, S. Kaneko, M. Hashimoto, K. Iwata, X. Zhao, Co-occurrence probability based pixel pairs background model for robust object detection in dynamic scenes, *Pattern Recognition* 48 (4) (2015) 1374–1390.
46. J. Rosell-Ortega, G. Andreu-Garcia, A. Rodas-Jorda, V. Atienza-Vanacloig, Background modelling in demanding situations with confidence measure, *IAPR ICPR* (2008).
47. O. Barnich, M. V. Droogenbroeck, ViBe: a powerful random technique to estimate the background in video sequences, *IEEE ICASSP* (2009), 945–948.
48. F. Tombari, A. Lanza, L. D. Stefano, S. Mattoccia, Non-linear parametric Bayesian regression for robust background subtraction, *IEEE MOTION* (2009).
49. T. Bouwmans, F. E. Baf, Modeling of dynamic backgrounds by Type-2 fuzzy Gaussians mixture models, *MASAUM Journal of Basic and Applied Sciences* 1 (2) (2009) 265–277.
50. Z. Zhao, T. Bouwmans, X. Zhang, Y. Fang, A. Fuzzy, Background modeling approach for motion detection in dynamic backgrounds, *International Conference on Multimedia and Signal Processing* (December 2012).
51. H. Zhang, D. Xu, Fusing color and gradient features for background model, *International Conference on Signal Processing, ICSP* 2 (7) (2006).
52. H. Zhang, D. Xu, Fusing color and texture features for background model, *FSKD 2006* 4223 (7) (2006) 887–893.
53. F. E. Baf, T. Bouwmans, B. Vachon, Foreground detection using the Choquet integral, *IEEE WIAMIS* (2008), 187–190.
54. P. Chiranjeevi, S. Sengupta, Interval-valued model level fuzzy aggregation-based background subtraction, *IEEE Transactions on Cybernetics* (2016).
55. S. Javed, S. Oh, A. Sobral, T. Bouwmans, S. Jung, Background subtraction via superpixel-based online matrix decomposition with structured foreground constraints, *Workshop on Robust Subspace Learning and Computer Vision, ICCV* (December 2015).
56. S. Javed, A. Mahmood, T. Bouwmans, S. Jung, Background-foreground modeling based on spatiotemporal sparse subspace clustering, *IEEE Transactions on Image Processing* (2017).
57. B. Rezaei, S. Ostadabbas, Background subtraction via fast robust matrix completion, *International Workshop on RSL-CV in conjunction with ICCV* (October 2017).
58. B. Rezaei, S. Ostadabbas, Moving object detection through robust matrix completion augmented with objectness, *IEEE Journal of Selected Topics in Signal Processing* (2018).
59. N. Vaswani, T. Bouwmans, S. Javed, P. Narayanamurthy, Robust PCA and robust subspace tracking: A comparative evaluation, *SSP* (June 2018).
60. S. Prativadibhayankaram, H. Luong, T. Le, A. Kaup, Compressive online video background foreground separation using multiple prior information and optical flow, *MDPI* (2018).
61. J. He, L. Balzano, A. Szlam, Incremental gradient on the Grassmannian for online foreground and background separation in subsampled video, *IEEE CVPR* (June 2012).
62. P. Rodriguez, B. Wohlberg, Incremental principal component pursuit for video background modeling, *Journal of Mathematical Imaging and Vision* 55 (1) (2016) 1–18.
63. H. Guo, C. Qiu, N. Vaswani, Practical ReProCS for separating sparse and low-dimensional signal sequences from their sum, *Preprint* (October 2013).

64. P. Narayanamurthy, N. Vaswani, A Fast and Memory-efficient Algorithm for Robust PCA (MEROP), *IEEE ICASSP* (April 2018).

65. S. Javed, T. Bouwmans, S. Jung, Stochastic decomposition into low rank and sparse tensor for robust background subtraction, *ICDP* (July 2015).

66. A. Sobral, S. Javed, S. Jung, T. Bouwmans, E. Zahzah, Online stochastic tensor decomposition for background subtraction in multispectral video sequences, *ICCV* (2015).

67. C. Lu, J. Feng, Y. Chen, W. Liu, Z. Lin, S. Yan, Tensor robust principal component analysis with a new tensor nuclear norm, *IEEE T-PAMI* (2019).

68. D. Driggs, S. Becker, J. Boyd-Graberz, Tensor robust principal component analysis: Better recovery with atomic norm regularization, *Preprint* (January 2019).

69. P. Gil-Jimenez, S. Maldonado-Bascon, R. Gil-Pita, H. Gomez-Moreno, Background pixel classification for motion detection in video image sequences. *International Work Conference on Artificial and Natural Neural Network, IWANN*, 2686 (2003) 718–725.

70. A. Tavakkoli, Foreground-Background Segmentation in Video Sequences Using Neural Networks, *Intelligent Systems: Neural Networks and Applications* (May 2005).

71. Z. Wang, L. Zhang, H. Bao, PNN based motion detection with adaptive learning rate. *CIS* (2009), 301–306,

72. D. Culibrk, O. Marques, D. Socek, H. Kalva, B. Furht, A neural network approach to Bayesian background modeling for video object segmentation, *IEEE Transactions on Neural Networks* 18 (6) (2007) 1614–1627.

73. L. Maddalena, A. Petrosino, A self-organizing approach to detection of moving patterns for real-time applications, *Advances in Brain, Vision and Artificial Intelligence* 47 (29) (2007) 181–190.

74. L. Maddalena, A. Petrosino, A self-organizing neural system for background and foreground modeling, *ICANN* (2008), 652–661.

75. L. Maddalena, A. Petrosino, Neural model-based segmentation of image motion, *KES* (2008), 57–64.

76. L. Maddalena, A. Petrosino, A self organizing approach to background subtraction for visual surveillance applications, *IEEE Transactions on Image Processing* 17 (7) (2008) 1168–1177.

77. L. Maddalena, A. Petrosino, Multivalued background/foreground separation for moving object detection, *International Workshop on Fuzzy Logic and Applications, WILF* (2009), 263–270.

78. L. Maddalena, A. Petrosino, A fuzzy spatial coherence-based approach to background/foreground separation for moving object detection, *NCA* (2010), 1–8.

79. L. Maddalena, A. Petrosino, The SOBS algorithm: What are the limits? *IEEE Workshop on Change Detection, CVPR* (June 2012).

80. Maddalena, A. Petrosino, The 3dSOBS+ algorithm for moving object detection, *Computer Vision and Image Understanding, CVIU* 122 (2014) 65–73.

81. M. Chacon-Muguia, S. Gonzalez-Duarte, P. Vega, Simplified SOM-neural model for video segmentation of moving objects, *IJCNN* (2009), 474–480.

82. M. Chacon-Murguia, G. Ramirez-Alonso, S. Gonzalez-Duarte, Improvement of a neural-fuzzy motion detection vision model for complex scenario conditions, *IJCNN* (2013).

83. G. Gemignani, A. Rozza, A novel background subtraction approach based on multi-layered self organizing maps, *IEEE International Conference on Image Processing* (2015).

84. N. Goyette, P. Jodoin, F. Porikli, J. Konrad, P. Ishwar, Change detection.net: A new change detection benchmark dataset, *IEEE Workshop on Change Detection, CDW* (2012).

85. L. Maddalena, A. Petrosino, 3D neural model-based stopped object detection, *International Conference on Image Analysis and Processing, ICIAP* (2009), 585–593.

86. L. Maddalena, A. Petrosino, Self organizing and fuzzy modelling for parked vehicles detection, *Advanced Concepts for Intelligent Vision Systems, ACVIS* (2009), 422–433.

87. L. Maddalena, A. Petrosino, Stopped object detection by learning foreground model in videos, *IEEE Transactions on Neural Networks and Learning Systems* 24 (5) (2013) 723–735.

88. R. Guo, H. Qi, Partially-sparse restricted Boltzmann machine for background modeling and subtraction, *ICMLA* (2013), 209–214.

89. Z. Qu, S. Yu, M. Fu, Motion background modeling based on context-encoder, *IEEE ICAIPR* (September 2016).

90. L. Xu, Y. Li, Y. Wang, E. Chen, Temporally Adaptive Restricted Boltzmann Machine for Background Modeling, *AAAI* (January 2015).

91. P. Xu, M. Ye, Q. Liu, X. Li, L. Pei, J. Ding, Motion detection via a couple of auto-encoder networks, *International Conference on Multimedia and Expo, ICME* (2014).

92. P. Xu, M. Ye, X. Li, Q. Liu, Y. Yang, J. Ding, Dynamic background learning through deep auto-encoder networks, *ACM International Conference on Multimedia* (November 2014).

93. M. Babaee, D. Dinh, G. Rigoll, A deep convolutional neural network for background subtraction, *Preprint* (2017).

94. C. Bautista, M. Dy, R. O. Manalac, M. Cordel, Convolutional neural network for vehicle detection in low resolution traffic videos, *TENCON* (2016).

95. M. Braham, M. Van Droogenbroeck, Deep background subtraction with scene-specific convolutional neural networks. *International Conference on Systems, Signals and Image Processing, IWSSIP* (2016).

96. P. Cinelli, Anomaly detection in surveillance videos using deep residual networks, *Master Thesis, Universidade de Rio de Janeiro* (February 2017).

97. K. Lim, W. Jang, C. Kim, Background subtraction using encoder-decoder structured convolutional neural network, *IEEE AVSS* (2017).

98. S. Choo, W. Seo, D. Jeong, N. Cho, Multi-scale recurrent encoder-decoder network for dense temporal classification, *IAPR ICPR* (2018), 103–108.

99. Choo, W. Seo, D. Jeong, N. Cho, Learning background subtraction by video synthesis and multi-scale recurrent networks, *ACCV* (December 2018).

100. A. Farnoosh, B. Rezaei, S. Ostadabbas, DeepPBM: deep probabilistic background model estimation from video sequences, *Preprint* (February 2019).

101. D. Zeng, M. Zhu, Combining background subtraction algorithms with convolutional neural network, *Preprint* (2018).

102. Y. Wang, Z. Luo, P. Jodoin, Interactive deep learning method for segmenting moving objects, *Pattern Recognition Letters* (2016).

103. S. Lee, D. Kim, Background subtraction using the factored 3-way restricted Boltzmann machines, *Preprint* (2018).

104. T. Nguyen, C. Pham, S. Ha, J. Jeon, Change detection by training a triplet network for motion feature extraction, *IEEE T-CSVT* (January 2018).

105. M. Shafiee, P. Siva, P. Fieguth, A. Wong, Embedded motion detection via neural response mixture background modeling, *International Conference on Computer Vision and Pattern Recognition* (2016).

106. M. Shafiee, P. Siva, P. Fieguth, A. Wong, Real-time embedded motion detection via neural response mixture modeling, *Journal of Signal Processing Systems* (June 2017).

107. Y. Zhang, X. Li, Z. Zhang, F. Wu, L. Zhao, Deep learning driven blockwise moving object detection with binary scene modeling, *Neurocomputing* (June 2015).

108. X. Zhao, Y. Chen, M. Tang, J. Wang, Joint background reconstruction and foreground segmentation via a two-stage convolutional neural network, *Preprint* (2017).

109. M. Shafiee, P. Siva, P. Fieguth, A. Wong, Embedded motion detection via neural response mixture background modeling, *International Conference on Computer Vision and Pattern Recognition* (2016).

110. Y. Chan, Deep learning-based scene-awareness approach for intelligent change detection in videos, *Journal of Electronic Imaging* 28 (1) (2019).

111. S. Ammar, T. Bouwmans, N. Zaghden, M. Neji, A Deep Detector Classifier (DeepDC) for moving objects segmentation and classification in video surveillance, *IET Image Process* (2020).

112. S. Ammar, T. Bouwmans, N. Zaghden, M. Neji, Moving objects segmentation based on DeepSphere in video surveillance, *ISVC* (2019).

113. K. Karmann, A. Brand, Moving object recognition using an adaptive background memory, *Time-Varying Image Processing and Moving Object Recognition*, Elsevier (1990).

114. M. Boninsegna, A. Bozzoli, A tunable algorithm to update a reference image, *Signal Processing: Image Communication* 16 (4) (2000) 1353–365.

115. D. Fan, M. Cao, C. Lv, An updating method of self-adaptive background for moving objects detection in video, *International Conference on Audio, Language and Image Processing* (2008) 1497–1501.

116. T. Chang, T. Ghandi, M. Trivedi, Computer vision for multi-sensory structural health monitoring system, *ITSC* (October 2004).

117. C. Wren, F. Porikli, Waviz: Spectral similarity for object detection, *IEEE International Workshop on Performance Evaluation of Tracking and Surveillance, PETS* (January 2005).

118. F. Porikli, C. Wren, Change detection by frequency decomposition: Wave-back, *International Workshop on Image Analysis for Multimedia Interactive Services, WIAMIS* (April 2005).

119. V. Cevher, D. Reddy, M. Duarte, A. Sankaranarayanan, R. Chellappa, R. Baraniuk, Compressive sensing for background subtraction, *ECCV* (2008).

120. J. Mota, L. Weizman, N. Deligiannis, Y. Eldar, M. Rodrigues, Reference-based compressed sensing: A sample complexity approach, *ICASSP* (2016).

121. D. Kuzin, O. Isupova, L. Mihaylova, Compressive sensing approaches for autonomous object detection in video sequences, *SDF* (2015) 1–6.

122. P. Jodoin, Motion detection: Unsolved issues and [potential] solutions, Invited Talk, *SBMI 2015 in conjunction with ICIAP* (September 2015).

123. T. Bouwmans, Z. Javed, M. Sultana, S. Jung, Deep neural network concepts for background subtraction: A systematic review and comparative evaluation, *Neural Networks* (2019).

124. M. Braham, S. Pierard, M. V. Droogenbroeck, Semantic Background Subtraction, *IEEE International Conference on Image Processing, ICIP* (September 2017).

125. D. Zeng, X. Chen, M. Zhu, M. Goesele, A. Kuijper, Background Subtraction with Real-time Semantic Segmentation, *Preprint* (December 2018).

126. P. Rodriguez, B. Wohlberg, Translational and rotational jitter invariant incremental principal component pursuit for video background modeling, *International Conference on Image Processing, ICIP* (2015).

127. N. Vaswani, T. Bouwmans, S. Javed, P. Narayanamurthy, Robust sub-space learning: Robust PCA, robust subspace tracking and robust subspace recovery, *Signal Processing Magazine* 35 (4) (2018) 32–55.

128. O. Karadag, O. Erdas, Evaluation of the robustness of deep features on the change detection problem, *IEEE Signal Processing and Communications Applications Conference, SIU* (2018) 1–4.

129. G. Silva, P. Rodriguez, Jitter invariant incremental principal component pursuit for video background modeling on the TK1, *Asilomar Conference on Signals, Systems, and Computers, ACSSC* (2015).

130. G. Chau, P. Rodriguez, Panning and jitter invariant incremental principal component pursuit for video background modeling, *ICCV* (2017).

131. J. He, D. Zhang, L. Balzano, T. Tao, Iterative Grassmannian optimization for robust image alignment, *Image and Vision Computing* (June 2013).

132. J. He, D. Zhang, L. Balzano, T. Tao, Iterative online subspace learning for robust image alignment, *IEEE Conference on Automatic Face and Gesture Recognition, FG* (2013).

133. B. Wohlberg, Endogenous convolutional sparse representations for translation invariant image subspace models, *IEEE International Conference on Image Processing, ICIP* (2014).

134. L. Lim, H. Keles, Foreground segmentation using a triplet convolutional neural network for multiscale feature encoding, *Preprint* (January 2018).

135. L. Lim, H. Keles, Foreground segmentation using convolutional neural networks for multi-scale feature encoding, *Pattern Recognition Letters* 112 (2018) 256–262.

136. L. Lim, l. Ang, H. Keles, Learning multi-scale features for foreground segmentation, *Preprint* 2018.

137. J. Zhu, S. Liao, Z. Lei, D. Yi, S. Li, Pedestrian attribute classification in surveillance: Database and evaluation. *IEEE CVPR* (2013) 631–338.

138. P. Golle, Machine learning attacks against the asirra captcha. *ACM conference on Computer and communications security*, 2008, 535–542.

139. S. Bhirud, V. Gohokar, Face recognition based on SVM and GABOR filter, *International Journal of Current Engineering and Technology*, 2014.
140. N. Zaghden, R. Mullot, M. Alimi, Categorizing ancient documents. *International Journal of Computer Science Issues (IJCSI)* 10 (2) (March 2013) 1694–0784.
141. N. Zaghden, R. Mullot, M. Alimi, Characterization of ancient document images composed by Arabic and Latin scripts. *IIT* (2011) 124–127.
142. S. Ammar, N. Zaghden, M. Neji, A framework for people re-identification in multi-camera surveillance systems. *International Conference on Cognition and Exploratory Learning in Digital Age* (2017) 319–322.
143. S. Ammar, N. Zaghden, M. Neji, An Effective Approach Based on a Subset of Skeleton Joints for Two-Person Interaction Recognition, In *Iberoamerican Congress on Pattern Recognition. CIARP*, Springer, Cham, (2018) Lecture vol. 11401.
144. Y. LeCun, B. Boser, J. S. Denker, D. Henderson, R. E. Howard, W. Hubbard, L. D. Jackel, Handwritten Digit Recognition with a Back-Propagation Network, In *Advances in neural information processing systems*, 2, MIT Press, Cambridge (1989) 396–404.
145. J. Long, E. Shelhamer, T. Darrell, Fully convolutional networks for semantic segmentation. *IEEE CVPR* (2015) 3431–3440.
146. M. Babaee, D. Tung Dinh, G. Rigoll, A deep convolutional neural network for video sequence background subtraction, *Pattern Recognition* (2018).
147. A. Radford, L. Metz, S. Chintala, Unsupervised representation learning with deep convolutional generative adversarial networks, *ICLR* (2016).
148. B. Liu, Y. Liu, K. Zhou, Zhou image classification for dogs and cats. *Image CF* (2014).
149. W. Li, H. Fu, L. Yu, P. Gong, D. Feng, C. Li, N. Clinton, Stacked Autoencoder-based deep learning for remote-sensing image classification: A case study of African land-cover mapping, *International Journal on Remote Sensors* 37 (2016) 5632–5646.
150. O. Zou, L. Ni, T. Zhang, Q. Wang, Deep learning based feature selection for remote sensing scene classification, *IEEE Geoscience Remote Sensors Letters* 12 (2015) 2321–2325.
151. X. Chen, S. Xiang, C. L. Liu, C. H. Pan, Vehicle detection in satellite images by hybrid deep convolutional neural networks, *IEEE Geoscience Remote Sensors Letters* 11 (2014) 1797–1801.
152. J. Donahue, J. Krähenbühl, T. Darrel, Adversarial feature learning. *International Conference on Learning Representations, ICLR* (2017).
153. S. Oh, A. Hoogs, A. Perera, N. Cuntoor, C. Chen, J. Lee, A large-scale benchmark dataset for event recognition in surveillance video. *IEEE Computer Vision and Pattern Recognition, CVPR* (2011).
154. C. Rosenberg, M. Hebert, H. Schneiderman, Semi-supervised self-training of object detection models. *IEEE WACV/MOTION'05* (2005).
155. T. Joachims, Transductive inference for text classification using support vector machines. *International Conference on Machine Learning* (1999) 200–209.
156. P. Diederik, J. Danilo, M. Shakir, W. Max, Semi-supervised learning with deep generative models, *Advances in Neural Information Processing Systems* (2014).
157. J. T. Springenberg, Unsupervised and semi supervised learning with categorical generative adversarial networks. *ArXiv* (2015).
158. T. Miyato, S. Maeda, M. Koyama, S. Ishii, Virtual adversarial training: A regularization method for supervised and semi-supervised learning, *IEEE Transactions on Pattern Analysis and Machine Intelligence* 41 (2017) 1979–1993.
159. T. Salimans, I. J. Goodfellow, W. Zaremba, V. Cheung, A. Radford, X. Chen, Improved techniques for training GANs. *CoRR* (2016).
160. A. M. Dai, Q. V. Le. Semi-supervised sequence learning. *International Conference on Learning Representations. ICLR* (2018).
161. A. Radford, R. Jozefowicz, I. Sutskever, Learning to generate reviews and discovering sentiment. *CoRR* (2017).
162. H. Seo, P. Milanfar, Face verification using the lark representation, *IEEE Transactions on Information Forensics Security* 6 (2011) 1275–1286.

163. A. Ghorbel, I. Tajouri, W. Aydi, N. Masmoudi, A Comparative Study of GOM, uLBP, VLC and Fractional Eigenfaces for Face Recognition, In *International Image Processing, Applications and Systems (IPAS)*, Hammamet, Tunisia, (November 2016), 5–7.

164. M. Abdullah, M. Wazzan, S. Bo-Saeed. Optimizing Face Recognition Using PCA. *ArXiv 1206.1515* (2012).

165. R. Johannes, S. Armin, Face recognition with machine learning in OpenCV fusion of the results with the localization data of an acoustic camera for speaker identification, *ArXiv 1707.00835* (2017).

166. M. Bhuiyan, Towards face recognition using eigenface, *International Journal of Advanced Computer Science and Applications* (2016).

167. M. Slavković, DubravkaJevtić, Face recognition using eigenface approach, *Serbian Journal of Electrical Engineering* 9 (1) (2012) 121–130.

168. A. Abd Rahman, M. A. Noah, R. S. Safar, N. Kamarudin. Human Face Recognition: An Eigenfaces Approach. *IntelSys* (2014) 42–47.

169. R. Saha, D. Bhattacharjee, S. Barman, Comparison of different face recognition method based on PCA, *International Journal of Management & Information Technology* (2014).

170. K. Simonyan, O. Parkhi, A. Vedaldi, A. Zisserman, Fisher Vector Faces in the Wild, *BMVC 2013*, Bristol, UK (September 2013).

171. B. Li, K. K. Ma, Fisherface vs. eigenface in the dual-tree complex wavelet domain. *The Fifth International Conference on Intelligent Information Hiding and Multimedia Signal Processing* (2009) 30–33.

172. Z. Abidin, A. Harjoko, A neural network based facial expression recognition using Fisherface, *International Journal of Computer Applications* 59 (3) (2012).

173. H. Gowda, G. Kumar, M. Imran, Multimodal biometric recognition system based on nonparametric classifiers, *Data Analysis Learning* 43 (2018) 269–278.

174. M. S. Bartlett, J. R. Movellan, T. J. Sejnowski, Face recognition by independent component analysis, *IEEE Transactions on Neural Networks* 13 (2002) 1450–1464.

175. R. Kong, Z. Bing, A new face recognition method based on fast least squares support vector machine, *Physics Procedia* 22 (2011) 616–621.

176. Z. Cui, W. Li, D. Xu, S. Shan, X. Chen, Fusing Robust Face Region Descriptors via Multiple Metric Learning for Face Recognition in the Wild, *CVPR*, Portland, OR (June 2013) 3554–3561.

177. S. A. Khan, M. Ishtiaq, M. Nazir, M. Shaheen, Face recognition under varying expressions and illumination using particle swarm optimization, *Journal of Computer Science* 28 (2018) 94–100.

178. Z. Dehai, D. Da, L. Jin, L. Qing, A PCA-based face recognition method by applying fast Fourier transform in pre-processing. *ICMT*, France (2013).

179. R. A. Vyas, S. M. Shah, Comparison of PCA and LDA techniques for face recognition feature based extraction with accuracy enhancement, *IRJET* 4 (2017) 3332–3336.

180. A. Azeem et al., A survey: face recognition techniques under partial occlusion, *International Arabic Journal on Information Technology* 11 (1) (2014) 1–10.

181. T. Le, B. Len, Face recognition based on SVM and 2DPCA. *ArXiv* (2011).

182. Z. Huang, W. J. Li, J. Shang, J. Wang, T. Zhang, Non-uniform patch based face recognition via 2D-DWT. *Image Vision Computing* 37 (2015) 12–19.

183. Z. Sufyanu, F. Mohamad, A. Yusuf, M. Mamat, Enhanced face recognition using discrete cosine transform. *Engineering Letters* 24 (2016) 52–61

184. M. Abdulrahman, Y. G. Dambatta, A. S. Muhammad, Face recognition using eigenface and discrete wavelet transform. *International Conference on Advances in Engineering and Technology* (2014).

185. S. S. Shanbhag, S. Bargi, K. Manikantan, S. Ramachandran, Face recognition using wavelet transforms-based feature extraction and spatial differentiation-based pre-processing. *ICSEMR* (2014) 1–8.

186. V. Perlibakas, Face recognition using principal component analysis and log-Gabor filters. *ArXiv* 2006).

187. S. Hafez, M. Selim, H. Zayed, 2D face recognition system based on selected Gabor filters and linear discriminant analysis LDA. *ArXiv 1503.03741* (2005).

188. Y. Ming, Q. Ruan, W. Xueqiao, Efficient 3D face recognition with Gabor patched spectral regression, *Computing and Informatics* 31 (4) (2012) 779–803.
189. L. Cament, F. Galdames, K. Bowyer, C. Perez, Face recognition under pose variation with local Gabor features enhanced by active shape and statistical models, *Pattern Recognition* (2015).
190. J. Fan, T. W. Chow, Exactly robust kernel principal component analysis, *IEEE Transactions on Neural Networks and Learning Systems* (2019).
191. E. Rublee, R. Vincent, K. Kurt, B. Gray, ORB: an efficient alternative to SIFT or SURF, In *IEEE International Conference on Computer Vision* (2011) 2564–2571.
192. A. Vinay, A. S. Cholin, A. D. Bhat, K. B. Murthy, S. Natarajan, An efficient ORB based face recognition framework for human-robot interaction, *Procedia of Computing Science* 133 (2018) 913–923.
193. K. Kim, M. Franz, B. Scholkopf, Iterative kernel principal component analysis for image modeling, *IEEE T-PAMI* 27 (9) (2005) 1351–1366.
194. J. Lu, K. Plataniotis, A. Venetsanopoulos, Face recognition using kernel direct discriminant analysis algorithms, *IEEE Transactions on Neural Networks and Learning Systems* 14 (2003) 117–126.
195. A. Vinay, S. Shekhar Vinay, K. N. Balasubramanya Murthy, S. Natarajan, Performance study of LDA and KFA for Gabor based face recognition system, *ICRTC*. 2015.
196. W. J Yang, Y. C. Chen, P. C. Chung, J. F. Yang, Multi-feature shape regression for face alignment, *EURASIP Journal of Advanced Signal Processing* 2018 (2018) 51.
197. II. Ouanan, M. Ouanan, B. Aksasse, Non-linear dictionary representation of deep features for face recognition from a single sample per person, *Procedia of Computing Science* 127 (2018) 114–122.
198. H. D. Vankayalapati, K. Kyamakya, Nonlinear feature extraction approaches with application to face recognition over large databases. *International Workshop on Nonlinear Dynamics and Synchronization* (2009) 44–48.
199. B. Devi, N. Veeranjaneyulu, K. Kishore, A novel face recognition system based on combining eigenfaces with Fisher faces using wavelets, *Procedia of Computing Science* 2 (2010) 44–51.
200. Y. Sun, D. Liang, X. Wang, X. Tang, Deepid3: Face recognition with very deep neural networks. *ArXiv 1502.00873* (2015).
201. H. Li, Z. Lin, X. Shen, J. Brandt, A convolutional neural network cascade for face detection, 2015, *IEEE Conference on Computer Vision and Pattern Recognition, CVPR* (2015).
202. S. Farfade, M. Saberian, L. Li, Multi-view face detection using deep convolutional neural networks. *ICMR* (2015).
203. A. Fathima, S. Ajitha, V. Vaidehi, M. Hemalatha, R. Karthigaiveni, R. Kumar. Hybrid approach for face recognition combining Gabor wavelet and linear discriminant analysis. *CGVIS* (2015) 220–225.
204. O. Barkan, J. Weill, L. Wolf, H. Aronowitz, Fast high dimensional vector multiplication face recognition. *IEEE ICCV* (2013) 1960–1967.
205. F. Juefei-Xu, K. Luu, M. Savvides, Spartans: Single-sample periocular-based alignment-robust recognition technique applied to non-frontal scenarios. *IEEE T-IP* 24 (2015) 4780–4795.
206. R. Sharma, M. S. Patterh, A new pose invariant face recognition system using PCA and ANFIS, *Optik* 126 (2015) 3483–3487.
207. M. Moussa, M. Hmila, A. Douik, A Novel face recognition approach based on genetic algorithm optimization, *Studies in Informatics and Control* 27 (2018) 127–134.
208. A. Mian, M. Bennamoun, R. Owens, An efficient multimodal 2D-3D hybrid approach to automatic face recognition, *IEEE Transactions in Pattern Analysis and Machine Intelligence* 29 (2007) 1927–1943.
209. H. Cho, R. Roberts, B. Jung, O. Choi, S. Moon, An efficient hybrid face recognition algorithm using PCA and Gabor wavelets, *International Journal of Advanced Robotics Systems* 11 (2014) 59.
210. J. Sing, S. Chowdhury, D. Basu, M. Nasipuri, An improved hybrid approach to face recognition by fusing local and global discriminant features. *International Journal of Biomedicine* 4 (2012) 144–164.

211. P. Kamencay et al., A novel approach to face recognition using image segmentation based on SPCA KNN method, *Radio Engineering* 22 (2013) 92–99.
212. J. Sun, Y. Fu, S. Li, J. He, C. Xu, L. Tan, Sequential human activity recognition based on deep convolutional network and extreme learning machine using wearable sensors, *Journal of Sensors* 10 (2018).
213. C. Ding, D. Tao, Robust face recognition via multimodal deep face representation, *IEEE Transactions on Multimedia* 17 (2015) 2049–2058.
214. E. Gonzalez-Sosa, J. Fierrez, R. Vera-Rodriguez, F. Alonso-Fernandez, Facial soft biometrics for recognition in the wild, recent works, annotation, and COTS evaluation, *IEEE Transactions on Information Forensics Security* 13 (2018) 2001–2014.
215. D. Yi, Z. Lei, S. Liao, S. Z. Li, Learning face representation from scratch. *ArXiv 1411.7923* (2014).
216. F. Bellakhdhar, K. Loukil, M. Abid, Face recognition approach using Gabor Wavelets, PCA and SVM, *IJCSI International Journal of Computer Science Issues* (2013) 201–206.
217. P. Khoi, L. H. Thien, V. H. Viet, Face retrieval based on local binary pattern and its variants: A comprehensive study, *International Journal of Advanced Computer Science Applications* 7 (2016) 249–258.
218. M. Xi, M. Chen, D. Polajnar, W. Tong, Local binary pattern network: A deep learning approach for face recognition. *IEEE ICIP* (2016) 3224–3228.
219. J. Phillips, H. Moon, S. Rizvi, P. Rauss, The FERET evaluation methodology for face-recognition algorithms, *IEEE T-PAMI* 22 (10) (2000) 1090–1104.
220. I. Laure Kambi Beli, C. Guo, Enhancing face identification using local binary patterns and k-nearest neighbors, *Journal of Imaging* 3 (2017) 37.
221. K. Bonnen, B. Klare, A. K. Jain, Component-based representation in automated face recognition, *IEEE Transactions on Information Forensics Security* 8 (2012) 239–253.
222. J. Ren, X. Jiang, J. Yuan, Relaxed local ternary pattern for face recognition, *IEEE ICIP* (2013) 3680–3684.
223. S. U. Hussain, T. Napoléon, F. Jurie, *Face Recognition Using Local Quantized Patterns*, HAL, India (2012).
224. M. Annalakshmi, S. Roomi, A. Naveedh, A hybrid technique for gender classification with SLBP and HOG features, *Cluster Computing* 22 (2019) 11–20.
225. M. Karaaba, O. Surinta, L. Schomaker, M. Wiering, Robust face recognition by computing distances from multiple histograms of oriented gradients. *IEEE Symposium Series on Computational Intelligence* (2015) 203–209.
226. O. Arigbabu et al., Soft biometrics: Gender recognition from unconstrained face images using local feature descriptor. *ArXiv 1702.02537* (2017).
227. I. Leonard, A. Alfalou, C. Brosseau, Face recognition based on composite correlation filters: Analysis of their performances, *Face Recognition*, London (2012).
228. T. Napoléon, A. Alfalou, Local binary patterns preprocessing for face identification/verification using the VanderLugt correlator. *Optical Pattern Recognition* (2014).
229. B. Heflin, W. Scheirer, T. E. Boult, For your eyes only. Proceedings of the *IEEE WACV* (2012) 193–200.
230. J. Parris et al., Face and Eye Detection on Hard Datasets. *Preprint of IJCB* (2011). Available at http://vast.uccs.edu/~tboult/PAPERS/IJCB11-Parris-et-al-FDHD.pdf.
231. X. Zhu, S. Liao, Z. Lei, R. Liu, S. Li, Feature correlation filter for face recognition. *International Conference on Biometrics* 4642 (2007) 77–86.
232. Y. Ouerhani, M. Jridi, A. Alfalou, C. Brosseau, Optimized pre-processing input plane GPU implementation of an optical face recognition technique using a segmented phase only composite filter, *Optics Communications* 289 (2013) 33–44.
233. D. Yi, Z. Lei, S. Liao, S. Z. Li, Shared representation learning for heterogeneous face recognition, *International Conference and Workshops on Automatic Face and Gesture Recognition* (2015) 1–15.
234. L. Lenc, P. Král, Automatic face recognition system based on the SIFT features, *Computer Electrical Engineering* 46 (2015) 256–272.

235. B. Kepenekci, Face Recognition using Gabor wavelet transform. Ph.D. thesis, The Middle East Technical University (2001).
236. A. Martinez, R. Benavente, The AR Face Database, Technical Report, Univerzitat Autonoma de Barcelona (1998).
237. G. Du, F. Su, A. Cai, Face Recognition Using SURF Features, *Pattern Recognition and Computer Vision; International Society for Optics and Photonics* 7496 (2009).
238. A. Vinay, D. Hebbar, V.S. Shekhar, K.B. Murthy, S. Natarajan, Two novel detector-descriptor based approaches for face recognition using sift and surf. *Procedia of Computing Science* 70 (2015) 185–197.
239. P. K. Shah, B. Anand, Face recognition using SURF features and SVM classifier, *International Journal of Electronics Engineering Research* 8 (1) (2016) 1–8.
240. M. Calonder, V. Lepetit, M. Ozuysal, T. Trzcinski, C. Strecha, P. Fua, BRIEF: Computing a local binary descriptor very fast, *IEEE Transactions on Pattern Analysis and Machine Intelligence* 34 (2011) 1281–1298.
241. A. Alahi, R. Ortiz, F. Vandergheynst, Freak: Fast retina keypoint. *IEEE CVPR* (2012) 510–517.

18

Human Detection and Tracking Using Background Subtraction in Visual Surveillance

Lavanya Sharma

Amity Institute of Information Technology, Amity University
Noida, India

CONTENTS

18.1 Introduction...317
18.2 Background Subtraction Technique...318
18.3 Background Models for Object Detection...320
18.4 Real-Time Challenges..321
18.5 Resources and Data Sets Used...322
18.6 Experimental Evaluation of Considered BGS Techniques...................322
18.7 Conclusion..323
References..324

KEYWORDS: *Gaussian mixture model, object detection and tracking, KLD, FLD, background subtraction, histogram, cloud computing, FG, BG, internet of things.*

18.1 Introduction

In recent times, motion-based object detection has become one of the major areas of attention of research in artificial intelligence (AI) applications [1, 2, 3]. Detection of an object is a vital step in any computer vision and machine learning applications because of its real-time applications in tracking of moving objects, visual surveillance, pedestrian detection, indoor/outdoor security, suspicious activity detection, logo detection, e-health department, traffic monitoring, location prediction using IP, cameras, defense, and automated driven cars. Several techniques have been developed to differentiate the foreground (FG) object from the background (BG) scene of a video sequence [4, 5, 6]. Usually, the BG contains insensate objects that remain static in the scene [1, 2, 7, 8]. These objects can be motionless such as change in lighting condition, room furniture, walls, doors, wavering bushes, escalators, slow leafy movement, or changing lights. In order to detect the moving objects in real-time applications, several methods are used such as optical flow and the background subtraction (BGS) method.

BGS is one of the most focused and effective techniques for detection of motion-based or moving objects in incessant video sequences from static or nonstatic cameras. BGS evaluates existing frames by subtracting it from a modeled or reference frame and updating the

FIGURE 18.1
Moving object detection from video frames.

modeled background on runtime to get better outcomes without false alarms. Basically, this technique aims to distinguish each and every pixel of a frame as either a BG pixel or an FG pixel [9, 10]. The most common challenging issues in BGS are the recognition and correct classification of nonstatic objects inside a frame from the static ones [8, 9, 11–14]. Such backgrounds are known as dynamic backgrounds and various BGS techniques have been developed to resolve these dynamic BG problems in both indoor and outdoor video sequences as shown in Figure 18.1 [15–32].

This chapter consists of seven sections. The first section deals with the introductory part. In Section 18.2, steps of basic background techniques are discussed. Section 18.3 presents brief information about various background subtraction techniques. In Section 18.4, several open challenges handled by several researchers to date are discussed. Section 18.5 provides details of some existing data sets available in literature with the number of video sequences provided. In Section 18.6, qualitative and quantitative outcomes of several existing data sets are discussed. In the last section, an overall summary of the paper is provided.

18.2 Background Subtraction Technique

BGS is a very crucial step in visual surveillance as it is first applied to detect the object without any a prior information. It deals with the detection of instances of nonstatic objects of several groups such as people, animals, insects, or automobiles before operating the complex process for tracking, counting of people, vehicle detection, and tracking [8, 9, 33, 34]. This technique has three phases:

1. **Initialization of Background:** The main aim is to build a BG model using a fixed number of frames. Haque [2, 35] takes an initial 50 frames to model the BG, whereas Sharma et al. [8, 34] take an initial 200 frames for background modeling depending upon the total number of frames in a frame sequence. This model can be designed by several methods such as averaging, mean, median, mode, fuzzy, neuro inspired, and many more.

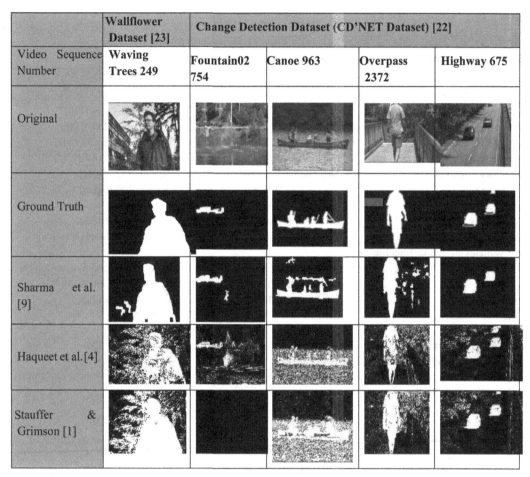

	Wallflower Dataset [23]	Change Detection Dataset (CD'NET Dataset) [22]			
Video Sequence Number	Waving Trees 249	Fountain02 754	Canoe 963	Overpass 2372	Highway 675
Original					
Ground Truth					
Sharma et al. [9]					
Haqueet et al. [4]					
Stauffer & Grimson [1]					

FIGURE 18.2
Performance analysis of considered BGS techniques.

2. **Background Detection:** In the next frame, a comparison between the existing or current frame with the background model frame is done [1, 8, 10, 36]. This process of subtraction leads to computation of the FG mask as shown in Figure 18.2.

3. **Background Maintenance** In this phase, after detection of the FG mask, the background model is updated at runtime by updating the learning rate, because the background is nonstatic, dynamic, and keeps on changing [10, 34, 37].

According to Bouwmans [38], in order to develop a BGS technique, researchers must design each step and select the important features with relation to the challenging issues they want to tackle in the particular applications. In this section, real-time challenging issues of visual surveillance of human detection and tracking are reviewed as shown in Table 18.1. The main goal of the BGS technique is to detect human-based activities in visual surveillance. Road surveillance requires detection of moving vehicles for counting the total number of vehicles crossing a particular road in a given interval of time, congestion

TABLE 18.1

Human-Based Activities in Visual Surveillance

Subcategories-Aims	Objects of Interest-Scenes	Authors-Dates
1) Road Surveillance	**1-Car**	
1.1) Vehicles Detection		
Vehicles Detection	Road Traffic	Zheng et al. (2006)[40]
Vehicles Detection	Urban Traffic (Korea)	Hwang et al. (2009)[41]
Vehicles Detection	Highways Traffic (ATON Project)	Wang and Song (2011)[42]
Vehicles Detection	CDNet data set 2012[40]	Hadi et al. (2014)[43]
Vehicles Detection	CDNet data set 2012[40]	Aqel et al. (2015)[44]
Vehicles Detection	CDNet data set 2012[40]	Aqel et al. (2016)[45]
Vehicles Detection	CDNet data set 2012[40]	Wang et al. (2016)[46]
Vehicles Detection	Urban Traffic (China)	Zhang et al. (2016)[47]
Vehicles Detection	CCTV cameras (India)	Hargude and Idate (2016)[48]
1.2) Vehicles Detection/Tracking		
Vehicles Detection/Tracking	Highways Traffic (India)	Sawalakhe and Metkar (2015)[49]
Vehicles Detection/Tracking	Highways Traffic (India)	Dey and Praveen (2016)[50]
Multi-Vehicles	CDNet data set 2012[40]	Hadi et al. (2016)[51]
Detection/Tracking	NYCDOT video/NGSIM US-101	Li et al. (2016)[52]
Vehicles Tracking	highway data set (USA)	
1.3) Vehicles Counting		
Vehicles Detection/Counting	Road (Portugal)	Toropov et al. (2015)[53]
Vehicles Counting	Lankershim Boulevard data set (USA)	Quesada and Rodriguez (2016)[54]
1.4) Congestion Detection		
	1-Car	
Congestion Detection	Aerial Videos	Lin et al. (2009)[55]
Free-Flow/Congestion Detection	Urban Traffic (India)	Muniruzzaman et al. (2016)[56]
	3-Pedestrians	
Pedestrian Abnormal Behavior	Public Roads (China)	Jiang et al. (2015)[57]

control, theft detection, road accidents, and many more as shown in Table 18.1. In order to achieve this goal, detection is also based on location and quality of camera. The videos in traffic surveillance can be classified as: (1) captured from a static camera at a high altitude, and (2) aerial surveillance having very high-resolution satellite images (Teutsch et al. [39]) Generally, cameras work with only 1 or 2 frames per second and a resolution of pixels at 100 per frame to decrease the cost and hard disk drive (HDD) storage. A low-quality camera can only generate information up to 1 GB to 10 GB per day.

18.3 Background Models for Object Detection

In literature, most of the authors used the BGS technique to model the background. This section provides a detailed description about the several problematic issues handled by various researchers until now [9, 11, 34]. This section also provides details about the color

TABLE 18.2

Parameters and Suitable Application for Visual Surveillance

Author	Color Channel	Camera Position	External Parameter Used	Major Challenges	Suitable Scenarios	BG Model
Stauffer et. al [1]	RGB	Static	μ, ω, α, T	Changes in BG	Outdoor	Gaussian
Zhou [58]	Ycbcr	Moving airborne camera	Φ, T, K	Changes in BG that lead to false alarm	Outdoor	BG subtraction
Haque et. al [35]	Gray	Static	σ, α, ω, μ, S	Gradual intensity change in BG	Indoor, Outdoor	GMM model
Haque et. al [2]	Gray	Static	σ, T	Sudden illumination change in BG	Remote surveillance System	Multimodal (Gaussian)
Oliver et. al [3]	Gray	Static	R, N, φ, #	Both indoor and outdoor	ViBe	Universal BG SubtractionTechnique
Yadav et. al [7]	Gray	Static	α, ω, T	Both indoor and outdoor	Indoor and Outdoor	BG subtraction
Yadav et. al [33]	Gray	Static	α, ω, T	Noise, outlier, and BG variations	Indoor and Outdoor	*Kullback*–Leibler divergence (KLD) based
Sharma et. al [8]	Gray	Static	α, t	Complex BG and illumination variation	Indoor and Outdoor	*Fisher's linear discriminant* (FLD)
Sharma et. al [9]	Gray	Static	α, ω, Th	Dynamic BG and illumination variation	Indoor and Outdoor	Gaussian mixture-based model and BGS technique
Sharma et. al [11]	Gray	Static	α, ω, Th	Dynamic BG and illumination variation	Indoor and Outdoor	Histogram model and BGS technique

channel with camera position either moving or static, parameters used, suitable applications, and model used by the authors for experimental analysis in FG detection as given in Table 18.2.

18.4 Real-Time Challenges

The concept behind all the real-time applications is the moving object detection on static or moving cameras. This section deals with various challenging issues explored on the basis of a nonstatic environment of a BG scene that often leads to false detection of a BG object as a foreground object. Some of the important problematic issues are discussed here:

- **Dynamic BG:** In real-time applications, a BG is not always simple; it is sometimes so complex that it becomes very difficult to distinguish an FG pixel or BG pixel and often leads to false classification due to a waving movement of leaves, a non-clear sky, and many more [2, 11, 33, 36].

- **Bootstrapping:** During the training phase of BG modeling, BG is sometimes absent, which leads to difficulty in computation of an illustrative BG [3, 10].

- **Intensity Variation:** Sometimes, there can be slow or gradual changes in the BG sequences that can lead intensity changes that often lead to misclassification of BG or FG pixels [7, 8, 10, 11].

- **Rippling of water, leaves, and cloudy skies:** Due to rippling of water, cloudy skies, or slow leafy movement, a BG sequence can be considered as a foreground and lead to misclassification of pixels as foreground or BG [10, 59].

- **Shadowing:** This is an active and immense area. The shadowing appearance with a motion-based object in computer vision often leads to depletion of reliability of tracking and detecting of an object [3, 60].

- **Inserted BG object:** In some cases, a new BG object is inserted in the video sequence, then this inserted object cannot be classified as an FG object due to absence of effective maintenance method [3, 10].

18.5 Resources and Data Sets Used

In literature, several resources and data sets are available to detect and track a motion-based object from a video sequence. These data sets provide real-time indoor and outdoor frame sequences with several problematic issues such as intensity variations, dynamic BG, shadowing, camera jitter, bootstrapping, and many more with their ground-truth images. Some of the data sets with a number of video sequences are listed in Table.18.3.

18.6 Experimental Evaluation of Considered BGS Techniques

In this section, both qualitative and quantitative analysis of considered BGS techniques are discussed [1, 2, 8] of literature. This work is implemented on MATLAB tool 2011b with 8 GB RAM. Experimental Evaluation is done on video sequences from two different data sets on the Wallflower data set [62] and CDNet data set [61] as shown in Figure 18.2.

The system performance of three methods on five video sequences from Wallflower [62] and CDNet [61] data sets are evaluated in terms of various performance metrics as shown in Table 18.4. where Tp is number of pixel's detected truly positive, Fp is falsely positive pixels, and Fn is falsely negative detected pixels.

TABLE 18.3

Data Set and Challenges for Visual Surveillance

Data Sets	Major Challenging Issues	Number of Video Sequences
Change Detection [61] Data Set	Camera Jitter, nondistinguishable BG, irregular motion of object, shadowing. (http://changedetection.net/)	31
Microsoft's Wallflowert[62]	Dynamic or complex BG, intensity variation, camouflage, foreground aperture, sudden or gradual changes (light switch on/off), bootstrap.	7
IBM[63]	Indoor and outdoor sequences from PET 2001. (http://www.research.ibm.com/peoplevision/performanceevaluation.html)	15
VSSN 2006 [59]	Animated BG, illumination changes and shadows. (http://mmc36.informatik.uni-augsburg.de/VSSN06 OSAC).	9 semi-synthetic videos
ETISEO [64]	Shadowing with same, different, and different illumination level (http://www-sop.inria.fr/orion/ETISEO)	80
CAVIAR [37]	Resolution problem (http://homepages.inf.ed.ac.uk/rbf/CAVIARDATA1)	80 staged indoor videos

TABLE 18.4

Quantitative Analysis Results of Considered BGS Techniques

Method	Precision	Recall	F-Measure	TPR	FPR	Accuracy	T_Error
Sharma et.al. [8]	0.8481	0.9209	0.8724	0.9210	0.0159	0.9835	1.5009
Haque et.al. [35]	0.3485	0.7971	0.4630	0.7967	0.1370	0.8656	8.7106
Stauffer and Grimsom [1]	0.3413	0.8280	0.4586	0.8284	0.1801	0.8457	10.0657

$$\text{Precision } (P) = Tp/(Tp + Fp) \tag{18.1}$$

$$\text{Recall } (R) = Tp/(Tp + Fn) \tag{18.2}$$

$$F\text{-Measure } (F\,1 - score) = 2 * (P * R)/(P + R) \tag{18.3}$$

$$F\,P_{Error} = FP * 100/rows * col \tag{18.4}$$

$$FN_{Error} = FN * 100/rows * col \tag{18.5}$$

$$T\_Error = F\,P_{Err} + FN_{Err} \tag{18.6}$$

It is clearly depicted from Table 18.4 that Sharma et al. [8] has less number of total errors as compared to the others and has better overall performance than other state-of-the-art methods. This leads to the conclusion that this method can handle the dynamic BG and intensity variation problem.

18.7 Conclusion

This chapter summarized several BGS techniques used for motion-based object detection in real-time applications. Some of the most commonly used BG techniques, various challenging or problematic issues, resources, and data sets with a number of video sequences provided for performance evaluation with their ground-truth images are discussed in this paper. This chapter also presented a comparative analysis of some considered work from literature. In the future, we will perform comparative analysis on various data sets with their challenging issues using cloud computing and Internet of Things (IoT).

References

1. Stauffer, C., Grimson, W.E.L.: Adaptive background mixture models for real-time tracking, *IEEE Computer Society Conf. on Computer Vision and Pattern Recognition*, June, pp. 246–252 (1999).
2. Haque, M., Murshed, M., Paul, M.: Improved Gaussian mixtures for robust Object Detection by adaptive multi-background generation, *19th International Conference on Pattern Recognition, IEEE*, pp. 8–11 (2008).
3. Barnich, O., Droogenbroeck, M.V.: Vibe: A universal background subtraction algorithm for video sequences. *IEEE Transactions on Image processing*, vol. 20, no. 6, pp. 1709–1724 (2011).
4. Kent, P., Maskell, S., Payne, O., Richardson, S., Scarff, L. Robust background subtraction for automated detection and tracking of targets in wide area motion imagery. *SPIE Security+ Defence*, pp. 85460Q–85460Q (2012).
5. Yadav, D.K., Singh, K.: Moving object detection for visual surveillance using Quasi-Euclidian distance. *IC3T-2015, LNCS, Advances in Intelligent Systems and Computing Series.* Springer, September, Vol. 381, pp. 225–233 (2015).
6. FatihSavaş, M. et.al.: Object detection using an adaptive background subtraction method based on block-based structure in dynamic scene. *Optik.* Elesvier, Vol. 168, September 2018, pp. 605–618 (2018).
7. Yadav, D.K, Sharma, L., Bharti, S.: Moving object detection in real-time visual surveillance using background subtraction technique. *IEEE, 14th International Conference in Hybrid Intelligent Computing (HIS-2014)*, Gulf University for Science and Technology, Kuwait, pp. 79–84 (2014).
8. Sharma, L., Yadav, D.K, Bharti, S.: An Improved Method for Visual Surveillance using Background Subtraction Technique. *IEEE, 2nd International Conference on Signal Processing and Integrated Networks (SPIN-2015)*, Amity Univ. Noida, India, pp. 421–426 (2015).
9. Sharma, L., Singh S., Yadav, D.K.: Fisher's linear discriminant ratio based threshold for moving human detection in thermal video. *Infrared Physics and Technology.* Elsevier, Vol. 78, pp. 118–128 (2016).
10. Sharma, L., Lohan, N.: Performance analysis of moving object detection using BGS techniques in visual surveillance. *International Journal of Spatio-Temporal Data Science, Inderscience*, vol. 1 no. 1, pp. 22–53 (2019).
11. Sharma, L., Yadav, D.K.: Histogram based adaptive learning rate for background modelling and moving object detection in video surveillance. *International Journal of Telemedicine and Clinical Practices, Inderscience*, vol. 2 no. 1, pp. 74–92 (2017).
12. Sengupta, S., Mittal, N.: Analysis of various techniques of feature extraction on skin lesion images, *Proceedings of 2017 6th International Conference on Reliability, Infocom Technologies and Optimization (Trends and Future Directions) (ICRITO)*, Noida, India, pp. 651–656 (2017).
13. Sen Gupta, S., Khan, M. S., Sethi, T.: Latest Trends in Security, Privacy and Trust in IOT, *2019 3rd International conference on Electronics, Communication and Aerospace Technology (ICECA)*, Coimbatore, India, pp. 382–385 (2019).
14. Sengupta, S.: A study of Bluetooth smart for medical application, *2015 4th International Conference on Reliability, Infocom Technologies and Optimization (ICRITO) (Trends and Future Directions)*, Noida, India, pp. 1–3 (2015).
15. UK Home Office. Data Set. Available at: http://www.homeoffice.gov.uk/science-research/hosdb/i-lids [accessed on Dec. 12, 2019].

16. Sharma, L., Garg, P. (Eds.): *From Visual Surveillance to Internet of Things*. Chapman and Hall/CRC, New York, NY (2019), https://doi.org/10.1201/9780429297922.

17. Sharma, L., Lohan, N.: Performance analysis of moving object detection using BGS techniques in visual surveillance. *International Journal of Spatiotemporal Data Science, Inderscience*, vol. 1, pp. 22–53 (January 2019).

18. Kumar, A., Jha, G., Sharma, L.: Challenges, potential & future of IOT integrated with block chain. *International Journal of Recent Technology and Engineering*, vol. 8, no. 2S7, pp. 530–536 (July 2019).

19. Liu, Y., Hou, R.: About the sensing layer in Internet of things [J]. *Computer Study*, vol. 5, p. 55 (2010).

20. Anand, A., Jha, V., Sharma, L.: An improved local binary patterns histograms techniques for face recognition for real time application. In *International Journal of Recent Technology and Engineering*, vol. 8, no. 2S7, pp. 524–529 (July 2019).

21. Sharma, L., Yadav, D. K.: Histogram based adaptive learning rate for background modelling and moving object detection in video surveillance. *International Journal of Telemedicine and Clinical Practices, Inderscience*, (June, 2016). DOI: 10.1504/IJTMCP.2017.082107.

22. Sharma, L., Lohan, N.: Performance analysis of moving object detection using BGS techniques. *International Journal of Spatio-Temporal Data Science, Inderscience*, (February, 2019).

23. Sharma, S., Verma, S., Kumar, M., Sharma, L.: Use of Motion Capture in 3D Animation: Motion Capture Systems, Challenges, and Recent Trends, in *1st IEEE International Conference on Machine Learning, Big Data, Cloud and Parallel Computing (Com-IT-Con)*, India, pp. 309–313, (14–16 Feb., 2019).

24. Sharma, L., Lohan, N.: Internet of things with object detection. In *Handbook of Research on Big Data and the IoT*. IGI Global, pp. 89–100 (March, 2019). DOI: 10.4018/978-1-5225-7432-3.ch006.

25. Sharma, L.: Introduction: From visual surveillance to Internet of things. *From Visual Surveillance to Internet of Things*. Chapman Hall/CRC, New York, NY, Vol. 1, p. 14 (2019).

26. Sharma, L., Garg, P. K.: Block based adaptive learning rate for moving person detection in video surveillance. *From Visual Surveillance to Internet of Things*. Chapman Hall/CRC, New York, NY, Vol. 1, p. 201 (2019).

27. Sharma, L., Garg, P. K.: Smart E-healthcare with Internet of things: Current trends challenges, solutions and technologies. *From Visual Surveillance to Internet of Things*. Chapman Hall/CRC, New York, NY, Vol. 1, p. 215 (2019).

28. Sharma, L., Garg, P. K., Agarwal, N.: A foresight on e-healthcare Trailblazers. *From Visual Surveillance to Internet of Things*. Chapman Hall/CRC, New York, NY, Vol. 1, pp. 235 (2019).

29. Makkar, S., Sharma, L.: A face detection using support vector machine: Challenging issues, recent trend, solutions and proposed framework. In: *Third International Conference on Advances in Computing and Data Sciences (ICACDS 2019, Springer)*. Inderprastha Engineering College, Ghaziabad, pp. 12–13 (April 2019).

30. Sharma, L., Garg, P. K.: Future of Internet of things. *From Visual Surveillance to Internet of Things*. Chapman Hall/CRC, New York, NY, Vol.1, p. 245 (2019).

31. Sharma, L., Garg, P. K.: IoT and its applications. *From Visual Surveillance to Internet of Things*. Chapman Hall/CRC, New York, NY, Vol. 1, p. 29 (2019).

32. Jha, G., Singh, P., Sharma, L.: Recent advancements of augmented reality in real time applications. In *International Journal of Recent Technology and Engineering*, vol. 8, no. 2S7, pp. 538–542 (July 2019).

33. Yadav, D.K., Singh, K.: A combined approach of Kullback-Leibler divergence method and background subtraction for moving object detection in thermal video. *Infrared Physics and Technology*. Elsevier, Vol. 76, pp. 21–31 (2015), 23, December 2017.

34. Sharma, L., Lohan, N.: Performance enhancement through handling of false classification in video surveillance. *Journal of Pure and applied Science & Technology*, vol. 7, no. 2, pp. 9–17 (July, 2017).

35. Haque, M., Murshed, M., Paul, M.: On stable dynamic background generation technique using Gaussian mixture models for robust object detection, *5th International Conference on Advanced Video and Signal Based Surveillance, IEEE*, September, pp. 41–48(2008).

36. Sheikh, Y., Javed, O., Kanade, T.: "Background subtraction for freely moving cameras, *IEEE 12th International Conference on Computer Vision*, pp. 1219–1225 (2009).

37. CAVIAR Data Set. Available at: http://homepages.inf.ed.ac.uk/rbf/CAVIARDATA1 [accessed on Jan. 16, 2019]

38. Bouwmans, T.: Traditional and recent approaches in background modeling for foreground detection: An overview. *Computer Science Review*, vol. 11, pp. 31–66 (May, 2014).

39. Sharma, L., Singh, A., Yadav, D. K.: Fisher's linear discriminant ratio based threshold for moving human detection in thermal video. *Infrared Physics and Technology*, Elsevier, vol. 78, pp. 118–128 (March, 2016).

40. Zheng, J., Wang, Y., Nihan, N., Hallenbeck, E.: Extracting roadway background image: A mode based approach. *Transportation Research Report*, pp. 82–88 (2006).

41. Hwang, P., Eom, K., Jung, J., Kim, M.: A statistical approach to robust background subtraction for urban traffic video. *International Workshop on Computer Science and Engineering*, pp. 177–181 (2009).

42. Wang, C., Song, Z.: Vehicle detection based on spatial-temporal connection background subtraction. *IEEE ICIA*, pp. 320–323 (2011).

43. Hadi, R., Sulong, G., George, L.: An innovative vehicle detection approach based on background subtraction and morphological binary methods. *Life Science Journal*, pp. 230–238 (2014).

44. Aqel, S., Sabri, M., Aarab, A.: Background modeling algorithm based on transitions intensities. *IRECOS 2015*, vol. 10, no. 4, (2015).

45. Aqel, S., Aarab, A., Sabri, M.: Traffic video surveillance: Background modeling and shadow elimination. IT4OD 2016, pp. 1–6 (2016).

46. Wang, K., Liu, Y., Gou, C., Wang, F.: A multi-view learning approach to foreground detection for traffic surveillance applications. IEEE T-VT, (2015).

47. Zhang, Y., Zhao, C., He, J., Chen, A.: Vehicles detection in complex urban traffic scenes using Gaussian mixture model with confidence measurement. IET ITS, (2016).

48. Hargude, S., Idate, S.: i-surveillance: Intelligent surveillance system using background subtraction technique. ICCUBEA 2016, pp. 1–5 (2016).

49. Sawalakhe, S., Metkar, S.: Foreground background traffic scene modeling for object motion detection. IEEE India Conference, INDICON 2014, pp. 1–6 (2014).

50. Dey, J., Praveen, N.: Moving object detection using genetic algorithm for traffic surveillance. ICEEOT 2016, pp. 2289–2293 (2016).

51. Hadi, R., George, L., Mohammed, M.: A computationally economic novel approach for real-time moving multi-vehicle detection and tracking toward efficient traffic surveillance. *Arabian Journal for Science and Engineering*, vol. 42, no. 2, pp. 817–831 (February, 2017).

52. Li, C., Chiang, A., Dobler, G., Wang, Y., Xie, K., Ozbay, K., Wang, D.: Robust vehicle tracking for urban traffic videos at intersections. IEEE AVSS 2016, (2016).

53. Toropov, E., Gui, L., Zhang, S., Kottur, S., Moura, J.: Traffic flow from a low -frame rate city camera. IEEE ICIP 2015, (2015).

54. Quesada, J., Rodriguez, P.: Automatic vehicle counting method based on principal component pursuit background modeling. IEEE ICIP 2016, (2016).

55. Lin, R., Cao, X., Xu, Y., Wu, C., Qiao, H.: Airborne moving vehicle detection for video surveillance of urban traffic. IEEE IVS 2009, pp. 203–208 (2009).

56. Muniruzzaman, S., Haque, N., Rahman, F., Siam, M., Musabbir, R., Hossain, S.: Deterministic algorithm for traffic detection in free-flow and congestion using video sensor, *Journal of Built Environment, Technology and Engineering*, vol. 1, (September. 2016) ISSN: 0128-1003.

57. Jiang, Q., Li, G., Yu, J., Li, X.: A model based method for pedestrian abnormal behavior detection in traffic scene. IEEE ISC2 2015, pp. 1–6 (2015).

58. Zhou, Y., Maskell, S.: Moving object detection using background subtraction for a moving camera with pronounced parallax. *IEEE Conference on Sensor Data Fusion: Trends, Solutions, Applications (SDF)*, Germany (2017).

59. IBM Data Set. Available at: http://www.research.ibm.com/peoplevision/performanceevaluation.html [accessed on Jan. 26, 2019]

60. Sharma, R. et.al.: Optimized dynamic background subtraction technique for moving object detection and tracking. *2017 2nd International Conference on Telecommunication and Networks (TEL-NET), IEEE*, pp. 1–3 (2017).

61. Changedetection.net. A New Change Detection Benchmark Data Set. Available from: https://www.researchgate.net/publication/232905474_changedetectionnet_A_New_Change_Detection_Benchmark_Dataset [accessed Jan. 26, 2019].

62. Toyama, K., Krumm, J., Brumitt, B., Meyers, B., Wallflower: Principles and practice of background maintenance. *Proc. IEEE Int. Conf. Computer Vision*, vol. 1, pp. 255–261 (1999).

63. VSSN Data Set. Available at: http://mmc36.informatik.uni-augsburg.de/VSSN06/OSAC [accessed on Jan. 26, 2019]

64. ETISEO Data Set. Available at: http://www-sop.inria.fr/orion/ETISEO [accessed on Jan. 26, 2019]

19

The Future of Smart Cities

Lavanya Sharma

Amity Institute of Information Technology, Amity University
Noida, India

Mukesh Carpenter

Department of Surgery, Alshifa Hospital
New Delhi, India

CONTENTS

19.1   Introduction 330
19.2   Technologies for a Smart and Innovative City 330
    19.2.1   Hybrid Energy Systems 330
    19.2.2   Multimodal Transport Systems 331
    19.2.3   Interoperable Software Platforms 331
19.3   Global Perspective for Smart Cities: Digital India 331
    19.3.1   Electronic Vehicles...332
    19.3.2   Agro-Tech and Warehouses 332
    19.3.3   Technology-Based Traffic Management 332
    19.3.4   Swachh Bharat Mission...332
19.4   Digital Innovation in the United States and Canada..............................333
    19.4.1   Data-Driven Communal Safety 333
    19.4.2   Resilient Energy and Infrastructure 333
    19.4.3   Intelligent Transportation System 333
    19.4.4   Multiple Categories...333
19.5   Smart Cities: Acceleration, Technology, Cases, and Evolutions............334
    19.5.1   Smart City Projects Ranking in IoT Deployments 334
    19.5.2   Real-Time Smart City Challenges..335
    19.5.3   Smart City and Technology Choices..335
    19.5.4   Smart City Applications: Broader Perspectives.........................336
19.6   Case Study: Role and Economy of Smart City Barcelona 336
    19.6.1   Street Lights..337
    19.6.2   Waste Disposal 337
    19.6.3   Bike System 337
    19.6.4   Bus Transit System 337
    19.6.5   Noise Sensors 337
    19.6.6   Irrigation System..337
    19.6.7   Fab Labs...338
19.7   Conclusion 338
References...338

KEYWORDS: *smart city, IoT, ICT, economy, transportation, healthcare, electronic vehicle, automated control systems, automated vertical farm, vehicle to everything, digital twins, public safety wearables, intelligent traffic management, water quality monitoring*

19.1 Introduction

According to a recent report provided by the United Nations, every week about 1.3 million residents are moving to cities and with this, urban populations will grow rapidly to 6.3 billion people by the end of 2050 [1–2]. Smart cities are using data that is collected from people, automobiles, and buildings from all over the globe to improve daily life and also minimize the environmental effect of the city itself by constantly sharing the data with itself to maximize efficiency [1–5]. These cities are fully connected, sustainable, and energy efficient and use their infrastructures to intelligently improve the way of living. Some of the key elements of these cities include:

- **Ubiquitous Wi-Fi:** Wireless internet facilities can be available to all nodes of the city.
- **Electric Vehicle Charging:** Charging station networks can be available within the city that support the development of electric vehicles
- **Connected Vehicle Infrastructure:** An infrastructure that provides full communication of vehicles with each other to prevent accidents.
- **Smart, Sustainable Electricity and Street Lightening:** Sharing of information also results in conserving energy resources and automatic lighting based on vehicles or residents also results in saving energy.
- **Smart Parking:** A lot of time is wasted in search for parking. By using smart sensor-based parking, time consumption gets reduced and also results in smooth traffic control.
- **Smart Water Management Systems:** Excess water flow detection or leak detection of water results in water storage management.
- **Wildfire Cameras:** The use of static and dynamic cameras can help in better surveillance systems to detect and track people or wildlife.

19.2 Technologies for a Smart and Innovative City

In today's scenario, cities are facing various challenging issues and because cities are basically communal and politically aware entities, communal or social issues are always at peak on the agenda for the residents and governing authorities that manage them. Therefore, it's about establishing the factual circumstances for a prosperous economy, one that produces and protects occupations and promotes communal equality in an era of digital transformation [2, 6–8].

19.2.1 Hybrid Energy Systems

Hybrid energy systems is where the production, storage, and consumption of renewable energy can flow "freely" between buildings, power grids, heat networks, and consumers.

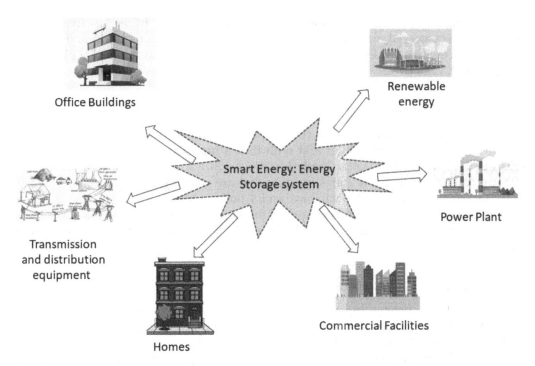

FIGURE 19.1
Hybrid energy system.

Ideally, this takes place through economic incentive schemes, such as tenant electricity models, which allow users to be both consumers and producers (Figure 19.1) [9–14].

19.2.2 Multimodal Transport Systems

Multimodal transport systems are largely based on power from renewables. These require not only conventional public transport systems, electric vehicles, and charging technologies, but also booking, routing, and information systems that make public mobility more appealing to users—thus helping make the private car obsolete for city travel [9, 10, 15, 16].

19.2.3 Interoperable Software Platforms

Interoperable software platforms are where all kinds of data can be combined, analyzed, and processed with the aim of improving urban services or launching new ones.

19.3 Global Perspective for Smart Cities: Digital India

India is becoming a progressively digitized country and sales of smart devices including smartphones are steeply rising. Some open challenges are still present like internet facilities and delivery of online-based shopping takes some time to deliver, pollution levels are increasing day by day, and traffic is also increasing rapidly. In the last five years, a new focus has emerged among central government related to automation and robotics for social places. This has led to experimentations with robotics in communal places and emergency services [17–20].

19.3.1 Electronic Vehicles

India is a developing country that is fully dependent on hydrocarbon deposits like petrol and diesel to fuel automobiles and with this, a high level of pollution is rising in urban cities. Maharashtra, Uttar Pradesh (UP), Andhra Pradesh (AP), Karnataka, and Goa are among the first few states in India that are working toward electric vehicles (EVs). Telangana is the fourth one to have an EV policy. Outside India, Bolivia is helping India to procure the lithium that is required for batteries. Surat is one of the major hubs for textiles and diamonds, and Gujarat has been declared as the first smart city in India [10, 15, 16, 21].

19.3.2 Agro-Tech and Warehouses

Testing of delivery drones and robots are collecting pace beyond the repository gateways. Automated control systems (ACS) are observing, managing, and optimizing traffic movements. In India, a suddenly prolific e-commerce culture has made it critical for the ITS and logistics industry to get artifacts right with immediate effect. An automated vertical farm (AVF) plays an important role in production of food in non-agricultural parts across the globe. The pillars of flyovers in India have vertical gardens to improve the city air. Advanced mobile health applications are also playing a significant role for the patient "beyond the hospital." Robots in social, restricted, and commercial places include police officers, defense, healthcare workers, organization staff, and restaurant waiters [9, 10, 15, 16, 18, 19]. The robot "Mitra" is the beginning of the robotics world.

19.3.3 Technology-Based Traffic Management

In terms of traffic, India is facing many traffic jam situations such as if two cars coming from the opposite side lead to a blockage of a complete lane. Self-driven cars with embedded sensors can outperform human drivers in seeing what surrounds them. Drones also help in security measures by monitoring and sensing traffic flow and can provide us with a world where ambulances will have free movement each time. Availability of Metros in cities is also one big revolution in urban cities for safe transportation such as the Delhi Metro Rail Corporation (DMRC) who are extending their routes to several interstate levels without leaving any carbon footprint. Electric cars will be upcoming in the future in India with proper policies [7, 8, 15, 16, 21–29].

19.3.4 Swachh Bharat Mission

This mission was launched by the Indian government in order to build a culture of responsible waste management that results in automated leftover or waste elimination. In smart cities, self-driving trash pick-up trucks can pick up the waste discharged or unmanageable trash from streets, lane sides, rivers, lakes, or industries. Startups related to waste disposal are already launched in India to make cities cleaner and pollution free. IMAGINE governance (IG) can access data to track the bin cycle and make this more efficient and more economical [18, 19, 30].

19.4 Digital Innovation in the United States and Canada

The United States and Canada are among leading technology innovators. According to IDC technologies, the North American region is projected to reach 32% of global smart cities' ICT spend by 2023. Some of the smart cities' fastest growing projects are Vehicle to Everything (V2X), Digital Twins, Public Safety wearables, Intelligent Traffic Management (ITM), and Water Quality Monitoring (WQM) [17, 31–35].

19.4.1 Data-Driven Communal Safety

Chicago's police department deployed a real-time crime center that leveraged gunshot detection data from "ShotSpotter" that detected more than 90% of gunfire events with a particular location within 60 seconds and a visual surveillance system to help officials to identify illegal activities more quickly. Since this deployment, there has been a sharp reduction by 40% in homicides and shootings.

19.4.2 Resilient Energy and Infrastructure

The city of New York is a leading smart city for various reasons such as smart monitoring of the city helps in managing resources more effectively and also results in financial savings. Automated Meter Reading (AMR) units provide accurate data on actual water consumption and also send warning or emergency messages related to leakage or non-payment of bills. Earlier leakage water detection has saved this city more than $73 million. WQM also sends an alert for quality issues if any are detected and protects residents from polluted water [3, 4, 31–36].

19.4.3 Intelligent Transportation System

The city of Pittsburgh, Pennsylvania, implemented a network of smart traffic lights for blocking or jamming reduction. Traffic is logged in time-sequenced groups of automobiles and artificial intelligence algorithms use that data to build a time plan that will pass all the transport via intersections in an efficient manner. Each light communicates with data it collected to adjacent lights and enables the system to adapt sequencing to minimize traffic buildup. This city estimates that intersection wait times have dropped by 41%, journey times by 26%, and emissions by 21% [1, 2, 9–20, 23–35, 37–40].

19.4.4 Multiple Categories

In Canada, Toronto is one of the fastest growing cities and has partnered with Alphabet's Sidewalk Labs to turn its seafront area into a high-tech-based smart city. This city plan includes involvement of robotics such as self-driven cars, heated cycle lanes, waste removal, roadside walks, and free Wi-Fi. Sensors gather all the information related to energy consumption, usage of buildings, and traffic flow for further analysis [18–20, 30].

19.5 Smart Cities: Acceleration, Technology, Cases, and Evolutions

By the end of 2019, about 40% of local and regional governments used IoT for infrastructure such as streetlights, traffic signals, and roads. Some of the important ongoing projects for cities that have already have been started in terms of "environment" include air quality monitoring to fight pollution in the city of Glasgow, UK, and a "smart flood alert context," an open source flood sensor network in the UK [2, 17, 31–35, 37, 38].

19.5.1 Smart City Projects Ranking in IoT Deployments

For smart cities, use cases include smart parking, smart traffic management, smart waste management, and smart street lighting. Sometimes, these use cases combine a combination of enhanced efficiency, urban problem solving, reduced cost, improved living standards in urban areas, and placing residents first for several reasons. In order to make a city smarter, the city should have an integrated approach where several projects are connected. Both information and platforms are combined together to get the complete benefits a smart city can make possible [2, 17, 31–35, 37, 38].

"Open technologies" and "open data platforms" are important keys to move forward to the next level. From the point of a global share of IoT analytics, smart city projects lie at the second IoT segment. According to IDC, "open data platforms" will appear as the next frontier in IoT platforms by the end of 2018. Germany-based IoT Analytics announced a report where 640 actual, real-life IoT projects are already existing and smart city projects are at the second segment and connected cities at the topmost segment as shown in Figure 19.2. In case of smart city IoT projects, the most popular applications are city safety, smart traffic, followed by smart utilities [17, 31].

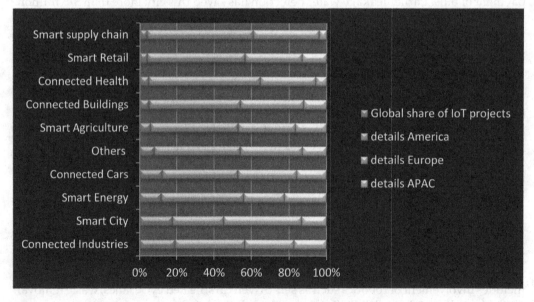

FIGURE 19.2
IoT segments with current IoT projects (IoT Analytics report) [34].

19.5.2 Real-Time Smart City Challenges

Smart cities have a more visionary approach. Presently, various smart city projects have been completed and new ones are being deployed, but it will take several more years to call a city really smart. In order to have a real smart city, there is a lot of work to be done in the future across various activities, assets, and infrastructure that can be turned into a smart version. Funding is one of the important aspects for cities for its smart city transformation. Other important aspects include a lot of legacy, new skills, and regulations. There is lots of alignment to do on various segments including city administration, transportation, local and central government agencies, education services, and many more as shown in Figure 19.3. In order to make a current ad hoc smart project more integrated in future, a roadmap should be based on expertise to learn from potential failures. Another open challenge is attitude and willingness to modify the things for the betterment of residents and the community. Financing of smart city initiatives is one of various additional stumbling blocks [32].

19.5.3 Smart City and Technology Choices

Smart city deployment selection needs to be prepared for scaling or integration purposes of a smart city and if required it can be replaced with advanced technologies such as IoT. Presently, IoT technology is comparatively easy and cost-effective as compared to other technologies for various use cases such as smart parking, smart traffic control, smart waste, and smart water management. Generally, urban ecosystems have good non-wired coverage for moving objects and tracking, cloud technology, and other related products designed especially for smart city projects. Even in several cities there is a low-power wide-area network (LPWAN) connectivity available that is sufficient for

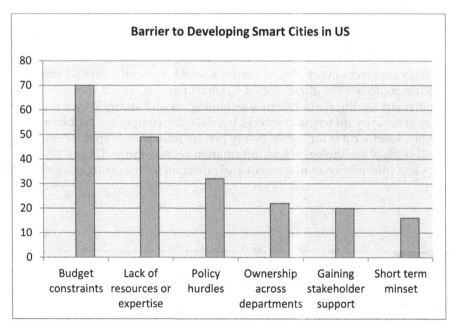

FIGURE 19.3
Barriers to developing smarter cities in the United States.

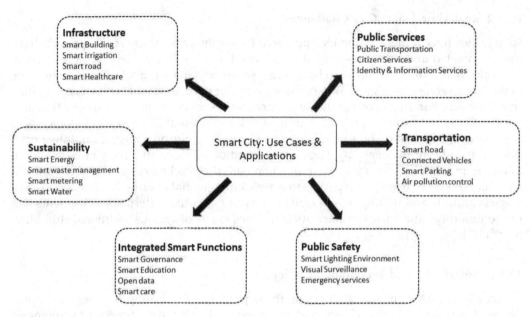

FIGURE 19.4
Smart city use cases and applications.

various real-time applications [3–8, 17, 22, 31–36, 41]. According to IoT Analytics, 59% of all LPWAN projects today are part of smart city initiatives as shown in Figure 19.4. Choices regarding network connectivity, data exchange, and IoT platforms evolve when moving to real scenarios.

19.5.4 Smart City Applications: Broader Perspectives

IoT technology is present everywhere in today's world. Presently, various smart city projects are going on across the globe related to smart parking, smart transportation, smart energy, and smart healthcare but from a technological and strategic viewpoint, we need to take care of security (in terms of safety), big data, fog computing, mobility (in terms of mobile ability, whether it is for public or any private transport or applications), the cloud, and the full stack of technologies and information-related things [24, 26, 27, 33, 34]. Data capabilities and information management are important for the smart cities of the present and future.

19.6 Case Study: Role and Economy of Smart City Barcelona

According to the Wikipedia, the gross domestic product (GDP) of the greater Barcelona metropolitan area makes it the 4th most economical powerful city of the European Union (EU). To make a city "smart," there is a need of a thriving economy and investments. This city is revising its strategies with a focus on the major point of the impact that smart cities and technologies will have on its residents in a fully resident-focused approach. The Barcelona region and Catalonia have a good economy and industry. Moreover, this city attracts a lot of foreign investments. This city is not only a smart city leader but it is also an economic leader. The Catalonian region is attracting the world's topmost foreign investors; in recent years, mostly from Middle Eastern countries. The role of residents and their actions are indeed crucial and so are the ways that any countries govern. The high-tech improvements seen throughout this city set a milestone for all other cities in order to improve their infrastructure in the same manner [3–16, 18–30, 36, 39–41]. Some of the major characteristics of this city that make it a smart city are listed here:

19.6.1 Street Lights

This city becomes more energy efficient, cost-effective, and also reduces the temperature produced by conventional lamping using LED-based lighting system solutions. Use of sensors make it more efficient in receiving data related to air pollution, noise pollution, energy, and the presence of residents [2, 34].

19.6.2 Waste Disposal

The use of a vacuum-based approach in smart bins slurps the waste material to underground storage, helping to reducing the bad odor of garbage and noise pollution from garbage trucks. It also helps in detection of waste that is collected from different regions. The incinerated waste can be used later to generate energy for heating systems [34].

19.6.3 Bike System

Barcelona is the first of the larger cities as compared to other cities to implement a bike system, called Bicing. The main aim of this system is to reduce the number of automobiles in the city. Apart from various occasional controversies, Bicing is still considered as a successful plan with over 120,000 users [34].

19.6.4 Bus Transit System

This system is implemented for sustainability, mobility, and lessening vehicles emissions using hybrid buses. This system also has smart bus shelters that utilize solar panels to deliver energy for the screens that display the waiting times [34].

19.6.5 Noise Sensors

Sensors that are easy to use and cost-effective benefit the residents of this city who had registered nighttime noise complaints for decades. These sensors can detect air pollution, noise levels, temperature, and humidity levels [34].

19.6.6 Irrigation System

Various sensors offer live data related to humidity, atmospheric pressure, wind velocity, and sunlight. For example, a gardener can check the needs and requirements of water content for plants based on this live data. It also helps in avoidance of overwatering [34].

19.6.7 Fab Labs

This is the first city across the globe to have an open network of Fab Labs, a small-scale workshop that offers digital fabrication. The principle of this initiative is "no smart city without smart citizens" [34].

19.7 Conclusion

Smart cities are fully connected, sustainable, and energy efficient and use their infrastructures to intelligently improve quality of life. Various smart city projects are currently going on across the globe related to smart parking, smart transportation, smart energy, and smart healthcare but from a technological and strategic viewpoint, we need to take care of security, big data, fog computing, mobility, the cloud, and the full stack of connected technologies and information-related things. This chapter provides a detailed overview of current challenging issues, technologies for smart and innovative smart cities, and the global perspective of smart cities. This chapter also provides a case study based on the role and economy of smart city Barcelona.

References

1. Future of Smart Cities. Available at: https://www.inc.com/soren-kaplan/the-future-of-smart-cities.html [accessed on May 20, 2020]
2. Smart Cities of the Future. Available at: https://www.bosch.com/stories/smart-cities-of-the-future/ [accessed on May 20, 2020]
3. Lavanya Sharma, P.K. Garg, (Eds.). (2019). *From Visual Surveillance to Internet of Things*. New York, NY: Chapman and Hall/CRC, https://doi.org/10.1201/9780429297922.
4. Lavanya Sharma, Nirvikar Lohan, "Performance Analysis of Moving Object Detection using BGS Techniques in Visual Surveillance," *International Journal of Spatiotemporal Data Science*, Inderscience, vol. 1, pp. 22–53, January 2019.
5. Anubhav Kumar, Gaurav Jha, Lavanya Sharma, "Challenges, Potential & Future of IOT Integrated with Block Chain," *International Journal of Recent Technology and Engineering*, vol. 8, no. 2S7, pp. 530–536, July 2019.
6. Akshit Anand, Vikrant Jha, Lavanya Sharma, "An Improved Local Binary Patterns Histograms Techniques for Face Recognition for Real Time Application," *International Journal of Recent Technology and Engineering*, vol. 8, no. 2S7, pp. 524–529, July 2019.
7. Lavanya Sharma, Dileep Kumar Yadav, "Histogram based Adaptive Learning Rate for Background Modelling and Moving Object Detection in Video Surveillance," *International Journal of Telemedicine and Clinical Practices*, Inderscience, June, 2016. DOI: 10.1504/IJTMCP.2017.082107
8. Lavanya Sharma, Nirvikar Lohan, "Performance Analysis of Moving Object Detection using BGS Techniques," *International Journal of Spatio-Temporal Data Science*, Inderscience, vol. 1, pp. 22–53, February, 2019.
9. Lavanya Sharma, P K Garg, "Future of Internet of Things," *From Visual Surveillance to Internet of Things*, New York, NY: Chapman Hall/CRC, vol. 1, p. 245, 2019.
10. Lavanya Sharma, P K Garg, "IoT and its Applications," *From Visual Surveillance to Internet of Things*, New York, NY: Chapman Hall/CRC, vol. 1, p. 29, 2019.

11. J. Jin et al., "An Information Framework for Creating a Smart City Through Internet of Things," *IEEE Internet of Things Journal*, vol. 1, no. 2, pp. 112–121, 2014.
12. A. Botta et al., "Integration of Cloud Computing and Internet of Things: A Survey," *Future Generation Computer Systems*, vol. 56, pp. 684–700, 2016.
13. S. Sicaria et al., "Security Privacy and Trust in Internet of Things: The Road Ahead," *Computer Networks*, vol. 76, pp. 146–164, 2015.
14. World Economic Forum, "*Industrial Internet of Things: Unleashing the Potential of Connected Products and Services*" (Report, Geneva, Switzerland) January 2015.
15. Lavanya Sharma, P K Garg, "Smart E-healthcare with Internet of Things: Current Trends Challenges, Solutions and Technologies," *From Visual Surveillance to Internet of Things*, New York, NY: Chapman Hall/CRC, vol. 1, p. 215, 2019.
16. Lavanya Sharma, P K Garg, Naman Agarwal, "A Foresight on e-healthcare Trailblazers," *From Visual Surveillance to Internet of Things*, New York, NY: Chapman Hall/CRC, vol. 1, p. 235, 2019.
17. IoT and Smart City Innovation. Available at: https://www.i-scoop.eu/internet-of-things-guide/smart-cities-smart-city/ [accessed on May 20, 2020]
18. Gauri Jha, Pawan Singh, Lavanya Sharma, "Recent Advancements of Augmented Reality in Real Time Applications," *International Journal of Recent Technology and Engineering*, vol. 8, no. 2S7, pp. 538–542, July 2019.
19. Lavanya Sharma, Annapurna Singh, Dileep Kumar Yadav, "Fisher's Linear Discriminant Ratio based Threshold for Moving Human Detection in Thermal Video," *Infrared Physics and Technology*, vol. 78, pp. 118–128, Elsevier, March, 2016.
20. T. Bouwmans, F. Porikli, B. Horferlin, A. Vacavant, *Handbook on Background Modeling and Foreground Detection for Video Surveillance*, CRC Press, Taylor and Francis Group, 2014.
21. C. Harrison, B. Eckman, R. Hamilton, P. Hartswick, J. Kalagnanam, J. Paraszczak et al., "Foundations for Smarter Cities," *IBM Journal of Research and Development*, vol. 54, no. 4, 2010.
22. H. Schaffers, N. Komninos, M. Pallot, B. Trousse, M. Nilsson, A. Oliveira, et al., "Smart Cities and the Future Internet: Towards Cooperation Frameworks for Open Innovation," *The Future Internet. FIA 2011. Lecture Notes in Computer Science*, Berlin, Heidelberg: Springer, 2011.
23. Shubham Sharma, Shubhankar Verma, Mohit Kumar, Lavanya Sharma, "Use of Motion Capture in 3D Animation: Motion Capture Systems, Challenges, and Recent Trends," in *1st IEEE International Conference on Machine Learning, Big Data, Cloud and Parallel Computing (Com-IT-Con)*, Faridabad, India, pp. 309–313, February 14–16, 2019.
24. Lavanya Sharma, Nirvikar Lohan, "Internet of Things with Object Detection," *Handbook of Research on Big Data and the IoT*, IGI Global, pp. 89–100, March, 2019. DOI: 10.4018/978-1-5225-7432-3.ch006
25. R. Nagarathna, R. Manoranjani, "An Intelligent Step to Effective e-Governance in India through E-Learning via Social Networks," *2016 IEEE 4th International Conference on MOOCs Innovation and Technology in Education (MITE)*, Madurai, India, pp. 29–35, December 9–10, 2016.
26. Lavanya Sharma, "Introduction: From Visual Surveillance to Internet of Things," *From Visual Surveillance to Internet of Things*, New York, NY: Chapman Hall/CRC, Vol. 1, p. 14, 2019.
27. Lavanya Sharma, P K Garg, "Block based Adaptive Learning Rate for Moving Person Detection in Video Surveillance," *From Visual Surveillance to Internet of Things*, New York, NY: Chapman Hall/CRC, Vol. 1, p. 201, 2019.
28. Andrea Caragliu, Chiara Del Bo and Peter Nijkamp, "Smart Cities in Europe," *Journal of Urban Technology*, vol. 18, no. 2, pp. 65–82, April 2011.
29. Vito Albino, Umberto Berardi and Rosa Maria Dangelico, "Smart Cities: Definitions Dimensions Performance and Initiatives," *Journal of Urban Technology*, vol. 22, no. 1, pp. 3–21, Feb 2015.
30. T. Bouwmans, N. Aybat, E. Zahzah, *Handbook on Robust Low-Rank and Sparse Matrix Decomposition: Applications in Image and Video Processing*, Taylor and Francis Group, 2016.
31. IoT Analytics. Available at: https://iot-analytics.com/top-10-iot-project-application-areas-q3-2016/ [accessed on May 22, 2020]

32. Smart City Use Cases and Challenges. Available at: https://www.businessinsider.com/the-smart-cities-report-driving-factors-of-development-top-use-cases-and-market-challenges-for-smart-cities-around-the-world-2016-10?IR=T [accessed on May 20, 2020]

33. Smart City Overview. Available at: https://www.i-scoop.eu/smart-city-active-citizen-participation/ [accessed on May 22, 2020]

34. Smart City Series: the Barcelona Experience. Available at: https://www.e-zigurat.com/blog/en/smart-city-barcelona-experience/. [accessed on May 22, 2020]

35. IoT for Smart Cities. Available at: https://www.visualcapitalist.com/iot-building-smarter-cities/ [accessed on April 12, 2020]

36. Applications of Smart Cities. Available at: https://www.digi.com/blog/post/iot-applications-in-smart-cities [accessed on April 12, 2020]

37. Global Perspective of Smart Cities. Available at: https://inc42.com/resources/the-future-of-smart-cities-a-global-perspective/ [accessed on May 20, 2020]

38. Smart City innovation in the US and Canada. Available at: https://blog.equinix.com/blog/2019/08/06/4-examples-of-smart-city-innovations-in-the-u-s-and-canada/ [accessed on May 20, 2020]

39. N. Dlodlo, P. Mbecke, M. Mofolo and M. Mhlanga, "The Internet of Things in community safety and crime prevention for South Africa," *International Joint Conference on Computers Information and Systems Sciences and Engineering CISSE*, University of Bridgeport, Bridgeport, CT, December 12–14, 2013.

40. A. Zanella and L. Vangelista, "Internet of Things for Smart Cities," *IEEE Internet of Things journal*, vol. 1, no. 1, 2014.

41. Yong Liu and Rongxu Hou, "About the Sensing Layer in Internet of Things [J]," *Computer Study*, vol. 5, pp. 55, 2010.

Index

A

adaptive neuro-fuzzy inference system 147
amyotrophic lateral sclerosis 62
application programming interface (API) 41,
    101, 258
Arduino microcontroller 261
artificial intelligence of things 128
artificial intelligence system 48, 61
artificial neural networks 59, 127, 222
augmented reality 84, 86, 257

B

background subtraction techniques (BGS)
    290–295, 318
backtracking 18
bandwidth allocation 17, 19, 24, 26, 27
big data 47, 79, 177
brain–computer interfaces 61

C

Change detection 294
cloud computing 178, 197, 200, 237, 244
CNNs 57, 293, 302
computation offloading 17
computer vision 104, 148, 181, 192, 193, 231
Continuous Aldohexose Monitor 259

D

dataset 47, 124, 133, 225
deep detector classifier (DeepDC) 293
Deep Dense Face Detector (DDFD) 301
deep learning 46, 56, 58, 290, 293, 295, 296
deep neural network 293
density functional theory 63
Discrete Cosine Transform (DCT) 294

E

electrocorticographic 63
electroencephalographic 61
electronic health records (EHR) 49
Enterprise resource planning (ERP) 47
Euclidian distance 302

F

face images 149, 154, 155, 157
fast Fourier transform 294
Fisherface and linear discriminative
    analysis 298
Fully convolutional networks 296
functional magnetic resonance
    imaging 63

G

Gaussian 152, 291, 303, 321
general regression neural network 292
generative adversarial networks 296
Global Positioning System (GPS) 15,
    36, 106
Global System for Mobile Communications
    (GSM) 36
gross domestic product 336

H

healthcare 8, 16, 25, 46, 332, 336, 338
high-performance computing 55

I

image processing 132, 144, 147, 148, 168
image recognition 110, 112, 113, 147
incremental synchronous learning 76
Independent component analysis
    (ICA) 298
information and communication technology
    36, 52
Infrastructure as a Service 49, 198,
    221, 237
Intelligent Traffic Management 333
Internet of Medical Things 49
Internet of Things (IoT) 197, 215
IR sensors 148, 261

K

Kinect Fusion 88, 89
K-means clustering 270, 272, 274, 275
k-nearest neighbors (KNN) 298

L

local binary pattern (LBP) 302
localized area potentials 63

M

machine learning 10, 25, 47, 290, 291, 317
Magic Medicine Cabinet (MMC) 46
magneto-encephalography (MEG) 63
Medicine Information Support System
 (MISS) 50
mobile cloud computing 55, 56, 67

O

object detection 78, 79, 133
object tracking 27, 318, 320

P

Platform as a Service 49, 198, 220, 237
principal component analysis 148, 291, 298

Q

quality of service 19, 26, 27, 56, 236, 258

R

radial basis function 138, 292
radial basis function neural network
 (RBFNN) 292
Radio-Frequency Identification (RFID) 36, 46,
 76, 122, 246
radon transform (RT) 301
rapid diagonistic test 138
rectified linear unit 111, 150
red blood cells 261, 269
reinforcement learning 124, 126
robotic arm 101, 280, 281, 284
robotic telesurgery 61
robotics 16, 48, 332, 333
robust kernel PCA (RKPCA) 300

S

Self Organizing Background Subtraction 292
sensors 24, 49–51, 102, 112, 146, 188, 197,
 228, 247
service-oriented architecture 76
smart city architecture 7
smart data 5, 6
smart education system 85, 87, 89
smart energy empowerment 6
smart healthcare 28, 46, 49
smart homes 50, 74, 112, 140, 182, 232
smart networks and connecting devices 6
smart quality of life 5, 7
smart transportation 130, 188, 336, 338
Software as a Service 49, 198, 237
Supervised Deep Learning 296
support vector machine 138, 148, 291
Surgery in Space 60
supervised learning 104, 126, 296, 297

T

Traffic Signalization Detector 107
transductive SVMs 297

U

Ubiquitous Wi-Fi 330
unsupervised learning 104, 126, 296, 295

V

video surveillance 155, 201, 206, 240, 242, 291
VIRECAR 85, 86
virtual private network 51
virtual reality 84, 178

W

wavelet transform 298, 299, 301
winner-take-all (WTA) 292
wireless body area networks 50
World Health Organization 269

Printed in the United States
by Baker & Taylor Publisher Services